M000073400

PRIVACY

THE LOST RIGHT

PRIVACY

THE LOST RIGHT

Jon L. Mills

OXFORD
UNIVERSITY PRESS

Oxford University Press, Inc., publishes works that further Oxford University's objective of excellence in research, scholarship, and education.

Oxford   New York
Auckland   Cape Town   Dar es Salaam   Hong Kong   Karachi   Kuala Lumpur   Madrid   Melbourne
Mexico City   Nairobi   New Delhi   Shanghai   Taipei   Toronto

With offices in
Argentina   Austria   Brazil   Chile   Czech Republic   France   Greece   Guatemala   Hungary   Italy
Japan   Poland   Portugal   Singapore   South Korea   Switzerland   Thailand   Turkey   Ukraine
Vietnam

Library of Congress Cataloging-in-Publication Data

Mills, Jon L.
   Privacy: the lost right / Jon L. Mills.
   p. cm.
       Includes bibliographical references and index.
       ISBN 978-0-19-536735-5 (alk. paper)
1. Privacy, Right of—United States. I. Title.
   KF1262.M55 2008
   342.7308'58—dc22

                                                                              2008016529

2 3 4 5 6 7 8 9

Printed in the United States of America on acid-free paper

Note to Readers
This publication is designed to provide accurate and authoritative information in regard to the subject
matter covered. It is based upon sources believed to be accurate and reliable and is intended to be current as
of the time it was written. It is sold with the understanding that the publisher is not engaged in rendering
legal, accounting, or other professional services. If legal advice or other expert assistance is required, the
services of a competent professional person should be sought. Also, to confirm that the information has not
been affected or changed by recent developments, traditional legal research techniques should be used,
including checking primary sources where appropriate.

*(Based on the Declaration of Principles jointly adopted by a Committee of the
American Bar Association and a Committee of Publishers and Associations.)*

You may order this or any other Oxford University Press publication by
visiting the Oxford University Press website at www.oup.com

To my mother, Marguerite, who taught me how to love learning,
to my wife, Beth, who shows me how to love life, and
to my children, Marguerite and Elizabeth, who teach
me how to love the world's endless possibilities.

CONTENTS

PREFACE

Privacy intrusions are not abstract. I remember working for the parents of children slain by the serial killer Danny Rolling. Their wishes to keep morbid pictures of their children out of the press were personal and their fears were real. When I worked for Dale Earnhart's widow, who devoted herself to stopping the release of her husband's autopsy photos, I saw her determination to protect her family and to spare other families the same pain. Intrusions hurt people deeply.

Intrusion is commonplace. Every single individual in today's society is at risk. In today's *Brave New World*, government monitors e-mail, data brokers sell your personal buying preferences, neighbors can research the value of your home and your political contributions, and an anonymous blogger can make up stories about your sexual habits and post them on the Internet. You have little recourse.

This book grew out of a number of personal, political, and professional experiences. I have introduced privacy policy as a legislator, litigated privacy controversies as a lawyer, and studied them as a professor. This book is an effort to synthesize these experiences and put privacy in a context that is understandable and useful to citizens while at the same time providing a resource to students and others with a more academic interest in these policies. I have included compelling stories and cases—some right out of the tabloids—that demonstrate important points. To streamline the text I included a detailed appendix on federal statutes as a reference for those who wish to see the entire scope of privacy policy.

Privacy is a concept we, as a society, are struggling to define, protect, and understand. Clearly, we want to protect our personal freedoms and personal information. But society is not headed in that direction. Technology, from camera phones to the Internet, facilitates our intrusiveness.

Our YouTube culture gives away more personal information and our government collects more information. Technology and culture combine to make this a very invasive world. The pace of change is not slowing. There are new inventions and intrusions coming daily.

A principal purpose of *Privacy: The Lost Right* is to place the contemporary loss of privacy in perspective historically, culturally, and legally. Our current remedies are inadequate and antiquated and cannot keep pace with intrusions. I suggest changes that can enhance privacy. But the major purpose of this book is to enhance the general understanding that generates the changes in our actions and policies to protect better all of us from this meddling world.

ACKNOWLEDGMENTS

I wish to thank Lenny Kennedy and Barbara Sieger for their diligence and patience over many years. I also wish to thank my diligent research assistants over the years of this book's creation: Steve Adamczyk, David Benjamin, Bonnie Daboll, Justin Duff, Brian Frankel, Lauren Gralnik, Andrew Hoffman, Josh Koehler, Ryan Koslosky, Jasmine McNeely, Jeremy Sahn, Dwayne Simpson, and Michelle Smith.

CHAPTER I

Introduction

A Day in the Life

Lenny wakes up in the morning, gets dressed and goes online to visit a couple of Web sites, while cookies[1] and spyware[2] track her browsing habits and gather her consumer information. She then gets in her car, which has a global positioning system ("GPS") and drives to work, while a "black box" sends data about the vehicle back to the automobile manufacturer. As she drives to work, RFID[3] technology from her E-Z Pass relays her payment information and the location of the car as it passes through a toll station. During her drive to work, Lenny has a conversation on her cellular phone that may be intercepted and publicly disclosed on the radio.[4] She arrives

---

[1] Luke J. Albrecht, Note, *Online Marketing: The Use of Cookies and Remedies for Internet Users*, 36 SUFFOLK U. L. REV. 421 (2003) (discussing the use of cookies and the collection of data from Internet users).

[2] Paul M. Schwartz, *Property, Privacy, and Personal Data*, 117 HARV. L. REV. 2055 (2004) (discussing a program that installs itself without your permission and can collect personal information).

[3] Radio Frequency Identification—implanted in merchandise, toll devices, pets, or people. *See* DANIEL J. SOLOVE, INFORMATION PRIVACY LAW 628–29 (2d ed. 2006).

[4] Further, technology can enable one to track a cell phone's location. "Cell phones can reveal very precise information about your location, and yet legal protections are very much up in the air." Ellen Nakashima, *Cell Phone Tracking Powers on Request*, WASH. POST, Nov. 23, 2007, at A01 (quoting Kevin Bankstone of Electronic Frontier Foundation).

at work and parks her car in a parking lot with camera surveillance. Once she is at her office desk, Lenny logs on to her computer and checks her e-mail, which is overseen by her employer.[5] In the afternoon, she visits a friend at a family-planning clinic and, unknown to her, her picture is taken and posted on a Web site by a "pro-life" group.[6] After work, Lenny and her colleagues are recorded going to a bar in a section of downtown where the city has recently installed a digital closed-circuit television ("CCTV") camera.[7] At the bar, Lenny buys a round of drinks with a credit card, and the transaction is monitored by her credit-card company, which then discloses Lenny's marketing information to a third party. After Lenny leaves the bar, a police detective picks up a piece of gum she left in an ashtray because Lenny generally fits the description of a murder suspect and the detective wants to check her DNA for a potential match.

The fictional societies in *Brave New World* and *1984* appalled readers with the specter of a dehumanized future world. Big Brother was omnipotent, privacy was scorned, and individuality was crushed. How do we stand today in the glare of instant communication, tabloid press, Internet intrusions,[8] data brokers, security cameras, and big government? Have individual freedoms been irretrievably altered by the omnipresent gaze of a modern-day panopticon?[9] What is left of individual privacy, and how

---

It was also recently revealed that there was a study conducted by Northeastern University which tracked the whereabouts of 100,000 people outside the United States through the use of their cell phones.Seth Borenstein, *Study secretly tracks cell phone users outside US*, ASSOCIATED PRESS (June 4, 2008), available at http://www.sfgate.com/cgi-bin/article. cgi?f=/n/a/2008/06/04/national/a100140D77.DTL (last visited June 11, 2008).

[5] Her employer may monitor the e-mails she sends or the Web sites she visits. Further, spyware implanted in her computer may allow outside parties to view her computer use, even the keystrokes. Kim Zetter, *Employers Crack Down on Personal Net Use*, PCWORLD, Aug. 25, 2006, http://www.pcworld.com/article/id,126835-c,workplace/article.html (last visited May 9, 2008).

[6] *See* abortioncams.com (last visited June 22, 2008). *See also infra* note 354 for other examples of citizens posting pictures on the Internet.

[7] *See* CLIVE NORRIS & GARY ARMSTRONG, THE MAXIMUM SURVEILLANCE SOCIETY: THE RISE OF CCTV (1999).

[8] For further discussion on the promise and problems of mass information on the Internet, see Tal Z. Zarsky, *Information Privacy in Virtual Worlds: Identifying Unique Concerns Beyond the Online and Offline Worlds*, 49 N.Y.L. SCH. L. REV. 231 (2004).

[9] *See* JEREMY BENTHAM, The PANOPTICON WRITINGS 29–95 (Miran Bozovic ed., Verso 1995) (suggesting the use of a panopticon design for a prison building, which aimed to create a prison atmosphere where prisoners could never know whether their actions were being monitored by guards at any given point in time). The mere possibility that a guard might be watching thus motivates inmates to regulate themselves as though

can it be saved? Is the protective ability of the law so far behind technology at this point that we cannot catch up? To understand privacy as it exists in this country today, we must answer a series of questions: what is privacy? what are the challenges to personal privacy in today's culture? what are our legal protections? and finally, how can we protect privacy better?

Individual identity is defined largely by the control of personal information and the exercise of personal autonomy. U.S. courts and writers refer to privacy in the most sacred of terms—as one of a person's most valued rights.[10] Indeed, privacy and personal autonomy are both cherished. We punish people by placing them in prison, thus taking away their autonomy and their ability to have private lives. We protect the right of citizens to live in a private home and carefully limit any intrusion into that home by either the government or other citizens. We usually allow people to choose which religious teachings to follow and which persons with whom to associate. However, in today's society, legal protections fail to match privacy's treasured status. Intrusions are allowed for a series of reasons: (1) protecting public security, welfare, and public health;[11] (2) upholding moral standards of society at a particular time;[12] (3) protecting other values such as access to public records and freedom of speech;[13] and (4) promoting commerce by allowing the gathering and wide dissemination of information.[14] The privacy right is hardly absolute. The importance of individual rights is balanced against the rights of the larger community. Amitai Etzioni devoted an entire book to describing the significance of honoring "communitarian theory" against modern concerns about individual privacy.[15] The book reminds us that we voluntarily give

---

someone was in fact observing their behavior. For a more thorough discussion of the panopticon effect, see *infra* Chapter III, § B-6.

[10] *See, e.g.,* Dalia v. United States, 441 U.S. 238, 250 n.9 (1979) ("[E]lectronic surveillance can be a threat to the 'cherished privacy of law-abiding citizens.'" (quoting United States v. U.S. Dist. Court, 407 U.S. 297, 312 (1972))); Quilici v. Village of Morton Grove, 695 F.2d 261, 280 (7th Cir. 1982) ("The right to privacy is one of the most cherished rights an American citizen has; the right to privacy sets America apart from totalitarian states in which the interests of the state prevail over individual rights.").

[11] *See, e.g.,* Sherr v. Northport-East Northport Union Free Sch. Dist., 672 F. Supp. 81 (E.D.N.Y. 1987) (holding that bogus and insincere religious beliefs are not grounds for exemption from New York's mandatory school inoculation program).

[12] *See, e.g.,* Loving v. Virginia, 388 U.S. 1 (1967). Miscegenation statutes of the past are one example of a prohibition that can only be based on a moral reason rather than other public purposes.

[13] The right to free speech justifies multiple private intrusions.

[14] *See* discussion *infra* Chapter III, § B-5(b).

[15] Amitai Etzioni, The Limits of Privacy (1999).

up some individual rights to protect our community from child molesters
and terrorists.

What does privacy mean? The word's etymology is from *privation*
and *deprivation*—two decidedly negative concepts.[16] But the words we
normally associate with privacy are independence, freedom, autonomy,
liberty, individuality, dignity, seclusion, and the absence of intrusion. All
of these are treasured concepts. However, we should be conscious that
just because something is protected by "privacy" does not automatically
mean that it is good and universally supported. Privacy can shield bad
acts. Feminist writers and others note that privacy was used to cloak
abuses by husbands in "disciplining" their wives.[17] So privacy can be, and
has been, used to cover up abuses.

There is a continuing struggle to define privacy. Some suggest that it
is not worth the struggle, because privacy cannot be understood as a uni-
fied concept. Privacy is hardly a one-dimensional concept and is probably
more akin to the "bundle of rights" we talk about when legally conceptualizing property rights. These property rights include the ability to own,
transfer, and exclude people from property. Privacy rights include the
right to exclude others, make choices, and exercise personal liberties.[18] It
is worthwhile to look at this entire bundle at one time.

Just as difficult as defining the term "privacy" is reaching agreement
on the origins of privacy as a legal concept. The legal status of privacy is
grounded in ancient natural-law principles of individual freedom and
liberty. These principles were articulated by philosophers from Aristotle
to Cicero to Thomas Aquinas. Evaluation of privacy law must begin with
these higher precepts. The principles of imposing limitations on the government and the sanctity of individuals are further described in the writings of John Stuart Mill, John Locke, and Thomas Hobbes. For example,
Mill said, "The only part of the conduct of anyone for which he is amenable
to society is that which concerns others. In that part which merely
concerns himself, his independence is, of right, absolute."[19] Sir William

---

[16] RICHARD A. GLENN, THE RIGHT TO PRIVACY: RIGHTS AND LIBERTIES UNDER THE LAW 3
(2003).

[17] The protection of a husband's ability to "discipline" his wife has been rightly critiqued
by contemporary feminist writers. *See* SOLOVE, *supra* note 3, at 69–73; *see also* Reva B.
Siegel, *"The Rule of Love": Wife Beating as Prerogative and Privacy*, 105 YALE L.J. 2117 (1996).

[18] *See* the "Four Spheres of Privacy" chart at page 6 and the accompanying text.

[19] JOHN STUART MILL, *On Liberty* 96 in UTILITARIANISM, LIBERTY, AND REPRESENTATIVE
GOVERNMENT, American ed., E.P. Dutton and Co., Inc. (1951); *see also* GLENN, *supra*
note 16, at 19.

Blackstone, as the first recorder of the common law, emphasized the importance of private property and the prerogatives of a family's privacy.[20]

Privacy thus has many theoretical progenitors. Even in early America,
the combination of rights protecting the home, the person, and personal
information provided a basis for protecting individual liberty.[21] Those
protections are based on the evolution of common-law protections. Even
before the landmark—and revered—article by Samuel D. Warren and
Louis D. Brandeis,[22] Thomas Cooley made an attempt to define privacy as
"a right of complete immunity: to be let alone."[23] And the Michigan
Supreme Court recognized the right when deciding that a young unmar-
ried man could be excluded from a room during childbirth because "[t]he
plaintiff had a legal right to privacy of her apartment at such a time and
the law secures to her this right by requiring others to observe it."[24]

The article by Warren and Brandeis galvanized this disparate history.
It is fair to say that they named privacy but did not invent it. The 1890
article expressed deep concern about the advent of photography, new
technologies, an intrusive society, and an invasive press as dangers to
individual privacy.[25] In fact, Warren may have been personally offended
by press coverage of his daughter's wedding.[26] In 1905, the first American
court identified "privacy" as a freestanding right.[27] In 1928, Brandeis, sit-
ting as a Supreme Court justice, dissented in *Olmstead v. United States*, a
case dealing with surveillance, arguing that the right to privacy is inherent
in the U.S. Constitution.[28] Brandeis's view would become law when *Katz
v. United States* overturned *Olmstead*, echoing his earlier dissent.[29]
Likewise, in *Mapp v. Ohio*, an important decision regarding the exclu-
sionary rule under the Fourth Amendment, the Court again returned to

---

[20] 2 WILLIAM BLACKSTONE, COMMENTARIES ON THE LAW OF ENGLAND 1–15 (1766).
[21] *See* GLENN, *supra* note 16, at 47.
[22] Samuel D. Warren & Louis D. Brandeis, *The Right to Privacy*, 4 HARV. L. REV. 193 (1890).
[23] GLENN, *supra* note 16, at 50 (noting that as early as the 1880s, Thomas Cooley was attempting to define privacy).
[24] DeMay v. Roberts, 9 N.W. 146, 149 (Mich. 1881).
[25] Warren & Brandeis, *supra* note 22 (asserting that individuals should have full protection of person and property).
[26] *See* GLENN, *supra* note 16, at 45. However, recent scholarship indicates that Warren's daughter could only have been as old as seven at the time of the publication and was not married until fifteen years later. *See* J. THOMAS McCARTHY, THE RIGHTS OF PUBLICITY AND PRIVACY 20 (2d ed. 2007).
[27] *See* Pavesich v. New England Life Ins. Co., 50 S.E. 68 (Ga. 1905).
[28] Olmstead v. United States, 277 U.S. 438, 473–76 (1928) (Brandeis, J., dissenting).
[29] Katz v. United States, 389 U.S. 347, 350–51 (1967).

Brandeis's ideas to support the finding that evidence obtained through unconstitutional means may not be used against a defendant.[30]

By the 1960s, legal protections derived from Warren and Brandeis had developed in three areas: the privacy torts, as articulated by William L. Prosser[31] and the *Restatement (Second) of Torts*; the search-and-seizure Fourth Amendment jurisprudence developed in *Katz v. United States*; and the now well-known "penumbral" rights identified in *Griswold v. Connecticut*. The Court in *Griswold* again cited Brandeis's dissent in *Olmstead*, including the phrase "the right to be let alone." In *Griswold*, Justice William O. Douglas recognized that privacy was not a new concept when he said ". . . the right of privacy which presses for recognition here is a legitimate one. . . . We deal with a right of privacy older than the Bill of Rights. . . ."[32]

Family Tree for Privacy in Contemporary U.S. Law

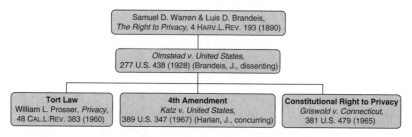

Samuel D. Warren & Luis D. Brandeis, *The Right to Privacy*, 4 HARV.L.REV. 193 (1890)

Olmstead v. United States, 277 U.S. 438 (1928) (Brandeis, J., dissenting)

Tort Law
William L. Prosser, *Privacy*, 48 CAL.L.REV. 383 (1960)

4th Amendment
Katz v. United States, 389 U.S. 347 (1967) (Harlan, J., concurring)

Constitutional Right to Privacy
Griswold v. Connecticut, 381 U.S. 479 (1965)

Though these areas of the law are different, each draws from the same well. The once seemingly novel idea that a "right to privacy" existed in the Constitution found footholds at various times through similar reasoning in Fourth Amendment jurisprudence, privacy torts, and constitutional penumbral rights.[33]

Today, the law protects privacy through a mixture of constitutional law, tort law, property law, and statutory law. Some of these legal protections are ancient and settled, whereas others are more modern and tend to be less effective. Constitutional law protecting personal autonomy in areas such as marriage, procreation, and child rearing is well developed, offering significant, though sometimes unpredictable, protection. However,

---

[30] Mapp v. Ohio, 367 U.S. 643 (1961).

[31] Prosser was something of a critic of privacy as it was articulated by Warren and Brandeis. He did not favor expansion. He did categorize privacy into four torts. *See* William L. Prosser, *Privacy*, 48 CAL. L. REV. 383 (1960).

[32] Griswold v. Connecticut, 381 U.S. 479, 485–86 (1965).

[33] *See* discussion *infra* Chapter III, § A-1.

the same cannot be said for constitutional law's effectiveness in the area of intrusions relating to personal information, by either private or governmental sources. For these types of intrusions, constitutional law provides a lower standard of protection. Furthermore, because the First Amendment specifically fosters individual expression by protecting most forms of speech, in some cases it can be a significant obstacle to an individual's *privacy interests*. Because individual privacy is impaired through the constitutional protection enjoyed by the media when disclosing private information, the First Amendment serves a critical dual role in privacy analysis. It provides both a basis for the "penumbra" protecting privacy and a justification for press and other free-speech intrusions.[34]

Tort law seeks to prevent the intrusiveness associated with unauthorized disclosure of personal information.[35] But tort protections are inadequate for the realities of modern life. Tort law fails to protect against the disclosure of personal information or to provide an adequate remedy to the victim once that information is disclosed. One reason for this result is the law's pervasive requirement in privacy cases, both information-related and autonomy-related, that an individual have a "reasonable expectation" of privacy in order to be eligible for any remedy.[36] Obviously, the law cannot provide redress for every perceived intrusion against the privacy of some oversensitive person. However, the reasonable expectation of privacy recognized by the law does not keep pace with the varying types of information disclosure afforded by rapidly advancing technologies, such as the Internet, digitally recorded closed-circuit television, and mobile communication devices. As a result, data that was once within the reasonable expectation of personal and private information has become readily available and easily disseminated—without a legal structure in place to protect the individual whose privacy has been invaded.

In comparison with the unclear and flimsy remedies associated with protecting information, the rights associated with protecting personal, real, and intellectual property and the rights protecting personal physical space are well developed and well established in most modern systems of law.

---

[34] *See* discussion *infra* Chapter IV.

[35] *See* Diane L. Zimmerman, *Requiem for a Heavyweight: A Farewell to Warren and Brandeis's Privacy Tort*, 68 CORNELL L. REV. 291, 295 n.11 (1983) ("The common law secures to each individual the right of determining, ordinarily, to what extent his thoughts, sentiments, and emotions shall be communicated to others."(quoting Samuel D. Warren & Louis D. Brandeis, *The Right to Privacy*, 4 HARV. L. REV. 193, 198 (1890)).

[36] *See* Katz v. United States, 389 U.S. 347, 360 (1967) (Harlan, J., concurring).

This book explores why personal information is less protected than personal autonomy and suggests theories of how protections could be improved. In particular, it explores how modern courts can and should expand tort remedies to comport with reality, how property theories offer an avenue for protecting personal information, and how governments might expand existing statutory privacy protection.[37]

The examples of actual cases in the next chapter help illustrate the importance and prevalence of privacy issues in our contemporary lives.

---

[37] *See* Warren & Brandeis, *supra* note 22, at 205.

CHAPTER II

A Perspective on the Reality of Privacy Issues Today

The loss of privacy is more than just an academic question. The complexity of today's society constantly generates both major and minor invasions of an individual's privacy rights. The following are real-life examples that will be referenced in various places in this book when the issues they illustrate are discussed. Some of these examples will also be examined in more depth in Chapter VI, where I will discuss the outcomes of the cases and how various reforms might improve such outcomes.

Twenty invasions:

1. After a series of savage murders of college students, the press seeks access to autopsy and crime-scene photographs.
2. The producers of the movie *The Perfect Storm* intentionally and inaccurately depict boat captain Billy Tyne as an unsuccessful and careless captain who took risks that cost his crew their lives. They market the film as a true story.
3. Two individuals talk on a cell phone about a labor dispute in Philadelphia. Their call is monitored and later broadcast on the radio.
4. A St. Patrick's Day parade committee in Boston denies a gay group their request to participate in the parade.
5. A woman writes an Internet blog revealing personal, embarrassing, and offensive details about a lover.

6. Terri Schiavo is found to be in a persistent vegetative state. A court finds that her intent was to be removed from life support in these circumstances. The legislature passes a statute requiring life support to be reattached.

7. An Internet Web site solicits salacious comments about individuals and promises anonymity to the writer.

8. Ms. Toni Ann Diaz is elected the first female president of her community-college student body in Oakland, California. The newspaper publishes the fact that she had previously undergone a sex-change operation.

9. During a child-custody dispute an estranged husband surreptitiously videotapes, through the open window of her house, his wife having sex with another woman.

10. The *New York Times* seeks NASA records of the audiotape of the crew's voices recorded during the Challenger crash.

11. The company that produces the video series *Girls Gone Wild* films a woman exposing herself in a public square and uses her image in nationwide advertising for the video.

12. The newsletter of the organization Jews for Jesus recounts the conversion of a Mrs. Rapp to Jesus. She says it never happened.

13. The Texas legislature passes a statute criminalizing homosexual behavior.

14. A Maryland database of medical records compiled for cost-containment purposes is sold to bankers who use the list to call in loans to patients with terminal cancer.

15. A school board requires random drug and alcohol testing of all students if they are going to participate in the school band.

16. The City of Miami Beach requires all applicants for city jobs to disclose whether they have smoked tobacco in the last year.

17. An unknown person in Berlin pretends to be an actress on a dating Web site. That person posts suggestive remarks and discloses the actress's home address and phone number.

18. A physician uses a patient's spleen cells to patent a cell line.

19. A fourteen-year-old boy dies of a drug overdose, and members of the local police department videotape the autopsy and show it to friends at parties.

20. A television production company contracts with a medical examiner in Nashville, Tennessee, to obtain access to accident sites and autopsies. After the death of a married couple who

apparently jumped out of the window of a Nashville hotel, the production company films the scene and then films the autopsy of the wife for the television show *True Stories from the Morgue.*

These incidents represent a cross section of intrusions into individuals' lives by the government, individuals, corporations, and the media. The span and depth of these intrusions should enrage citizens. But the fact is that we as citizens are largely unaware of just how invasive this society can be.[38] Some of these scenarios have legal remedies—others do not. As examples, they begin to provide the context of our contemporary intrusive society.

---

[38] *See* Joseph Turow, Lauren Feldman, and Kimberly Meltzer, *Open to Exploitation: American Shoppers Online and Offline,* Annenberg Public Policy Center of the University of Pennsylvania, June 1, 2005. This poll indicated wide ignorance of the law and business practices affecting personal information. Cited, *available at* http://epic.org/privacy/survey/ (last visited June 22, 2008). 64% believed falsely that their supermarket is barred by law from selling customer data. 72% believed falsely that charities are barred by law from selling personal information without permission. 73% believed falsely that banks are barred by law from sharing information with other companies and affiliates. 75% believed falsely that the presence of a privacy policy on a Web site means that the company cannot sell customers' information to others. 76% believed falsely that the Federal Trade Commission will correct errors in credit reports.

CHAPTER III

Privacy and Its Contemporary Context: Why Privacy Is Disappearing

Today's society is more intrusive than at any other time in modern history. The information industry, the modern press, and governments are increasingly intrusive. Each has strong motivations to intrude on personal privacy. And they do. Whether we are directly harmed or not, individuals are at risk. Do we as citizens understand the vast scope of intrusion, the potential ill effects, and the burden of living in the contemporary "panopticon?"

A. Defining Privacy

Individual privacy is at the core of personal identity and personal freedom. When we assent to becoming a member of society, we agree to give up some freedom and independence. That freedom that remains is what constitutes our common notion of individual privacy. Yet a threshold challenge is to formulate a comprehensive definition of privacy. Such a formulation necessarily involves multiple aspects of privacy. Four broad categories of legal doctrine provide individuals with a basic blanket of privacy protection from intrusions by the government, private entities, or individuals: freedom of personal autonomy; the right to control personal information; the right to control property; and the right to control and protect personal physical space.[39] Commentators have often divided privacy into "informational and decisional" privacy.[40] The bundle of rights that makes up privacy protects a broader set of "privacy interests" represented by the four areas. These categories of privacy are not entirely separate and may more appropriately be visualized as overlapping spheres of protection. In the following graphic depiction, the concept of imprisonment, or the loss of all privacy, functions as a common point that links all four spheres together in a total denial of privacy.

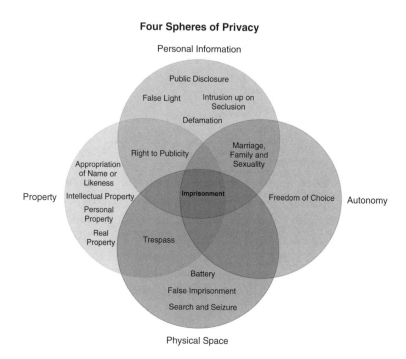

Four Spheres of Privacy

Personal Information

Public Disclosure

False Light   Intrusion up on Seclusion

Defamation

Right to Publicity   Marriage, Family and Sexuality

Appropriation of Name or Likeness

Property   Intellectual Property   Imprisonment   Freedom of Choice   Autonomy

Personal Property

Real Property   Trespass

Battery

False Imprisonment

Search and Seizure

Physical Space

It is necessary to consider these various rights as representing the universe within which privacy remedies exist, because intrusions on privacy do not fall neatly into legal categories. For instance, intruding on one's "right to publicity" by commercially using an individual's persona

---

[39] These four areas of legal doctrine operate to protect information, protect liberty in decision making, and protect against spatial intrusions to our person or property.

[40] See Dorothy J. Glancy, *Privacy on the Open Road*, 30 Ohio N.U. L. Rev. 295, 321 (2004); Alan Kato Ku, *Talk Is Cheap but a Picture Is Worth a Thousand Words: Privacy Rights in the Era of Camera Phone Technology*, 45 Santa Clara L. Rev. 679, 681 (2005). Some have suggested five areas, adding freedom of association to the above-mentioned four. See Anita L. Allen, Privacy Law and Society 5 (2007).

without permission implicates an invasion not only of that individual's right to personal information but also of that individual's property rights. Additionally, constitutional concerns penetrate into each of the spheres to varying degrees. A legal scholar wants to know what types of constitutional, tort, common-law, or statutory issues are raised, but the average citizen just wants relief. Relief probably will not come easily or through a single path. The spheres above are useful in organizing and defining the nature of intrusions and how they may be remedied.

1. The Autonomy Sphere: The Personal Freedom to Make Decisions

The autonomy sphere is fundamental to individual freedom and identity. Our ability to make some decisions, such as what clothes to wear and how to style our hair, is completely personal and basically unregulated.[41] Other decisions, such as whom to marry, whether to have children, how to raise our children, what organizations to join, where to live, which religion to practice, what medicine to take, and even how to die, have all either currently or historically been subject to governmental control or regulation.[42] Interestingly, traditional areas protected by privacy law such as procreation and dying are becoming increasingly complex with new technologies that enable artificial reproduction and provide new ways of sustaining human life.[43]

We give up the right to make many decisions as part of the social contract. Being a citizen grants certain rights to individuals as citizens but also entails giving up certain rights to the government.[44] The government

---

[41] However, even clothes and hair length are regulated in some settings, for example, in the military. *See* Goldman v. Weinberger, 475 U.S. 503 (1986) (upholding military ban on wearing yarmulkes while in uniform).

[42] *See, e.g.*, Buck v. Bell, 274 U.S. 200, 207 (1927) (supporting sterilization of the mentally ill, stating that "[t]hree generations of imbeciles are enough"). For an example of sterilization procedure, see Amy Burkholder, "'Pillow Angel' Surgery Broke Law," CNN.com, May 8, 2007, http://www.cnn.com/2007/HEALTH/05/08/ashley.ruling/index.html. "Ashley" was born with static encephalopathy, which rendered her unable to function in any decision-making capacity. At her parents' request, the six-year-old underwent surgery to remove her breast buds and uterus, freezing her growth at 4 feet 5 inches and 75 pounds. A panel with federal investigative authority found that Ashley's constitutional and common-law rights were violated, since Washington law requires zealous advocacy on the child's behalf and a court order before a sterilization procedure may take place.

[43] *See* discussion *infra* Chapter III, § B-3.

[44] *See* Jon Mills, *The Rewards of Citizenship and the Perils of Identity: How the Law Defines You in the Globalized World*, 2 WARSAW U. L. REV. 95 (2004). An individual's identity may affect his or her human rights as a citizen in various countries and as a global citizen.

gives us many rules that conform to its view of morality, that serve other public purposes, or occasionally, that reflect paternalistic concern.[45] However, the U.S. courts have a well-developed jurisprudence that deals with the right of individuals to make personal decisions. Privacy is a constitutionally created "penumbra"—a combination of freedom of speech, freedom of religion, and freedom of association and the Ninth Amendment's reservation of "other" rights to the people.[46] For the government to intrude on these freedoms requires a showing of a compelling governmental interest.[47] The most prominent constitutional privacy interests continually cited by the U.S. Supreme Court deal with procreation, marriage,[48] and family.[49] Such freedoms also are protected through federal and state statutes. Other liberty interests related to personal autonomy have been found in, for example, the right to refuse medical treatment.[50] Thus, individuals have significant legal options for protecting their right to make personal decisions.

2. The Personal-Information Sphere: Protecting Personal Data

Control of personal information is the least developed sphere of privacy and the sphere with the least legal protection. Individuals seek to protect information either by preventing its release or by recovering damages for a wrongful release of information. Some ability to control personal information is afforded by constitutional and statutory law.

For example, a woman will have different human rights depending on her citizenship and nationality. Her rights will be greater in some countries than in others.

[45] See CAL. VEC. CODE § 21212 (2007) (California bicycle-helmet law); FLA. STAT. § 316.614 (2007) (Florida safety-belt law); FLA. STAT. § 316.211 (2007) (Florida helmet law).

[46] See Griswold v. Connecticut, 381 U.S. 479 (1965).

[47] An intrusion upon a reasonable expectation of privacy requires a showing by the government of a compelling governmental interest that has been furthered by the least intrusive means. See, e.g., Roe v. Wade, 410 U.S. 113 (1973).

[48] Even prison inmates have a constitutional right to marry. Turner v. Safley, 482 U.S. 78 (1987).

[49] See Griswold, 381 U.S. at 479; Roe, 410 U.S. at 113; Troxel v. Granville, 530 U.S. 57 (2000) (holding that a law granting grandparents' right to visit against wishes of parents is unconstitutional). The Society of Sisters case struck down compulsory "public education" to allow for private schools. Currently, home schooling is allowed but can be regulated by states. See State v. Schmidt, 505 N.E.2d 627 (1987), cert. denied, 484 U.S. 942 (1987). See Meyer v. Nebraska, 262 U.S. 390 (1923), and Pierce v. Society of Sisters, 268 U.S. 510 (1925). These early cases indicate that the government cannot intrude on certain family decisions, particularly related to educating children.

[50] Cruzan v. Director, Mo. Dep't of Health, 497 U.S. 261 (1990).

There is recognition by the courts that guarding information can be constitutionally protected. The Supreme Court concluded that constitutional privacy includes not only an "interest in independence in making certain kinds of important decisions" but also "an individual interest in avoiding disclosure of personal matters."[51] However, personal information is protected by a lower standard than that for personal autonomy. Termed "rational-basis scrutiny,"[52] the standard for personal information requires a legitimate governmental interest in the intrusion upon informational privacy, whereas the government must show a "compelling governmental interest" to intrude on autonomy interests.

In addition to being protected by constitutional and statutory law, personal information can be protected through tort-law principles such as false light, defamation, public disclosure of private facts, and intrusion upon seclusion. Each is based on a "reasonable expectation" of privacy against the specific intrusion.[53] Still, the law will bend to allow the disclosure of personal information under the First Amendment when the social value of such information is "newsworthy." This standard allows significant intrusions and will be analyzed in more detail later.[54]

Different types of personal information are subject to varying levels of control. Some information remains completely private and undisclosed, such as a personally held belief, and is unknown and uncontrolled. Once a belief is expressed in words or actions, however, it may or may not be protected by privacy principles. Other information is known to some individuals but not to all. Such information includes disclosures to priests, lawyers, doctors, and spouses that we do not expect to become public knowledge. Personal information becomes more widely available in several ways.

---

[51] Whalen v. Roe, 429 U.S. 589, 599–600 (1977). "We are not unaware of the threat to privacy implicit in the accumulation of vast amounts of personal information in computerized data banks or other massive government files. . . . [There is] a concomitant statutory or regulatory duty to avoid unwarranted disclosures. . . . [I]n some circumstances, that duty arguably has its roots in the Constitution. . . ." *Id.* at 605.

[52] *See* Heller v. Doe, 509 U.S. 312, 319 (1993) (holding that rational-basis review applies when there is neither a fundamental right at stake nor a suspect classification). Rational-basis scrutiny requires a legitimate state purpose and a rational relationship between the regulation and the purpose. Courts usually defer to the legislature. *See, e.g.,* Thornburgh v. Am. Coll. of Obstetricians & Gynecologists, 476 U.S. 747, 789 (1986), *overruled on other grounds by* Planned Parenthood of Se. Pa. v. Casey, 505 U.S. 833 (1992) (asserting that there is heavy deference to the legislature when rational-basis review applies and that fundamental liberties receive greater substantive protection than general liberties).

[53] A "reasonable expectation" of privacy is determined by defining what a rational person would expect to be confidential. *See* discussion of tort protections *infra* Chapter IV § D.

[54] *See* discussion of newsworthiness *infra* Chapter VII, § B-4.

First, we volunteer information or agree to disclose it to governmental and commercial entities as a prerequisite for obtaining a license, going to court, traveling, buying property, acquiring a car, finding a job, obtaining credit, receiving medical care, or even being born or giving birth. Even if such information is voluntarily disclosed, individuals may not have consented to the "aggregation" or assembling of the various dispersed or obscure pieces of information.[55] Information also is gathered from us without our permission when the government is authorized to conduct wiretaps, investigations, mail inspections, and e-mail interceptions.[56] Finally, information disclosure may be mandated by rule or law; for example, you must disclose your birth date to obtain a driver's license.

All these methods of disclosure increase the availability of information. Further, modern technology makes this information easier to collect, easier to collate and file, and easier to disseminate. Both governmental and private entities use "data mining" for purposes ranging from advanced security to commercial gain.[57] Thus, the level of control an individual may exercise over personal information inevitably conflicts with security and commercial interests. The need for some form of balancing becomes crucial to individual privacy concerns. The ultimate question is, what societal values do we wish to protect through keeping information private? This identification of values will guide us in defining the types of information we want to keep private.[58]

---

[55] *See* Chapter III, § B-4(c).

[56] In the interest of homeland security, the federal government is working closely with private companies to collect large quantities of personal information on American citizens. *See* discussion *infra* Chapter V, § A-2.

[57] *See* ROBERT O'HARROW, JR., NO PLACE TO HIDE (2005) (discussing emerging dangers of data gathering techniques).

[58] Examples of the types of information we want to keep private are the exceptions to the disclosure of public records established by the states and federal government: medical information, personal financial information, children's abuse records. A good indicator of what a society or government views as appropriately confidential is its list of exceptions to or exemptions from public-records disclosure. In other words, what information in government records should be protected from general distribution because of its private nature? A study done by a team of Levin College of Law faculty and students classified Florida's thousand-plus exemptions into fourteen categories. Florida has one of the most stringent open-records laws in the country and is the only state to grant the right of public access in its constitution. Consequently, Florida has extensive case law and analysis of public-records and open-meeting policies. The list of exemptions to protect privacy should be representative of other states.

1. Private financial (e.g., estates, donors, tax returns)
2. Government financial (e.g., contracts, bidding)
3. Personal medical

3. The Personal-Property Sphere: Protecting Private Property

Freedom to control property is the third sphere of privacy and is perhaps the oldest and best-protected private legal right under Western jurisprudence. Like the freedom to control personal information, the freedom to control property is partially regulated by tort law that compensates damage to property. Control over real and personal property is vindicated by the tort of trespass. A person can own and control a home and personal property like an automobile. Also, like the freedom to control personal autonomy, the freedom to control property can be protected by constitutional law, which provides a means to prevent government takings of property interests.

Generally, the types of rights that are protected include the right to use property, to sell property, and to exclude others from the enjoyment of property. The type of ownership, for example, leasehold or fee simple, determines the extent of control over the property, subject to some limitations in use based on government regulations.[59] Clearly, a major sector of privacy-related protection relates to "place" and ownership.

Theories of property law are also used to guard certain types of information. For example, property-based law protects information rights in copyrights, patents, and trademarks and is used as a theoretical basis for the "appropriation of personality" and "right to publicity" torts that protect individuals from the misuse of their name or image.

---

4. Sensitive personal and identification information (e.g., Social Security number, driver's license number, credit card information, and library records)
5. Public-safety information (e.g., building plans, port or power plant facilities)
6. Sensitive information about victims or third parties (e.g., names, photos)
7. Proprietary information (e.g., trade secrets, whether government or private)
8. Investigatory material (e.g., investigations by police and other agencies, usually only ongoing)
9. Personnel information (e.g., employment records, employee reviews and evaluations)
10. Age-sensitive information (e.g., juvenile records)
11. Family-related personal information (e.g., parental rights, adoption, custody)
12. Certain judicial or court proceedings (e.g., mediation, arbitration, grand jury)
13. Professional disciplinary proceedings (e.g., Florida bar, Judicial Qualifications Commission, medical peer review, professional organizations, supervising agencies)
14. Legislative exemption (e.g., legislative records made confidential and exempt)

See Warren & Brandeis, supra note 22. See also SOLOVE, supra note 3 (listing various categories of protected information in the table of contents, including health and genetics; government records; business and financial records; and privacy at home, school, and work).
59 For example, zoning laws constitute government limitations on private and commercial use of property.

4. The Control-of-Physical-Space Sphere: Protecting the Person

The fourth sphere of privacy, freedom to control physical space, is distinct from the freedom to control property. Physical space connotes a completely personal right. It is protected by criminal-law and tort-law principles. Even in societies that have no private property ownership rights, control of physical space is protected.[60] A portion of this right is derived from ancient legal principles used to protect against assault, battery, and trespass. Such freedom is directly related to our ability to control the space that we choose to physically occupy. Legal protections for such control derive from search-and-seizure constitutional jurisprudence and intrusion-upon-seclusion torts. Relief has been sought under this theory for intense surveillance of Ralph Nader by General Motors,[61] intrusive "news gathering" about Jacqueline Kennedy Onassis by the paparazzi,[62] and video voyeurism.[63] In each case, the publication of information is not the basis for the violation; instead, it is the intrusion upon the person that is the basis for the case. There are also statutory protections from personal invasions, including stalking laws and false-imprisonment policies.

These four categories, when viewed as overlapping spheres of legal protection, may help define privacy expectations in modern society.

5. The Personal and Societal Context of Privacy: The Individual in Our Society

Despite multiple general definitions, privacy is a subjective and highly personal concept. We humans are highly self-aware of our individuality,

---

[60] For example, in North Korea, the government refuses to recognize individual property rights. However, the country's constitution protects the inviolability of person and residence, although government officials often fail to respect such rights in practice. BUREAU OF DEMOCRACY, HUMAN RIGHTS & LABOR, U.S. DEP'T OF STATE, COUNTRY REPORTS ON HUMAN RIGHTS AND PRACTICES: DEMOCRATIC PEOPLE'S REPUBLIC OF KOREA (2004), *available at* http://www.state.gov/g/drl/rls/hrrpt/2003/27775.htm.

[61] *See* Nader v. General Motors Corp., 25 N.Y. 2d 560 (N.Y. 1970).

[62] *See* Galella v. Onassis, 487 F.2d 986 (2d Cir. 1973) (holding that certain photographers could not come within twenty-five feet of Mrs. Onassis). The word *paparazzi*, as applied to the modern day meaning, is derived from a photographer named "Paparazzo" (playing off the word which literally means buzzing insect) in Federico Fellini's movie *La Dolce Vita* in 1960.

[63] *See* Video Voyeurism Prevention Act of 2004, 18 U.S.C.A. § 1801 (West 2004). This federal legislation prohibits the recording by any means or the dissemination of images of an individual's "private areas" without consent, under circumstances in which that individual has a reasonable expectation of privacy, regardless of whether the individual is in a private or public location.

and some even argue that we are the only animals that are self-aware.[64] In legal terms, however, the individual does not get to define his or her own boundaries in modern society. The legal system cannot respond to and redress harm according to an individual's view of his or her privacy rights. Legal recognition of privacy is based on a reasonable expectation of privacy rather than a personal subjective perception.[65]

As society changes, so too does its reasonable expectation of privacy, thereby making the task of setting a permanent definition of privacy impossible. Multiple factors exist that influence a "society" for purposes of defining reasonable expectations of privacy: family, religion, wealth, political structure, history, climate, work habits, geography, ideology, urbanization, cultural norms, and technology. Each of these factors affects a particular society's expectation of personal privacy[66] and influences individuals' expectations. Thus, expectations of privacy must be placed in context before one can address the level of legal privacy protection enjoyed by individuals living in different societies or countries. The Alaska Supreme Court, for example, focusing on place and time to determine whether there was a reasonable expectation of privacy, held that the private use of marijuana in Alaska was protected by privacy because

---

[64] See Michael D. Rivard, *Toward a General Theory of Constitutional Personhood: A Theory of Constitutional Personhood for Transgenic Humanoid*, 39 UCLA L. Rev. 1425, 1433 (1992) (theorizing that "[i]f the average, mature member of a species exhibits the capacity for self-awareness, then all members of the species are entitled to a rebuttable presumption of constitutional personhood"); *see also* DANIEL DENNETT, FREEDOM EVOLVES 2 (2003) ("If we find this astonishing, it is because we human beings, unlike all other species on the planet, are knowers. We are the only ones who have figured out what we are, and where we are, in this great universe.").

[65] Katz v. United States, 389 U.S. 347, 360 (1967) (Harlan, J., concurring) ("A person has a constitutionally protected reasonable expectation of privacy. . . . [T]here is a twofold requirement, first that a person have exhibited an actual [subjective] expectation of privacy and, second, that the expectation be one that society is prepared to recognize as 'reasonable.' Thus a man's home is, for most purposes, a place where he expects privacy, but objects, activities, or statements that he exposes to the 'plain view' of outsiders are not 'protected' because no intention to keep them to himself has been exhibited. On the other hand, conversations in the open would not be protected against being overheard, for the expectation of privacy under the circumstances would be unreasonable.").

[66] See Daniel J. Solove, *Conceptualizing Privacy*, 90 CAL. L. REV. 1087, 1094 (2002). Solove attempts to "conceptualize" privacy and differentiates the conceptualization of privacy from the mere use of the term. *Id.* He explains that a conception is a category, and thus requires that we look at the modern usage of the word *privacy* while identifying the common elements that are unique to privacy. *Id.* at 1096. Solove defines privacy in terms of "practices," or activities, customs, norms, and traditions. *Id.* at 1126. Solove's conceptualization of privacy is thus useful to an analysis of privacy law that accounts for societal changes.

"of the nature of the culture of the people of Alaska and their reverence for individuality."[67]

Among various cultures and societies there is a vast range in the value placed on the individual and hence in reasonable expectations of privacy. Some cultures have placed a different value on individuality in practice and in legal doctrine than has American culture.[68] One example comes from Nazi Germany. There, individuality was subsumed by ideology that came to define one's privacy interests without reference to individual rights or community standards.[69] Instead of individuals defining privacy interests for themselves, it was decided for them.[70] In Nazi Germany, there was a total lack of privacy, with such basic choices as one's spouse and procreation activities driven by Nazi ideology, namely, the protection and expansion of the "Aryan" race.[71] Thus, where the state has a powerful enough grip on its people, ideology can overtake and eliminate any semblance of individual privacy.

How a given society defines individuality in relation to the public also influences the meaning given to privacy. In small or closely knit societies that depend on or greatly emphasize a specific cultural element, individuals' privacy expectations are likely to differ from those in more populated and heterogeneous cultures. For example, Eskimo culture is greatly affected by the frigid climate, with little in the way of modern conveniences or technology. The Eskimo family[72] is the main social unit where people work and live together in tight, often dangerous, spaces.[73] Although familial closeness certainly impedes on individual privacy among family members, it also strengthens the expectation of privacy between the family unit and outsiders.[74] Eskimo culture illustrates that where a

---

[67] Ravin v. State, 537 P.2d 494, 504 (Alaska 1975).
[68] *See, e.g.*, Amanda Stallard, *Joining the Culture Club: Examining Cultural Context When Implementing International Dispute Resolution*, 17 OHIO ST. J. ON DISP. RESOL. 463, 472 (2002) (labeling North American and Northern European cultures as "low context," "characterized by individualism, heterogeneity, and overt communication" and Latin American and Asian cultures as "high context," "focus[ed] on collective identity, homogeneity, and covert communication").
[69] *See* Jon Mills, *Sex, Lies and Genetic Testing: What Are Your Rights to Privacy in Florida?*, 48 FLA. L. REV. 813, 819–20 (1996); *see also* GEORGE L. MOSSE, NAZI CULTURE: INTELLECTUAL, CULTURAL AND SOCIAL LIFE IN THE THIRD REICH xx (1966).
[70] *See* Mills, *supra* note 69, at 819.
[71] *See id.*
[72] *See* BARRINGTON MOORE, JR., PRIVACY: STUDIES IN SOCIAL AND CULTURAL HISTORY 3–80 (1984); Mills, *supra* note 69, at 817–18.
[73] *See* Mills, *supra* note 69, at 817–18.
[74] *Id.*

particular natural element, rather than governmental or societal influences, plays a critical role in everyday life, that factor can define an individual's expectation of privacy and influence choices concerning personal matters.

Similarly, religion can play a critical role in an individual's expectation of privacy. In ancient Hebrew society, for example, individual privacy was subordinated to the larger society as a whole.[75] Religion defined an individual in relation to society, placing the highest values on God and the solidarity of the Hebrew community.[76] Because individual sin was believed to affect the community as a whole, religion influenced personal decisions, with little or no autonomy left to the individual.[77] The Hebrews' religion did prohibit the arbitrary use of a leader's power solely for personal gain, but this prohibition did little to distinguish between the individual and public realms.[78]

Americans often say that our culture represents the pinnacle of support for individual autonomy and potentially the greatest extension of reasonable expectations of privacy. But is that true today? The constitutional underpinnings of free speech, free association, and the penumbras of the Bill of Rights cloak American citizens with significant privacy rights. However, the definition of privacy in America today is elusive because the concept is no more static than the concept of democracy or freedom. For instance, privacy today is a different concept than it was in colonial America. The New England colonists valued being alone and being with family in intimate settings.[79] Privacy was highly valued right as early as the sixteenth century.[80] Personal correspondence was generally given privacy protections.[81] Also, the notion that a "man's home is his castle" was generally accepted in colonial America.[82] Courts generally provided protections against unwanted intrusions of the privacy of the home.[83] Indeed, the law was established at the time of independence that

---

[75] *See id.* at 821–22; Ellis Weinberger, *Privacy, Database, and Jewish Law available at* http://www.cus.cam.ac.uk/~ew206/dissertation.html (last visited May 9, 2008).

[76] *Id.*

[77] *Id.*

[78] *Id.*

[79] DAVID H. FLAHERTY, PRIVACY IN COLONIAL NEW ENGLAND 6–7 (1967).

[80] *See id.* at 10–13 (citing examples of early use of the word *privacy*).

[81] *Id.* at 116 (stating that "[w]hen friends carried the mail the privacy of the contents was normally assured").

[82] *Id.* at 85–88.

[83] *Id.* at 89 (noting that an early complaint "for hovering about his house, peeping in at the window" occurred in 1680); *see also* State v. Williams, 2 Tenn. (2 Overt.) 106, 106–07 (1808) (recognizing a common law indictment for eavesdropping).

eavesdropping on an individual's home could be remedied through common law nuisance.[84]

Nonetheless, Puritan morality and religious beliefs limited, to some degree, individual privacy. Government surveillance and church-fostered communitarian efforts to promote pious behavior restricted the privacy inherent in individuals' lives. For instance, individuals were expected to conform to religious practice including observation of the Sabbath and maintaining their familiar hierarchies. Yet in practice, surveillance affected, but did not seriously threaten, individual privacy because of social norms necessitating a certain level of privacy.[85] As the significance of Puritanism in colonial New England diminished, other values, such as individualism, flourished.[86] The value placed on personal autonomy legitimated privacy claims as well.[87]

Furthermore, as the population grew and economic conditions improved, larger houses became more common, allowing anonymity in living space and enabling personal privacy.[88] Privacy also was available because of working conditions (farming in solitude), a slower pace of life (allowing for more rest), and the lack of intrusive technology. The availability of privacy coupled with the changing culture resulted in higher expectations of privacy. Early American societies likely did not have a conscious appreciation for threats to personal privacy, because privacy was unlikely to be invaded. Further, intrusions often could be remedied on a personal level, making recourse to the courts unnecessary.[89] Thus, privacy could be viewed as a cultural norm, merely a part of other legal concepts, rather than a distinct notion.[90] Perhaps the inherent expectation

---

[84] See 4 WILLIAM BLACKSTONE, COMMENTARIES ON THE LAWS OF ENGLAND 169 (1769) (stating that "Eaves-droppers, or such as listen under walls or windows or the eaves of a house, to hearken after discourse, and thereupon to frame slanderous and mischievous tales, are a common nuisance and presentable at the court-leet: or are indictable at the sessions, and punishable by fine and finding sureties for their good behaviour.").

[85] See FLAHERTY, supra note 79, at 243–44.

[86] Id. at 244.

[87] Id. But can strong religious beliefs and absolute personal autonomy be harmonized? Most monotheist religions call for a complete devotion of self to God, or some higher being. If this is the case, can there ever truly be private autonomy when all one's secrets are revealed to God? However, there are few things more personal and private than one's relationship with God. Therefore, if this is the only cause of the loss of privacy, how much autonomy is really sacrificed?

[88] Id. at 245.

[89] See id. at 246–48. Additionally, when privacy invasions mandated involvement of the courts, the remedies available often were adequate for the types of cases brought, such as trespass, search and seizure, and defamation. Id. at 248.

[90] See id. at 248.

of privacy and individuality that prevailed among early Americans explains why there is no explicit privacy protection in the text of the U.S. Constitution.[91]

Overall, the societal and legal definition of privacy relies almost completely on the context and culture in which privacy rights are being examined. Today's culture has evolved to a point where individuality and privacy are challenged by virtually all aspects of contemporary society.

6. The Importance of Privacy to the Individual and to Society

Brandeis called privacy "the right most valued by civilized men."[92] We acknowledge our belief in its importance with wide-ranging and weighty terms used to define it—for example, liberty, freedom, individuality, solitude, and seclusion. Although privacy can be thought of in those terms, it is not synonymous with any one of them. We have deemed it important and defined it in grandiose terms that include almost all aspects of being a person. Why do we consider it so important? It seems more real when we get specific and talk about freedom to choose our spouse, to define activities in our home, to control our body, to define our own sexual conduct, or to keep secret our finances, health needs, and buying habits. People will have subjective views on the relative importance of different categories of privacy rights—secrecy of medical treatments, the right to own a gun, the right to watch obscene movies in one's home, or the right to have homosexual relations. The importance of a specific privacy right is in the eye of the beholder and depends on what brand of privacy an individual values most. Individual priorities most certainly affect an individual's support for or opposition to a particular privacy protection. A person might see no contradiction in strenuously supporting privacy of medical information and vehemently opposing homosexual adoption.

We have our own symbols of privacy. We can go to a political rally, ride a motorcycle, wear jeans, read a book on knitting while attending a football game, marry our sweetheart privately, bungee jump off a bridge, or hate a television show and tell others why. The absence of privacy is the

---

[91] See Olmstead v. United States, 277 U.S. 438, 478 (1928) (Brandeis, J., dissenting) (suggesting that the right to privacy is inherent in the U.S. Constitution). For a more detailed discussion of the right to privacy embodied in the First Amendment, see *infra* Chapter V, § B.

[92] *Olmstead*, 277 U.S. at 478.

loss of control of one's identity, living space, conduct, dress and hairstyle, personal information, and thoughts. We all know that we give these things up in increments to be part of society.[93] When we lose control of more of these choices, we become concerned with "privacy."

Sometimes we willingly relinquish control. When we join the armed services we give up our choice in clothes, hairstyle, daily activities, and private showers. Sometimes privacy is taken, as in totalitarian states where privacy is the enemy of the government. Our Constitution protects a number of rights that are incapable of precise or succinct definition, for example, equality, due process, and freedom of speech. We do not need a benefit to be precisely defined to accept it as an important right. Does privacy go beyond a "noninstrumentalist" value to a tangible public good? In other words, does privacy have a tangible value, or is it just a good thing?

Writers have seen a need for some privacy to preserve "public mental health."[94] To enhance well-being a person must have a private place. Free will is necessary for political innovation against unwelcome changes and for mental health. Privacy is not just an abstract right in need of protection; it is part of a social environment that fosters creativity, thought, and growth beyond the protected status quo and in broader terms, it fosters "the pursuit of happiness." It is an antidote to the pressure of the status quo to preserve sameness.

Privacy is an integral part of the amalgamation of values that define a healthy society. Specifically, privacy promotes *individuality, intimacy,* and *liberty*.[95] Individuality allows people to *be themselves,* as opposed to always *being respectable,*[96] in a world made of glass walls. It allows the freedom to express views or to remain anonymous. Intimacy allows us choices

---

[93] *See* Pierre-Joseph Proudhon, General Idea of the Revolution in the Nineteenth Century 293–94 (2004) ("To be governed is to be watched, inspected, spied upon, directed, law-driven, numbered, regulated, enrolled, indoctrinated, preached at, controlled, checked, estimated, valued, censured, commanded, by creatures who have neither the right nor the virtue nor the wisdom to do so. To be governed is to be at every operation, at every transaction noted, registered, counted, taxed, stamped, measured, numbered, assessed, licensed, authorized, admonished, prevented, forbidden, reformed, corrected, punished.").

[94] Sydney M. Jourard, *Some Psychological Aspects of Privacy*, 31 Law & Contemp. Probs. 307–18 (1966); *see also* Robert Ellis Smith, Privacy 328 (1979).

[95] Paul Chadwick, Victorian Privacy Commissioner, Law Week 2006 Address at the State Library of Victoria: The Value of Privacy (May 23, 2006), *available at* http://www.privacy.vic.gov.au/ (search for "The Value of Privacy").

[96] Jourard, *supra* note 94, at 310.

to reveal ourselves to some, but not to others. The value of intimacy is tarnished when relationships are defined by outside sources and databases rather than personal molds that grow and shrink at the discretion of the parties to the relationship.[97]

Liberty is a precondition to the freedom of expression.[98] If you deny someone the necessary privacy, you deny them the capacity to express themselves to others and to associate with others. These personal values are very much a part of First Amendment freedoms in the United States.

The loss of privacy, therefore, not only is a loss to each of us as individuals, but also impairs creativity in art, science, and living. The loss of privacy can hurt each of us and all of us. So privacy serves utilitarian principles and existentialist principles. It is useful to society and the individual. Can it be true that we will act the same and feel the same if we know there is the electronic equivalent of a police officer taking notes twenty-four hours a day?[99] Will we choose not to go into a certain store or bar? When we know that our e-mails are monitored, are we discouraged from writing e-mails to a friend?

Orwellian "thought police" and *Brave New World*'s punishment for "thought crime" makes us nervous. How much of ourselves should be public knowledge or government monitored. In Franz Kafka's, "The Trial," Joseph K. is arrested and prosecuted for unknown crimes. Daniel Solove aptly compares Joseph K's plight to today's citizens who may have been turned down for a job or been denied a credit card, and they do not know how, why, or who the accuser is.[100]

B. Challenges to Privacy

Our intrusive society requires and keeps more information on individuals, and requires permits, licenses, and permission for a myriad of actions. There is apparently a hunger for more and more data. Information is available in photos, in videos, on DVDs, in audiotapes, in camera phones,

---

[97] *See* Chadwick, *supra* note 95, at 5.

[98] *See* Madhavi Sunder, *Authorship and Autonomy as Rites of Exclusion: The Intellectual Propertization of Free Speech in* Hurley v. Irish-American Gay, Lesbian and Bisexual Group of Boston, 49 STAN. L. REV. 143 (1996).

[99] *See* Christopher Slobogin, *Transaction Surveillance by the Government*, 75 MISS. L.J. 139 (2005).

[100] *See* SOLOVE, *supra* note 3.

over the Internet,[101] over the airwaves, and through the written word on paper. Each form is slightly different in effect and impact. Today's society seems to crave voyeuristic publications[102] and other media far beyond paper, such as YouTube. At the same time that the media are claiming broad protections, the very nature of media intrusiveness has changed. Not only is the government collecting more information about individuals, but government policies allow greater disclosure of that information to others. And now, the same government information is more readily available through Internet search engines.[103] In sum, if our society's desire is for more privacy protection, its actions are conflictingly schizophrenic.[104]

A sign that today's society has elements of exhibitionism and voyeurism is the success of modern condominiums designed specifically to allow passersby to see into people's lives.[105] Not only are there glass walls, but there are "peekaboo" features like a window between the kitchen and the bathroom and a bathroom that is a glass cube. Architecture is catching up with the personal displays on Facebook and YouTube.

---

[101] *See* Paul M. Schwartz, *Internet Privacy and the State*, 32 Conn. L. Rev. 815 (2000) (arguing that the Internet is the greatest threat to informational privacy and discussing the inadequacy of current remedies).

[102] *See* Jeffrey Scott Shapiro, *Fair Comment: Why Are the Tabs Ganging Up on Kobe Bryant's Accuser?*, Insight on the News, Apr. 26, 2004 (discussing the invasive and voyeuristic tactics of modern tabloids).

[103] *See, e.g.*, USA People Search, http://www.usa-people-search.com (last visited May 7, 2008) (allowing, for a fee, access to such information as addresses, telephone numbers, and criminal and court records).

[104] However, it may be more correct to assert that although any given member of society wants more privacy for himself or herself, an individual is more than willing to sacrifice the privacy of others for his or her own personal gain. As game theory teaches, there may exist a prisoners' dilemma of privacy. *See generally* Duncan Luce & Howard Raiffa, Games and Decisions 47 (1983). Each player in the game values the theoretical right of privacy, but not absolutely. The highest "payoff" is to have one's own privacy fully respected while retaining the right to uncover information about others. The lowest payoff, then, is to have one's privacy rights violated while being unable to gather information about others. A game-theoretic approach to privacy recalls an appropriate analogy to First Amendment protections for free speech, as scholars have noted the tendency of those of all political persuasions to champion censorship for others' views while advocating nearly unlimited free-speech rights for themselves. *See* Nat Hentoff, Free Speech for Me but Not for Thee (1993). The recent boom in technology has, of course, increased the stakes in the privacy game.

[105] Penelope Green, *Yours for the Peeping*, N.Y. Times, Nov. 4, 2007, § 3, at 1, *available at* http://www.nytimes.com/2007/11/04/weekinreview/04green.html (last visited May 7, 2008).

1. The Evolution of More-Intrusive Technology

Available technologies, including CCTV, camera phones,[106] GPS locators,[107] national identification cards,[108] identity chips,[109] interactive television,[110] and the Internet,[111] represent an explosion of potential privacy intrusions. These technologies have a series of impacts on privacy: (1) technology makes it easier to gather information through spike mikes,[112] search engines, infrared sensors, CCTV, and long-distance cameras; (2) technology makes it easier to file, assemble, and collate mountains of previously dispersed and obscure data; (3) our use of technology such as cell phones, the Internet,[113] a GPS, or even a printer[114] makes it easier to track us; and

---

[106] Camera phones have given rise to such previously unthought-of signs as "No camera phones in the locker room" in health-club facilities. *See* Jo Napolitano, *Hold It Right There, and Drop That Camera*, N.Y. Times, Dec. 11, 2003, *available at* http://www.nytimes.com (search for "Hold It Right There and Drop That Camera").

[107] *See* Road User Fee Task Force, Office of Innovative Partnership & Alternative Funding, The Oregon Mileage Fee Concept: Discoveries 2003–2004 (2004), *available at* http://www.oregon.gov/ODOT/HWY/OIPP/docs/ruftf_2004dec21_discoveries.pdf (last visited May 9, 2008). Courts have allowed employers to track employees with a GPS in company cars, *see* Elgin v. St. Louis Coca-Cola Bottling Co., No. 4:05CV970-DJS, 2005 WL 3050633 (E.D. Mo. Nov. 14, 2005), but courts have said that placing a GPS on a rental car without notice is a violation of the leasee's privacy, *see* Turner v. American Car Rental, Inc., 92 Conn. App. 123 (2005).

[108] *See* Jamie Colby, *The Real ID Act*, Fox News, Feb. 5, 2005, http://www.foxnews.com/story/0,2933,249900,00.html (last visited May 9, 2008). The Real ID Act of 2005 requires states to include personal information in a magnetic strip attached to every driver's license. Intended as a tool to improve national security, the Real ID will include an individual's sex, address, digital photo, and fingerprints. However, the May 2008 deadline for implementation, along with various privacy concerns, has caused many states to pass resolutions against the Real ID Act.

[109] *See* Barnaby J. Feder & Tom Zeller, Jr., *Identity Chip Planted under Skin Approved for Use in Health Care*, N.Y. Times, Oct. 14, 2004, *available at* http://www.nytimes.com (search for "Identity Chip Planted under Skin").

[110] *See* Katz, Note, *infra* note 124, at 163.

[111] *See* Elbert Lin, *Prioritizing Privacy: A Constitutional Response to the Internet*, 17 Berkeley Tech. L.J. 1085, 1090 (2002) (arguing that the Internet requires a constitutional right to protect informational privacy).

[112] Spike mikes are microphones usually mounted at the end of a spike or probe and can allow for remote monitoring or recording of conversations. Paul Brookes, Electronic Surveillance Devices 22 (Newnes Pocket Books 2001) (1996).

[113] *See* Michael R. Siebecker, *Cookies and the Common Law: Are Internet Advertisers Trespassing on Our Computers?*, 76 S. Cal. L. Rev. 893 (2003).

[114] *See* Electronic Frontier Foundation, *Is Your Printer Spying on You?*, http://www.eff.org/issues/printers (last visited May 9, 2008). A study by the Electronic Frontier Foundation found that some laser printers encode each page with identifying information that can identify the printer a document came from. In an effort to identify counterfeiters, the U.S. government persuaded printer manufacturers to use such identifiers. Recently, E.U. policymakers expressed concern about the practice. Commissioner Franco Frattini

(4) new technology makes it easy to distribute information worldwide in an instant. It is simply a fact that privacy is more in jeopardy today because of modern technology. Although there once was a time where spoken words disappeared and newsprint merely turned to dust, "[t]oday, our pasts have become etched like a tattoo into our digital skin."[115]

Among the myriad consequences, these technologies facilitate businesses' creation of consumer profiles, using personal information and demographics, to aid in marketing, sales research, and solicitation.[116] Although arguably privacy is violated[117] when companies track Internet use or collect consumer information, consumers usually must "opt out,"[118] or provide consent, to prevent disclosing personal information. But often, as in the case of a routine Internet purchase, consumers may not consider the information provided to be embarrassing or revealing and may thus readily grant consent. The Internet provides an open pipeline for the flow of personal information. A user may unwittingly transmit information to a third party simply by browsing the Internet,[119] or because of certain

---

said that although the European Commission could not uncover a specific law against the dots themselves, "to the extent that individuals may be identified through material printed or copied using certain equipment, such processing may give rise to the violation of fundamental human rights, namely the right to privacy and private life. It also might violate the right to protection of personal data." Posting of Danny O'Brien to Deeplinks Blog, EU: Printer Tracking Dots May Violate Human Rights, http://www.eff. org/deeplinks/2008/02/eu-printer-tracking-dots-may-violate-human-rights (Feb. 13, 2008).

[115] J.D. Lasica, *Digital Footsteps*, SALON MAGAZINE, Nov. 1998, *available at* http://www. jdlasica.com/articles/digital.html (last visited May 9, 2008).

[116] *See* Siebecker, *supra* note 113, at 896–900.

[117] *Cf.* FRED H. CATE, PRIVACY IN PERSPECTIVE 9–17 (2001) (discussing beneficial uses of information, including reducing the cost of consumer credit, identifying and meeting consumer needs, enhancing customer convenience and service, promoting competition and innovation, preventing and detecting fraud, informing the electorate, and protecting public health and safety).

[118] There are two types of rules concerning the choice to provide personal information. Under an "opt-in" rule, the consumer must affirmatively agree to the use of his or her information. An "opt-out" rule allows the data broker to use a consumer's information unless the consumer requests that it remain confidential. *See generally* PAUL H. RUBIN & THOMAS M. LENARD, PRIVACY AND THE COMMERCIAL USE OF PERSONAL INFORMATION xx–xxi (2002) (arguing that "[a]n opt-in rule would dramatically reduce the amount of information available to the economy and impose substantial costs on consumers").

[119] A cookie, which is a text file generated by a Web site and stored on a user's computer, may store information about a user's use of a Web site. Although some cookie data can be considered harmless (e.g., color-scheme preferences, a session ID so that a user does not need to login to a password-protected Web site each time the user attempts to load a new Web page), some information that can be stored in cookies may present a threat to privacy. For example, cookies may be used by third parties to display advertising on the basis of a user's prior browsing habits. A third-party advertising provider may be

software installed (potentially without the user's knowledge or consent) on a computer.[120] Several cases have challenged the legality of "cookies" under the Wiretap Act[121] and the Stored Communications Act.[122] Generally, if a third-party advertiser's actions are undertaken with the Web site operator's prior consent, the advertiser's acts do not violate the law.[123] Courts tend to uphold the legality of transmitting information via cookies.

In addition to cookies, there is now a wealth of data flowing from watching television. Interactive TV (ITV)[124] is distinct from cable because it allows customers to navigate, record, and replay. One example is the popular TiVo function. In the future, customers may be able to pick camera angles or purchase an item directly through their television. Also, the provider can monitor channel clicks and determine favorite shows

---

able to track a user's browsing habits across multiple Web sites. Although this information typically does not link browsing habits across sites with personally identifiable information, it is likely possible. Browsing habits within a single site can easily be tracked and linked to personal information. For example, a user may shop and have an account at a hypothetical onlinestore.com. When logged in to the site, the online store may track the items the user views and purchases and may use this information to create a customer profile. In this case, cookies may be used to link personally identifiable information with browsing habits.

[120] "Adware" or "malware" may be installed unwittingly on a user's computer. This installation may happen, for example, when the software is bundled with other software in a single installation package, when reporting functions of otherwise legitimate software are undisclosed or hidden in lengthy user agreements, or when a nefarious individual exploits a bug in a Web browser, plug-in, or other computer program to install software on a user's computer. These programs, which sometimes behave similarly to computer viruses, may track a user's computer use even outside of the Web (e.g., what programs are running, the file names of documents in use) and may even be used to log a user's keystrokes. The transmission of information obtained by such software may constitute a significant threat to privacy. Therefore, it is very important to keep installed software up to date with the latest security patches.

[121] Wiretap Act, 18 U.S.C. §§ 2510–2522 (2000).

[122] Stored Communications Act, 18 U.S.C. §§ 2701–2712 (2000).

[123] *See* Bruce Boyden, *Privacy of Electronic Communications, in* PROSKAUER ON PRIVACY § 6:2.4[B][3] (Christopher Wolf ed., 2006) (discussing legal challenges to cookies used in online advertising); *see also* Siebecker, *supra* note 113 (arguing that cookies constitute a common-law trespass). *See, e.g., In re* DoubleClick Inc. Privacy Litigation, 154 F. Supp. 2d 497, 510–11 (S.D.N.Y., 2001) (holding that the Electronic Communications Privacy Act (ECPA) did not extend to "cookies" placed by Internet advertisers on computer hard drives in order to select advertisements to display to users).

[124] Interactive television is described as a means to transform television into an "on-demand, participatory, non-linear, infotainment, advertising targeted, broadband, two-way communication platform." David Katz, Note, *Privacy in the Private Sector: Use of the Automotive Industry's 'Event Data Recorder' and Cable Industry's 'Interactive Television' in Collecting Personal Data*, 29 RUTGERS COMPUTER & TECH. L.J. 163, at 182 (2003).

and potential purchases.[125] The industry is growing fast. There are 18 million hook ups today and more coming. The technology could ultimately tailor advertisements to the specific individual watching TV at the time-instant marketing. All of this feedback of information gives a large amount of data to the service provider. And none of this information is subject to the same restrictions that cable TV providers must follow.[126] The privacy concerns are huge.[127]

Because of marketing potential, companies collecting personal information can and do profit from its sale.[128] Information sold on the Internet includes detailed information accumulated from public records and packaged for sale on Web sites that sell background information.[129] In his book *No Place to Hide*, Robert O'Harrow describes the common world of data assembly and surveillance.[130] O'Harrow notes that consumers are often willing, if not eager, to accept such corporate surveillance of their habits.[131] Nonetheless, O'Harrow explains that such acceptance ends when these data brokers are caught selling their information to thieves or the brokers' own databases are raided by

---

[125] Farhood Manjoo, *Your TV Is Watching You*, SALON.COM, May 8, 2003, http://dir.salon.com/story/tech/feature/2003/05/08/future_tv (last visited on May 7, 2008).

[126] Section 631 of the 1934 Communications Act (47 U.S.C. 551), known as the Cable Act, proscribes privacy protections for cable television operators. Currently, digital broadcast satellite providers and providers of digital recording services are not considered cable television operators and therefore "do not currently have to comply with the privacy protections in section 631 because such provisions apply only to cable operators." *See* H.R. 3511 [108th]: Video Programming Consumer Privacy Protection Act of 2003, *available at* http://www.govtrack.us/congress/bill.xpd?bill=h108-3511 (last visited on May 7, 2008). Congressman Edward Markey [D-MA] introduced a bill in 2003 to effectively bring these activities under the regulation of cable television providers, but the bill did not pass and has not been reintroduced. *Id.*

[127] CENTER FOR DIGITAL DEMOCRACY, TV THAT WATCHES YOU: THE PRYING EYES OF INTERACTIVE TELEVISION 6 (2001), *available at* http://people.virginia.edu/~qw2d/STS402/resourses/IPTV--privacyreport.pdf (last visited on May 7, 2008).

[128] *See* Bethany R. Harrison, *When Companies Sell Information Gathered Through the Internet*, BUS. L. TODAY, Nov.-Dec. 2004, at 13, 14.

[129] *See, e.g.*, PeopleFind, http://www.peoplefind.com/background_search.htm (last visited May 9, 2008) (discussing information available, including property owned, names of neighbors and relatives, any civil or criminal records, demographics of neighborhood, value of property).

[130] *See* O'HARROW, *supra* note 57.

[131] *See id.* at 62 (noting that data brokers like Acxiom are marketed to the public as trusted third parties that oversee personal information). Acxiom's "privacy officer," Jennifer Barrett, asserts that her company "helps provide individuals with more shopping opportunities, quicker loan approvals, targeted marketing promotions, and an array of conveniences. . . . [M]ost people don't know or care how their information is used to generate these Information Age benefits, as long as they keep coming." *Id.*

outsiders.[132] The reporting of the security breaches of ChoicePoint, Acxiom, and the LexisNexis subsidiary Seisint, through which thousands of individuals' personal information was stolen, has heightened public awareness of the inherent problems in the mass gathering of personal information.

Many of these data brokers are heavily involved in the security business. ChoicePoint, for instance, gathers criminal records of thousands of individuals for use by police departments and other governmental agencies to help police the community.[133] Where such governmental agencies lack the resources, will, or ability to create an identity database on their own, private industry and private information profilers can step in to do what the government, for political or other reasons, will not.[134] The problems for society arise when such information is provided to those outside the governmental sphere, either intentionally or unintentionally, or when overreaching members of the government and law-enforcement community use it to achieve personal gain, harass innocent citizens, or curtail otherwise lawful behavior.

Even without the intentional misuse of personal information, the danger posed by the practice of data gathering is significant. The dissemination or sale of personal information is highly invasive, sometimes causing emotional harm, financial losses, or further invasions of privacy.[135] Moreover, large quantities of personal information can be easily transferred to others with the click of a mouse, which increases the likelihood that individual harm will result from the collection of personal data.[136] Yet the First Amendment's right to free speech likely protects the collection and distribution of personal information provided voluntarily

---

[132] In 2003, a computer hacker gained access to Acxiom's encrypted files and stole names, credit-card numbers, Social Security numbers, addresses, and other details involving an estimated 20 million people and collectively valued at $1.9 million. *Id.* at 71–72.

[133] *See id.* at 92 (describing ChoicePoint's many uses, including "data mining, fingerprints, high-technology cards, and an ever-expanding network of checkpoints to verify that someone was who they claimed to be").

[134] *See id.* Post-September 11 antiterrorism efforts have spawned the development of security systems like "Matrix," which combines privately collected individual information with financial records, credit-card activity, and criminal history, through the use of federal subpoenas, giving investigators the new power to discern patterns and apply models that single out potential terrorists and supporters on the basis of precise and layered characteristics. *Id.* at 107–08.

[135] *See* discussion *infra* Chapter VII, § C.

[136] *See* Jonathan P. Graham, Note, *Privacy, Computers, and the Commercial Dissemination of Personal Information*, 65 Tex. L. Rev. 1395, 1398 (1987).

by the consumer.[137] Furthermore, many of the sources of individual information are public records. But the nature of such information changes
dramatically when it is compiled and made readily available to both
government and private viewers. New Web sites are now devoted exclusively to gathering consumers' personal information such as prior arrests,
addresses, and neighborhood income levels.[138]

Convenient and efficient advances in technology tend to diminish
privacy. Whether this convenience is worth the price is certainly arguable,
but individual expectations of privacy are nevertheless affected by technology. For instance, in his book *The Naked Crowd*, Jeffrey Rosen documents the psychological alterations in expectations of privacy created by
the explosion of the Internet.[139] Rosen explains that modern individuals
in American society are less often seeking acceptance from societal norms,
but instead have begun to choose to gain acceptance from the faceless
crowd of the Internet.[140] To do this, Rosen claims, individuals are forced to
"reveal details of their personal lives without being able to gauge the audience's reaction."[141] It is this process that has led to a devaluation of privacy
in America, a trend Rosen sees as dangerous and fraught with peril.[142] Given
the many technological advances and their impact on individual privacy, it
seems obvious that adequate and flexible legal remedies are needed.[143]

---

[137] *See, e.g.*, Dwyer v. Am. Express Co., 652 N.E.2d 1351, 1354 (Ill. App. Ct. 1995) (stating
that the voluntary use of a credit card gives the information to the company, and thus,
the company has not committed an unauthorized intrusion by compiling and then
renting out the information). "By using the American Express card, a cardholder is
voluntarily, and necessarily, giving information to defendants that, if analyzed, will
reveal a cardholder's spending habits and shopping preferences. We cannot hold that a
defendant has committed an unauthorized intrusion by compiling the information
voluntarily given to it and then renting its compilation." *Id.* These disclosures are now
regulated more closely. See the discussion of ECPA Chapter III, § B-4(a).

[138] For an example of such a Web site, *see* http://www.intelius.com (last visited May 9,
2008), which, for a fee, will perform background checks and inform paying customers
of personal information.

[139] Jeffrey Rosen, *The Naked Crowd*, SPIKED, July 19, 2004, http://www.spiked-online.com/
Articles/0000000CA5FF.htm (last visited May 9, 2008).

[140] *See id.*

[141] *Id.*

[142] *See id.* Rosen believes that the growing "culture of self-revelation" will eventually cause
a suffocating atmosphere of conformity that will undermine the individualistic history
and traditions of America. *See id.*

[143] For a general discussion on individual rights in personal information, see ANNE W.
BRANSCOMB, WHO OWNS INFORMATION? FROM PRIVACY TO PUBLIC ACCESS (1994).
Branscomb argues that if information were given the full protection of property law,
the following legal principles would emerge:

1. Secrecy: the right to prevent disclosure of information

However, certain remedies have been limited for years. With the advent of the Internet came the question of who bears liability for its content. To address this question, Congress acted to ensure that Internet service providers ("ISPs") could continue to provide access to information without fearing liability for the content its users posted online using its service. ISPs are generally not liable for third-party communications published on the Internet.[144] The majority of federal circuits have interpreted the federal Communications Decency Act ("CDA") as establishing broad federal immunity from any cause of action that would otherwise make service providers liable for information that originates from a third-party user of the service.[145] In other words, the CDA precludes courts from placing an ISP in a publisher's role. Additionally, where a state law contradicts the CDA, the state law is deemed preempted.[146] These policies limit the remedies available to parties harmed by information published on the Internet.

2. Different Media—Different Intrusion

Another important issue is the recognition that information conveyed or available through different modes has different effects. Photos have a different impact than written words, and video has a different impact than photos, as a mode of intrusion. This realization is the contemporaneous

---

   2. Privacy: the right to prevent unwelcome and unauthorized intrusions
   3. Confidentiality: the right to release information with restrictions and to prevent others from obtaining the information without the subject's consent
   4. Publicity: the right to release information into the public domain at a time and place of one's own choosing
   5. Commerciality: the right to sell information for fair value
   6. Accessibility: the right to obtain information
   7. Reciprocity: the right to receive value in exchange for value given
   8. Integrity: the right to control the accuracy and reliability of information
   9. Interoperability: the right to transparency in the transfer of information
   10. Responsibility: the duty to act responsibly
   11. Liability: the right to have grievances redressed
   12. Commonality: the right to share information in the public domain
   13. Equity: the right to have no wrong go unrighted
   Id. at 180–83.
[144]   47 U.S.C.A. § 230(c) (West 1998).
[145]   Almeida v. Amazon.com, Inc. 456 F.3d 1316, 1321 (11th Cir. 2006); *see* Zeran v. America Online, Inc. 129 F.3d 327 (4th Cir. 1997) (certiori denied); *see* Zeran v. America Online, Inc. 524 U.S. 937 (1998), which declares much of the CDA unconstitutional but leaves ISP immunity intact.
[146]   *See Zeran*, 129 F.3d at 334–35.

recognition of the Marshall McLuhan theory that "the medium is the message."[147]

Recall that Warren and Brandeis were concerned with the intrusive nature of the medium of photography.[148] Today, images can be acquired and portrayed through written words, developed pictures, digital files, videotapes, and video broadcasts. Those images can then be sent to or made available to every computer in the world. There is no doubt that the impact of information disclosure on individual privacy varies depending on the medium of disclosure involved. For example, an autopsy photograph has a different effect on the observer than does the written report describing it. Although a transcript of voices during a tragic accident may be painful, listening to actual broadcast voices of a loved one would be far worse.

Courts have recognized the differences among the various mediums for delivering information and their impact on personal privacy. The medium in which personal information is conveyed matters to and bears on the level of privacy protection given by courts. For example, in *New York Times Co. v. NASA*, the U.S. Court of Appeals for the D.C. Circuit held that the final voice recordings of the Challenger astronauts could not be released.[149] Because such recordings were held to be of an invasive nature to the families of the astronauts, the court held that their privacy interests were protected under the federal Freedom of Information Act.[150] However, the court allowed the release of a written transcript of the recordings because it would be less intrusive in nature. The court recognized that although the written words and the spoken words were the same, the impact on the privacy interests of the family were very different.

Another example of evolving protection based on the medium of conveyance is Florida legislation that compels a showing of good cause by anyone wishing to observe autopsy pictures.[151] The statute was upheld

---

[147] MARSHALL MCLUHAN, UNDERSTANDING MEDIA: THE EXTENSIONS OF MAN (1964).
[148] *See* Warren & Brandeis, *supra* note 22, at 14–15.
[149] *See* New York Times v. NASA, 782 F. Supp. 628, 631 (D.D.C. 1991) (holding that disclosure of an audiotape recording, containing the Challenger astronauts' voices and background noise before the shuttle exploded, would constitute a "clearly unwarranted" invasion of personal privacy, pursuant to the exemption for disclosure provided by the Freedom of Information Act).
[150] *See id.* at 632–33; *see also* Campus Commc'n. Inc. v. Earnhardt, 821 So. 2d 388 (Fla. Dist. Ct. App. 2002) (holding that a publishing company seeking autopsy photographs of a famous racecar driver did not establish good cause to gain access to view or copy the autopsy report and that the privacy interest of the driver's family prevailed).
[151] A significant number of states restrict access to autopsy photos. *See infra* note 1304.

against various First Amendment and public-records challenges.[152] Again, the court and the statute recognized the difference between the release of a written autopsy report, which is permitted, and autopsy photos that visually depict an individual.

What the judges in these cases have recognized is that alternative means of disseminating information about the same factual circumstances can have divergent impacts on personal privacy. Privacy policies should mitigate a potentially harmful impact by requiring that the disclosure of information be made in the least harmful way when compelling interests justify lowering the privacy shield at all. Further, privacy policies must be technologically rational and consider the effects and intrusions caused by different means of communication.

3. New Technology and New Decisions on Birth, Life, and Death

The advent of new medical and biological technologies has changed how the law must deal with the age-old issues of birth, life, and death. The law is asked to answer questions it never had to address before concerning traditional personal decisions. Because these technologies are so new, the law in these areas is developing. Moreover, the issues of birth, death, and genetics are emotional and controversial and deal with basic human values and religious beliefs.

In the past, reproductive decisions did not involve contracting for a baby using sperm or eggs from people other than the parents or having an embryo carried by someone other than the mother. The right to die did not involve dealing with life-sustaining machines that perpetuate a life when an individual is incapable of breathing or eating. It falls to the law to balance and determine the human consequences of these technological changes.

a. Procreation

Procreation is an area of human decision making where the law has given the individual great discretion. Controversy began when technology modified human decisions. Contraceptives have been around, in one

---

[152] Earnhardt v. Volusia County, Office of the Med. Exam'r, No. 2001-30373-CICI (Fla. Cir. Ct. July 10, 2001); *Campus Commc'n.*, 821 So. 2d at 392–95.

form or another, for thousands of years,[153] but in the early 1960s, when the first oral contraceptive pill was introduced, many states reacted by making it illegal to give married couples advice about the use of contraceptives. Use of contraceptives is, of course, still contrary to some religious beliefs.

The availability of contraceptives was the catalyst for one of the landmark privacy cases. In *Griswold v. Connecticut*, the Court found that contraception was such a personal decision that it is protected by a constitutional right to privacy.[154] Soon thereafter, in *Roe v. Wade* the Court recognized that the state could not make it illegal for a woman to terminate her pregnancy. *Griswold* and *Roe* represent some of the cornerstones of privacy jurisprudence relating to autonomy. These cases demonstrate the deference the Court has given to personal decisions dealing with procreation and childbearing. Now technology is presenting a new set of issues that would have been hard to predict even fifty years ago.

Today the new questions in reproductive issues relate to what is termed alternative reproductive technology. New terms such as "fertility tourism" have been coined to refer to the phenomenon of individuals shopping for jurisdictions whose laws relating to reproduction allow them to accomplish their individual reproductive goals.

With the advent of alternative reproductive technology, couples can use a third party's donated sperm or egg to conceive. People can also contract with a third party who agrees to be a surrogate and carry the child through gestation. As many as five parties could be involved in the production of a child: two prospective parents desiring a baby who contract with a surrogate and with both egg and sperm donors. Like traditional adoption, this method leads to parenthood without any genetic relation to the child.

It is easy to see the myriad problems that may arise from a five-party "transaction" involving the production of a child. Imagine a scenario in which a couple contracts with a surrogate who, after two months, decides she wants an abortion. The husband and wife, who desired the child and perhaps contributed the gametes, would assert a privacy interest as genetic parents in the decision making with regard to the child. However, it is not

---

[153] PLANNED PARENTHOOD FEDERATION OF AMERICA, A HISTORY OF BIRTH CONTROL METHODS (2002), *available at* http://www.plannedparenthood.org/resources/research-papers/bc-history-6547.htm (last visited May 9, 2008).

[154] Griswold v. Connecticut, 381 U.S. 479 (1965); *see also* Eisenstadt v. Baird, 405 U.S. 438 (1972) (extending the rights at issue in *Griswold* to single persons).

difficult to see that their interest would surely give way to the surrogate's autonomy to make decisions about her own body.[155] The couple might be limited to a breach-of-contract action against the surrogate.

There have been federal statutory attempts to create a uniform policy approach to reproductive technology, but there is no existing national policy.[156] Few states have adopted the uniform statutes, and state law regarding assisted reproduction varies considerably.[157]

The issue will not go away or get less complicated. Right now, an American soldier preparing to deploy to Iraq can leave his sperm behind at home, preserving the ability to have a child even if he dies.[158] This humane and thoughtful option may give rise to a number of legal conundrums. Some state statutes protect the right of children "conceived" before the death of a father but do not contemplate this possibility of artificial insemination after his death. What are the consequences? Can this child be a legal heir?

The law dealing with reproductive technology is inconsistent, scattered, and unsettled. Given the lack of uniformity and the complicated and novel nature of many of the problems likely to spring from assisted reproduction, courts in the United States are likely to see. Privacy issues relating to parents, children, siblings, donors, and hosts will arise continually. It will be up to the courts to sort out these issues.

b. Death and Dying

The issue of death is one that confronts the law with some frequency. The case of Terri Schiavo is the most famous recent example of a court's grappling with the "right to die." American courts have necessarily had to confront the difficult problem of suicide and assisted suicide.

Suicide and dying raise questions of personal autonomy, individual dignity, liberty, and privacy. Death is uniquely private. Penney Lewis points out that suicide is often described as "the ultimate exercise of one's right to privacy."[159] Although suicide used to be a crime, it is no longer.

---

[155] *See generally* MARY A. FIELD, SURROGATE MOTHERHOOD: THE LEGAL AND HUMAN ISSUES (1990).

[156] *See generally* Helene S. Shapo, *Assisted Reproduction and the Law: Disharmony on a Divisive Social Issue*, 100 Nw. U. L. REV. 465 (2006).

[157] *Id.*

[158] *See* Frank Buckley, *Insurance Policy: Soldiers Freezing Sperm*, CNN.COM, Jan. 30, 2003, http://www.cnn.com/2003/HEALTH/01/30/military.fertility/index.html (last visited May 9, 2008).

[159] Penney Lewis, *Rights Discourse and Assisted Suicide*, 27 AM. J.L. & MED. 45 (2001).

However, it is a crime to assist another in suicide. The most famous case is the criminal conviction of Dr. Jack Kevorkian for participating in the suicide of others.[160]

The Supreme Court has surgically defined the right to refuse medical treatment, without recognizing a right to assisted suicide.[161] In *Cruzan*, the Court stated that "for the purposes of this case, we assume that the United States Constitution would grant a competent person a constitutionally protected right to refuse lifesaving hydration and nutrition."[162] This assumption was later reiterated in *Glucksberg*, in which the Court stated that it had not only assumed but "strongly suggested" as well that the right existed.[163] In Justice William J. Brennan's dissent in *Cruzan*, he argued that not only should this right exist, but it should be fundamental. However, the majority did not agree. The explanation for this tentative recognition of a right to refuse medical treatment is a desire to resist a proliferation of cases of assisted suicide involving third parties and the ambiguous consequences of involving others.

The right to refuse medical treatment is a private right that, under this interpretation, involves no other person who causes the death of the patient. The Supreme Court has consistently upheld the right of states to prohibit assisted suicide.[164] In *Glucksberg* and *Vacco*, the Court looked to history and tradition, finding that no fundamental right to commit suicide exists under the Constitution. Furthermore, the Court emphasized the difference between *allowing* a patient to die from an illness and *causing* that person to die by procedure.

An important part of the process in end-of-life decisions is the principle of "substituted judgment." Although no one else is allowed to make the decision to terminate an individual's life other than that person, sometimes that decision is not clearly written and conveyed. In these cases courts can be asked to determine what the patient would do, through substituted judgment. This task is obviously profound and difficult but one that ultimately will fall to the courts when the wishes of the patient are disputed by relatives. In fact, that was the situation in the famous Schiavo case, in which the court found through "clear and convincing

---

[160] Michigan v. Kevorkian, 527 N.W.2d 714 (Mich. 1994).

[161] *See* Cruzan v. Director, Mo. Dep't of Health, 497 U.S. 261 (1990).

[162] *Id.* at 279.

[163] Washington v. Glucksberg, 521 U.S. 702, 719 (1997).

[164] *See id.* (holding that Washington statute did not violate due process); Vacco v. Quill, 521 U.S. 793 (1997) (holding that New York statute did not violate equal protection).

evidence" that Terri Schiavo would have wanted to end her life because of her persistent vegetative state.[165]

An individual may constitutionally refuse medical treatment, although the Court has reluctantly stated this principle. However, there is no constitutionally protected right to assisted suicide, and states are free to criminalize participation in this activity. But now it appears that states may allow alternative procedures to accomplish suicide. Oregon passed what is essentially an assisted-suicide provision that provides a procedure for two doctors to prescribe end-of-life pharmaceuticals. The statute was challenged by the Justice Department and upheld by the Supreme Court.[166] So it appears that individuals may be granted more autonomy in end-of-life decisions by state statutes in the future.

There is no doubt that this issue will continue to be emotional and controversial. Patients and families faced with long and painful deaths have sought assistance from the law. In *Krischer v. McIver*, an AIDS patient sought, in the face of a statute against assisted suicide, the constitutional right to seek assistance in ending his life.[167] The court denied him that right even under Florida's more expansive right to privacy. The dissent made an eloquent argument that will certainly be heard again:

> To my mind, the right of privacy attaches with unusual force at the death bed. This conclusion arises in part from the privacy our society traditionally has afforded the death bed, but also from the very core of the right of privacy—the right of self-determination even in the face of majoritarian disapproval. What possible interest does society have in saving life when there is nothing of life to save but a final convulsion of agony? The state has no business in this arena.[168]

---

[165] *In re* Guardianship of Schiavo, 780 So. 2d 176, 180 (Fla. Dist. Ct. App. 2001).

[166] The Oregon statute was challenged under a federal statute, but the U.S. Supreme Court held that the federal law could not, under the guise of drug enforcement, override a state statute. *See* Gonzales v. Oregon, 546 U.S. 243, 274–75 (2006).

[167] 697 So. 2d 97 (Fla. 1997). The facts in this case were compelling but not unique. Believing that his AIDS affliction was so agonizing that he had no hope of feeling better and that his life would be a continued agony, Mr. Hall wanted the ability to die at a time and place of his choosing. He wanted to consult a physician to provide a prescription that he could self-administer and that would result in painless death. He was concerned that any attempt to take his own life might be unsuccessful or worsen his condition.

[168] *Id.* at 111 (Kogan, J., dissenting).

c. Genetic Information

A person's genetic information is the ultimate manifestation of personal identity. It is cellular, invisible to the naked eye, and most often not known by anyone, including its host. Analyzing someone's DNA is equivalent to having a confidential open book about that person. Genetic information can reveal someone's gender or a predisposition to certain illnesses and contains the basic "building blocks" of a person's existence. In the right hands, this information can be used to help prevent certain illnesses or to treat them. In the wrong hands, however, this data can be used to intrude on a person's most private information.[169]

For example, a privacy issue of profound importance is the use or misuse or genetic information by employers and insurance companies. A person's predisposition to a disease could be used to deny employment or health insurance. The increased possibility that the individual will contract a disease makes that person a liability to an institution that provides health insurance or invests time and resources in that person's training and employment.[170]

Legislators and courts continue to wrestle with invasions of privacy based on genetics.[171] The Genetic Information Nondiscrimination Act (GINA)[172] recently passed both houses of Congress and was signed into law by President George W. Bush. Passage was delayed due to Senator Tom Coburn's (R–OK) previous hold on the bill because it contained an exception allowing discrimination based on genetic information from embryos and fetuses.[173] Professor Anita L. Allen pointed out that "[i]n

---

[169] See infra note 184 and accompanying text. For a contemporary update on genetic privacy issues, see Who Owns Your Body, http://whoownsyourbody.org (last visited May 9, 2008).

[170] NATIONAL HUMAN GENOME RESEARCH INSTITUTE, GENETIC DISCRIMINATION IN HEALTH INSURANCE, http://www.genome.gov/10002328 (last visited Nov. 21, 2007).

[171] For instance, it is now possible to swab the inside of your mouth with a cotton swab and mail the swab to laboratories across the country for various DNA testing. Companies such as Genelex (http://www.healthandDNA.com) charge a fee to customers to provide various services including paternity tests, predictive genetics tests, and ancestry DNA tests. The Food and Drug Administration currently has jurisdiction to oversee all laboratory tests under the Federal Food, Drug and Cosmetic Act, 21 U.S.C. §§ 331–360m (2000), that involve the delivery of a "device" across state lines. Genetic testing kits would appear to fall within the FDA's jurisdiction. However, when the customer merely delivers the swab, the swab fails to qualify as a medical device under the FDA's regulation. See Julie Han, The Optimal Scope of FDA Regulation and Genetic Tests: Meeting Challenges and Keeping Promises, 20 HARV. J.L. & TECH. 423, 430 (2007).

[172] H.R. 493, 100th 110th Cong. (2008).

[173] Editorial, Discrimination in the Genes, BOSTON GLOBE, May 2, 2007, available at http://www.boston.com/news/globe/editorial_opinion/editorials/articles/2007/05/02/discrimination_in_the_genes/ (last visited May 9, 2008).

tandem with HIPAA [the Health Insurance Portability and Accountability Act of 1996], the law would prescribe heightened confidentiality protections for genetic information maintained in health records, and also provide safe-guards against collection and disclosure."[174] However, there are various shortcomings in the legislation. The law does not explicitly prevent genetic information from being obtained by third parties. Furthermore, GINA does not apply to the military.

Since 1991, thirty-four states have passed laws protecting genetic information.[175] Although only a handful of states legislatively deem genetic information to be private property,[176] the majority of states with genetic privacy laws typically restrict certain parties, usually insurers or employers, from certain actions without consent.[177] For example, Florida requires public and private entities to, with specified exceptions, obtain informed consent from persons for DNA analysis (defined to include genetic testing) and keep the results confidential. The Florida statute also requires persons who perform or receive DNA analysis to notify the person tested of the results and of any use made of those results. The genetic information is exempt from Florida's sunshine law, and Florida imposes criminal penalties for violations of the statute.[178] California imposes penalties on any health-care service plan that willfully or negligently discloses genetic test results without written authorization.[179] Cali-fornia also has legislation prohibiting insurers and underwriters from disclosing individually identifiable medical or genetic information regarding a customer to a third party for purposes of granting credit.[180]

Information about health and gender may affect parents' decisions about an unborn child. Likewise, the same information at birth could affect parents' decisions in raising the child. If, for instance, a doctor told

---

[174] ALLEN, *supra* note 40, at 587.

[175] *See id*. at 584.

[176] These states are Florida, Alaska, Louisiana, Colorado, and Georgia. Other states, such as Michigan, expressly recommended against granting property rights in genetic information because doing so may lead to confusion and conflict with malpractice laws and the Federal Clinical Laboratory Regulations. *See* MICHIGAN COMM'N ON GENETIC PRIVACY & PROGRESS, FINAL REPORT AND RECOMMENDATIONS (1999), *available at* http://www.michigan.gov/documents/GeneticsReport_11649_7.pdf (last visited May 9, 2008).

[177] For a database of state legislation relating to genetic privacy, see National Conference of State Legislatures, State Genetic Privacy Laws, http://www.ncsl.org/programs/health/genetics/prt.htm (last visited Jan. 9, 2008).

[178] FLA. STAT. § 760.40 (2006).

[179] CAL. CIV. CODE § 56.17 (2007).

[180] *Id*. § 56.265.

parents that their child was predisposed to Huntington's disease, it could well have an impact on their decisions about how to, or whether to, raise the child.[181] And, now there is some research that suggests DNA can indicate whether a person may have violent tendencies.[182]

Wrongfully subjecting individuals to genetic testing can result in liability. In 2002, Burlington Northern Santa Fe Railway paid $2.2 million to settle claims by employees.[183] The company, suspicious of claims of carpal tunnel syndrome, required the employees who filed claims for the condition to submit blood samples for genetic DNA testing. The U.S. Equal Opportunity Employment Commission ("EEOC") successfully argued that giving the test to demonstrate a genetic predisposition for carpal tunnel syndrome violated the rights of the workers.

The concept of ownership and control of DNA, however, is not settled in the law. Do doctors have the right to test genes for purposes such as schizophrenia when the original *stated* purpose was to test for diabetes?[184] Also, doctors have patented a patient's genes and used them for their own purposes.[185] Can genes become a commodity to be sold for the modification of human characteristics? In his novel *Next*, Michael Crichton raises genetic engineering possibilities reminiscent of the science-fiction novel

---

[181] *See* Janet A. Benton, *Are Your Genes Protected? Federal Legislation and Genetic Discrimination*, 10 J. GENDER RACE & JUST. 285 (2007).

[182] Research indicates that the MAOA gene is responsible for an enzyme secreted in the brain that mops up neurotransmitters carrying signals from one nerve cell to another. One study indicates that a particular mutation in the MAOA gene is responsible for an increase of violent men in one extended family in Holland. *See* Steve Connor, *Genetic Test May Identify Boy Who Will Grow to Be Violent*," THE INDEPENDENT. Aug. 2, 2002, *available at* http://www.independent.co.uk/news/science/genetic-test-may-identify-boys-who-will-grow-to-be-violent-638555.html (last visited on May 5, 2008).

[183] *See* ALLEN, *supra* note 40, at 585.

[184] Can scientists do genetic research on your tissues without your consent? That is the essential question in a lawsuit pending before Judge Janet E. Barton of the Maricopa County Superior Court in Arizona. Members of the Havasupai Tribe allege that researchers from Arizona State University and the University of Arizona collected four hundred blood samples from tribal members for diabetes research, but that those same samples were used for additional unauthorized research on schizophrenia, inbreeding, and population migration. The tribe asserts that research on schizophrenia and inbreeding stigmatizes them and that they would not have authorized any migration research because it conflicts with their religious origin story.

[185] *See* discussion of *Moore v. Regents infra* Chapter VI, § J. Patients who donate tissues to a researcher or university may lose all legal rights to those tissues even if signed documents exist saying that the patients retain certain rights. That is the meaning of a recent court ruling in St. Louis involving the internationally famous prostate surgeon William Catalona. *See* Who Owns Your Body, *supra* note 169.

Brave New World's "predestination room," where humans can be genetically designed to fit certain specifications for the government.[186]

It is not science fiction to say that parents can select sperm or egg donors on the basis of physical traits such as hair or eye color so that, for example, their child will have blond hair.[187] At what point should the government intervene in personal decisions to do that which is scientifically possible but conflicts with current norms and values? Take cloning, for example.[188] As technology develops, the ability to analyze genetic information may well move out of the laboratory and become more commonplace.[189] The future complexities are beyond speculation.

The three issues discussed here, reproduction, death, and genetic engineering and mapping, are emblematic of the ongoing struggle for law, and privacy law in particular, to keep up with evolving technology. It is important to understand these issues because there is absolutely no question that the law will be required to resolve these most personal of human decisions.

4. The Increasing Demand for and Availability of Information

"Information" entails obtaining, collecting, and communicating or receiving data or knowledge.[190] The advent of new technologies creates more information sources and changes the way we acquire and disseminate personal information. A lot of information becomes available because of the voluntary or unconscious acquiescence of the public. In everyday life, individuals relinquish information to identify themselves, transact business, and obtain benefits. We give information to private businesses, individuals, and the government. Of course, if we wish to release information and expect it to be public, no remedy is needed. Sometimes, however, giving this information is a requirement of living in

---

[186] MICHAEL CRICHTON, NEXT (2006). In his novel, geneticists used human genes in animals, designed certain humans to be transgenic apes, and held as property the genes of individuals with special characteristics.

[187] *See* Michael D. Lemonick, *Designer Babies*, TIME, Jan. 11, 1999, *available at* http://www.time.com/time/magazine/article/0,9171,989987,00.html (last visited May 9, 2008).

[188] *See* Bonnie Steinbock, *Reproductive Cloning: Another Look*, 2006 U. CHI. LEGAL F. 87 (discussing some of the moral issues of cloning).

[189] Chris Gajilan, *Mapping Own DNA Changes Scientist's Life*, CNN.COM, Sept. 4, 2007, http://www.cnn.com/2007/HEALTH/09/04/dna.venter/index.html (last visited May 9, 2008).

[190] WEBSTER'S NINTH NEW COLLEGIATE DICTIONARY 620 (1985).

modern society. We are compelled or coerced to give information to the government that then becomes public information. Information given to private actors may be made available to marketers or may be acquired by the government, sometimes without a warrant. Much of this accumulation and trading of personal information goes on without our knowledge or consent even though we may have voluntarily given pieces of information over time. The chart below represents a simple way to determine how information is being treated. The release of information may be voluntary or involuntary.

Nature of Disclosure of Information

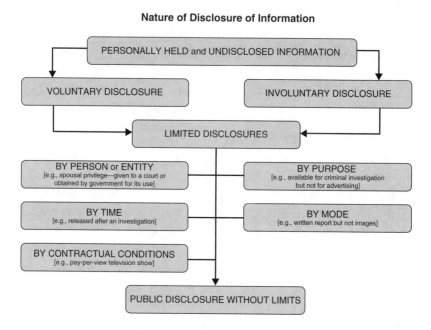

The government accrues information for a variety of purposes, ranging from licensing to compiling statistics. At one end of the scale of information gathering is obtaining information about citizens without their knowledge. This intrusion can occur with or without judicial supervision.[191] One of the most unregulated forms of governmental information gathering is what has been termed "transaction surveillance."[192]

---

[191] Leslie Cauley, *NSA Has Massive Database of Americans' Phone Calls*, USA TODAY, May 5, 2006, *available at* http://www.usatoday.com/news/washington/2006-05-10-nsa_x.htm (last visited May 9, 2008).

[192] Slobogin, *supra* note 99.

a. Transaction Surveillance: How the Government Watches Us

Governments have been in the surveillance business for a long time. They gather information for security purposes, for law enforcement, and for other reasons good or bad. The U.S. Constitution specifically protects against government searches and seizures, as does a long line of cases defining the limits of government conduct. Certain information is obtainable without probable cause or "reasonable suspicion" or any type of Fourth Amendment scrutiny whatsoever. These Fourth Amendment doctrines mean that we as citizens are particularly concerned about the government, with all its various powers, gathering information on us. And today, the government has better technological means than ever to facilitate intrusions.

Transaction surveillance is governmental monitoring of "written and digitized records, housed in private businesses, government agencies, and other institutions."[193] Other forms of information gathering used by the government, such as searches of houses, persons, documents, and effects, are subject to Fourth Amendment safeguards and usually require a warrant issued by a judge. Governmental authorities conducting these types of searches traditionally must meet a probable-cause standard—an articulable set of facts that lead an officer to reasonably believe that a crime has occurred, is occurring, or is about to occur—before attempting to gather the desired information.[194] Other less invasive forms of searches, such as stop-and-frisk actions, require that police first have a reasonable suspicion of criminal activity, which is a lower standard than probable cause.[195] Among the types of searches that fall under the reasonable-suspicion standard are those that arise in "special needs" situations, such as searches of school children and employees, drug testing, health and safety inspections, and roadblocks, requiring only minimal, yet still reasonable, suspicion.[196]

Governmental transaction surveillance, on the other hand, requires neither probable cause nor reasonable suspicion. "At most, government agents seeking transactional information need either a subpoena or a subpoena duces tecum issued by a grand jury, or an 'administrative subpoena' issued by a government agency which is valid as long as the information

---

[193] *Id.*

[194] *Id.* at 149–50.

[195] Terry v. Ohio, 392 U.S. 1 (1968).

[196] New Jersey v. T.L.O., 469 U.S. 325 (1985); Slobogin, *supra* note 99, at 150.

it seeks is 'relevant' to a legitimate (statutorily-authorized) investigation."[197] Regarding these venues for subpoenas, the Supreme Court defined "relevance" to be an extremely low standard, requiring only a "possibility" of relevance to the "general subject" of a subpoena duces tecum[198] and mere "official curiosity" to satisfy relevance for purposes of an administrative subpoena.[199] Although these venues for subpoenas may be challenged, such challenges are rarely successful.[200]

Still, subpoena requirements do not represent the lowest standard of scrutiny for governmental intrusions. Once the government is no longer conducting a "search or seizure," Fourth Amendment protection disappears completely. Although real-time government interception of communications requires both probable cause and a warrant, the acquisition of transaction information (identifying features of communications like names, phone numbers, e-mail addresses, and IP addresses) is virtually unrestricted.[201] The Ninth Circuit reasoned that Internet users have "no expectation of privacy in the to/from addresses of their messages or the IP addresses of the websites they visit because they should know that this information is provided to and used by Internet service providers for the specific purpose of directing the routing of information."[202] The Ninth Circuit's decision is rooted in well-settled Supreme Court case law.[203] Further, even bank records, logically considered sensitive,[204] are not protected,

---

[197] Slobogin, *supra* note 99, at 150–51. *See* Uniting and Strengthening America by Providing Appropriate Tools Required to Intercept and Obstruct Terrorism (USA PATRIOT) Act of 2001, Pub. L. No. 107-56 § 505, 115 Stat. 272, 365–66 (codified at 12 U.S.C. § 3414(a)(5)(A)).

[198] Slobogin, *supra* note 99, at 151(citing United States v. R. Enterprises, Inc., 498 U.S. 292, 301 (1991)).

[199] *Id.* (citing United States v. Morton Salt, 338 U.S. 632, 651–52 (1950)).

[200] *Id.* at 151.

[201] *See* United States v. Forrester, 512 F.3d 500, 510–11 (9th Cir. 2008).

[202] *Id.* at 510. *See also* Thygeson v. U.S. Bancorp, No. CV-03-467-ST 2004 WL 2066746, at *22 (D. Or. Sept. 15, 2004) (holding that Fourth Amendment protection does not extend to phone numbers and Web sites because callers and Internet surfers have "no reasonable expectation of privacy").

[203] *See* Smith v. Maryland, 442 U.S. 735, 742 (1979) (holding that there is no reasonable expectation of privacy in phone-company logs).

[204] *See* Christopher Slobogin, *Government Data Mining and the Fourth Amendment*, 75 U. CHI. L. REV. 317 (2008). In a survey conducted by Professor Slobogin, participants were asked to rank twenty-five scenarios in terms of their level of intrusiveness. With a police roadblock as the floor and the search of a bedroom the ceiling, surveillance of bank records was the second most intrusive scenario. The bedroom search received a mean intrusiveness score of 81.2 (out of 100); bank-record surveillance received a score of 80.3.

because the information was voluntarily given to a third party and therefore there is no reasonable expectation of privacy.[205]

In the Electronic Communications Privacy Act of 1986 ("ECPA")[206] and later, in the Patriot Act of 2001,[207] Congress chose to impose some level of statutory restraint on phone-number and Internet surveillance. Under the ECPA, "all the government agent must do is certify to a court facts that show the information is 'relevant to an ongoing investigation' and is 'likely to be obtained by [the surveillance].'"[208] Similarly, under the Patriot Act, the government need only certify that the information to be collected is relevant to a current investigation.[209] Under both statutes, the court *must* issue an order of authorization to use pen registers and trap-and-trace devices ("devices that obtain dialing, routing, addressing, or signaling information utilized in the processing and transmitting of wire or electronic communications") once the burden of showing relevance has been met.[210]

Another type of transaction surveillance is data mining. Data mining involves the use of private and public-records databases to accumulate and synthesize information about individuals or groups.[211] The process involves the analysis of enormous sums of information—bank records, credit-card activities, phone records, real-estate records, tax returns, travel itineraries, and more.[212] From these records, the government and private entities isolate specific behavioral patterns.[213] These patterns can then be used in many ways, from the development of suspect lists for crimes such as identity theft to the creation of lists of possible terrorists and persons who pose a potential risk to commercial flights.[214]

It is clear that current law allows data mining to gather vast amounts of information on individuals. For example, some fifty-two agencies,

---

[205] United States v. Miller, 425 U.S. 435, 443 (1976).

[206] PUB. L. No. 99-508, 100 Stat. 1848 (codified at 18 U.S.C. § 2510).

[207] Uniting and Strengthening America by Providing Appropriate Tools Required to Intercept and Obstruct Terrorism (USA PATRIOT) Act of 2001, Pub. L. No. 107-56, 115 Stat. 272.

[208] Slobogin, *supra* note 99, at 153 (citing 18 U.S.C. § 3123(a)(1) (2000)).

[209] *Id.* (citing 18 U.S.C. § 3121(c) (2000)).

[210] *Id.*

[211] U.S. GEN. ACCOUNTING OFFICE, REP. No. GAO-04-548, DATA MINING: FEDERAL EFFORTS COVER A WIDE RANGE OF USES 7 (2004), *available at* http://www.gao.gov/new.items/d04548.pdf (last visited May 9, 2008).

[212] *See* Slobogin, *supra* note 204, at 148–49.

[213] *Id.* at 148.

[214] *Id.* at 180–81.

from the Defense Department to the National Security Agency, are gathering data.[215] There were programs called Total Information Awareness (later, Terrorism Information Awareness) and others targeted to gather data on citizens. Although Congress has acted to limit some of the programs, large-scale data mining continues.

The long-term issue is how to define limits on the government's expansive appetite for information. Federal statutes have addressed some of the issues but have not created broad protections, perhaps because of continuing public concern with terrorism and security.[216] So a more effective solution may be interpretations of the Fourth Amendment that provide limitations and protections against broad government searches.[217]

b. Public Records: Government Information and Its Accessibility

In contrast to the relatively low level of protection against government surveillance of transaction information, most publicly held records are simply not protected at all. Openness of public records is a policy that was developed to improve government accountability. The modern reality is that these records are the largest source of information about individuals. The vast majority of information requests at the federal level are by businesses for commercial purposes.[218] The major search engine Google recognizes the value of public records. The company has partnered with four states—Arizona, California, Utah, and Virginia—to remove technical barriers that had prevented its search engine from accessing public records dealing with education, real estate, health care, and the environment.[219] The result clearly will be a further increase in the vast amounts of information available on the Internet.

Law-enforcement officials are not required to obtain any form of certification or permission to buy or acquire information collected by

---

[215] See U.S. GEN. ACCOUNTING OFFICE, *supra* note 211, at 2.

[216] In an ABC/*Washington Post* poll in March 2006, 62 percent favored the FBI having additional authority in surveillance, wiretaps, and the like. PollingReport.com, http://www.pollingreport.com/terror3.htm (last visited May 9, 2008).

[217] These interpretations, Slobogin argues, coupled with the prodding of legislators by courts, will lead to greater constitutional privacy protections in an area virtually unchecked at present. Slobogin differentiates between several types of searches: target driven, match driven, and event driven. *See* Slobogin, *supra* note 204, at 188–89.

[218] Patricia M. Wald, *The Freedom of Information Act: A Short Case Study in the Perils and Paybacks of Legislating Democratic Values*, 33 EMORY L.J. 649, 667 (1984).

[219] Associated Press, *Google Pushes U.S. States to Open Public Records*, TANNEWS, Apr. 30, 2007, http://tannews.blogspot.com/2007/04/google-pushes-us-states-to-open-public.html (last visited May 9, 2008).

private companies. Firms like Matrix, ChoicePoint, Acxiom, and Seisint can compile shockingly detailed and in-depth information about an individual through the use of vast computer networks. "In fact, law enforcement officials need consult *no* other entity (certainly not a court, and not even a prosecutor) before obtaining such information."[220] In the event that either a governmental agency or a private company administering a system of records for the government does not hold the records that the government is attempting to obtain, the only obstacle to complete government access to all data collected and maintained by commercial data brokers is the price government is willing to pay for information.[221] As a result, data brokers like ChoicePoint and Matrix offer electronic bundles of collected personal information to the government at prices that reflect this government need. Furthermore, the government itself has gone into the information-selling business. For example, states have sold personal information obtained from driver's licenses to individuals and businesses.[222]

As noted above, courts agree that when individuals voluntarily disclose information to third parties, these individuals assume the risk that anyone can view the information, and they have no reasonable expectation of privacy.[223]

Some access to federal public records is regulated by the Privacy Act of 1974.[224] (Federal statutory protections will be discussed more comprehensively later.[225]) The Privacy Act protects the privacy of individuals that are identified in computerized information systems maintained by federal agencies and attempts to prevent the misuse of such information.[226] In doing so, the act recognizes the need for federal agencies to collect information on individuals and balances this need against those individuals' right of privacy. The act provides individuals with the opportunity to control the gathering, dissemination, and accuracy of information about themselves contained in government files.[227] To be protected under

---

[220] Slobogin, *supra* note 99, at 155.

[221] *Id.* at 156–57.

[222] *See* Reno v. Condon, 528 U.S. 141 (2000) (holding constitutional the Driver's Privacy Protection Act of 1994, a restriction on states' ability to sell private information without a driver's consent).

[223] *See* United States v. Miller, 425 U.S. 435 (1974) (holding that the Fourth Amendment does not prohibit such transfer of information to third parties).

[224] 5 U.S.C. § 552a (2000).

[225] *See* discussion *infra* Chapter IV, § C.

[226] Thomas v. U.S. Dep't of Energy, 719 F.2d 342 (10th Cir. 1983).

[227] Vymetalik v. FBI, 785 F.2d 1090 (D.C. Cir. 1986).

the act, information must be personal and must reflect upon individuals' private affairs and not their public responsibilities.[228]

Although the Privacy Act of 1974 limits a private individual's access to public records, law-enforcement officials are afforded a much higher degree of access. So long as the head of the agency that is seeking the information from the public records makes a written request to the agency that holds the records (detailing the reason the record is needed), access will be granted to the investigating agency.[229] Congress chose not to include any standard of relevance or requirement of judicial approval in the act.[230] Furthermore, the act applies only to federal documents, leaving the regulation of state public records to state law.

Access to public information, or "transparency," is generally considered a hallmark of modern democracies.[231] However, scholars now are challenging whether openness is necessarily a universally good public policy.[232] Wide access poses a potential threat to personal privacy. To make matters worse, the possibility for intrusion through public records is far greater today than it was fifty years ago, in large part because of advances in modern technology. Once something is a public record, courts will hold that its general publication is protected speech. For example, a newspaper reported that a woman was sterilized while in a mental institution.[233] She had no recourse against the newspaper because that information was a public record.

Easier and more affordable access to public records increases the likelihood of invasion of one's privacy. Public records containing personal

[228] Windsor v. Fed. Executive Agency, 614 F. Supp. 1255 (M.D. Tenn. 1983), aff'd, 767 F.2d 923 (6th Cir. 1985) (Tenn. Ct. App. 1985).
[229] 5 U.S.C. § 552a(b)(7) (2000).
[230] See id.
[231] See, e.g., Rodrigo Labardini, The Fight Against Corruption in Mexico, 11 U.S.-MEX. L.J. 195, 199–200 (2003) (discussing how the new Ley Federal de Transparencia y Acceso a la Información Pública Gubernamental or Federal Transparency and Access to Public Government Information Law is aiding the Mexican government's fight against corruption); see also Matthew I. Van Horn, Investigating Slovakia's Business Climate After the "Velvet Revolution," 5 TULSA J. COMP. & INT'L L. 365, 375 (1998) (discussing how Slovakia's decrease in access to public information has stunted the country's growth in democracy and capitalism).
[232] See generally Mark Fenster, The Opacity of Transparency, 91 IOWA L. REV. 885 (2006) (A newspaper wrote a story criticizing a health care facility and stated that woman had been involuntarily sterilized as a child while a resident at Jasper County Home. The court held that under the Iowa Freedom of Information Act, documents reviewing plaintiff's sterilization were in the public domain, so that disclosure of plaintiff's sterilization was not actionable. This case occurred before the passage of HIPPA. This kind of record should be confidential under HIPPA today).
[233] Howard v. Des Moines Register & Trib. Co., 283 N.W.2d 289, 300 (Iowa 1979).

information were once housed only in physical locations, requiring an individual to travel in person to many locations to obtain information. Today, many public records are accessible online, enabling easier searching and viewing of others' personal information.[234] And more public information is put online continually. For example, Google is providing free software and assistance to help state governments make public records that are basically unavailable or difficult to find easily available on the Internet.[235] As in the case of consumer information revealed on the Internet, access to one or two public records alone may not be sufficient to determine an individual's identity or to learn enough about someone to actually have invaded his or her privacy. But the current availability and compilation of public records from multiple sources can enable the discovery of personal, sensitive information in a matter of minutes. Research can show the criminal history and birthdates[236] the value of a person's home,[237] their political contributions,[238] and their personal pages and social-networking web participation.[239] This information is public but these sites make information easy to compile. Zaba CEO Nick Matzorkis says public information online is "a 21st century reality with or without ZabaSearch."[240]

Court records and court proceedings are rich sources of public information. The facts gathered in court proceedings concern intimate private

---

[234] For a discussion of the "practical" protection of personal information contained in public records, see Victoria S. Salzmann, *Are Public Records Really Public? The Collision Between the Right to Privacy and the Release of Public Court Records over the Internet*, 52 BAYLOR L. REV. 355, 377 (2000) (explaining that public documents remaining in a "quasi-public" state, such as court records located in court filing cabinets, could protect personal information from online exploitation); John Kennedy, *Online Access Vexes Clerks*, ORLANDO SENTINEL, June 27, 2003, at B1 (noting that "practical obscurity" historically has provided safeguards against the revelation of personal information contained in public records housed only at the courthouse); COMM. ON PRIVACY & COURT RECORDS, SUPREME COURT OF FLORIDA, FINAL REPORT: EXAMINATION OF THE EFFECTS OF ADVANCED TECHNOLOGIES ON PRIVACY & PUBLIC ACCESS TO COURT RECORDS AND OFFICIAL RECORDS (2003), a*vailable at* http://www.flcourts.org/gen_public/stratplan/privacy.shtml (last visited May 9, 2008).

[235] *See* Dibya Sarkar, *Google Helps States Make Public Records Easier to Find*, ASSOCIATED PRESS, *available at* http://seattlepi.nwsource.com/business/313638_google30.html (last visited May 15, 2008).

[236] Zabasearch.com (last visited May 18, 2008).

[237] Zillow.com (last visited May 18, 2008).

[238] Fundrace.huffingtonpost.com (last visited May 18,2008).

[239] Spokeo.com (last visited May 18,2008), wink.com (last visited May 18, 2008).

[240] Vauhini Vara, Wall Street Journal, *New Sites Make it Easier to Spy on Your Friends*, May 13, 2008; Page D1. For example, this article reports that a person discovered through spokeo.com that a friend added to her wish list on amazon.com a disposable pad that protects mattresses from bedwetters.

details of family, finance, and health. Because of the risks of disclosing sensitive information, several states have evaluated privacy and Internet access to court documents.[241] A Florida committee was charged with recommending strategies that will reduce the amount of private information included in court records, categories of information that should be exempted from public records, and policies that will regulate the release of electronic court records.[242] The final report included an overall acceptance of Internet access, but also policies designed to restrict access to the most sensitive records and methods to avoid the collection of unnecessary and intrusive information.[243]

Electronic access to court records engenders concerns of identity theft, as well as fears that highly sensitive information will be made publicly available to anyone with Internet access.[244] Some of the most sensitive types of information are included in family-law cases, such as Social Security numbers, financial documentation, medical records, and mental-health evaluations.[245] Criminal cases also contain highly personal information, including mental-competency evaluations, and victim identities or descriptions. Public access to the courts is an essential component of the justice system and should not be deterred by the availability of electronic access to court records. Private information also can be gathered involuntarily, such as when information is compelled during discovery in the course of a criminal or civil proceeding.[246] Naturally, a party affected by these disclosures may seek closure of the records.

---

[241] *See, e.g.,* COMM. ON PRIVACY & COURT RECORDS, *supra* note 234.

[242] *See* Request for Input, http://www.flcourts.org/search.shtml (search for "Request for Input"; then follow "Corel Office Document") (last visited May 12, 2008) http://www.flcourts.org/gen_public/stratplan/bin/PUBLIC%20COMMENT%20NOTICE.pdf and http://www.flcourts.org/gen_public/stratplan/bin/Request%20for%20Input.pdf (last visited May 9, 2008).

[243] *See* COMM. ON PRIVACY & COURT RECORDS, *supra* note 234. A number of states such as New York, Minnesota, and North Dakota formed similar committees to investigate placing court records on the Internet and came to the same conclusions as the Florida committee. For a state-by-state comparison of policies regarding Internet access to court records, see Justice Management Institute and National Center for State Courts, State Information, http://cdt.org/publications/02082courtrecords.shtml (last visited May 19, 2008).

[244] *See* Laurie Cunningham, *Access Depends on Study Balancing Interests,* 79 MIAMI DAILY BUS. REV., Sept. 29, 2004, at 12.

[245] *See id.*

[246] *See, e.g.,* Post-Newsweek Stations, Florida, Inc. v. Doe, 612 So. 2d 549, 552 (Fla. 1992) (holding that the names of a prostitute's customers could be revealed, because the clients had no privacy interest in the secrecy of their names).

In *Barron v. Florida Freedom Newspapers, Inc.*, a newspaper contested the closing of a divorce proceeding.[247] The Supreme Court of Florida stated that "*all* trials, civil and criminal, are public events and there is a strong presumption of public access to these proceedings and their records, subject to certain narrowly defined exceptions."[248] This is the position held throughout the United States, including state and federal court systems. Therefore, the Florida court found that although the trial court records contained medical reports, which generally are protected by the right to privacy, the records were no longer protected when the medical condition became an integral part of the civil proceeding.[249] The court outlined five factors to be considered when analyzing a request for closure of a civil proceeding, noting that (1) there is a strong presumption in favor of openness; (2) the public and the media have standing to challenge a closure order, and the burden of proof rests on the party seeking closure; (3) court proceedings should be closed only in certain circumstances, but the context of the information may invoke constitutional privacy protection; (4) court proceedings should be closed only when no reasonable alternative is available to accomplish the desired result; and (5) the presumption of openness continues through the appellate review process. Thus, in a civil case, obtaining closure is difficult, even when it involves information that is ordinarily considered to be protected as private.[250]

In the criminal context, obtaining closure of proceedings is again quite difficult. In *Post-Newsweek Stations, Florida Inc. v. Doe*, "John Does" listed on a prostitute's client list sought to limit public access to pretrial discovery materials in a criminal prostitution case.[251] The Supreme Court of Florida held that although the "Does" had standing to seek an order denying public access to the evidence revealing their names, they lacked a constitutional privacy interest[252] in their names and addresses.[253] The court noted that in *Florida Freedom Newspapers, Inc. v. McCrary*,[254] it held that pretrial discovery information becomes public record once the state

---

[247] 531 So. 2d 113 (Fla. 1988).
[248] *Id.* at 114 (emphasis added).
[249] *See id.* at 119.
[250] *Id.* at 118–19.
[251] 612 So. 2d 549 (Fla. 1992).
[252] *See* Fla. Const. art. I, § 23 (Florida's privacy amendment).
[253] *See Doe*, 612 So. 2d at 553.
[254] 531 So. 2d 113 (Fla. 1982).

gives the requested information to the defendant, but further explained that the statutory right of public access must be balanced against the individual's constitutional right to privacy.[255]

However, the *Doe* court concluded that the Does failed to show good cause to prohibit disclosure of the names and addresses of individuals on the witness list.[256] Justice Kogan, dissenting, opined that because the Does had not been charged with any crime, their private lives should not be subjected to public scrutiny.[257] Justice Kogan further stated that although a person does not have the right to refuse a lawful summons to appear at a deposition or to testify at a trial, the right to protect one's good name "prohibits the news media and others from using a state-created method of gathering information as a means of prying into the personal lives of private individuals or of transforming unsubstantiated rumor into tabloid headlines."[258] The court system's intrusion into one's private information can be based on involuntary investigation, as in *Doe*, or by becoming a party to a case, as in *Barron*. These Florida cases are representative of the basic openness of courts across the various states and also demonstrate the peril presented to privacy by court proceedings and records.

c. The Aggregation Effect and "Practical Obscurity": How Technology Creates a Dossier out of Tidbits of Information

The upshot of technology and the increased supply and demand for information is a massive amount of information that is easily accessible. That which was lost in "practical obscurity" is available online and instantly. The effect of these circumstances is an aggregation of information that is easily available and that is different in nature from the same information that exists in practical obscurity. In fact, courts have recognized the difference. A court held that an aggregation of information was owned by the CIA because the agency had brought that information together through its own efforts.[259] Certainly the marketplace recognizes

---

[255] *See Doe*, 612 So. 2d at 551.

[256] *See id.* at 553.

[257] *See id.* at 554 (Kogan, J., dissenting).

[258] *Id.*

[259] Pfeiffer v. CIA, 60 F.3d 861 (D.C. Cir. 1995) (reasoning that the report belonged to the CIA because "it was created at government expense, with government materials and on government time").

the value of accumulated information, as evidenced by the purchases and sales of such data.[260]

Individuals voluntary disclose information in small quantities constantly.[261] For example, if a person is the subject of unwanted publicity, each individual invader may not have played a significant enough role in the collection of information to have "unreasonably" invaded that person's privacy.[262] However, the totality of the minor invasive actions is enough to constitute a significant invasion, although there is no single person to blame.[263] Data brokers can turn these puzzle pieces into a digital biography that may or may not have parts missing or may be inaccurate.

The debate among those with an interest in aggregated-information questions is whether the aggregated information is different from the separate parts. One argument is that the assembly of small pieces of information otherwise available is no different from and no more subject to protection than the individual pieces. The opposing argument is that the assembled information has greater value, as evidenced by the marketing of aggregated data, and therefore must be treated differently.

In the wake of such widespread data gathering, choosing whether to reveal personal information is certainly of interest to most individuals. One reason people want to maintain autonomy is the possibility of mischaracterization if personal information is collected or shared by others.[264] If others obtain only a small piece of information, it "can easily be confused with knowledge."[265] Thus, truly accurate knowledge, obtained through

---

[260] Federated Department Stores, the owner of Macy's, offered to sell access to 1.5 million cardholder names. The price was $90 per 1,000 names, with a minimum order of 50,000 names and $15 for additional names. The list included age, income, and ages of children. *See* Russell Gold, *Latest Privacy Mailings Are Hard to Decipher*, WALL ST. J., May 30, 2002, *available at* http://online.wsj.com/article_print/SB1022703971467032160.html (last visited May 13, 2008).

[261] *See* Daniel J. Solove, *Identity Theft, Privacy, and the Architecture of Vulnerability*, 54 HASTINGS L.J. 1227, 1233 (2003).

[262] *See id.*

[263] *See id.* (describing this "aggregation problem").

[264] *See* James P. Nehf, *Recognizing the Societal Value in Information Privacy*, 78 WASH. L. REV. 1, 24 (2003). Another example of the impact of mistakes was a woman who lost three jobs because her record was not cleared after she was wrongly arrested. Eugene Meyer, *Md. Woman Caught in Wrong Net; Data Errors Link Her to Probes, Cost 3 Jobs*, WASH. POST, Dec. 15, 1997, at C1.

[265] Nehf, *supra* note 264, at 24 (quoting JEFFREY ROSEN, THE UNWANTED GAZE: THE DESTRUCTION OF PRIVACY IN AMERICA 8 (2000)). Nehf further remarks that the tangible harm associated with mischaracterization is what someone other than the intended recipient does with the information once it is obtained. *Id.* at 26–27. For example, misinformation could affect one's ability to obtain a job or a loan. *Id.* at 26.

information collection, paradoxically may come only through full disclosure or discovery.

In day-to-day interactions, people constantly disclose information, whether in the form of a name, an address, a phone number, another identifying piece of data, or something more intimate shared with a friend. Balancing the necessity of disclosure in some instances with the right to confidentiality in others affects the value placed on personal information.[266] Furthermore, the value of information affects how it is shared with others and alters the desire to keep some information private.

The context of the disclosure plays an important role in determining the value of information to the owner or the extent to which the owner feels that an invasion of privacy has occurred. If personal information is obtained illegally, or obtained legally and then used without consent, the owner of the information should be afforded some legal remedy in the absence of a public reason for disclosure, such as the protection of the First Amendment or public safety. Thus, the manner by which information is obtained is central to considering how to protect it.

Information can be obtained in four ways: from voluntarily disclosure without limitations,[267] from disclosure with conditions,[268] from disclosure in exchange for a benefit,[269] or from involuntary disclosure without consent.[270] In each of these cases, the reasonable expectation of privacy differs. Any disclosure without consent gives rise to privacy concerns because consent or personal autonomy is a core principle of privacy.[271]

In sum, information is given and accumulated in the private and public sector. A combination of policies and technology makes that information more vulnerable to intrusion today than ever before.

---

[266] See, e.g., Taylor v. Best, 746 F.2d 220 (1984) (holding that a prisoner's privacy interest in keeping his family history confidential during a screening interview with the staff psychologist was outweighed by the public interests in prison safety, the prisoner's effective rehabilitation, and the psychologist's promise of confidentiality).

[267] For example, disclosure of a name to a reporter writing a story.

[268] For example, disclosure of information to a lawyer knowing it is confidential.

[269] For example, disclosure of personal information to obtain a business location.

[270] For example, obtaining information through a wiretap warrant.

[271] See FTC, PRIVACY ONLINE: A REPORT TO CONGRESS (1998), available at http://www.ftc. gov/reports/privacy3/toc.htm (last visited May 9, 2008). In 1990, the governments of the United States, Canada, and various European countries conducted multiple studies addressing informational privacy issues. These governments compiled reports and promulgated codes regarding fair information practices, and, from these reports and codes, five core principles of information use, collection, and dissemination were derived: (1) notice/awareness; (2) choice/consent; (3) access/participation; (4) integrity/security; and (5) enforcement redress.

5. Institutional Privacy Practices

Just as states and the federal government hold large amounts of information, so too do private institutions. In some of the more personally sensitive areas such as health care, consumer information, and financial information, the principal repository of information is the private sector. Another group of institutions that control vast amounts of sensitive information include our private and public education systems. Finally, there is the enterprise that can generally be described as the "news business," which has as its central goal the distribution of information. There are particular laws and practices that relate to each of these institutions in efforts to promote privacy.

Because of privacy concerns, there are multiple statutory and regulatory directives at the state and federal levels that attempt to control private information. The plethora of these controls gave rise to a new class of employees who focus on information issues in their institutions: the privacy officer. In fact, there is an organization called the International Association of Privacy Professionals (formerly the Association of Privacy Officers).[272] The organization's Web site shows the broad number of fields in which members work and provides options for training and education.

The following sections discuss how enterprises in the private sector deal with information under the existing regulatory scheme.

a. The Health-Care Industry

The health-care industry is a bit unusual because confidentiality has long been a principle of the medical profession. The Hippocratic oath recognizes the importance of patient confidentiality.[273] Interestingly, the health-care industry has sought government controls to maintain confidentiality. One such control is the Health Insurance Portability and Accountability Act ("HIPAA"),[274] which was enacted on August 21, 1996, in an effort to safeguard personal medical information.

---

[272] *See* International Association of Privacy Professionals, http://www.privacyassociation. org (last visited May 9, 2008).

[273] The oath states in part, "Whatever, in connection with my professional practice or not, in connection with it, I see or hear, in the life of men, which ought not to be spoken of abroad, I will not divulge, as reckoning that all such should be kept secret." University of New South Wales Library, http://info.library.unsw.edu.au/biomed/pdf/hippocrati-coath.pdf (last visited May 15, 2008).

[274] Pub. L. No. 104-191, 110 Stat. 1936 (1996). (codified as amended in scattered sections of 42 U.S.C.). *See* Appendix I.

Today, all health-care organizations must pay close attention to the release of any personal information. HIPAA is comprehensive. For example, a person's prescriptions and hospital records, and even conversations among medical personnel about a person's treatment, are supposed to be confidential.

However, medical information has been subject to exploitation and serious abuse. A Maryland database of medical records compiled for cost-containment purposes was sold to overzealous bankers, who called in loans made to patients with terminal cancer.[275] Medical students in Colorado profited by selling the medical records of patients to malpractice lawyers.[276] A convicted child rapist employed at a hospital in Newton, Massachusetts, used a former employee's computer password to access nearly a thousand patient records to make vulgar phone calls to young girls.[277] Finally, a state health-department worker in Florida forwarded the names of nearly four thousand patients who tested positive for HIV to local newspapers.[278]

HIPAA requires that all health plans, providers, and clearinghouses establish and maintain "reasonable and appropriate administrative, technical, and physical safeguards" to protect the integrity, confidentiality, and availability of health information.[279] HIPAA aims to improve the portability and continuity of health insurance coverage, combat waste, simplify the administration of health insurance, and eliminate fraud and abuse in health-insurance delivery.[280]

HIPAA is an improvement from the policies of the past because it protects against "reasonable anticipated threats or hazards to the security or integrity of the information."[281] The electronic compilation of such massive amounts of information benefits patients as well as research institutions because records may be accessed instantly, which reduces costs and increases efficiency.[282]

---

[275] Booth Gunter, *It's No Secret: What You Tell Your Doctor—and What Medical Documents Reveal About You—May Be Open to the Scrutiny of Insurers, Employers, Lenders, Credit Bureaus, and Others*, TAMPA TRIB., Oct. 6, 1996, at Commentary1.

[276] Donna E. Shalala, U.S. Sec'y of Health & Human Servs., Speech at the National Press Club, Washington, D.C. (July 31, 1997).

[277] Matthew Brelis, *Patients' Files Allegedly Used for Obscene Phone Calls*, BOSTON GLOBE, Apr. 11, 1995, at Metro1.

[278] Doug Stanley & Craig S. Palosky, *HIV Tracked on Unauthorized Lists*, TAMPA TRIB., Oct. 35, 1996, at Florida/Metro1.

[279] 42 U.S.C. § 1320d-2 (2000).

[280] *Id.*

[281] *Id.*

[282] Phillip Buttell, *The Privacy and Security of Health Information in the Electronic Environment Created by HIPAA*, 10 KAN. J.L. & PUB. POL'Y 399, 405 (2000).

However, such administrative simplifications also raise privacy issues in the transmission of data. With increased accessibility, health-care information is communicated to other health-care providers, billing services, third-party payers, research organizations, and public-health agencies.[283] This immense diffusion of private medical information poses new privacy issues as technology advances and such information becomes widely accessible.[284] Advancing technology in genetics is already a conundrum. Information that can predict health issues and assist health professionals could, if made available to employers or insurance companies, create tremendous problems for the patient. For example, if genetic tests reveal a predisposition to heart disease or diabetes, would not an employer aware of that information be reluctant to hire that individual for a stressful job?[285]

Privacy concerns have medical consequences. Patients may not disclose all medical conditions for fear that their medical records may not be secure. Doctors also might not record a patient's entire record in the file to maintain the physician-patient relationship. The increased desire for immediate access to such information along with the high implementation costs of conforming to HIPAA create an atmosphere rich in opportunities to violate privacy through access to personal medical records.

b. The Consumer-Information Industry and Credit Reporting

Our society lives on credit and supplies that industry with as much information as we need to in order to obtain loans and other financing. Individuals are used to responding to any question to obtain credit. Although this industry is related to the banking industry, as a society we use credit in ways that usually do not involve banks. The information generated is not only what we disclose to get credit but also the information we create when we use credit cards. Tracking the use of one's credit card provides a detailed life history of travel, personal preferences, and purchasing practices. That information is valuable to marketers who want to know how to sell us things we want to buy or how to persuade us to buy them. So an industry exists around not only granting credit but also selling the information about the use of credit. Acxiom stated on its

---

[283] Patricia Carter, *Health Information Privacy: Can Congress Protect Confidential Medical Information in the "Informational Age"?*, 25 WM. MITCHELL L. REV. 223, 225 (1999).

[284] *See* Buttell, *supra* note 282, at 406.

[285] *See* discussion *supra* Chapter III, § B-3(c).

Web site that it has compiled demographic and lifestyle information on 111 million households or 176 million individuals in its "Infobase" list.[286]

Regulation of consumer information is a complex subject. There are different entities, such as retailers and credit-card companies. There are different types of information, including the types of goods purchased and the record of payment. The law is different depending on the entity holding the information and the type of information. Although certain types of information are protected, huge amounts of data are still available to the data industry. The result is a large and profitable industry trading in consumer information and profiles.

Consumers give out information about their personal interests, hobbies, buying patterns, income, families, and purchase potential. This exchange of information is often done without the consumer's knowledge of its importance or the manner in which the information will be used. For example, consumer data is often collected by retailers, grocery stores, newspapers and magazines, product manufacturers, nonprofit organizations, surveys, and contests.[287] There are several methods by which retailers and other entities collect consumer information.

One method is through the use of discount cards. When individuals regularly shop at grocery stores, they are often offered discount cards, which are scanned when consumers make purchases. The discount cards (also used widely by other major retailers) are usually assigned after the customer fills out an application. The applications often request information such as the individual's name, address, e-mail address, phone numbers, and age, at least. Since the card is presented upon purchase, a record of purchases is available to the retailer. As of 2002, six out of every ten supermarkets either collected or planned to begin collecting consumer data through the use of discount cards.[288] One company, Catalina Marketing Corporation had at that time a database with "shopping preferences of thirty million households."[289]

Another common method of obtaining consumer information is through the use of surveys and contests. Often, when enticed with the

---

[286] Acxiom, http://www.acxiom.com (last visited May 9, 2008).
[287] CANADIAN INTERNET POL'Y & PUB. INT. CLINIC, ON THE DATA TRAIL: HOW DETAILED INFORMATION ABOUT YOU GETS INTO THE HANDS OF ORGANIZATIONS WITH WHOM YOU HAVE NO RELATIONSHIP (2006), *available at* http://www.cippic.ca/documents/May1-06/DatabrokerReport.pdf (last visited May 9, 2008).
[288] Allison Kidd, *A Penny Saved, a Lifestyle Learned? The California and Connecticut Approaches to Supermarket Privacy*, 4 N.C. J.L. & TECH. 143 (2002).
[289] *Id.* at 289.

possibility of winning a free cruise, an individual may hurriedly fill out a contest form requesting information ranging from one's address and e-mail to hobbies, interests, income, number of children, and career.

Buying patterns, demographics, and even interests or dislikes represent a valuable commodity to other entities who wish to market their products to individuals. Information gathered in any of the transactions described above may be sold to others for marketing use. The information may be made available to entities affiliated with the information collector. The information may also be sold to data brokers, who in turn assimilate and sell the information to interested companies. The collecting entity may also sell the information directly to other companies.[290]

The law regulating this type of distribution of information differs depending on who collects the information, to whom they sell it, and what kind of information it is. Because the distribution of consumer information is narrowly regulated, much of the information individuals (often unwittingly) disclose about themselves is fair game and for sale.

The consumer-finance industry has seen an increase in federal and state legislation in the last decade to balance increased demands for information on consumer trends and spending.[291] As the desire for more consumer profiles increases, the industry wants to create a "physically linked world" where every item in your shopping cart will be traceable to your credit card.[292]

The major federal legislation is the Gramm-Leach-Bliley Act of 1999 ("GLBA"),[293] which seeks to strike a balance between consumer privacy interests and industry goals.[294] The GLBA significantly changed the scope of permissible activities of the financial industries.[295] The projected outcome of the GLBA was an increase in large financial conglomerates,[296] and the debate in Congress reflected significant concern over the protection

---

[290] Robert O'Harrow, Jr., *Prescription Sales, Privacy Fears: CVS, Giant Share Customer Records with Drug Marketing Firm*, WASH. POST, Feb. 15, 1998, at A1.

[291] There are also more groups reporting on and advocating privacy—for example, the Electronic Privacy Information Center (EPIC), http://www.epic.org, and Privacy Rights Clearinghouse, http://www.privacyrights.org (last visited May 9, 2008).

[292] M.K. Shankar, *Algorithm Ensures Unique Object ID*, NIKKEI ELECTRONICS ASIA Apr. 2001.

[293] Pub. L. No. 106-102, 113 Stat. 1338 (1999) (codified at 15 U.S.C. §§ 6801–6809).

[294] Dolores S. Smith & James H. Mann, *The New Consumer Financial Privacy Regulations: Balancing the Interests of Consumers and Industry*, 17 N.Y.L. SCH. J. HUM. RTS. 93 (2000).

[295] Paul J. Polking & Scott A. Cammarn, *Overview of the Gramm-Leach-Bliley Act*, 4 N.C. BANKING INST. 1 (2000).

[296] Robert W. Dixon, *The Gramm-Leach-Bliley Act: Why Reform in the Financial Services Industry Was Necessary and the Act's Projected Effects on the Banking Community*, 49 DRAKE L. REV. 671 (2001).

of consumer financial data with the projected increase in cross-industry mergers and technology.[297]

Under the GLBA, three significant privacy provisions apply broadly to any financial institution engaged in financial activities.[298] First, unless pursuant to an exception, financial institutions may not disclose to a nonaffiliated third party any "nonpublic personal information."[299] Second, financial institutions may not disclose an account number or similar access number or code for a credit card or deposit account of a consumer to any nonaffiliated third party for use in telemarketing, direct-mail marketing, or other marketing through electronic mail.[300] Third, financial institutions must provide disclosures describing their privacy policies to consumers annually and whenever they establish a customer relationship with a consumer.[301]

Although the GLBA provides little regulation regarding the sharing of nonpublic consumer information among an institution's affiliates, states such as California are taking affirmative steps to provide more security for consumers than the GLBA provides.[302] The California Financial Information Privacy Act ("CFIPA")[303] took effect in July 2004 and generally requires that financial institutions allow consumers to "opt out" before financial institutions are allowed to transmit personal financial information to affiliates.[304] The California financial industry challenged the CFIPA on the grounds that the Fair Credit Reporting Act of 1970 ("FCRA")[305] preempts state regulation of information sharing among affiliates.[306] The court rejected the plaintiff's argument, holding that the FCRA's preemptive effect was limited to regulations on the sharing of consumer credit

---

[297] AM. BANKERS ASS'N, FINANCIAL MODERNIZATION: GRAMM-LEACH-BLILEY ACT SUMMARY 22 (1999).
[298] Gramm-Leach-Bliley Act § 509.
[299] Id. § 502(a).
[300] Id. § 502(d).
[301] Id. § 503(a).
[302] Stephen F. Ambrose, Jr. & Joseph W. Gelb, Consumer Privacy Litigation and Enforcement Actions, 60 BUS. LAW 723, 724 (2005).
[303] CAL. FIN. CODE §§ 4050–4060 (West Supp. 2005).
[304] Id. § 4053.
[305] 15 U.S.C. §§ 1681–1681u (2000).
[306] Am. Bankers Ass'n v. Lockyer, No. CIV S 04-0778 MCE KJM, 2004 U.S. Dist. LEXIS 12367 (E.D. Cal. June 30, 2004). Generally, the FCRA "does not annul, alter, affect, or exempt any person subject to the provisions of [the act] from complying with the laws of any State with respect to the collection, distribution, or use of any information on consumers, except to the extent that those laws are inconsistent with any provision of [the act], and then only to the extent of the inconsistency." 15 U.S.C. § 1681t(a).

reports.[307] The battle over regulating consumer information is far from over.

c. The Financial Industry

By the nature of their business, banks and other financial-services institutions have and retain sensitive personal information. Personal financial information historically has been considered private. Banks have prided themselves on protecting their clients' information.[308] Bankers have reasons to want financial information kept secret. Although the habits, opinions, and associations of the individual may be revealed, businesses could lose strategic position in their market if costs of supplies, dates, and amounts of purchases were disclosed.[309]

The nature and quantity of financial information has expanded in contemporary society through bank credit cards, online banking, and online financial services. Private bank records can provide the reader with a "virtual current biography" of the individual.[310]

Abuses of personal financial information over the last thirty years have raised individual concerns and calls for enhanced financial-industry regulation. Over this period of time, policymakers have sought to balance individual privacy interests with the government's need for financial information for security and criminal-justice reasons.

The 1970 Bank Secrecy Act[311] requires the banking industry to maintain records and submit reports of large currency transactions.[312] Intended initially as a vehicle to track money laundering and curtail drug transactions, the Bank Secrecy Act requires institutions to report credit extensions over $10,000 not secured by real property and all transactions involving

---

[307] *Id.* at *19–*20.

[308] *See, e.g.*, TCF Privacy Policy, http://www.tcfexpress.com/Footer/footer_privacy.jsp (last visited May 9, 2008).

[309] Mary Catherine Green, *The Bank Secrecy Act and the Common Law: In Search of Financial Privacy*, 7 Ariz. J. Int'l & Comp. L. 261, 263 (1990).

[310] Burrows v. Superior Court, 13 Cal. 3d 238, 247 (1974) (holding that unconsented disclosure of customer information by a bank to law-enforcement agents was the product of an unlawful search and seizure).

[311] 31 U.S.C. §§ 5311–5330 (2000).

[312] Note, *The 1970 Bank Secrecy Act and the Right of Privacy*, 14 Wm. & Mary L. Rev. 929 (1973). The record-keeping requirement of the act applies to insured banks, various financial institutions, a number of noninsured businesses, and a number of individuals. The act also requires the reporting of the export or import of monetary instruments and the secretary of the treasury is empowered to request the identity and addresses of the parties to the transaction, the legal capacities of the parties, and a description of the transaction.

the exchange of foreign currency.[313] The act was upheld by the Supreme Court in *California Bankers Association v. Shultz*.[314] The Court held it is reasonable to require banks to keep such records because banks are integral parties to transactions involving negotiable instruments, and not innocent bystanders.[315]

Surprisingly, as mentioned previously in the section on transaction surveillance, certain bank records are easily obtained by government investigators. The Supreme Court again found in *United States v. Miller* that a person has no reasonable expectation of privacy in records that are in the possession of the bank as a third party.[316] In response to the *Miller* decision, Congress passed the Right to Financial Privacy Act of 1978 ("FPA").[317] Congress was concerned with the growing preference of the courts for disclosure of financial records and the political atmosphere surrounding the Watergate break-in scandal.[318] The stated purpose of the FPA is to "protect the customers of financial institutions from unwarranted intrusion into their records while at the same time permitting legitimate law enforcement activity."[319] Under the FPA, records may be accessed under five circumstances: voluntary authorization by the customer; administrative summons; search warrants; judicial subpoena; and formal written request.[320]

However, the FPA poses significant undisclosed privacy risks to individuals. The formal-written-request loophole allows governmental agencies that do not have administrative-summons authority to receive personal financial information without a court order. According to the *New York Times*, the Department of Defense has issued over five hundred "national security letters," which are legal under the FPA and are used to access personal bank records of U.S. citizens to search for terrorist activity.[321] The government calls this practice the Terrorist Financial Tracking

---

[313]   *Id.* at 930.

[314]   416 U.S. 21 (1974).

[315]   *Id.* at 48–49.

[316]   425 U.S. 435 (1976).

[317]   12 U.S.C. §§ 3401–3422 (2000).

[318]   M. Elizabeth Smith, *The Public's Need for Disclosure v. The Individual's Right to Financial Privacy: An Introduction to the Financial Right to Privacy Act of 1978*, 32 ADMIN. L. REV. 511, 529 (1980).

[319]   H.R. REP. No. 95-1383, at 33 (1978), *as reprinted in* 1978 U.S.C.C.A.N. 9273, 9304.

[320]   George B. Trubow & Dennis L. Hudson, *The Right to Financial Privacy Act of 1978: New Protection from Federal Intrusion*, 12 J. MARSHALL J. PRAC. & PROC. 487, 494 (1979).

[321]   Eric Lichtblau & Mark Mazzetti, *Military Expands Intelligence Role in U.S.*, N.Y. TIMES, Jan. 14, 2007, *available at* http://www.nytimes.com/2007/01/14/washington/14spy.html (last visited May 9, 2008).

Program and claims that it is entirely legal. However, an audit released by the Justice Department in March 2007 revealed numerous improper uses of the national security letters by the FBI.[322] The FBI apologized to the country for the illegal applications, which included the accessing of personal data and telephone records without proper authorization or cause.

In addition to the balance between federal and individual privacy interests, the common law recognizes an implied term of contract not to reveal financial information unless disclosure is required under compulsion of law, from a duty to the public, or to protect the bank's interest, or is made with the express or implied consent of the customer.[323] Some states that provide a constitutional right to privacy have rejected the common-law tradition. The Florida Supreme Court rejected the holding in *Miller* on the grounds that financial privacy is included in Florida's constitutional privacy protection and requires a compelling state interest for the disclosure financial records held by banks.[324]

The financial industry will continue to be a focal point of privacy concerns in the future as technology continues to facilitate the amalgamation and transmission of personal financial information.

d. Educational Institutions

Private and public educational institutions collect massive amounts of sensitive and personal information on individuals. Our employment and personal futures are tied to our educational records. So we have great interest in their integrity, accuracy, and availability. Making certain grades and records available to designated recipients is vital, but there are some records that should not be generally public. Whether we were put in "time out" when we were in second grade should not be a public issue.

Educational institutions are expert at creating records. There is information about grades, conduct, discipline, attendance, health, finance, athletics, personal activities, and actions that cover the entire gamut of human conduct. Academic institutions have great power over their students regarding evaluations, admission, and retention. Because of this general power and the sensitivity of records, federal and state laws have intervened to control actions.

---

[322] John Solomon & Barton Gellman, *Frequent Errors in FBI's Secret Records Requests: Audit Finds Possible Rule Violations*, WASH. POST, Mar. 9, 2007, at A1.

[323] Tournier v. Nat'l Provincial & Union Bank of England, [1924] 1 K.B. 461.

[324] Winfield v. Div. of Pari-Mutual Wagering, 477 So. 2d 544 (Fla. 1985).

The Family Educational Rights and Privacy Act of 1974 ("FERPA")[325] is the central controlling policy. It applies to all schools that directly or indirectly receive federal funds, including grants or loans to students in attendance.[326] Therefore, virtually all schools are affected. FERPA requires generally that schools keep student records (1) confidential to third parties absent parental consent; (2) accessible upon parental request; and (3) challengeable by parents if the records are claimed to be misleading, inaccurate, or in violation of students' privacy rights.[327]

FERPA, however, is not absolute and contains a number of exceptions to confidentiality, such as permitting access by "other school officials, including teachers," who the school has determined have a legitimate educational interest.[328] Further, student records may be disclosed in the event of a health emergency or to potential schools that the student seeks to attend.[329] And section 507 of the Patriot Act amends FERPA to permit schools to disclose educational records to the attorney general in response to terrorist investigations, without any knowledge or notice to the student.

There are limited claims under FERPA for violations of the statute, but a student may have a claim under state tort law. In 2002, the Supreme Court ruled in *Gonzaga University v. Doe* that students may not recover damages under 42 U.S.C. § 1983 for violations of FERPA.[330] In *Gonzaga*, a former undergraduate student was refused certification to teach in Washington because a university administrator reported Doe by name to the state teacher-certification agency after overhearing rumors of sexual misconduct involving the student.[331] Without federal remedies for FERPA

---

[325] 20 U.S.C. § 1232g (2000); *see also* 34 C.F.R. pt. 99 (2007). FERPA is also known as the Buckley Amendment.

[326] Winona Zimberlin, *Who's Reading Johnny's School Records?*, GPSOLO, April/May 2006, at 30.

[327] Dixie Snow Huefner & Lynn M. Daggett, *Recognizing Schools' Legitimate Educational Interests: Rethinking FERPA's Approach to the Confidentiality of Student Discipline and Classroom Records*, 51 AM. U. L. REV. 1, 4 (2001).

[328] There are other statutes that currently affect student privacy, including the Patriot Act. *See* Zimberlin, *supra* note 326, at 33.

[329] *See* Huefner & Daggett, *supra* note 327, at 7–8. Other important exceptions include judicial orders or subpoenas, cases involving litigation with parents, disclosure of the final results of a disciplinary proceeding at a postsecondary institution to the victim of a crime of violence or a sex offense; disclosure of the final results of a disciplinary proceeding at a postsecondary institution if the alleged perpetrator is a student and has violated the school's rules; and disclosure to the parent of a student under twenty-one years of age who violated rules regarding alcohol or a controlled substance at a postsecondary institution.

[330] 536 U.S. 273 (2002).

[331] *Id.*; Campus Commc'ns, Inc. v. Earnhardt, 821 So. 2d 388, 391–92 (Fla. Dist. Ct. App. 2002).

violations, victims are limited to state-law actions such as invasion of privacy or injunctive relief to stop a school from improperly releasing records.[332]

e. The News Business

Unlike most other industries, the news business has as its goal the disclosure of information, and its ability to disclose information is protected by policy and the Constitution. I will not belabor here what has been previously discussed about the substantive rights of the press. What is interesting is the industry's procedures for and practice of reviewing information and deciding whether to publish it.

As opposed to other industries with laws and guidelines about the release of information, a newspaper or news outlet must analyze the myriad cases on First Amendment law and the range of cases dealing with liability for privacy intrusions. Because of the substantial protections of the First Amendment, news businesses are rarely found liable.

In fact, the press generally is very aware of potential liability for privacy intrusions and has practices and procedures to guard against breaches. *The First Amendment Handbook*, first produced in 1986 by the Reporter's Committee for Freedom of the Press, includes and describes various forms of defamation and defenses and cites case law. It also provides strategies on gaining access to private places and private information.[333]

In defense of the press, the press has a long-established code of ethics,[334] and many media outlets work hard to adhere to that code. Editors and reporters argue vigorously about a story's veracity and importance before printing the story. Reporters tell of instances in which they did not publish a story because it would have been embarrassing and harmful to the subjects of the story and the story was not "important enough."[335] This internal debate may be augmented by conversations with the media organization's attorney. Media attorneys advise their clients of the law and the risks, but acknowledge that it is the editors who make the final decision. The attorneys say that they should not tell a paper not to publish something.

---

[332] Zimberlin, *supra* note 326, at 33.

[333] REPORTERS COMM. FOR FREEDOM OF THE PRESS, THE FIRST AMENDMENT HANDBOOK (2003), *available at* http://www.rcfp.org/handbook/index.html (last visited May 9, 2008).

[334] *See* Society of Professional Journalists, Code of Ethics, https://www.spj.org/ethicscode. asp (last visited June 19, 2007).

[335] University of Florida Center for Governmental Responsibility Symposium on Privacy Law, Jan. 23, 2007. Symposium material is available in CGR Office.

The landscape of the press has changed, and the mainstream press knows it. Today, the press consists of blogs, Web sites, tabloids, and reality shows. All will claim the cloak of First Amendment protection. It is clear that many of these members of the new press do not sit in editors' offices and debate the propriety and ethics of publication.[336]

The debate over what rights a blogger has in comparison with those of the traditional press is a hot topic. Bloggers are increasingly moving into the sphere once occupied solely by traditional journalists and are, in some cases, rivaling these journalists for the scoop on many stories. A recent *Harvard Law Review* article analyzes whether bloggers should be treated as journalists.[337] According to the article, bloggers will most likely receive protection under the constitutional "qualified journalist" privilege, as that privilege has been found to extend to anyone who, when gathering information from qualified sources, intended to disseminate that information to the public.[338] So it may be that in this contemporary society, bloggers will be legally almost equal to the *New York Times*. It is a fair statement that the contemporary "news industry" is a source of many intrusions on personal privacy.

6. The Panopticon Effect

The totality of current technology and the demand for information creates what can be termed a "panopticon effect." In the late 1700s, Jeremy Bentham, a British legal scholar and founder of British utilitarianism,

---

[336] One example of the differences in editorial oversight and decision making is the controversy over Dale Earnhardt's autopsy photos. *See* Campus Commc'ns, Inc. v. Earnhardt, 821 So. 2d 388 (Fla. Dist. Ct. App. 2002). In this case the operator of a Web site featuring autopsy photographs of celebrities sought those of Mr. Earnhardt. The *Orlando Sentinel*, on the other hand, decided not to publish them after mediation with the medical examiner and the Earnhardts. Another example occurred after the death of Princess Diana. Although British newspapers did not show postcrash photographs of the princess, the Italian magazine *Chi* published photographs of Princess Diana breathing from a respirator, dying. *See* Michael Holden, *Princess Diana Documentary Photos Spark Anger,"* REUTERS, May 28, 2007, http://www.reuters.com/article/entertainmentNews/idUSL2823650520070528 (last visited May 9, 2008).

[337] Note, *Developments in the Law of Mass Media*, 120 HARV. L. REV. 990 (2007). *See also* Grant Penrod, *What About Bloggers?*, NEWS MEDIA & THE LAW, Summer 2005, at 14.

[338] Note, *supra* 337, at 999. Bloggers may be less successful in seeking protection for confidential sources under statutory shield laws. Some shield laws specifically define the types of news organizations protected, and courts have declined to extend the shied to bloggers. If, however, the shield law contains language that can be interpreted broadly, as most shield laws do, then a court may extend protection. *See id.* at 1000-04.

embarked on a wide campaign for prison reform. He championed the concept of "the Panopticon,"[339] which literally translates as a building with a comprehensive or panoramic view.[340] The utility of such a structure lies in its design—a circular prison structure with a large, open interior and an observation tower in the center.

Panopticon Effect

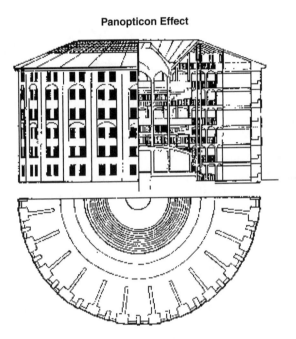

Prison cells are stacked and arranged around the perimeter such that they constitute the entire thickness of the structure's walls. Because of the building's circular design, each and every cell is visible from the central tower. The windows of the tower provide 360-degree visibility from within and block all visibility from without, allowing the guards to monitor the prisoners but preventing the prisoners from seeing the guards. Consequently, each and every cell occupant is subject to constant scrutiny by guards in the tower. This design creates a round-the-clock surveillance machine. Prisoners never know whether they are being watched at any point in time, and guards can use that element of uncertainty to their advantage. Because of psychological pressure, prisoners are forced to conform their behavior to acceptable standards at all times, effectively becoming their

---

[339] BENTHAM, *supra*, note 9, at 29–95.
[340] THE COMPACT EDITION OF THE OXFORD ENGLISH DICTIONARY 2066 (1987).

own warden, despite the fact that guards may only be selectively monitoring the prisoners' behavior.

Facilitating what could be compared to George Orwell's *1984* "Big Brother" form of crime control, digital closed-circuit television ("CCTV") cameras are now trained on the public in a multitude of locations, such as public streets, public parks, parking lots, and metropolitan centers. These public cameras are constantly increasing in sophistication and number, and thus continually altering modern notions of privacy in public places. "[C]amera technology is likely to increase exponentially in the next decade . . . [and] the law is not likely to keep up."[341] Yet it is not the actual viewing or recording of an individual that poses the only threat to reasonable expectations of privacy in public places. The mere chance that one's public movements are being monitored is enough to alter an individual's behavior, regardless of whether anyone is actually watching. Of course, there are individuals who apparently do not mind being observed or want to be observed. One example is the success of glass-walled apartments built to allow exhibitionism and voyeurism at the same time.[342] That tendency for exhibitionism, however, is not yet shared by the majority of society.

Professor Christopher Slobogin compares the effect of public CCTV surveillance to that of Bentham's panopticon prison,[343] describing this phenomenon as "panopticism" and a form of "subtle coercion."[344] Noting the disquieting effect that the act of staring at an individual can cause, he posits that "the cyclopean gaze of the camera eye may be equally disquieting, and perhaps more so, given the anonymity of the viewer and the unavailability of countermeasures, such as staring back or requesting the starer to stop."[345] Just as a prisoner's conduct is either altered or completely arrested by Bentham's panoptic effect, so too is the public conduct of an individual who know that there is a chance that someone is watching what the cameras are recording.

---

[341] Christopher Slobogin, *Public Privacy: Camera Surveillance in Public Places and the Right to Anonymity*, 72 MISS. L.J. 213, 219 (2002). Cameras have also been placed on public billboards to monitor the types of people viewing the advertisement. Stephanie Clifford, *Billboards That Look Back*, N.Y. TIMES, May 31, 2008, at C2, available at http://www.nytimes.com/2008/05/31/business/media/31billboard.html?ex=13699728 00&en=3426ddfada55ea69&ei=5124&partner=permalink&exprod=permalink (last visited June 11, 2008).

[342] *See supra* note 105 and accompanying text.

[343] Slobogin, *supra* note 341, at 245.

[344] *Id.* at 237.

[345] *Id.* at 236.

The effect of panopticism can be stretched even further, depending on degrees of access to the images that CCTV cameras are capturing. In Britain, CCTV monitoring has become commonplace, prying into all aspects of life.[346] However, as private citizens are granted access to these cameras from home computers and televisions, the psychological effect becomes even more constricting. By granting public access to the camera feeds, the government increases the general public's perceived notion that someone may be watching at any time. Additionally, private citizens are given the opportunity to spy on each other and report suspicious behavior to government officials. This new form of panoptic control has been termed "little brother,"[347] an offshoot of the original "Big Brother" concept of control envisioned by Orwell.

Here in the United States, CCTV cameras are multiplying in numbers. Microphones are being installed in public, under the pretext of detecting the sound of gunshots, but they are powerful enough to pick up the private conversation of two teenagers on a street corner. Global positioning systems are being installed in our vehicles, and radio frequency identification devices ("RFIDs") are being tagged to the products we purchase.[348] RFID is an expanding technology that facilitates business for inventory and product tracking yet has properties for massive privacy intrusions.[349] A key to protecting abuse is to prevent "skimming," the use of scanners to steal information from RFID chips. A skimmer could walk by you with a scanner and pick up information from your credit cards and drivers license if they have RFID chips.[350] And law enforcement can

---

[346] See NORRIS & ARMSTRONG, *supra* note 7.

[347] Janet Kornblum, *Prying Eyes Are Everywhere*, USA TODAY, Apr. 13, 2005, *available at* http://www.usatoday.com/tech/news/2005-04-13-spyware_x.htm (last visited May 9, 2008).

[348] RFID can either be passive or active. The difference affects the distance from which a reading of the information can be obtained. It was first used to identify planes in WW II through the use of transponders and radars. Frequently Asked Questions, RFID Journal, *available at* http://www.rfidjournal.com/faq (last visited on May 5, 2008).

[349] IBM's patent application for the RFID states "Based on the results of the correlation, the exact identity of the person or certain characteristics about the person can be determined. This information is used to monitor the movement of the person through the store or other areas." IBM US Patent Application, *available at* http://www.spychips.com/documents/ATT00075.pdf (last visited on May 5, 2008).

[350] Several states have enacted anti-RFID laws. For example, a recently-enacted Washington state law criminalizes the unauthorized scanning of another person's RFID without that persons consent for criminal purposes such as fraud, identity theft or stalking. Claire Swedberg, *Washington State Governor Signs Anti-Skimming Law*, RFID Journal, March 27, 2008 *at* http://www.rfidjournal.com/article/articleview/3988/ (last visited on May 5, 2008).

place an RFID device on your car, without a warrant, to facilitate their tracking your movements.[351]

There are even options to insert RFIDs in humans.[352] As technology advances, the potential for panoptic surveillance seems to have no end. And although there is indeed some benefit to be derived from any system of crime surveillance to the extent that criminal activity is effectively deterred, there remains the potential that perfectly lawful activity will be chilled because of a collective fear that someone (possibly a police officer or even the next-door neighbor) may be watching. Suddenly, the lawful act of visiting a bar frequented by homosexuals, or an abortion clinic,[353] becomes a decision wrought with potential danger.

Contemporary American society has a lower expectation of privacy because of both the frequency with which and the manner in which personal information is disclosed. Information or topics once secret may no longer be considered taboo. Modern means of intrusion are faster, cheaper, and more revealing.

The new constant gaze of our society supports what can be termed the new army of "citizen spies." Because of technology and the Internet, virtually anyone who is perturbed by someone's conduct can post it on the Internet. In fact, there are Web sites that facilitate posting for bad driving, bad parking, leaving dog droppings, leering at women, littering, loud talking on cell phones, and yelling at children.[354] Once information

---

[351] See, e.g., U.S. v. Knott, 460 U.S. 276 (1983); U.S. v. McIver, 186 F.3d 1119 (9th Cir. 1999).

[352] For a history and discussion on the possible uses of RFIDs in the future, see Todd Lewan, *Microchips Everywhere: A Future Vision*, Assoc. Press, Jan. 29, 2008, *available at* http://seattletimes.nwsource.com/html/businesstechnology/2004151388_apchippingamericaiii29.html?syndication=rss (last visited May 9, 2008). The RFID would replace the bar code on items we purchase; individual products could then be tagged to their purchaser-owner, and people could be traced as they move. An alternative to RFID technology is the use of massive FBI databases containing our individual characteristics to biometrically track and record our movements and activities. The FBI is citing national-security concerns as justification for the use of such biometric tracking. *See* Kelli Arena & Carol Cratty, *FBI Wants Palm Prints, Eye Scans, Tattoo Mapping*, CNN.com, Feb. 4, 2008, http://www.cnn.com/2008/TECH/02/04/fbi.biometrics/index.html (last visited May 9, 2008).

[353] See United States v. Vazquez, 31 F. Supp. 2d 85 (D. Conn. 1998). This case involved prosecution of Carmen Vazquez for violating the Freedom of Access to Clinic Entrances Act, 18 U.S.A. § 248 (2000) ("FACE"). Vazquez had videotaped individuals entering an abortion clinic. The U.S. government sought to permanently seal the videos, which had been used as evidence, against public disclosures. The court denied the government's motion and the videos remained public records.

[354] See, e.g., http://www.platewire.com (last visited May 9, 2008) (bad driving); http://www.niceparkingdude.com (last visited May 9, 2008) (bad parking); http://www.hollabacknyc.blogspot.com (last visited May 9, 2008) (leering); http://www.litterbutt.com (last visited

is posted, more information may follow. A license plate number of a bad driver can soon be converted into a name and address. These comments and charges may be and usually are anonymous. There is even a Web site that allows and encourages the anonymous posting of innuendo or gossip about college students.[355]

There are also online encyclopedias such as Wikipedia that are authored by visitors to the site. Wikipedia is classified as a service provider under section 230 of the federal Communications Decency Act and therefore is not susceptible to liable suits,[356] unlike online publishers such as CNN.com.[357] However, the actual author of libelous statements may be found liable for incorrect statements published on service providers, although the prosecution of any claims against the author will probably encounter substantial impediments to legal action.[358] Web sites and ISPs are now taking affirmative steps to solidify the anonymity of the actual writer.[359] When an ISP is sued, there are cases where the writer is unknown

---

May 9, 2008) (littering); http://www.rudepeople.com (last visited May 9, 2008) (bad behavior). *See also* The Wall Street Journal, *No one too obscure for these online exposés*, GAINESVILLE SUN, Jan. 13, 2007, at 7B.

[355] *See* Associated Press, *Web Site Sparks Juicy Campus Battle*, GAINESVILLE SUN, Feb. 18, 2008, at 1A.

[356] For example, in February 2007, professional golfer Fuzzy Zoeller sued the owner of an IP address that posted improper remarks about Zoeller on Wikipedia. *See* Associated Press, *Golfer Fuzzy Zoeller Sues Consulting Firm over Wikipedia Entry*, FOX NEWS, Feb. 22, 2007, http://www.foxnews.com/story/0,2933,253829,00.html (last visited May 9, 2008).

[357] Daniel Terdiman, *Is Wikipedia Safe from Libel Liability?*, CNET NEWS.COM, Dec. 7, 2005, http://news.com.com/Is+Wikipedia+safe+from+libel+liability/2100-1025_3-5984880.html (last visited May 9, 2008).

[358] Lyrissa Barnett Lidsky & Thomas F. Cotter, *Authorship, Audiences, and Anonymous Speech*, 82 NOTRE DAME L. REV. 1537 (2007) (discussing the constitutional and practical problems of identifying anonymous authors).

[359] The Juicycampus.com privacy policy states, "It is not possible for anyone to use this website to find out who you are or where you are located. We do not collect any information directly from you. You've never given us your name or email address, and we don't want it. We do not track any information that can be used by us to identify you." Juicy Campus, http://www.juicycampus.com (last visited May 16, 2008). There are even ISP services such as Whosarat.com that allow users to publically post the names and faces of confidential government informants. *See* Jason Trahan, *Web site that rats out informants worries Dallas officials: Local officials weigh sealing some plea deal data to protect identities*, THE DALLAS MORNING NEWS, Mar. 29, 2008, *available at* http://www.dallasnews.com/sharedcontent/dws/news/localnews/stories/DN-whosarat_30met.ART.North.Edition1.470d70c.html (last visited on May 8, 2009). By posting such information, users are essentially placing a bulls-eye on the backs of the people they reveal whether their information has any credibility or not. The privacy policy for whosarat.com states that the purpose of the site is for entertainment only and that "In no event shall this web site and this web site owner be liable to a user or third party for any slander, libel, damages, *injuries or death* resulting from the use or inability to use

and never can be held accountable.[360] Currently, some sophisticated parties are able to receive some sort of relief and make ISPs take down information by using the Digital Millennium Copyright Act[361] ("DMCA"). The "notice and takedown" provision of the DMCA allows a party to notify an ISP and demand the removal of information the party believes to be covered by its copyright. The ISP may face liability if it fails to act.[362]

Technology facilitates intrusions and the assembly of information and simplifies the mass distribution of that information. The overall effect is to lower expectations of privacy. Modern society seems to have achieved a panopticon for all of us and a "perfect storm" of intrusiveness:

1. Technology, such as CCTV, facilitates intrusions and the collection of more information.
2. Society demands more information.
3. Public files are more easily accessed and contain more information.
4. Expanded concerns for public safety and security justify more intrusions.
5. Segments of the modern press seek more-intrusive information and disseminate that information more quickly and carelessly.
6. "Citizen spies" post information on individuals on the Internet.

All the circumstances previously discussed conspire to make our contemporary society a very intrusive place, seemingly devoid of privacy. As Scott McNealy, the CEO of Sun Microsystems, admonished us, "[y]ou have zero privacy. . . . Get over it."[363] For those of us who do not wish to surrender totally, we need to evaluate our existing legal protections.

If we accept that privacy is important to us personally and to our society, the question becomes, how is society protecting that right globally and in the United States?

---

the information or materials in this site." (emphasis added). Who's a Rat Legal Information, http://www.whosarat.com/disclaimer.php (last visited May 16, 2008).

[360] See, e.g., Carafano v. Metrosplash.com, Inc., 339 F.3d 1119 (9th Cir. 2003) (a dating Web site was held not liable for an offensive posting. The unknown person who actually posted the material on a computer in Berlin, Germany, was not identified and not a party).

[361] 17 U.S.C. § 512(c) (2000).

[362] See 17 U.S.C. § 512(c) and (g); see also H.R. Rep. No. 105-551, at 52-62 (2000) (describing the DMCA's take-down and put-back procedures).

[363] See Polly Sprenger, Sun on Privacy: Get Over It, WIRED, Jan. 26, 1999, http://www.wired.com/news/politics/0,1283,17538,00.html (last visited May 9, 2008).

C. Privacy: Global Differences and Consequences

Privacy is a global issue. Every nation that purports to care about individual rights must protect individual privacy. Reality is as widely varied as the nations and cultures that define and implement privacy policies. There are also international and transnational policies on privacy.[364] In other words, privacy standards are now part of the global norm in human-rights issues. Any country that participates as part of the global community and is a signatory of various treaties is expected to protect individual privacy.[365] The effects of globalization on international treaties, trade, travel, and security compel us to look beyond national laws and consider how privacy rights are treated across borders and in the borderless Internet. This section will address international standards and treaties relating to privacy, the policies and laws within certain nations, and international guidelines. Finally, the section will address the status of privacy in the European Union, Latin America, and Asia.

1. Sources of Privacy Law and Policy

a. International Treaties, Conventions, and Frameworks

Virtually all twentieth-century treaties and declarations containing human-rights provisions have included some explicit recognition of privacy rights.[366] For example, Article 12 of the Universal Declaration of

---

[364] *See* discussion *infra* Chapter III, § C-1(a).

[365] For example, the preamble to the Council of Europe's Convention for the Protection of Individuals with Regard to Automatic Processing of Personal Data states "that it is desirable to extend the safeguards for everyone's rights and fundamental freedoms, and in particular the right to the respect for privacy" and "that it is necessary to reconcile the fundamental values of the respect for privacy and the free flow of information between peoples." Convention for the Protection of Individuals with Regard to Automatic Processing of Personal Data, Jan. 1, 1981, Europ. T.S. No. 108 [hereinafter Convention 108].

[366] For example, the five major international privacy policies are the Organization for Economic Cooperation and Development ("OECD") Guidelines on the Protection of Privacy and Transborder Flows of Personal Data (1980), *available at* http://www.oecd. org/document/18/0,2340,es_2649_34255_1815186_1_1_1_1,00.html (last visited May 9, 2008); the U.N. Guidelines for the Regulation of Computerized Personal Data Files, G.A. Res. 45/95, U.N. Doc. A/RES/45/95 (Dec. 14, 1990); Convention 108, *supra* note 365; Directive 95/46/EC of the European Parliament and of the Council on the Protection of Individuals with Regard to the Processing of Personal Data and on the Free Movement of Such Data, 1995 O.J. (L 281) 31 [hereinafter E.U. Directive]; and

Human Rights states, "No one shall be subjected to arbitrary interference with his privacy, family, home, or correspondence."[367] Furthermore, Article 17 of the International Covenant on Civil and Political Rights declares, "No one shall be subjected to arbitrary or unlawful interference with his privacy, family, home or correspondence, nor to unlawful attacks on his honor and reputation."[368]

The privacy issues faced by nations with a free press and basic personal freedoms are similar. Of course, some jurisdictions are less concerned with personal privacy issues.[369] Those jurisdictions that are concerned face the challenges of the free press, new technology, the Internet, government security, information needs, and a generally intrusive public. Con-sequently, broad global privacy statements confront a complex matrix of different national policies and new global realities.

In a world where territory is the basis for governmental control, privacy is difficult to protect internationally. Laws, including those aimed at protecting privacy, are generally enforced by national governments. These national governments control defined territory, and it is often difficult for them to exercise control beyond their borders. Modern developments, like the rise of the Internet, the rapid growth of outsourcing services to developing nations, and the continued expansion of power vested in multinational corporations contribute to a situation in which the enforcement of national-based privacy protections is difficult.

This complicated web of national jurisdictions is exacerbated by the dominance of the borderless Internet as a primary means of communication.[370]

---

the Asia-Pacific Economic Cooperation ("APEC") Privacy Framework (2005), *available at* http://epic.org/redirect/apf12407.html (last visited May 13, 2008).

[367] Universal Declaration of Human Rights, G.A. Res. 217A, art. 12, U.N. Doc. A/810, at 71 (Dec. 10, 1948).

[368] International Covenant on Civil and Political Rights art. 17, *opened for signature* Dec. 19, 1966, 999 U.N.T.S. 171.

[369] The human-rights group Privacy International issues an annual report called the *International Privacy Ranking*, which judges nations on the basis of a variety of factors. In 2007, the report classified Malaysia, China, Russia, Singapore, Taiwan, Thailand, the United States, and the United Kingdom as "endemic surveillance societies," the worst ranking. Greece received the best score and was thus considered to have "adequate safeguards against abuse." The report does not rank all the nations in the world and excludes, among others, North Korea, Cuba, Zimbabwe, and most of the former republics of the Soviet Union. *See* EPIC & PRIVACY INT'L, THE 2007 INTERNATIONAL PRIVACY RANKING (2007), *available at* http://www.privacyinternational.org/article.shtml?cmd[347]=x-347-559597 (last visited May 9, 2008).

[370] The network's functioning is controlled by private organizations such as the Internet Engineering Task Force ("IETF"), the Internet Corporation for Assigned Names and

The technology of the Internet and its international nature make its regulation on a national level very difficult.[371] The Internet is not aligned with geography, and users have access to information without regard to the territorial origin of data.[372] The Internet, because it is a network-based system, requires multinational oversight to provide effective enforcement.[373] Nations working with each other to prosecute violations (including of their citizens' privacy) rely on treaties, agreements, or extralegal mechanisms to bring about justice.[374] When agreements and cooperation between nations are fragmented, attempts to safeguard privacy are undermined.

Both the United Nations and the Organization for Economic Co-operation and Development ("OECD") help guide the development of international privacy protection.[375] In both the Universal Declaration of Human Rights and the International Covenant on Civil and Political Rights, the United Nations declared a right to privacy.[376] Additionally, in its Guidelines for the Regulation of Computerized Personal Data Files, the United Nations stressed that data collected should be secure, accurate, limited, and accessible to the data subject for inspection and correction.[377] However, these declarations and guidelines are not binding on U.N. members.

The OECD also issues guidelines for international privacy protection. The OECD works with its thirty member countries and seventy other countries to address economic and social issues.[378] The OECD tries to foster good governance and produces instruments, decisions, and recommendations to help develop a consistent global legal framework.[379] OECD efforts include the development and publication of the following:

1. Guidelines on the Protection of Privacy and Transborder Flows of Personal Data

---

Numbers ("ICANN"), and the World Wide Web Consortium ("W3C"). Andrew T. Kenyon, New Dimensions in Privacy Law 9 (2006).

[371] Jon L. Mills, *Internet Casinos*, 19 Dick. J. Int'l L. 77, 96 (2000).

[372] *Id.* at 84.

[373] *Id.*

[374] *Id.* at 85.

[375] In addition, APEC and the European Union have guidelines on privacy policy. *See supra* note 366.

[376] Jody R. Westby, ABA International Guide to Privacy 82 (2004).

[377] *Id.*

[378] *See* Organization for Economic Cooperation and Development, http://www.oecd.org/ (last visited May 9, 2008).

[379] *Id.*

2. Guidelines for the Security of Information Systems and Networks: Towards a Culture of Security
3. The International Guide to Cyber Security[380]

The OECD and the U.N. efforts, though not binding, represent the introduction of important ideas into the conversation between nations, show possible progress toward greater harmonization of national standards, and leave the door open for establishing customary international law.

Prime examples of regional transnational privacy policy are found in Article 8 of the European Convention on Human Rights, which protects "the right to respect for private and family life," and the E.U. Charter of Fundamental Rights, which has articles on respect for private and family life and protection of personal data.[381] By comparison, the United States has no comprehensive legislation on privacy rights.[382] Some commentators suggest the basic difference in policy is because of a basic difference in philosophy.[383] They suggest that Americans focus on the sanctity of the home and actions by governmental actors but less on intrusions by the media and private actors. By comparison, the Continental culture focuses more on dignity and personal respect. This distinction is a tangible example of the theory discussed above that culture defines privacy policy.[384] Therefore, we can expect very different sets of privacy protections across the world.

b. National Constitutions, Laws, and Policies Protecting Privacy

Privacy laws and policies vary greatly among nations. Worldwide, countries have increasingly placed privacy as a specific textual right in their constitutions. When evaluating a nation's privacy framework, one should take care not to interpret strict protections on paper as translating into strict

---

[380] WESTBY, *supra* note 376, at 82–87.
[381] Charter of Fundamental Rights of the European Union art. 8, 2000 O.J. (C 364) 1.
[382] *See* Donald C. Dowling, Jr. & Jeremy M. Mittman, *International Privacy Law*, in PROSKAUER ON PRIVACY, *supra* note 123, § 14:1, § 14:2-3 ("By international standards, the United States takes an almost *laissez faire* 'sectoral' approach to privacy law, concentrating on a handful of specific areas of data management. . . . Even with all its privacy laws, the United States leaves most areas of personal data processing largely unregulated.").
[383] James Whitman, *The Two Western Cultures of Privacy: Dignity Versus Liberty*, 113 YALE L.J. 1151 (2004).
[384] *See, e.g., id.* at 1161–62.

enforcement.[385] As previously stated, the United States has no textually explicit constitutional privacy right. And without a written constitution, the United Kingdom obviously has no textual right.

The constitutions of countries such as Nepal[386] and Paraguay,[387] however, explicitly protect their citizens against invasions of privacy, including informational intrusions.[388] The enforcement of these binding provisions, though, is uncertain. There is no doubt that in application, the right to privacy will vary from nation to nation. The continued expansion of the development of privacy laws around the globe is spurred by economic realities and demands. It is in the interests of large economies, such as those of the United States and the European Union, to promote data protection. It is likewise in the interest of countries that wish to trade with those large economic powers to provide privacy and data protection.

Even though E.U. privacy law originates from a common source, each member state has a unique national privacy law. Because each state interprets its own laws, privacy rights are interpreted differently, even among E.U. member states.

Clearly there will be conflict between nations' policies on privacy. Because of increased global commerce and communications, those conflicts will become more frequent. Global communication makes worldwide libel possible, for example. The fact that there are different consequences in different countries puts a new face on liability for Internet distribution.

---

[385] See SOLOVE, *supra* note 3, at 929.

[386] NEPAL CONST. art. 22 ("Except as provided by law, the privacy of the person, house, property, document, correspondence or information of anyone is inviolable.").

[387] See PARA. CONST. art. 36, § 1 ("Personal documents are inviolable. Records, regardless of the technique used, accountings, printed matter, correspondence, writings, telephonic communication, telegraphic communication, or any other type of communication, collections or reproductions, testimonies or objects of testimonial value, as well as their respective copies, cannot be reviewed, reproduced, intercepted, or seized unless a court order is issued in specific cases established in the law, and then only when actions are essential for clearing up matters falling within the jurisdiction of the respective competent authorities.").

[388] See also CONSTITUIÇÃO FEDERAL [C.F.] art. 5, § X (Braz.); POL. CONST. ch. II, art. 49; SLOVK. CONST. art. 19, § 3 ("Everyone has the right to protection against the unwarranted collection, publication, or other illicit use of his personal data."); CONSTITUCIÓN [C.E.] art. 18, § 4 (Spain) ("The law shall limit the use of information, to guarantee personal and family honor, the privacy of citizens, and the full exercise of their rights."); BUNDESVERFASSUNG DER SCHWEIZERISCHEN EIDGENOSSENSCHAFT [BV], CONSTITUTION FÉDÉRALE DE LA CONFÉDÉRATION SUISSE [Cst] [Constitution] April 18, 1999, SR 101, RO 101, art. 13, ¶ 2 (Switz.) ("Every person has the right to be protected against abuse of personal data.").

Because of national and cultural differences, universal agreement on specific privacy policies beyond broad principles is unlikely. We therefore should expect continuing conflicts. However, the privacy policy of the European Union is an example of a regional policy worth examining.

2. The European Union: A Comprehensive Privacy Policy

The European Union has implemented the most comprehensive and substantial example of privacy protection, a data-protection regime that could serve as the cornerstone for the gradual spread of effective data protection worldwide because of its far-reaching economic and trade impact. For example, the European Union questioned whether its privacy standards were being violated by the data-retention policy of the worldwide search engine Google.[389] By putting that policy under a microscope, the European Union may have an impact far beyond its borders.

The current E.U. data-protection regime is contained in a comprehensive body of legislation, adopted by its Council of Ministers on October 24, 1995, entitled European Union Directive on the Protection of Individuals with Regard to the Processing of Personal Data and on the Free Movement of Such Data ("E.U. Directive").[390] The E.U. Directive, which requires its member states to adopt national legislation pursuant to its provisions,[391] is the culmination of over fifty years of Europe's "devotion to recognizing, maintaining, restoring, and ensuring personal privacy."[392]

---

[389] In May 2007, the Article 29 Data Protection Working Party wrote a letter to Google expressing the working party's view that Google's data-retention policies did not meet the E.U. standards. Google stores information about every search conducted on its engine, including the search query, the date and time of the search, and the physical location of the computer from which the search took place. Google retains the data for eighteen to twenty-four months, a length of time that the European Union found unsatisfactory. *See* Frederick Lane, *E.U. Questions Data Retention Policies*, NewsFactor. com, May 28, 2007, *available at* http://www.newsfactor.com/news/EU-Questions-Google-Data-Retention/story.xhtml?story_id=13000BY3SQIU; Kevin J. O'Brien & Thomas Crampton, *European Union Warns Google on Possible Violations of Privacy Law*, N.Y. Times, May 26, 2007, at C3, *available at* http://www.nytimes.com/2007/05/26/business/26google.html?ex=1337832000&en=9bcd1d8790e9cc83&ei=5090&partner=rssuserland&emc=rss.

[390] *See* E.U. Directive, *supra* note 366.

[391] *Id.* art. 4.

[392] Marsha Cope Huie et al., *The Right to Privacy in Personal Data: The E.U. Prods the U.S. and Controversy Continues*, 9 Tulsa J. Comp. & Int'l L. 391, 441 (2002).

a. Basic Principles of the E.U. Data-Protection Regime

The E.U. Directive sets forth eight principles governing the collection and use of personal identifiable information: purpose limitation, data quality, data security, sensitive data protection, transparency, data transfer, independent oversight, and individual redress.[393] Its main objective is to "protect the fundamental rights and freedoms of natural persons and in particular their right to privacy with respect to the processing of personal data."[394] The E.U. Directive requires entities that control data-processing operations to adhere to its principles when processing an individual's personal data.[395] In its broadest form, the E.U. Directive states that personal data cannot be processed without the individual's authorization unless the processing either is necessary to perform a contract between the individual and the entity or falls within a specific exception.[396]

The European Data Protection Supervisor ("EDPS") monitors the processing of personal data within the European Union, advises on policies and legislation that affect privacy, and cooperates with other data-protection authorities to promote consistent data protection throughout the European Union.[397] The EDPS is an independent entity created by the European Parliament and Commission.[398] The primary responsibilities of the EDPS are to receive and investigate data-privacy-violation complaints and provide advice to the European Community regarding data-protection matters.[399] The EDPS has broad authority regarding data practice, which has helped render it an effective enforcement mechanism.[400] Each E.U. member state has its own data-protection authority with powers to advise, investigate, and impose penalties for violations of data-protection law.[401]

---

[393] See JACQUELINE KIOSEK, DATA PRIVACY IN THE INFORMATION AGE 39–35 (2000) (providing an in-depth discussion of the articles of the E.U. Directive).

[394] E.U. Directive, *supra* note 366, art. 1(1); *see also id.* art. 2(a) (defining "personal data" as "any information relating to an identified or identifiable natural person").

[395] *Id.* art. 3.

[396] Ryan Moshell, Comment ... *And Then There Was One: The Outlook for a Self-Regulatory United States Amidst a Global Trend Toward Comprehensive Data Protection*, 37 TEX. TECH. L. REV. 357, 369 (2005).

[397] See European Data Protection Supervisor, http://www.edps.europa.eu/EDPSWEB/webdav/site/mySite/shared/Documents/EDPS/Publications/Brochures/brochure_edps_en.pdf (last visited May 9, 2008).

[398] Moshell, *supra* note 396.

[399] *Id.*

[400] *Id.* at 370.

[401] See Regulation (EC) No. 45/2001 of the European Parliament and of the Council, 2001 O.J. (L 8) 1; E.U. Directive, *supra* note 366. Article 24 of Regulation 45/2001 states that "each Community institution and Community body shall appoint at least one person

b. Transfer of Personal Data to Third Countries Under the E.U. Regime

The E.U. Directive not only requires that its member states enact national laws ensuring personal data privacy within their respective borders but also creates specific guidelines regulating the export of personal data to "third countries."[402] According to Article 25, which seeks to exercise jurisdictional extraterritoriality in this regard,[403] such transfer of data can occur only when the receiving country has promulgated standards ensuring "adequate" compliance with the principles set forth in the E.U. Directive.[404] This compliance mechanism greatly affects the United States as a third country engaging in business with the European Union, indirectly compelling U.S. businesses to embrace E.U.-like privacy standards. Critics have opposed the E.U. Directive's influence on U.S. privacy laws in terms of its extraterritorial effect, with one commentator observing that the European Union "has gone so far as to give an ultimatum to Washington: adopt strong privacy laws, or stand the risk of losing countless trillions of dollars with Europe."[405] Because the current data-protection regime in the United States includes a large component of industry self-regulation, such extraterritorial application of the E.U. Directive to U.S. companies has the potential to dampen the ability of such companies to do business with E.U. member states.

c. Safe Harbor Agreements: A Model for Globalization of Privacy?

Because of the potential threat to U.S. business interests, the U.S. Department of Commerce developed a certification program for companies seeking to do business with the European Union. The United States' experience in establishing a framework for a personal-data-protection regime

---

as data protection officer." Article 28 of the E.U. Directive requires each E.U. member state to provide one or more independent public authorities with the power to investigate, intervene, and participate in legal action under the directive.

[402] *See* E.U. Directive, *supra* note 366, art. 25.

[403] Moshell, *supra* note 396, at 372.

[404] *See* E.U. Directive, *supra* note 366, art. 25 (stating in part that "[E.U.] Member Sates shall provide that the transfer to a third country of personal data . . . may take place only if . . . the third country . . . ensures an adequate level of protection").

[405] John R. Vacca, *The European Data Protection Directive: A Roadblock to International Trade?*, in THE PRIVACY PAPERS: MANAGING TECHNOLOGY, CONSUMER, EMPLOYEE, AND LEGISLATIVE ACTIONS 569, 570 (Rebecca Herold ed., 2002).

acceptable to the European Union may be instructive as to how such regimes could be established with other non-E.U.-member countries on a worldwide basis. Unlike the centralized and tightly controlled data-protection system employed by the European Union, the data-protection regime in the United States tends to be fragmented and highly dependent on industry self-regulation. In an effort to bridge the two contrasting data-protection regimes, the U.S. Department of Commerce and the European Commission reached a compromise, agreeing to a safe harbor[406] that seeks to assure the E.U. of the adequacy of protection for data processed by U.S. businesses.[407] U.S. companies agreeing to the terms of, and joining, the safe-harbor program are deemed to have adequate data-protection policies.

Because membership in the program is voluntary, the safe harbor could serve as a viable option for other nations seeking to open business opportunities within the European Union. Nations not willing to enact E.U.-adequate data-protection laws themselves may enable companies to do business with the European Union by allowing a company to individually commit to the E.U. data-protection principles. Such a gradual expansion of E.U. privacy principles within a third nation could lead to a progressive warming of the climate toward data protection.

I. MECHANISM OF OPERATION

The safe harbor was approved by the European Union in July 2000.[408] Under the safe harbor, there is a presumption of the "adequacy" of privacy protection under the E.U. Directive for any U.S. organization that can demonstrate that it complies with the principles embodied in the E.U. Directive. Robert LaRussa, acting undersecretary of the International Trade Administration, described the overall purpose of the safe harbor as "a landmark accord for e-commerce. It bridges the differences between E.U. and U.S. approaches to privacy protection and will ensure that data flows between the U.S. and the E.U. are not interrupted. As a result,

---

[406] *See generally* Issuance of Safe Harbor Principles and Transmission to European Commission, 65 Fed. Reg. 45,666 (July 24, 2000), *relevant portion available at* http://www.export.gov/safeharbor/SHPRINCIPLESFINAL.htm.

[407] *See* Letter from David L. Aaron, U.S. Dep't of Commerce, to Industry Representatives (Nov. 4, 1998), *available at* http://www.ita.doc.gov/td/ecom/aaron114.html.

[408] *See generally* Commission Decision 2000/520/EC, 2000 O.J. (L 215) 7.

the Safe Harbor should help ensure that e-commerce continues to flourish."[409]

II. BASIC PRINCIPLES

The safe harbor sets forth seven principles with which U.S. organizations must comply in order to qualify for the safe harbor and the presumption of "adequacy" that such compliance imparts. These principles entail: (1) notice; (2) choice; (3) onward transfer; (4) security; (5) data integrity; (6) access; and (7) enforcement.[410]

1. Notice: Adherence to the safe-harbor agreement requires that an organization provide an individual with proper notice about the collection and dissemination of information practices. Specifically, an individual must be informed about the purposes of the collection and use of his or her personal information, ways to contact the organization with regard to inquiries or complaints, and any choices or means that may be available to the individual for limiting the use and disclosure of his or her personal information. Furthermore, if an individual's information is disclosed to a third party, the individual must be provided with information regarding the identity of that party. The language of the notice must be clear and conspicuous. Such notice must be provided when an individual is first requested to provide the organization with personal data or as soon thereafter as is practicable. But in any event, the notice must be provided before the organization uses the information "for a purpose other than that for which it was originally collected or processed by the transferring organization or discloses it for the first time to a third party."[411]

2. Choice: Individuals must have the opportunity to decide whether their personal information can be submitted to a third party or whether it can be used "for a purpose that is incompatible with the purpose[s] for which it was originally collected."[412] Two types of choice-consent regimes are recognized: opt-in and opt-out regimes. An opt-in regime requires affirmative steps by the individual to allow the collection or use of personal information. Such a regime is required to be offered in regard to "sensitive information (i.e., personal information specifying medical or

---

[409] Memorandum from Robert S. LaRussa, Acting Undersecretary for the Int'l Trade Admin., to Colleagues (July 21, 2000), http://www.export.gov/safeharbor/larussacovernote717.htm.

[410] Issuance of Safe Harbor Principles, 65 Fed. Reg. 45,666, *relevant portion available at* http://www.export.gov/safeharbor/SHPRINCIPLESFINAL.htm.

[411] *Id.* at 45, 667.

[412] *Id.*

health conditions, racial or ethnic origin, political opinions, religious or philosophical beliefs, trade union membership or information specifying the sex life of the individual)."[413] An opt-out regime requires affirmative steps to prevent the collection or use of personal information and must be available in regard to nonsensitive information.[414]

3. Onward transfer: If an organization wishes to disclose information to a third party, it must adhere to the notice and choice principles.[415] Furthermore, the third party to whom the information will be transferred must provide at least the same level of privacy protection as is required by the relevant safe-harbor principles.[416]

4. Security: "Organizations creating, maintaining, using or disseminating personal information must take reasonable precautions to protect it from loss, *misuse and unauthorized access, disclosure, alteration and destruction*."[417]

5. Data integrity: "An organization may not process personal information in a way that is incompatible with the purpose for which it has been collected or subsequently authorized by the individual. To the extent necessary for those purposes, an organization should take reasonable steps to ensure that data is reliable for its intended use, accurate, complete, and current."[418]

6. Access: An individual must be able to access the personal information that an organization holds about that individual and must be able to correct, amend, or delete such information where inaccurate.[419]

7. Enforcement: There must be a mechanism in place to ensure compliance with the aforementioned principles, recourse for individuals who are harmed by an organization's noncompliance with these principles, and consequences to organizations that fail to follow these principles.[420]

d. The Consequences of E.U. Data Protection

The safe-harbor mechanism may offer a long-term solution as a cornerstone of and framework for an eventual worldwide personal-data-protection regime. However, the experience of the United States during the past

---

[413] *Id.* at 45, 668.
[414] *Id.* at 45, 667.
[415] *Id.* at 45, 668.
[416] *Id.*
[417] *Id.* (emphasis added).
[418] *Id.*
[419] *Id.*
[420] *Id.*

several years indicates that for success, there must be strong and positive involvement of the government, as well as willingness and ability on the part of private organizations to fully participate.[421] As a result of the unevenness of the application of the safe harbor in the United States, consumer groups in the European Union have had reservations about the resulting personal data protections as compared with those under the E.U. Directive itself.[422] For instance, U.S. organizations appear to have had difficulty in translating the basic principles of the safe harbor into their own individual data-handling policies and procedures.[423] Thus, to have a chance of success worldwide in protecting personal data, both the government and organizations must overcome the existing stumbling blocks toward successful implementation of the safe harbor in the United States. If this happens, a large step will have been taken toward a successful worldwide personal-data-protection regime.

Commentators are rationally skeptical about full-scale implementation of these lofty principles in a setting where commercial pressure is high.[424] Interestingly, all the principles are espoused in either statutory or common-law-based remedies in the United States. But the distinctions between the U.S. approach and the E.U. approach—including First Amendment protections and the availability of public information—are substantial, making the United States quite a different setting. So although the safe-harbor principles certainly are bringing common ground to global privacy issues, the individual national values and laws are still of central importance.

In fact, the European Union has more substantial privacy protections against intrusions by the press[425] and intrusions by private entities.[426] The general principles also would appear to provide more protection in the

---

[421] Sylvia Mercado Kierkegaard, *Safe Harbor Agreement—Boon or Bane?*, 1 SHIDLER J.L. COM. & TECH. 10 (2005), *available at* http://www.lctjournal.washington.edu/vol1/a010Kierkegaard.html. Note that Kierkegaard concludes that this lofty goal is unlikely to be attained. See *id.*

[422] *Id.*

[423] *Id.*

[424] *See, e.g.,* Tracey DiLascio, Note, *How Safe is the Safe Harbor? U.S. and E.U. Data Privacy Law and the Enforcement of the FTC's Safe Harbor Program*, 22 B.U. INT'L L.J. 399, 423–24 (2004); Kyle Thomas Sammin, Note, *Any Port in a Storm: The Safe Harbor, The Gramm-Leach-Bliley Act, and the Problem of Privacy in Financial Services*, 36 GEO. WASH. INT'L L. REV. 653, 653–54 (2004).

[425] *See* discussion *infra* Chapter III, § C-6(e).

[426] *See* discussion *supra* Chapter III, § C-2.

European Union than Fourth Amendment principles provide in the United States.[427]

Privacy issues in the global setting are likely to be involved in an increasing number of conflicts for the same reasons there are increasing conflicts within each nation, that is, technology, commercial motivations to intrude, an intrusive society, and an intrusive press. The additional factor that will clearly foster even more conflict among nations is the existence of varied cultures, constitutions, and legal contexts among the nations of the world. Regional and global polices by organizations such as the European Union and the United Nations must confront these realities.

3. Great Britain

Privacy policy is unclear in Great Britain since it has no history of privacy torts. Further since Britain has no constitution, there is obviously no constitutional privacy right. Although the Human Rights Act of 1998 and the Data Protection Act of 1998 together provide the statutory basis for privacy protection,[428] the primary common-law theory used is "breach of confidence."[429] This theory allows action for a breach even where there is no preexisting relationship between parties, only an implied one. In other words, you have an actionable right if another person or party discloses information about you when that person knows or ought to know that you reasonably expect that information to be confidential. So a photographer taking an unauthorized picture of the private celebrity wedding of Michael Douglas and the publication of that picture would be a breach of confidence.[430] But the courts have not established clear criteria for the kind of disclosure of personal information that invokes the protection for breach of confidence.[431]

---

[427] For example, Fourth Amendment protection in the United States turns on the question of whether one has a "reasonable expectation of privacy." This nebulous concept sometimes produces questionable results. *See* discussion *infra* Chapter VII, § B-1.

[428] Raymond Wacks, *Why There Will Never Be an English Common Law Privacy Tort*, *in* NEW DIMENSIONS IN PRIVACY LAW: INTERNATIONAL AND COMPARATIVE PERSPECTIVES 154 (Andrew Kenyon & Megan Richardson eds., 2006).

[429] Andrew Kenyon & Megan Richardson, *New Dimensions in Privacy: Communications Technologies, Media Practices and Law*, *in* NEW DIMENSIONS IN PRIVACY LAW, *supra* note 428, at 1, 7.

[430] Douglas v. Hello! Ltd, [2001] Q.B. 967; Douglas v. Hello! Ltd [2003] 3 All E.R. 996; Douglas v. Hello! Ltd [2005] H.R.L.R. 27.

[431] See Wacks, *supra* note 428, at 165. By comparison, American courts have established many tests to determine what kind of information is protected and what is not. *See* Chapter IV, § D-5.

A comparable situation in the United States might result in a suit for public disclosure of private facts or intrusion upon seclusion, or other statutory causes of action.[432]

British courts have been very reluctant to identify a distinct "privacy" right, and British commentators have criticized the absence of a clear privacy right.[433] Nonetheless, the existence of the E.U. Article 8 right (in the European Convention on Human Rights) and continual pressures of circumstance have built up a body of case law that aims to protect individuals against intrusions. British law directs courts to consider Article 8 obligations for human rights as a logical support for protecting privacy values. In fact, the court in the *Douglas* case noted that "there is no watertight division between the two concepts" of privacy and confidentiality.[434]

Indeed, cases illustrate the common interests between the two concepts. For example, after the *Daily Mirror* disclosed that Naomi Campbell, a model, was receiving treatment at Narcotics Anonymous, the House of Lords upheld Campbell's claim against the newspaper but made it clear that the action was for breach of confidence.[435] In doing so, however, the judges made reference to Campbell's "right to privacy," as weighed against freedom of expression.[436] Another case involved a man recorded on a public street by CCTV holding a knife that he had used to slit his wrists. A local authority distributed the footage to the media. The European Court of Human Rights found that the man had no remedy under the British regime.[437] The court explained that breach of confidence did not cover a recording by CCTV on a public street. There was no rational expectation that what he did in public was confidential. Therefore, his Article 8 privacy rights were not violated.

---

[432] Steinbuch v. Cutler, 518 F.3d 580 (Ark. 2008) (Professor Steinbuch brought action for invasion of privacy and intentional infliction of emotional distress for private facts of a sexual liaison, originally being published on a weblog, and developed into a novel and potential television series).

[433] Wacks, *supra* note 428, at 155–56. Wacks says that there are seven reasons privacy torts will not be created in England: (1) the advance of the equitable remedy for breach of confidence; (2) the impact of the Human Rights Act of 1998; (3) the dominance of freedom of expression; (4) the impact of the Data Protection Act 1998; (5) media self-regulation; (6) the incoherence of the concept of privacy; and (7) judicial preference for legislation. *Id.*

[434] *Id.* at 159 (quoting Douglas v. Hello! Ltd. [2001] Q.B. 967, ¶ 165 (Keene, L.J.)).

[435] Campbell v. MGN Ltd. [2004] 2 A.C. 457, ¶ 82 (Hope, L.J.), ¶¶ 132–33 (Lady Hale, J.).

[436] *Id.* ¶ 36 (Hoffman, L.J.), ¶ 92 (Hope, L.J.).

[437] Peck v. United Kingdom, 36 Eur. H.R. Rep. 41, ¶ 10 (2003).

Although commentators criticize the failure to acknowledge an explicit privacy right, a lawyer from the United States will notice similar debates occurring in breach-of-confidence cases as in privacy-rights actions. A court must first determine if the expectation (of confidence or privacy) was reasonable. Second, in Great Britain, the court must determine whether the disclosure was of "important public information."[438] In the United States, the issue is whether the disclosure was protected First Amendment speech. Although the second inquiries in Great Britain and the United States are similar, the results may be different. The First Amendment protects more disclosures. For example, the disclosure of drug treatment in the Naomi Campbell case would very likely be considered protected speech in the United States.[439]

4. Latin America: Privacy in Developing Economies

Privacy protections are developing in Latin America and across the world. Trade groups and economic cooperatives have developed privacy and data-protection guidelines to help foster economic activity within their regions.[440] Although nothing prohibits a Latin American nation from adopting one of the previously developed privacy frameworks, the frameworks were

---

[438] For example, in Leeds City Council v. Channel Four Television Corp., [2007] 1 F.L.R. 678, *available at* 2005 WL 5353814 (Fam. Div.), the court balanced the intrusion of the media's surreptitious filming of the student discipline problem in a local school with the "important public interests" of concerned citizens, taxpayers, and members of public authorities to be informed about the education of students, which was being hampered by the school's inability to control students' behavior. The court stated that the surreptitious filming appeared to be the only way to expose the matter of concern and thus outweighed the students' and parents' claims of confidence. In Long Beach Ltd. v. Global Witness Ltd., [2007] EWHC (QB) 1980, *available at* 2007 WL 2187029, a Hong Kong court required a secretarial company to disclose to a judgment creditor documents addressing the business affairs of the son of the president of the Republic of the Congo. The documents were referred to at a public hearing in Hong Kong. Global Witness Ltd., a nonprofit English company that campaigned against corruption, obtained the documents and posted them on its Web site. The plaintiff sued, claiming confidentiality. The court ruled against the plaintiff and stated, "Once there was good reason to doubt the propriety of the financial affairs of a public official, there was a public interest in those affairs being open to public scrutiny."

[439] *See* Florida Star v. B.J.F., 491 U.S. 524 (1989) (holding that the newspaper's publication of information it obtained lawfully regarding the name of a rape victim was protected by the First Amendment). Arguably, the disclosure of a celebrity's drug treatment is less offensive than the disclosure of a private citizen's status as a rape victim, which *Florida Star* holds is protected by the First Amendment.

[440] *See, e.g.,* sources cited *supra* note 366.

developed to suit member nations within the North American, European, Asian, and Oceanic continents. The only Central and South American members of international organizations that produced privacy frameworks are Mexico (OECD), Chile, and Peru (both APEC members). In other words, Latin America has no privacy or data-protection guidelines that reflect their common interests and histories, and therefore data protections are inconsistent across the continent.

Attempting to resolve this matter, the Spanish Data Protection Agency established the Ibero-American Data Protection Network ("IDPN") to "serve as a vehicle for encouraging the exchange of experience and for strengthening mutual and continuous cooperation in data protection matters."[441] Spain, however, is an E.U. member, and its data-protection law is therefore based on the E.U. Directive. Recognizing the importance of having a nation's data-protection laws and practices be judged adequate by the European Commission, Spain has worked to develop E.U.-style data-protection laws within the IDPN. Although the IDPN appears to be the only regional group seeking to establish a privacy framework for Latin America, it does not appear so strong that it could not be overtaken by another group's concerted push toward privacy-framework development.

Because privacy concerns may not be as deep-rooted within Latin American culture as in the European Union and the United States, sweeping privacy legislation may be of questionable benefit at the moment.[442] Furthermore, the lack of resources in many Latin American nations may undermine the effectiveness of any potential data-protection authority. In Argentina, where E.U.-style laws were implemented, the designated privacy authority is not independent but rather can be appointed and removed by the president. Also, the Argentinean governing law does not provide for an independent audit of the authority's efficacy.[443] Therefore, independence may be in doubt.

---

[441] The IDPN is open to all Latin American nations. At a minimum, Argentina, Brazil, Chile, Costa Rica, El Salvador, Spain, Guatemala, Mexico, Nicaragua, Peru, Portugal, and Uruguay have participated in the network. *See* La Antigua Declaration, *available at* https://www.agpd.es/upload/Declaracion_La%20Antigua.ing.PDF (last visited May 13, 2008).

[442] *See* Margaret P. Eisenhauer, *Developments in Latin America Privacy Laws*, 5 Privacy & Security L. Rep. (BNA) 521 (Apr. 10, 2006).

[443] Rafael del Villar, Alejandro Díaz de León & Johanna Gil Hubert, *Regulation of Personal Data Protection and of Reporting Agencies: A Comparison of Selected Countries of Latin America, the United States and European Union Countries* (Feb. 2001) (unpublished manuscript), *available at* http://www1.worldbank.org/finance/assets/images/Regulation_of_Personal_Data_Protection.pdf.

The lack of a harmonized privacy framework, however, does not mean that privacy and autonomy over one's personal information receives no protection in Latin America. In fact, many Latin Americans have constitutional rights that U.S. citizens do not have. The Latin American region is unique in that citizens are afforded a constitutional right of *habeas data*, a right that has no counterpart elsewhere in the world. Although the right varies by nation, "it is designed to protect, by means of an individual complaint presented to a constitutional court, the image, privacy, honour, information, self-determination and freedom of information of a person."[444] *Habeas data* rights generally codify several of the fair-information principles: at a minimum, the right to obtain information about oneself and to correct inaccurate information. Generally, *habeas data* complaints may only be brought by the individual whose privacy has been violated. The right of *habeas data* first appeared in the 1988 Brazilian constitution, and several South American nations followed Brazil's lead and adopted *habeas data* rights in their constitutions: Paraguay in 1992, Peru in 1993, Argentina in 1994, Ecuador in 1996, Colombia in 1997, and Venezuela in 1999.[445] All these provisions grant access to publicly held data, and several explicitly grant access to private data as well.

Beyond *habeas data* rights, several Latin American constitutions recognize a broader right to privacy,[446] and others have provided privacy protections by statute. For example, Mexico has a freedom-of-information law[447] encompassing only the federal government. In Brazil, a 1997 law clarifies and regulates the constitutional right of *habeas data*.[448] Chile, Argentina, Uruguay, and Colombia have data-protection laws. Chile's law is applicable only to government databanks and provides for individual

---

[444] Andrés Guadamuz, *Habeas Data vs. The European Data Protection Directive*, 3 J. INFO. L. & TECH. (2001), *available at* http://www2.warwick.ac.uk/fac/soc/law/elj/jilt/2001_3/guadamuz/.

[445] *See* Alejandra Gils Carbo, Prosecutor, Argentine Attorney General's Office, Speech at the Twenty-third International Conference on Data Commissioners: One World, One Privacy (Sept. 26, 2001), *available at* http://www.cnil.fr/conference2001/eng/contribution/gils_contrib.html (last visited May 13, 2008).

[446] For example, the constitutions of Venezuela (article 28), Colombia (article 15), Chile, Peru, and the Dominican Republic.

[447] Ley Federal de Transparencia y Acceso a la Información Pública Gubernamental [Federal Transparency and Access to Public Government Information Law], 11 de Junio de 2002 (Mex.), *available (in English) at* http://www.gwu.edu/~nsarchiv/NSAEBB/NSAEBB68/laweng.pdf.

[448] Lei No. 9.507, de 12 de novembro de 1997, D.O.U. de 13.11.1997 (Brazil), *available (in Portuguese) at* http://www.planalto.gov.br/ccivil_03/leis/l9507.htm.

enforcement of the rights the law provides.[449] Uruguay's law, however, protects only personal data used for commercial purposes and exempts the public sector.[450] Argentina is the first Latin American nation to meet the European Union's data-protection adequacy requirement, and its data-protection law is applicable both to public and private entities.[451] Mexico,[452] Brazil,[453] and Colombia,[454] have sectoral laws providing limited privacy protections in limited contexts, like the laws of the United States. Although these nations have constitutional and statutory rights, respect for and enforcement of these rights is a challenge in many of these developing nations.[455]

5. Asia

Because of the cultural differences and varying political landscapes across Asia, privacy is dealt with very differently. For example, China has had a policy of keeping close track of its citizens, a practice dating back to the fourth century B.C.[456] This tradition is reflected today, for example, in its censoring of, and monitoring citizens' use of, the Internet.[457] In its ongoing transition

---

[449] Ley Sobre Protección de la Vida Privada [Law for the Protection of Private Life], Ley No. 19.628 Diario Oficial de 28 de agosto de 1999 (Chile), *available (in Spanish) at* http://www.sernac.cl/leyes/compendio/docs_compendio/Ley19628.pdf.

[450] Protección De Datos Personales Para Ser Utilizados En Informes Comerciales Y Acción De Habeas Data Ley 17.838 was enacted in September 2004, *available (in Spanish) at* http://www.clearing.com.uy/clearing/Ley17838.pdf.

[451] *See* Personal Data Protection Act, Law No. 25.326, Oct. 4, 2000, *available (in English) at* http://www.proteocciondedatos.com.ar/law25326.htm, *and (in Spanish) at* http://info-leg.mecon.gov.ar/infolegInternet/anexos/70000-74999/70368/norma.htm.

[452] EPIC & PRIVACY INT'L, *United Mexican States, in* PRIVACY AND HUMAN RIGHTS 2006, *available at* http://www.privacyinternational.org/article.shtml?cmd[347]=x-347-559515.

[453] *See, e.g.,* Lei No. 9.472, de 16 de Julho de 1997, livro I, art. 3, para. IX, D.O.U. de 17.7.1997 (Brazil), *available (in Portuguese) at* http://www.planalto.gov.br/ccivil_03/leis/l9472.htm.

[454] EPIC & PRIVACY INT'L, *Colombia, in* PRIVACY AND HUMAN RIGHTS 2006, *available at* http://www.privacyinternational.org/article.shtml?cmd[347]=x-347-559548.

[455] *See, e.g.,* AMNESTY INTERNATIONAL, 'I AM NOT ASHAMED!': HIV/AIDS AND HUMAN RIGHTS IN THE DOMINICAN REPUBLIC AND GUYANA, http://www.amnestyusa.org/news/document.do?id=ENGAMR010022006 (last visited May 13, 2008) (suggesting that the right to privacy in the Dominican Republic is not respected); Eisenhauer, *supra* note 442 (explaining that although the Chilean data-protection law is comprehensive in scope, it does not create an independent data-protection authority and relies on individuals for private enforcement and that the Argentine law, which is very comprehensive, has presented difficulties in implementation).

[456] EPIC & PRIVACY INT'L, PRIVACY AND HUMAN RIGHTS 2005, at 252 (2006).

[457] *See id.* at 254–58.

to the rule of law from the rule of person, "contradictory trends and isolated improvements" abound.[458]

Although the Chinese constitution does state that the personal dignity of its citizens is inviolable and that insult, libel, false accusation, and false incrimination directed against citizens by any means is prohibited,[459] this protection is left in the hands of the judiciary to enforce.[460]

Although Chinese citizens traditionally have not sought privacy protection,[461] attitudes today are evolving. According to Professor Lu Yaohuai from China's Central South University, traditional living arrangements, whereby families of several generations lived together in small homes, were not conducive to privacy.[462] However, as living conditions improve and people obtain more personal space, attitudes toward privacy are changing.[463] These changing attitudes toward privacy, however, have not stopped the Chinese government's surveillance activities. For example, China continues to increase video surveillance in public areas.[464] Businesses too are pursuing activities antithetical to privacy. For example, marketers are using information about consumers' credit histories and buying habits, and employers monitor their employees' activities on the Internet.[465] These concerns are very similar to concerns expressed by citizens in the United States.

Across the East China Sea lies Japan. Although the Japanese constitution has no textually explicit right to privacy, the Supreme Court recognized this substantial right in 1963.[466] Japan has a data-protection law that applies to both the public and private sectors.[467] The law promotes

---

[458] *Id.* at 248.

[459] XIAN FA [Constitution] art. 38 (P.R.C.), *available (in English) at* http://english.peopledaily.com.cn/constitution/constitution.html (last visited May 13, 2008).

[460] *See generally* Guobin Zhu, *The Right to Privacy: An Emerging Right in Chinese Law*, 18 STATUTE L. REV. 208, 211 (1997) (discussing Chinese legal scholars' work to advance the meaning of privacy, as well as providing a brief discussion of early cases applying the right of reputation to matters implicating privacy).

[461] For example, the Chinese word *yinsi* means both "shameful secret" and "privacy." *Id.*

[462] *The Long March to Privacy; China*, ECONOMIST, Jan. 14, 2006, at 45–46.

[463] *Id.*

[464] *Id.*

[465] *Id.*

[466] *See* EPIC & PRIVACY INT'L, *supra* note 456, at 429.

[467] *See generally* Miriam Wugmeister, *Privacy Law: Data Protection: Developments in Asia*, *in* PRIVACY AND SECURITY LAW INSTITUTE (EIGHTH ANNUAL): PATHWAYS TO COMPLIANCE IN A GLOBAL REGULATORY MAZE 569 (PLI 2007) (discussing recent developments in Japanese privacy law and policy, including the application of the data-protection law).

self-regulation but authorizes the creation of a protection organization within the private sector to handle complaint settlement.[468] Complementary laws establish data protection for both paper-based data as well as computer data. Criminal provisions apply for government officials who leak personal information "without proper justification."[469]

Japan also established a "privacy mark" system, whereby a government ministry will issue a mark to an organization committed to handling personal data in accordance with its guidelines.[470] The system presumes that market forces will penalize businesses not carrying the mark.[471] By June 13, 2005, 1,562 companies had been awarded privacy marks.[472] An E.U. study, however, suggests that there were serious shortcomings in the system.[473]

Government surveillance is also increasing in Japan. Wiretapping had been considered a violation of the right of privacy and was scarcely authorized before a 1999 law authorizing wiretaps was approved by a district court judge.[474] Courts have awarded damages for people who are illegally wiretapped.[475] License plates now carry smart chips, and densely populated public areas of Tokyo are being monitored by surveillance cameras, as are Japan's international airports.[476] In business, personal-data leaks are a problem for Japan, as well. At least one court has responded by awarding compensatory damages as well as damages for emotional distress.[477]

Although privacy and data-protection rights are still emerging in Asia, the continued growth of the Asian economy will probably drive the development of additional rights and remedies.

6. Examples of International Privacy Disputes

a. Passenger Information and National Security

What happens when treaties protecting privacy confront national-security policies designed to prevent terrorists from traveling to a particular nation?

---

[468] EPIC & PRIVACY INT'L, *supra* note 456, at 430.
[469] *Id.* at 431.
[470] *Id.* at 431–32.
[471] *Id.*
[472] *Id.*
[473] *Id.*
[474] *Id.* at 433.
[475] *Id.* at 434.
[476] *Id.* at 433–35.
[477] Wugmeister, *supra* note 467, at 573.

A conflict arose between U.S. requirements for information from airlines and E.U. requirements protecting E.U. citizens from disclosure of information.[478] Pursuant to the Aviation and Transportation Security Act ("ATSA"),[479] the United States requires access to detailed information about passengers flying into the United States. After passage of the ATSA, European airlines were in a Catch-22. The airlines faced being prohibited from landing unless they provided the information and being prohibited from operating out of Europe if they did. Although this situation has been resolved after years of legal challenges and political battles, this conflict foreshadows future conflicts, as no remedial actions have been taken to address the policy and cultural differences underlying the conflict. In a world with increasing concern about terrorism and varying standards for privacy, it is unlikely that privacy will prevail.

b. International Financial Transactions (SWIFT)

The United States maintained a secret program by which the Department of Treasury issued broad administrative subpoenas on a back-end financial messaging service used by banks, called SWIFT. SWIFT, a Belgian cooperative, maintained an office in the United States, where it mirrored the data stored on its European servers. As in the example relating to passenger's names, SWIFT faced diametrically opposed laws: the United States required SWIFT to turn over the information,[480] but the European Union prohibited the transfer of the data. The European authorities' chief concern was that information about E.U. citizens was being processed by the U.S. government without the citizens' consent. After investigations by the Belgian Privacy Protection Commission and the EDPS, SWIFT revised its privacy and data-protection policies. SWIFT applied for and was granted safe-harbor registration, and it now provides protections in line with the E.U. requirements.

---

[478] See Ioannis Ntouvas, *Air Passenger Data Transfer to the USA: The Decision of the ECJ and Latest Developments*, 16 Int'l J.L. & Info. Tech. 73 (2008) (providing a comprehensive review of the U.S.-E.U. conflict regarding the sharing of passenger information).

[479] Pub. L. No. 107-71, 115 Stat. 597 (2001) (codified as amended in scattered sections of 49 U.S.C.). The ATSA requires domestic and foreign airlines to provide a passenger and crew manifest to U.S. Customs. This requirement is in opposition to and conflicts with the E.U. Directive, which offers strict rules on data transfers like the ones required by the ATSA.

[480] SWIFT could have challenged the subpoena in court but chose not to.

c. Outsourcing Data Management

Imagine a scenario in which customer service for a large computer manufacturer is conducted out of multiple call centers in South Africa, the United States, India, and Canada. Imagine that each call center uses voice-over-the-Internet technology to allow customers and customer-service representatives to communicate. Also imagine that the consumer data from each customer-service phone conversation is entered into computers in each of these different nations and then archived in backup systems located in other nations.

Corporations in search of lower costs have outsourced a number of functions that implicate personal information including credit card management, bank transactions and medical records. Under current U.S. legislation a corporation must have a contractual commitment to confidentiality with a foreign company. If that foreign company breaches confidentiality, the American company may not be liable and the foreign company may be.[481] This (practice) is a problem since 62% of U.S. companies outsourcing have experienced data breaches.[482]

If there is an exchange of data that raises privacy concerns, at what geographic point can it be identified as occurring? Which nation's laws would govern? What if each nation's laws allow different types or levels of information to be legally shared? Which nation would be charged with addressing privacy violations? Would a nation be required to enforce a court ruling against a party who was convicted of violating privacy legislation in a different nation?[483] The answers to these questions rely on

---

[481] In one instance, the U.S. government prosecuted a Russian computer hacker under the Computer Fraud and Abuse Act for accessing personal data of Americans while abroad, 18 U.S.C. § 1030(a)(2). A federal court in Connecticut reasoned that "the intent to cause effects within the United States... makes it reasonable to apply to persons outside United States territory a statute which is not expressly extraterritorial in scope." United States v. Ivanov, 174 F. Supp. 2d 367, 370 (D. Conn. 2001) quoting United States v. Muench, 694 F.2d 28 (2d Cir. 1982). However, in terms of liability for corporations in the U.S., both HIPAA and GLBA are designed to protect against privacy breaches by entities initially receiving information. Therefore, when personal data is outsourced abroad, the U.S. companies may shield themselves from liability and the U.S. statutes may be inapplicable. *See* Jennifer Skarda-McCann, Note & Comment, *Overseas Outsourcing of Private Information & Individual Remedies for Breach of Privacy*, 32 Rutgers Computer & Tech. L.J. 325, 353–54 (2006).

[482] Larry Ponemon, *Privacy, Data Protection and Security Considerations in Outsourcing Decisions*, The Bureau of National Affairs, 7 Privacy Law Watch., 22 Oct. 2007.

[483] The answer to this and the preceding four questions might lie in the use of binding corporate rules ("BCRs"), which allow a company to establish legally enforceable rules for intraorganizational, cross-border transfers of personal data. However, BCRs are

the finite details of a given situation. But, as is often the case, different nations can interpret the same facts to have vastly different meanings, which can lead to problems of privacy protection on an international level.

d. Internet Defamation

Defamation has taken on global characteristics with the advent of the Internet. Now a publisher can defame someone in any country or every country. The interesting legal issue in the global context is the difference in free-press rights and defamation laws in different countries. What is protected speech in one country may be libel or slander in another.

Australia's Joseph Gutnick sued the *Wall Street Journal* for distributing a story he read in Australia on wsj.com. Seventeen hundred Australians subscribed to wsj.com. The Australian high court, employing a completely different standard from that of the American First Amendment, held the company liable and said that the place where the person downloads the materials "will be the place where the tort of defamation is committed."[484]

e. Different Approaches to the Right to Privacy Within the European Union

Princess Caroline of Monaco fought a long battle in multiple European courts to protect her right to prevent the publication of unauthorized photographs taken of her engaging in private activities. The German federal constitutional court (Bundesverfassungsgerichtshof), interpreting German law, enjoined the publication of those photographs that included images of her children, finding that a parent's relationship with her children needed more privacy protection.[485] The images of Princess Caroline shopping and relaxing on the beach, however, were not protected.[486]

---

still only "loosely defined," although the European Union appears receptive to allowing the use of BCRs in international data transfers within an organization. *See* David Bender & Larry Ponemon, *Binding Corporate Rules for Cross-Border Data Transfer*, 3 RUTGERS J.L. & URB. POL'Y 154, 161, 162 (2006).

[484] Dow Jones & Co. v. Gutnick, [2002] H.C.A. 56, 2002 (Austl.); *see also* JACK L. GOLDSMITH & TIM WU, WHO CONTROLS THE INTERNET: ILLUSIONS OF A BORDERLESS WORLD (2006).

[485] Von Hannover v. Germany, 2004-III Eur. Ct. H.R. 294, § 25. (Section 25 of the European Court of Human Rights opinion is a reproduction of the relevant portions of the decision by the German federal constitutional court).

[486] *Id.*

The court considered Princess Caroline a public figure,[487] and the photographs showed her in public places.[488]

She appealed to the European Court of Human Rights, which held that the German court violated her right to privacy under the European Convention on Human Rights.[489] The court weighed her Article 8 "right to respect her private life" against the Article 10 right of freedom of expression.[490] The substance of the photographs themselves tipped the balance in favor of her right to privacy. The court classified the photographs as depicting Caroline in "activities of a purely private nature such as engaging in sport, out walking, leaving a restaurant or on holiday."[491] The decisive factor for the court was that the photographs did not "contribute to a debate of general public interest."[492] The court emphasized that Princess Caroline performed no official function and that the pictures related only to her private life.[493]

This ruling illustrates analytical differences between the European Union and its member states, as well as between European and American courts. The photographs at issue in Caroline's case would almost surely fall under the protection of the First Amendment in the United States. Notice also the court's willingness to differentiate between what types of subject matter may contribute to a debate of general public interest and what does not. The German court and, indeed, American courts are not willing to engage in that sort of determination.[494] American courts prefer to allow speech and to err on the side of newsworthiness when confronted with a First Amendment issue, often to the detriment of privacy rights.[495]

---

[487] German case law refers to a "figure of contemporary society 'par excellence.'" *Id.*
[488] *Id.*
[489] *Id.*
[490] *Id.* § 58.
[491] *Id.* § 61.
[492] *Id.* § 76.
[493] *Id.*
[494] Compare the court's analysis with that of the German federal constitutional court, which took a view more akin to that of the United States:
> Nor can mere entertainment be denied any role in the formation of opinions. That would amount to unilaterally presuming that entertainment merely satisfies a desire for amusement, relaxation, escapism or diversion.
> Entertainment can also convey images of reality and propose subjects for debate that spark a process of discussion and assimilation relating to philosophies of life, values, and behavior models. In that respect, it fulfils important social functions. The same is true of information about people.

Id. § 25.
[495] *See* discussion *infra* Chapter IV, § A.

In other words, the European court's balancing of the freedom of expression against the right to privacy when interpreting the European Convention on Human Rights simply has no practical analogue in the United States at this time.

The German courts and the European Court of Human Rights took different approaches as well. Although both courts balanced the same underlying freedom of expression and privacy rights, the courts reached different conclusions. Given this disharmony between the E.U. courts and those of its member states, these different interpretations of privacy law may continue until uniformity is achieved by legislation.[496]

f. International Appropriation of Personality

A Texas family is suing Australia's Virgin Mobile phone company.[497] The company used a photograph of Alison Chang on posters and billboards in an advertising campaign in Australia.[498] The company downloaded her picture from Flickr, a popular Yahoo photo-sharing site. Flickr was a Canadian company that was sold to Yahoo.[499] Virgin Mobile received no permission to use the picture, and Ms. Chang was not notified. Among other tag lines in the ad was the line, "Free text virgin to virgin."[500]

The suit is seeking libel damages.[501] It also seems that the suit could seek the common-law remedy of appropriation of personality.[502] The advertising agency and the company took a picture that was in the public domain and used it for their financial gain a continent away from where the subject lived.[503]

Each of the above examples presents procedural legal issues and choices. This area of law is termed "conflict of law," and there are state and federal policies dealing with these issues. A U.S. citizen who suffers an alleged harm at the hands of an international entity may choose to sue in the United States or a foreign jurisdiction. If the person sues in the United

---

[496] *See* Daniel Kaboth, *Germany: The Publicity of Privacy*, LEGAL WK., July 29, 2004, *available at* http://legalweek.com/Articles/120821/Germany+The+publicity+of+privacy.html.

[497] Associated Press, *Dallas Family Sues Virigin Mobile for Illegal Use of Teen in Advertising Campaign*, FOXNEWS.COM, Sept. 21, 2007, http://www.foxnews.com/story/0,2933,297545,00.html.

[498] *Id.*

[499] *Id.*

[500] *Id.*

[501] *Id.*

[502] *Id.*

[503] *Id.*

States, the threshold question is whether a court has jurisdiction over the defendant. If the court has jurisdiction, the second question to ask is what law to apply to the transaction. In a diversity suit, even one involving international parties, state law governs choice of law.[504] State laws, however, are not uniform. Some states follow what is termed the "territorial" test in the *Restatement of Conflict of Laws*, whereas the majority follow the *Second Restatement*, which provides an "interest" analysis.[505] Still other states ask which jurisdiction has the greatest interest in the dispute. In other words, there is little certainty in determining which law will apply in a suit.

The U.S. citizen could also sue in a foreign jurisdiction, where the law may be more favorable. Assuming the foreign court has jurisdiction over the case, the judgment is enforceable in that jurisdiction only to the extent that the defendant has assets there. If the plaintiff is not able to collect on the judgment in the jurisdiction where it brought the action, the plaintiff could seek to enforce the judgment in the United States. Foreign judgments typically are recognized and given effect in state and federal courts, with certain exceptions. Most states follow the Uniform Foreign Money-Judgments Recognition Act of 1962, which essentially states that judgments should be recognized if the proceedings leading to the judgment comported with due process. However, some states require reciprocity of recognition, that is, the jurisdiction from which the judgment originated must also recognize judgments entered by the state where the judgment is sought to be enforced.[506] In the example of the Virgin Mobile advertising case, Ms. Chang could sue either in Texas or in Australia. If she sued in Texas, the laws of Texas on right of publicity could be used. However, Virgin Mobile, an Australian company, could potentially dispute jurisdiction in Texas.

Texas follows the *Restatement (Second) of Conflict of Laws*.[507] In a tort case, such as the Chang example, the relevant question is which state "has

---

[504] Success Motivation Institute of Japan, Ltd. v. Success Motivation Institute, Inc., 966 F.2d 1007, 1010 (5th Cir. 1992).

[505] RESTATEMENT (SECOND) OF CONFLICT OF LAWS § 6, at 10 (1971). Factors considered under the *Restatement's* analysis include "(a) the needs of the interstate and international systems, (b) the relevant policies of the forum, (c) the relevant policies of other interested states and the relative interests of those states in the determination of the particular issue, (d) the protection of justified expectations, (e) the basic policies underlying the particular field of law, (f) certainty, predictability and uniformity of result, and (g) ease in the determination and application of the law to be applied." *Id.*

[506] *See* 13 U.L.A. 149 (1986); EUGENE F. SCOLES ET AL., CONFLICT OF LAWS § 24.36 n.1, at 1312 (4th ed. 2004).

[507] Gutierrez v. Collins, 583 S.W.2d 312, 318 (Tex. 1979).

the most significant relationship to the occurrence and the parties."[508] In assessing this question, a court should look toward "(a) the place where the injury occurred, (b) the place where the conduct causing the injury occurred, (c) the domicile, residence, nationality, place of incorporation and place of business of the parties, and (d) the place where the relationship, if any, between the parties is centered."[509]

If we apply the *Restatement (Second)* analysis to the Chang case, it is not clear where the injury occurred. Chang lives in the United States, but the advertising campaign using her image was run only in Australia. How Chang came to learn of the use of her image may bear on this question. The answer to this question also depends on what Chang claims her injury is. For example, if Chang alleges appropriation of personality, the injury probably occurred in Australia. But if Chang learned of the use of her image when she was in Texas and the advertisement was made available outside Australia, it is possible that the injury occurred in Texas.

As for the second question, it appears more straightforward that the conduct causing the injury occurred in Australia: Virgin Mobile downloaded Chang's photograph and chose to use it in its advertising campaign. In other words, the decision to use Chang's photo, which led to the injury, occurred in Australia. The third factor does not cause the scale to tilt in either party's favor: Chang is a U.S. citizen, and Virgin Mobile is an Australian company. Finally, the two parties had no prior relationship. Accordingly, there is no central location of a relationship that does not exist. The lack of clarity in this analysis shows the difficulty that often arises in choice-of-law problems.

Obviously, these choices and decisions may determine the outcome of cross-border conflicts. For example, the same speech that the First Amendment protects in the United States might constitute a tort in Australia. It seems certain that the number of these international privacy conflicts will be on the rise.

7. Conclusion

Privacy issues relating to the use of personal data will continue to be the topic of international debate. Approaches to privacy vary worldwide, and

---

[508] RESTATEMENT (SECOND) OF CONFLICT OF LAWS § 145 (1971).
[509] *Id.*

even within the European Union, despite the common source of data protection. An end to the conflicts regarding privacy is not on the horizon. Because of globalization and international trade, the conflict and debate regarding privacy is, and will most likely continue to be, about personal information. However, privacy is recognized as a fundamental human right in several international political documents, and increased privacy protections ostensibly could be worked into trade agreements as required undertakings, just as labor and environmental policies have been inserted in various agreements.[510]

Individual nations have their own policies and interests in protecting the privacy of their citizens. As the examples above demonstrate, there are a wide range of policies affecting individuals in different nations. The twin issues of autonomy and protection of information have become issues in international treaties and policies over the past fifty years. Trade issues will continue to compel the consideration of privacy issues across borders. Because of the central nature of personal information in international trade, global policies affecting personal information are much more likely than global standards on personal-autonomy issues such as abortion, assisted suicide, and homosexual marriage. Although these volatile topics relate to human-rights policies, those issues are likely to remain issues controlled by local sovereigns according to the cultural context of each nation.

A nation has an interest in protecting the rights of its citizens. Following the E.U. example, a state must concern itself with the transfer of information outside its jurisdiction. Although future agreements could focus on non-commerce-related privacy, such matters implicating individual autonomy have traditionally been addressed under domestic law. Because its own citizens' rights are at stake, a state is concerned about how foreign states treat its citizens' data. Therefore, privacy will continue to be a critical issue within individual nations as well as an international issue affecting global relations.

---

[510] For example, an E.U.-Mexico bilateral trade agreement includes two nonbinding articles on data protection. Article 41 of the agreement states, "[T]he Parties agree to cooperate on the protection of personal data in order to improve the level of protection and avoid obstacles to trade that requires transfers of personal data." Economic Partnership, Political Coordination and Cooperation Agreement, E.U.-Mex., Oct. 28, 2000, 2000 O.J. (L 276) 45, *available at* http://trade.ec.europa.eu/doclib/docs/2004/june/tradoc_117711.pdf. Article 51 further states, "The Parties agree to accord a high level of protection to the processing of personal and other data, in accordance with the standards adopted by the relevant international organizations and the Community." *Id.* at art. 51.

CHAPTER IV

Legal Tools for Privacy Protection

As discussed in Chapter III, four broad legal concepts constitute the bulwark of privacy protection: autonomy in personal decision making, control of personal information, control of property rights, and control of physical space. Protection for these different, yet related, interests comes in various forms.

The right to make decisions related to self and family is protected through the right of privacy explicit in some state constitutions and implicit in the U.S. Constitution, articulated as a zone of privacy or freedom of association.[511] Control of physical space is protected by tort law, under

---

[511] Roe v. Wade, 410 U.S. 113 (1973). The U.S. Constitution does not explicitly mention any right of privacy. However, in a line of decisions going back as far as Union Pacific Co. v. Botsford, 141 U.S. 250, 251 (1891), the U.S. Supreme Court has recognized that a right of personal privacy, or a guarantee of certain areas or zones of privacy, exists under the Constitution. In varying contexts, the Court or individual Justices have found at least the roots of that right in the First Amendment, Stanley v. Georgia, 394 U.S. 557, 564, (1969); in the Fourth and Fifth Amendments, Terry v. Ohio, 392 U.S. 1, 8–9, (1968); Katz v. United States, 389 U.S. 347, 350 (1967); Boyd v. United States, 116 U.S. 616 (1886); Olmstead v. United States, 277 U.S. 438, 478 (1928) (Brandeis, J., dissenting); in the penumbras of the Bill of Rights, Griswold v. Connecticut 381 U.S. 479, 484–85 (1965); in the Ninth Amendment, *id.* at 486 (Goldberg, J., concurring); or in the concept of liberty guaranteed by the first section of the Fourteenth Amendment, Meyer v. Nebraska, 262 U.S. 390, 399 (1923). These decisions make it clear that only personal rights that can be deemed "fundamental" or "implicit in the concept of ordered liberty," Palko v. Connecticut, 302 U.S. 319, 325 (1937), are included in this guarantee of personal privacy. They also make it clear that the right has some extension to activities relating to marriage, Loving v. Virginia, 388 U.S. 1, 12 (1967); procreation,

the torts of trespass and intrusion upon seclusion, or by search-and-seizure jurisprudence.[512] Control of personal information may be protected under state constitutions or the U.S. Constitution in the case of governmental intrusion, or through tort law, such as defamation, false light, and public disclosure of private facts, in the case of a private intrusion. Control of property rights in the privacy context may be protected by statute or through the use of the tort of appropriation of name or likeness. The principle underlying each privacy remedy is legal protection of a right related to privacy, but the actual effectiveness varies dramatically.

The law struggles with remedies to respond to modern intrusions unheard of a hundred years ago. Trespass, defamation, and other common-law remedies evolved before privacy emerged as a distinct concept. Globally, modern constitutions virtually always include privacy as a textual right. However, without an explicit textual right to privacy in the U.S. Constitution, the American federal right of privacy remains subject to continual interpretation. Therefore, it must evolve from the well-known, yet implied, "penumbra of rights."[513]

As described in the section on defining privacy in Chapter III,[514] a consequence of the evolution of society and the random development of legal remedies for invasions of privacy is that finding a consistent defining principle is difficult. Each of the remedies to protect privacy has a distinct history and legal basis. And in each of these areas, changes in society have directly affected the remedies. In some cases, the impact may be from technology or culture, and in others it may be from the shifting definition of "reasonable expectations" of privacy.

In a constitutional analysis, an invasion of decisional privacy invokes the strict-scrutiny test, whereas an invasion of informational privacy invokes only a balancing test. One possible explanation for this difference is that intrusions in decisional privacy, such as those relating to family, procreation, and the sanctity of the home, somehow seem more tangible

---

Skinner v. Oklahoma, 316 U.S. 535, 541–42 (1942); contraception, Eisenstadt v. Baird, 405 U.S. 438, 453–54 (1972) (White, J., concurring in result); family relationships, Prince v. Massachusetts, 321 U.S. 158, 166 (1944); and child rearing and education, Pierce v. Society of Sisters, 268 U.S. 510, 535 (1925).

[512] There is a whole body of Fourth Amendment law dealing with searches and seizures by the government. Fourth Amendment analysis has evolved to deal with electronic intrusions into personal space in the context of criminal investigations. Fourth Amendment protections are not the focus of this book, however.

[513] See Griswold, 381 U.S. at 483.

[514] See discussion supra Chapter III, § A.

and intrusive than disclosures of personal information. This perception may not match reality, however, since some informational disclosures may be very intrusive and horribly destructive.[515]

The law appears to recognize gradations of informational privacy, giving certain information greater protection. For example, information pertaining to the intimate details of a person's life, including medical records and financial information, is often protected by statute.[516] Nevertheless, such statutory protections are typically subject to exceptions, as in the case where personal information becomes part of a criminal investigation or civil trial, and thus eventually ends up in a public record.[517] Furthermore, information related to individual habits or conduct is often afforded lesser protection in light of overriding public concerns such as openness, accountability, the public's "right to know," and public safety.[518] Although decision-making and information rights are distinct, they are related. Frequently, personal decisions regarding matters such as health, family, and procreation generate information that we may wish to keep private. The right to protect personal autonomy in making decisions is important, but so is the right to control sensitive information about oneself.

The law has several avenues to analyze and protect individual privacy. For example, constitutional principles (including those of the First Amendment), tort protection, federal and state statutory protection, and even a recognition of informational privacy as a property interest all work to create the legal framework for both analyzing and protecting privacy.

---

[515] *See, e.g.*, Diaz v. Oakland Trib., Inc., 139 Cal. App. 3d 118, 130 (Ct. App. 1983) (stating that the jury was within its right to find the information published by the paper regarding an individual's sex change operation of an "offensive" nature); *see also* discussion *infra* Chapter VII.

[516] *See, e.g.*, 5 U.S.C. § 552a (2000).

[517] *See, e.g., id.* § 552(b)(7) (This FOIA provision dealing with criminal records or information says the data will be public unless one of a series of conditions is met such as disclosing a confidential source or a be an unwarranted invasion of personal privacy); FLA. STAT. §§ 119.07(1) (2007); FLA. STAT. § 119.07(6) (2007); FLA. STAT. § 119.011(3) (2007) (discussing how criminal investigative information becomes a nonexempt public record when the state provides the information to the criminal defendant).

[518] For example, the Florida Supreme Court has held that applicants for governmental jobs do not have a reasonable expectation of privacy under the Florida Constitution in keeping information about their smoking habits private. City of N. Miami v. Kurtz, 653 So. 2d 1025 (Fla. 1995).

A. The Role of the First Amendment: Bulwark or Bludgeon of Liberty?

Under the Constitution, freedom of speech and freedom of the press, protected by the First Amendment, are often in direct conflict with informational privacy rights. Personal details such as a politician's personal financial dealings may be newsworthy. Furthermore, as described above, privacy rights concerning personal information, rather than decision making, receive a lower standard of constitutional protection. Therefore, free-speech and free-press rights almost always trump informational privacy rights.

The intent, history, and context of the First Amendment dictates that freedom of the press does not and should not always override privacy interests. The right to privacy and First Amendment freedoms are not mutually exclusive, but instead rest on the same principle: freedom of expression. An individual's right to privacy is inherent in the spirit of the First Amendment's protection of the expression of ideas. The right to privacy protects an individual's personal and private ideas and thoughts by allowing the individual to have autonomy and control over his or her own expression. It also ensures that the individual will have the freedom to make independent choices about the direction of his or her own life. Undoubtedly, the freedom to express oneself without fear of public censure fosters self-expression and the freedom to withhold self-expression from public view.

Without the right to privacy, individual expression may be chilled. Furthermore, although the First Amendment is essential in protecting democracy and self-government, democracy and self-government value the worth and dignity of the individual. Thus, the means for obtaining democracy should not outweigh the values for which democracy stands. In light of the First Amendment's role in the Constitution as a whole, courts should place greater emphasis on whether the particular speech at issue fosters individual freedom of thought and expression. If individual expression is chilled by the publication of private facts, the spirit of the First Amendment has been violated.[519]

The current balancing approach of the courts, which tends to favor the media's First Amendment right to publish private information over

---

[519] Bartnicki v. Vopper, 532 U.S. 514, 541–56 (2001) (Rehnquist, C.J., dissenting).

an individual's privacy rights, may actually chill individual expression, positioning the collective good over the rights of the individual. This end result is at odds with the Constitution, especially the First Amendment and other individual liberties protected by the Bill of Rights. Thus, the First Amendment should not limit an individual's right to informational privacy, but instead should actually protect such privacy. This view is consistent with the spirit of the First Amendment, which fosters self-expression and the protection of ideas. The freedom to speak or not to speak and to control information about oneself is central to protecting the essence of the First Amendment: freedom of individual expression.

In establishing our system of government, the framers of the Constitution specifically rejected an authoritative governmental system that placed the ruling power in the hands of a select few. Instead, our government is based on a written constitution of enumerated and reserved powers, sometimes referred to as a social contract.[520] The doctrine of social contract expresses the belief that our government should exist only by the consent of the governed. The Constitution commands that the only valid powers of the government be those delegated by the people.

The Bill of Rights constitutes another body of limitations on govern-mental authority. However, instead of dictating when the government is empowered to act, the Bill of Rights demarcates a sphere in which the government is precluded from acting. James Madison advocated including the Bill of Rights in the Constitution because he feared that the majority would suppress minority rights.[521] He cautioned that wherever the real power of government lies, there is a danger of oppression. But under our constitutional system, the real power lies with the majority acting through governmental powers.[522] In the new United States, Madison emphasized, the greatest danger to liberty is to be found "in the body of the people, operating by the majority against the minority."[523] In other words, the creators of the Bill of Rights believed that there were some rights so fundamental to the individual that they should not be stamped out even by the majority's will.[524]

---

[520] *See, e.g.*, LAURENCE H. TRIBE, AMERICAN CONSTITUTIONAL LAW §§ 14-3 to -5 (2d ed. 1988).

[521] NAT HENTOFF, THE FIRST FREEDOMS 74 (1980).

[522] *Id.*

[523] *Id.*

[524] Edward J. Eberle, *Hate Speech, Offensive Speech, and Public Discourse in America*, 29 WAKE FOREST L. REV. 1135, 1148–49 (1994) ("According to John Locke, who greatly

Freedom of the press and freedom of speech were included as the first of those rights deemed by the framers to be fundamental to an individual, as well as to a democracy. No doubt, one of the goals of the First Amendment, especially the "freedom of the press" clause, is to ensure the existence of an informed citizenry in order to foster democracy. In "On Freedom of Speech," an essay in *Cato's Letters* that significantly influenced the framers, the author wrote, "Whoever would overthrow the liberty of the nation, must begin by subduing the freedom of speech ...."[525] Echoing this strong belief in the importance of freedom of speech to our democratic society, Madison wrote that "the right of free discussion... [is] a fundamental principle of the American form of government."[526] Today, few would dispute the proposition that freedom of expression, as well as freedom of the press, embodied in the First Amendment, is essential to a democratic society.[527]

However, the freedoms of speech and the press are essential to a democratic society not only because they ensure an informed citizenry, but also because they ensure the individual's autonomy over his or her own thoughts and expression. These freedoms define the difference "between the individual and the collective—between self and society."[528] These individual rights allow the development of independent-minded citizens, and consequently foster firmer, better-constructed, informed individual opinions.[529] Through the free exchange of ideas, the political process of democracy or self-governance is realized. And through this political process, certain individual liberty values are realized, such as the

---

influenced the Framers of the Constitution, individuals enter into a social contract with government to secure their lives, liberty, and property, but expressly withhold consent to state authority to interfere in other areas of their lives. Locke places control of religious beliefs and expression outside the ambit of official authority, and this vision took root in the framing of the Constitution." (citing Kent Greenawalt, *Free Speech Justifications*, 89 COLUM. L. REV. 119, 147–48 (1989))).

[525] JOHN TRENCHARD & THOMAS GORDON, *No. 15, Of Freedom of Speech, Feb. 4, 1720, in* CATO'S LETTERS 110, 110 (Ronald Hamowy ed., 1995) [hereinafter CATO'S LETTERS, No. 15]. (As Clinton Rossiter once observed, *Cato's Letters* "was the most popular, quotable, esteemed source of political ideas in the colonial period." Published anonymously by the Englishmen John Trenchard and Thomas Gordon in the *London Journal* from 1720 to 1723, the 144 letters provide a compelling theoretical basis for freedom of conscience and freedom of speech).

[526] New York Times Co. v. Sullivan, 376 U.S. 254, 275 (1964) (citing *The Report of the Virginia Resolutions* in 4 ELLIOTT'S DEBATES 546 (1861)).

[527] *See, e.g.,* David A. Anderson, *The Origins of the Press Clause*, 30 UCLA L. REV. 455, 533 (1983).

[528] THOMAS I. EMERSON, THE SYSTEM OF FREEDOM OF EXPRESSION 545 (1970).

[529] *See id.*

freedom to develop one's faculties and express one's own individual thoughts. Thus, democracy and individual liberty are interconnected.

Although it is true that freedom of the press and freedom of expression are ultimately beneficial to society because they ensure that the voting public is informed and knowledgeable, these freedoms are an important value apart from their value to the collective society. The framers sought to protect individual freedom as an end unto itself. Our Constitution, through the Bill of Rights, recognizes the worth and dignity of the individual, apart from the state.

This proposition is clearer when freedom of the press and freedom of expression are read in conjunction with the other individual liberties secured by the First Amendment. The First Amendment also protects freedom of religion and the right to petition the government for grievances.[530] It can scarcely be deemed an accident that each of these individual liberties is contained in the same amendment, for they all have a common theme—liberty of conscience and thought and freedom of self-realization. The right to petition the government for grievances recognizes the right of an individual to be heard. Freedom of religion secures the individual's freedom to follow the dictates of his or her own conscience. Freedom of the press ensures that the individual has access to information and knowledge in order to make informed choices not only at the polls but also in his or her own life. Taken together, all the liberties secured by the First Amendment protect the individual's autonomy over the development and expression of his or her intellect, interests, tastes, and personality.[531]

Justice Brandeis recognized the value of our constitutional system of government as a means for securing happiness for individuals:

> The makers of our Constitution undertook to secure conditions favorable to the pursuit of happiness. They recognized the significance of man's spiritual nature, of his feelings and of his intellect. They knew that only a part of the pain, pleasure and satisfactions of life are to be found in material things. They sought to protect Americans in their beliefs, their thoughts, their emotions and their

---

[530] U.S. CONST. amend. I ("Congress shall make no law respecting an establishment of religion, or prohibiting the free exercise thereof; or abridging the freedom of speech, or of the press; or the right of the people peaceably to assemble, and to petition the government for a redress of grievances.").

[531] Doe v. Bolton, 410 U.S. 179, 209 (1973) (Douglas, J., concurring).

sensations. They conferred, as against the government, the right to be let alone—the most comprehensive of rights and the right most valued by civilized men.[532]

Justice Brandeis also voiced this proposition in *Whitney v. California* when he wrote that in a liberal democracy, "the final end of the State [is] to make men free to develop their faculties" and that the founders "valued liberty both as an end and as a means."[533]

Many commentators who advocate strong protection for the media under the First Amendment cite the famous quote, originating in *Cato's Letters*, that "freedom of speech is the great bulwark of liberty."[534] But it is important to examine what it means to be a bulwark of liberty. Proclaiming that it simply means that freedom of speech is fundamentally important as a value in and of itself is to ignore the plain meaning of the phrase. The phrase "bulwark of liberty" implies, and the authors of *Cato's Letters* as well as the Founding Fathers understood, that in protecting freedom of speech, there are other liberties at stake.[535] Thus, there are other liberties that are valued in our society, which must be protected, and the First Amendment is a means of protecting them. When a court protects freedom of the press without consideration of the individual liberties also at stake in the same case, it transforms the First Amendment from a bulwark into a bludgeon of liberty.

Although *Cato's Letters* are often quoted for the proposition that freedom of speech should not be limited, including by privacy concerns, what is often left out when these important and influential letters are cited is crucial to understanding the goal of the First Amendment. In *Cato's Letters No. 15*, "Of Freedom of Speech," the author wrote, "Without Freedom of thought, there can be no such thing as wisdom; and no such things as public liberty, without freedom of speech: Which is the right of every man, *as far as by it he does not hurt and control the right of another; and this is the only check which it ought to suffer, and the only bounds which it ought to know*."[536] Thus, *Cato's Letters* acknowledged that freedom of speech should not impose on the individual liberties of another.

---

[532] *See* Olmstead v. United States, 277 U.S. 438, 478 (1928) (Brandeis, J., dissenting).
[533] 274 U.S. 357, 375 (1927).
[534] CATO'S LETTERS No. 15, *supra* note 525, at 110.
[535] *Id.*
[536] *Id.* (emphasis added).

Professor Martin Redish, an eminent First Amendment scholar, echoed this idea when he cautioned, "Political democracy is merely a means to—or, in another sense, a logical outgrowth of, the much broader value of individual self-realization. We must not confuse one means of obtaining the ultimate value with the value itself."[537] The aspiration of a democratic society lies in the liberty of each individual to develop his or her life in the direction that he or she chooses. A free press is a means of ensuring that individuals make informed choices in every aspect of their lives. A free press also ensures that the government will not oppress the people from whom it derives its power. However, sacrificing individual liberties of the governed to ensure that the government will protect those same individual liberties is illogical and inconsistent with the First Amendment.

Traditional justifications of free speech emphasize its importance for the pursuit of truth or for the exercise of self-government. Justice Oliver Wendell Holmes's "marketplace of ideas" theory rests upon this principle.[538] Alexander Meiklejohn, a leading First Amendment scholar of the 1940s and 1950s, believed that the First Amendment simply entails a public interest in speech leading to an informed electorate.[539] The primary purpose of the First Amendment, according to Meiklejohn, is to enable members of the public to fully participate in self-government by understanding the problems and issues that face the body politic.[540] Although Meiklejohn eventually interpreted political speech broadly,[541] he specifically rejected the idea that the First Amendment was concerned with the "private freedom of this or that individual."[542]

By contrast, in the last few decades, scholars increasingly have defended free speech in the name of individual fulfillment and self-expression. For instance, David A. Richards argues that the government must be neutral toward the views of its citizens in order to respect "the ultimate moral sovereignty of persons."[543] Edwin Baker believes that the

---

[537] Martin H. Redish, *The Value of Free Speech*, 130 U. Pa. L. Rev. 591, 601 (1982).

[538] Abrams v. United States, 250 U.S. 616, 630 (1919) (Holmes, J., dissenting).

[539] Alexander Meiklejohn, Free Speech and Its Relation to Self-Government 88–89 (1948).

[540] *Id.*

[541] *See* Alexander Meiklejohn, *The First Amendment Is an Absolute*, Sup. Ct. Rev. 245, 255–57 (1961) (interpreting political speech to include philosophy and the sciences, literature, and the arts).

[542] Meiklejohn, *supra* note 539, at 88.

[543] David A.J. Richards, Toleration and the Constitution 168 (1986); *see also* Robert Nozick, Anarchy, State and Utopia 33 (1977) ("The moral side constraints upon what we may do, I claim, reflect the fact of our separate existences. They reflect

focus of self-fulfillment emphasizes "the source of the speech in the self, and make[s] the choice of the speech by the self the crucial factor in justifying protection."[544]

In fact, in the previous three decades, the Supreme Court has referred to the idea of self-expression as a primary purpose of the First Amendment. For instance, in *Cohen v. California*, the Court reversed the conviction of a man who wore a jacket exhibiting offensive language.[545] Although the jacket concededly may have shocked many members of the community, the Court reasoned that an individual's right to express himself or herself as he or she saw fit was fundamental to the First Amendment.[546] The Court reasoned that "no other approach would comport with the premise of individual dignity and choice upon which our political system rests."[547] Additional Supreme Court opinions have protected, under the First Amendment, the need to "assure self-fulfillment for each individual" and the right to "autonomous control over the development of one's intellect, interests, tastes, and personality."[548] Furthermore, Justice Brennan reasoned that freedom of speech was "intrinsic to individual dignity," especially "in a democracy like our own, in which the autonomy of each individual is accorded equal and incommensurate respect."[549] Thus, a full, sincere, and robust freedom of expression depends on an individual right to privacy. Undoubtedly, one's identity, in essence who one chooses to be and how one chooses to portray oneself to the world, is a significant form of expression.

For instance, in *Diaz v. Oakland Tribune, Inc.*, a columnist for the *Oakland Tribune* wrote a piece disclosing that the plaintiff, a student body president of a local community college, used to be a man but had gone through gender reconstruction surgery.[550] The plaintiff took affirmative

---

the fact that no moral balancing act can take place among us; there is no moral out-weighing of one of our lives by others so as to lead to a greater overall social good. There is no justified sacrifice of some of us for others.").

[544] C. Edwin Baker, *Scope of the First Amendment Freedom of Speech*, 25 UCLA L. REV. 964 (1978).

[545] 403 U.S. 15 (1971). Paul Robert Cohen was convicted of violating section 415 of the California Penal Code, which prohibits "maliciously and willfully disturb[ing] the peace or quiet of any neighborhood or person . . . by . . . offensive conduct," after he was observed in a Los Angeles county courthouse wearing a jacket emblazoned with the words "F__k the Draft." *Id.* at 16.

[546] *Id.* at 24.

[547] *Id.*

[548] Doe v. Bolton, 410 U.S. 179, 211 (1973) (Douglas, J., concurring).

[549] Herbert v. Lando, 441 U.S. 153, 183 n.1 (1979) (Brennan, J., dissenting).

[550] 139 Cal. App. 3d 118 (Ct. App. 1983).

efforts to keep her past gender secret, including moving across the country, changing her Social Security records, obtaining a new driver's license, and disclosing the information only to her family and very close friends.[551] The plaintiff brought a tort action against the newspaper for public disclosure of private facts, and the newspaper defended its actions on the ground that the publication was protected under the First Amendment right to a free press.[552]

The plaintiff testified at trial that she always had the feeling of being a woman.[553] She also testified that after the surgery, "she looked and behaved as a woman and was accepted by the public as a woman."[554] According to her therapist, "her physical and psychological identities were now in harmony."[555] In other words, the plaintiff had chosen to express herself as a woman.

Ultimately, the court decided that the story was not protected speech and that Diaz's privacy had been invaded.[556] The *Diaz* decision is one example, and an unusual one, in which a court concluded that an accurate written story had failed the newsworthiness test, and thereby protected the individual's right to vindicate the intrusion on her identity and autonomy.

As a further protection of individual autonomy, the First Amendment not only protects the right to speak, but it generally protects the right not to speak as well.[557] The Supreme Court has recognized that "[t]he right to speak and the right to refrain from speaking are complementary components of the broader concept of 'individual freedom of mind.'"[558] Likewise, the First Amendment protects the right not to associate when expressive association is involved, as well as the right to associate.[559] This line of First Amendment cases acknowledges that compelled speech constitutes as much of a burden on free expression as does infringement of affirmative speech. Individuals not only have a right to speak, but they have a right to

---

[551] *Id.* at 132.

[552] *Id.* at 124–25.

[553] *Id.* at 123.

[554] *Id.*

[555] *Id.*

[556] *Id.* at 137.

[557] *See* McIntyre v. Ohio Elections Comm'n, 514 U.S. 334, 342 (1995); Miami Herald Publ'g Co. v. Tornillo, 418 U.S. 241 (1974).

[558] Wooley v. Maynard, 430 U.S. 705, 714 (1977) (quoting Board of Education v. Barnette, 319 U.S. 624 at 637 (1943).

[559] *See, e.g.,* Roberts v. United States Jaycees, 468 U.S. 609, 617–18 (1984); Boy Scouts of Am. v. Dale, 530 U.S. 640, 648 (2000).

choose the manner, context, and setting in which to express themselves. Just as the plaintiff in *Diaz* has a right to express her identity in the means she chooses, she also should have the concurrent right to choose not to express her past identity.

Instead of looking at the right to privacy as limiting the First Amendment, it is perhaps more accurate to look at the right to privacy as a way of interpreting guarantees conveyed by the First Amendment and the values it ultimately protects. In other words, the right of private individuals to conceal personal details about their lives actually enhances, rather than limits, freedom of expression. Privacy allows individuals to think their own thoughts, have their own secrets, live their own lives, and reveal only what they want to the outside world. Without privacy, the free flow of information will not enable individuals to decide anything for themselves. Individuals may never realize the essence of truly free expression without the right to be let alone. The right to privacy is a necessary precondition for and part of freedom of expression.

In *Turner Broadcasting System v. FCC*, the Supreme Court held that "[a]t the heart of the First Amendment lies the principle that each person should decide for himself or herself the ideas and beliefs deserving of expression, consideration, and adherence. Our political system and cultural life rest upon this ideal."[560] In fact, the federal constitutional right to privacy was established in part from the oft-cited penumbras emanating from the Bill of Rights. In *Griswold v. Connecticut*, the Court reasoned that the First Amendment created a penumbra that included the right to privacy.[561] The Court explained that "specific guarantees in the Bill of Rights have penumbras, formed by emanations from those guarantees that help give them life and substance.... Various guarantees create zones of privacy."[562] The Court further noted that the First Amendment specifically protected the penumbral right of freedom of association.[563]

If the First Amendment actually includes a right to privacy, then using it to protect expansive invasions of individual privacy turns it on itself and chills self-expression. Civil libertarians often cringe at the idea of intrusive state power that infringes upon individual freedoms, heralding the First Amendment as a check on governmental limitation of speech.

---

[560] 512 U.S. 622, 641 (1994).
[561] 381 U.S. 479, 483 (1965).
[562] *Id.* at 484.
[563] *Id.*

But the First Amendment, when read without the right to privacy, actually prevents the government from protecting speech.

The Supreme Court offered a clear example of this proposition in *Bartnicki v. Vopper*.[564] In *Bartnicki*, a private cell-phone conversation between two individuals was intercepted and publicly disclosed on the radio.[565] The plaintiffs, whose conversation had been intercepted and publicized, sued the radio journalist under both federal and Pennsylvania wiretap statutes.[566] The *Bartnicki* Court held that a private action under the federal Wiretap Act[567] for disseminating the contents of an illegally intercepted cell-phone conversation violated the First Amendment.[568] In analyzing the constitutionality of the statute's provision for private relief, the Court applied strict scrutiny to a purportedly content-neutral statute.[569] The Court found that the content of the conversation was a matter of public concern, and thus held that the media's freedom-of-speech interest outweighed the plaintiffs' privacy interest.[570] The Court stated that the statute implicated the core purposes of the First Amendment because it imposed penalties on the publication of truthful information of public concern.[571]

The dissent chastised the majority, arguing that protecting disclosure of private conversations "diminishes, rather than enhances, the purposes of the First Amendment, thereby chilling the speech of the millions of Americans who rely upon electronic technology to communicate each day."[572] Chief Justice William Rehnquist's dissent correctly acknowledged that "[b]y 'protecting the privacy of individual thought and expression,' these statutes further the 'uninhibited, robust, and wide-open' speech of the private parties."[573] The dissent found that the government's interest in protecting private conversations by drying up the market for illegally intercepted communications created only an "incidental restriction on

---

[564] 532 U.S. 514, 553 (2001).

[565] *Id.* at 518–19.

[566] *Id.* at 520.

[567] 18 U.S.C. § 2511 (2000).

[568] 532 U.S. at 527–35.

[569] *Id.* at 527.

[570] *Id.* at 535.

[571] *Id.*

[572] *Id.* at 542 (Rehnquist, C.J., dissenting).

[573] *Id.* at 553–54 Rhenquist citing: By "protecting the privacy of individual thought and expression," *United States v. United States Dist. Court for Eastern Dist. of Mich.*, 407 U.S. 297, 302(1972), these statutes further the "uninhibited, robust, and wide-open" speech of the private parties, *New York Times Co. v. Sullivan*, 376 U.S. 254, 270 (1964).

alleged First Amendment freedoms that is no greater than essential to further the interest of protecting the privacy of individual communications."[574] Fewer people would speak candidly in private conversation about matters of public concern if they knew that all their views would be subject to public disclosure.[575]

In essence, the majority opinion in *Bartnicki* held that freedom of the press will trump the privacy interests of the individual speaker almost every time. Certainly, the speech of the individuals who were party to the private telephone conversation was chilled by the Court's decision. Fewer people would speak candidly in private conversation about matters of public concern if they knew that all their views would be subject to public disclosure. Again, however, the majority incorrectly assumed that the only First Amendment interests at stake are those of the press.

Perhaps the best example of the subordination of individual freedom to a broad and expansive community interest can be found in the Supreme Court's adoption of the newsworthiness doctrine. The general proposition of the newsworthiness doctrine is that publication of a newsworthy item of information is protected speech. The newsworthiness doctrine is evaluated in depth in Chapter VII.[576]

Of course, the First Amendment must protect the media's right to publish information that furthers the goals of the First Amendment and provides individuals with access to needed information. But perhaps, consistent with the First Amendment's concurrent protection of individual expression, including the right to privacy, courts should draw the line closer to protecting privacy than it is currently drawn. Accordingly, some scholars advocate stronger constitutional protection of informational privacy.[577]

The First Amendment's effect is complex. It operates as a basis for constitutional privacy protections and as a protection of speech that may infringe on privacy. With that fact as perspective, the next section examines the total scope of federal constitutional protections.

---

[574] *Id.* at 551.

[575] *Id.* at 554 Rhenquist said:" The chilling effect of the Court's decision upon these private conversations will surely be great: An estimated 49.1 million analog cellular telephones are currently in operation." (That was in 1999).

[576] *See* discussion *infra* Chapter VII, § B-4.

[577] *See, e.g.,* Edward J. Eberle, *The Right to Information Self-Determination,* 2001 Utah L. Rev. 965 (proposing constitutional protection of the right to "information self-determination" under substantive due process rights and suggesting that the level of scrutiny used to evaluate personal information should be based on its level of intimacy).

B. Constitutional Protections

Privacy as a constitutional right is asserted to protect a wide range of conduct and prerogatives. As previously stated, legally recognized constitutional privacy interests are generally separated into two classes: (1) interests in making intimate personal decisions or conducting personal activities without observation, intrusion, or interference (decisional privacy) and (2) interests in precluding dissemination or misuse of sensitive and confidential information (informational privacy).

1. Categories of Constitutional Protection for Personal Autonomy

Privacy jurisprudence regarding personal autonomy has evolved through the years into several categories of decision making that society has deemed most intimate to individuals.[578] The basic categories are procreation, family, marriage, and the home. There has been some expansion of these categories to include other personal choices that can be seen as extensions of these four categories, such as contraception, child rearing, abortion, and end-of-life decisions. This evolution took place in a relatively short period of time. Individuals maximize their constitutional privacy protection by arguing that an intrusion falls into one of these sensitive categories. These categories can further be described as including personal decisions relating to control of one's own body (such as the decision to terminate a pregnancy or refuse medical care); decisions relating to private sexual conduct between consenting adults (such as the decision

---

[578] See 62A Am. Jur. 2d Privacy § 8 (2008); Lawrence v. Texas, 539 U.S. 558 (2003) (protecting decisions in matters pertaining to sex); Roe v. Wade, 410 U.S. 113 (1973) (holding that the right of personal privacy includes the abortion decision); Eisenstadt v. Baird, 405 U.S. 438 (1972) (recognizing the individual right to privately decide whether or not to bear children); Loving v. Virginia, 388 U.S. 1 (1967) (holding that the freedom of choice to marry may not be infringed by the state); Griswold v. Connecticut, 381 U.S. 479 (1965) (protecting decision making within a marriage and asserting that a zone of privacy is created by various guarantees found in the Bill of Rights); Meyer v. Nebraska, 262 U.S. 390 (1923) (protecting parents' right to decide matters concerning their children's education). The decisional right to privacy also has been found to include the right to parent a child carried by a surrogate mother, Johnson v. Calvert, 85 P.2d 776 (Cal. 1993); the right to refuse medical treatment, Cruzan v. Director, Mo. Dep't of Health, 497 U.S. 261 (1990); and the right to possess marijuana in the privacy of one's home, Ravin v. State, 537 P.2d 494 (Alaska 1975) (interpreting the Alaska state constitutional right to privacy).

to engage on homosexual activity); decisions relating to procreation (such as decisions regarding sterilization and contraception); decisions relating to child rearing (such as decisions regarding education and health); decisions relating to marriage; and perhaps a number of other decisions that take place within the home. Clearly, the government still regulates activities within these categories. Issues such as polygamy, euthanasia, ownership of embryos, and same-sex marriage can be described as relating to these categories. These controversial topics are emotionally charged and involve legislative restrictions and ultimately judicial review. Emotional conflicts between prevailing views and individual volition typify the history and evolution of privacy rights and make accurate predictions of ultimate legal outcomes very difficult.

There are a series of areas in which courts generally have supported governmental control of personal conduct:

- Public safety: speed limits, gun control
- Public health: vaccination, drugs, alcohol (Prohibition)
- Public employment: drug testing, smoking[579]
- Paternal protection: safety belts, children's safety seats, motorcycle helmets[580]
- Public morality: prostitution, adultery, miscegenation, homosexuality, polygamy, the right to die[581]
- Public welfare: compulsory education

In all these areas, courts have found that the government has or had a prevailing or compelling interest to regulate private conduct.

It appears that privacy will continue to operate in the areas of family, procreation, marriage, and the home. However, it is also clear that simply because an issue *can* fall under a protected category does not mean that it will be protected. For example, restrictions on polygamy remain in place and constitutional.[582]

What is critical in a court's determination whether an activity is protected is the way the court chooses to frame the issue—for example,

---

[579] *See* City of N. Miami Beach v. Kurtz, 653 So. 2d 1025 (Fla. 1995).
[580] These statutes may be justified by the protection of citizens as well as potential utilitarian considerations such as the public-health costs associated with serious injuries. *See* State v. Eitel, 227 So.2d 489 (Fla. 1969).
[581] *See* discussion *infra* Chapter IV, § B-2.
[582] The Supreme Court described polygamy as a "barbarous practice." Mormon Church v. United States, 136 U.S. 1, 49–50 (1980); *see also* State v. Holm, 137 P.2d 726 (Utah 2007). In the not-too-distant past, interracial marriage was illegal. *Loving*, 388 U.S. 1 (1967).

"Is there a fundamental right to homosexual sodomy?" or "Is there a right to privacy in consensual sexual conduct in the privacy of one's home?" Is the question, does a person have the right to terminate his life? or is it, can a person can refuse medical treatment? In the latter instance, the Court found a liberty interest in refusing treatment but distinguished that decision from active voluntary euthanasia, in which the state has a compelling interest.[583]

Three of the most volatile contemporary issues centering on personal autonomy are sexual orientation, abortion, and the right to die. Each of these issues exists in every culture and is highly emotional, intensely personal, and charged with theological doctrine. The views of policymakers and tribunals regarding these issues have evolved over time. There is a central lesson: courts struggle when compelled to mix science, morality, and politics. But the corollary is that it seems that ultimately the courts must make the hardest decisions.

The case of Terri Schiavo is a painful and perfect example.[584] Ms. Schiavo had sustained brain injuries, and doctors had diagnosed her as being in a persistent vegetative state. There is no recovery from this condition, according to her doctors. The husband and parents of Ms. Schiavo bitterly disagreed as to what action should be taken, and the courts, legislature, and governor of Florida became involved.

Ms. Schiavo's husband felt that consistent with her wishes, she should be removed from life support and allowed to die. Her parents vehemently disagreed. The public debate ranged from the pope to the president.

State law said that in the absence of written directives, a court would determine by clear and convincing evidence what the will of the patient was or would be. In this case, the courts, in a painful exercise, determined that Ms. Schiavo would have wanted her life terminated in these conditions.[585] Following the court's decision, her life support was removed, but as a result of legislative and gubernatorial action, she was reattached to

---

[583] *Cruzan*, 497 U.S. at 279–80.

[584] *In re* Guardianship of Schiavo, 851 So. 2d 182 (Fla. Dist. Ct. App. 2003). The Florida Second District Court of Appeals described this difficulty in its fourth ruling on the Schiavo matter. "Each of us . . . as our own family, our own loved ones, our own children . . . we understand why a parent who had raised and nurtured a child from conception would hold out hope that some level of cognitive function remained. If Mrs. Schiavo were our own daughter, we could not but hold to such a faith. But in the end, this case . . . is about Theresa Schiavo's right to make her own decision." *Id.* at 186–87.

[585] *In re* Guardianship of Schiavo, 780 So. 2d 176, 180 (Fla. Dist. Ct. App. 2001).

life support. The courts were called upon again to review the legislation authorizing these actions, and a Florida court declared the legislation unconstitutional. Ms. Schiavo was again detached from life support and subsequently died.

All of this was an exercise to protect Ms. Schiavo's privacy right to make her own personal decisions and reject treatment, but the circumstances show how excruciatingly difficult protecting that right can be. There will be continuing controversies in these three areas and, undoubtedly, personal-autonomy decisions that we have not yet confronted. These cases teach us that the courts are unpredictable in particular fact situations. The cases also teach us that the way the court frames the question dictates its opinion—or, their views dictate the way they frame the question.

2. The Role of Morality and the Evolving Definition of Fundamental Rights and Privacy

The evolution of decisional privacy rights is frequently a clash of moral values and the evolution of those values.[586] For example, laws forbidding the use of contraception, prohibitions on abortion, and the criminalization of sexual conduct by homosexuals all furthered the belief held by a majority of citizens at the time that such acts were immoral. Indeed, as Judge Posner observed, "[a] traditional purpose of criminal punishment is to express moral condemnation of the criminal's acts."[587] Some would even argue that "[e]very political decision of consequence reflects a moral judgment," that legislation is always "based on someone's notion of what is right or wrong, just or unjust, fair or unfair."[588] Yet in *Lawrence v. Texas*, the Supreme Court declared that "the fact that the governing majority in a State has traditionally viewed a particular practice as immoral is not a

---

[586] These controversies also generate the argument between "originalists" and those who argue for a "living constitution." *See* Lawrence v. Texas, 539 U.S. 558, 562 (2003) (describing the case as involving "liberty of the person both in its spatial and in its more transcendent dimensions); *see also id.* at 605–06 (Thomas, J., dissenting) (quoting Justice Stewart's dissent in Griswold v. Connecticut, 381 U.S. 479, 530 (1965) and saying that he could "find [neither in the Bill of Rights nor any other part of the Constitution a] general right to privacy").

[587] Milner v. Apfel, 148 F.3d 812, 814 (7th Cir. 1998). Judge Posner went on to observe, "How else to explain prohibitions against gambling, prostitution, public nudity and masturbation, fornication, sodomy, the sale of pornography, sexual intercourse with animals, desecration of corpses, and a variety of other 'morals' offenses?"

[588] Commonwealth v. Wasson, 842 S.W.2d 487, 511 (Ky. 1992) (Wintersheimer, J., dissenting).

sufficient reason for upholding a law prohibiting the practice."[589] But clearly legislatures enact laws based on morality.[590]

The issue ends up being, what is the nature of the decisional privacy interest impaired, affected, or curtailed by morals legislation, and does it fall into one of the protected categories of autonomy? If the affected privacy interest is not *deemed* by a court to fall within a category of fundamental rights, then the government may well survive the lower rational-basis review for intruding upon "nonfundamental" rights. In these instances, it is clear that legislatures likely are able to legislate morality successfully. However, if the affected privacy interest is deemed by a court to fall within a category of fundamental decisions, then the government must show a compelling interest to impair that right through morals legislation.[591]

For example, the antimiscegenation laws struck down in *Loving v. Virginia* seemingly expressed the majoritarian view of the Virginia General Assembly that marriage between a black man and a white woman was immoral.[592] Nevertheless, the *Loving* Court recognized both the overt racially discriminatory purpose of the laws and that marriage is a fundamental decision. Likewise, in *Lawrence v. Texas*, the Court reaffirmed the fundamental nature of decisions by adults on how to "conduct their private lives in matters pertaining to sex."[593]

As the debate over same-sex marriage continues, the definition of the issue is central to its determination. Is morality the basis for laws and constitutional provisions prohibiting same-sex marriage?[594] If so, what is the nature of the right affected by the prohibition? Is the right simply the "right to marry," or is it the right to marry in a traditional American cultural sense? If marriage is one of the categories of fundamental decisions, then

---

[589] *Lawrence*, 539 U.S. at 577.

[590] *Id.* at 599 (Scalia, J., dissenting) (arguing that the majority's decision "effectively decrees the end of all morals legislation").

[591] For example, although assisted suicide may fall into the category of control of one's own body, courts have found the governmental interest in prohibiting this decision to be compelling. Although personal decisions relating to marriage are protected, the government's interest in prohibiting incest and bigamy are compelling. Indeed, our culture has approved a number of restrictions on personal decision making, reinforcing the notion that individual citizens are part of a social contract and consequently must forgo certain decisions in order to be a part of society.

[592] 388 U.S. 1 (1967).

[593] 539 U.S. at 572.

[594] *See* Lofton v. Kearney, 157 F. Supp. 2d 1372 (S.D. Fla. 2001) (upholding a Florida law that denies homosexuals the right to adopt). Other states have reached a different conclusion.

can a legislature show a compelling governmental interest in restricting same-sex marriage?

3. Constitutional Balancing Applied to Informational Privacy

The categories that are protected by informational-privacy jurisprudence may relate to information about some of the topics protected under personal-autonomy jurisprudence. Informational privacy may encompass an individual's interest in avoiding disclosure of personal matters, such as personality, name, likeness, and intimate and identifying details. However, the *constitutional* protection against public dissemination of information is limited and extends only to highly personal matters representing "the most intimate aspects of human affairs."[595]

Furthermore, the Constitution only protects individuals from privacy invasions by governmental actors.[596] However, a private actor can be classified, for constitutional purposes, as a governmental actor when that private actor serves a traditionally sovereign function or is so entangled with the government that its actions should be attributable to the government.[597] Therefore, it is perhaps obvious to note that virtually all decisional privacy-invasion claims are made against a governmental body,[598] whereas informational privacy-invasion cases based on constitutional

---

[595] Eagle v. Morgan, 88 F.3d 620, 625 (8th Cir. 1996).

[596] *See* United States v. Morrison, 529 U.S. 598 (2000); The Civil Rights Cases, 109 U.S. 3 (1883).

[597] *See, e.g.*, Jackson v. Metro. Edison Co., 419 U.S. 345 (1974) (stating that a private utility company, though it was heavily regulated and monopolistic, did not have a sufficient nexus with the government of Pennsylvania to qualify it as a state actor when it turned off the plaintiff's power).

[598] For an example of a decisional privacy-invasion claim against a private entity, see Chico Feminist Women's Health Ctr. v. Butte Glenn Med. Soc'y, 557 F. Supp. 1190 (D.C. Cal. 1983), in which an abortion clinic sued private individuals for interfering so much with operations that it was forced to close, and claimed an invasion of privacy (interference with women's right to have an abortion) under 42 U.S.C. §§ 1983, 1985(3), the federal Constitution, and the California Constitution. The court held that the clinic could not establish state action for purposes of obtaining relief under § 1983 or § 1985(3). *Id.* at 1197. Additionally, the court asserted that the plaintiffs could not state a claim for violation of the Fourteenth Amendment, because California had a specific statute that addressed the issue. *Id.* at 1197–98. The court did, however, hold that the plaintiffs were able to allege facts sufficient to state a claim for invasion of privacy under the California Constitution. *Id.* at 1201–05. The court also held that the privacy provision of the California Constitution protects against invasions by both governmental and nongovernmental entities. *Id.; see also* CAL. CONST. art. I, § 1 ("All people are by nature free and independent and have inalienable rights. Among these

and tort actions are brought against both governmental and private actors, including the press and private persons.[599]

The Supreme Court, in *Whalen v. Roe*, distinguished between decisional and informational privacy.[600] In *Whalen*, the Court determined that no Fourteenth Amendment violation occurred as a result of the enforcement of a New York statute requiring doctors and pharmacists to disclose to the state certain information, including the name, address, and age of patients who received certain prescriptions.[601] In analyzing the patient's right to informational privacy, the Court applied a balancing test, proclaiming that no constitutional violation had occurred.[602] This balancing-test analysis is arguably a rational-basis review that places informational privacy among the interests outside of the fundamental rights and substantive due process analysis.[603]

The *Whalen* decision has been cited in subsequent circuit court cases in which the courts also applied a balancing test to analyze informational privacy. For example, in *Doe v. City of New York*, the Second Circuit applied a balancing test, citing *Whalen*, and concluded that an HIV-positive individual filing a conciliation agreement had a constitutional right to privacy regarding the publication of his condition.[604] However, the court also held that the New York Administrative Code, which allowed publication of conciliation agreements, was valid because it gave the City of New York Commission on Human Rights discretion not to publicize all agreements.[605] The court further noted that the individual's right to privacy was no more absolute than the right to control other types of information and stated that the city's interest in disseminating

---

are enjoying and defending life and liberty, acquiring, possessing, and protecting property, and pursuing and obtaining safety, happiness, and privacy.").

[599] For an example of an informational privacy-invasion claim brought against a governmental actor, see Flaskamp v. Dearborn Pub. Sch., 385 F.3d 935, 944–46 (6th Cir. 2004), in which a teacher sued a school board for invasion of privacy under section 1983 of the Civil Rights Act. The teacher claimed that by asking her about her relationship with a graduated student, the school's principal violated her right to informational autonomy. *Id.* at 940. The Sixth Circuit held that the questioning was a legitimate attempt to shed light on the prior relationship. *Id.* at 946–47; *see* Owassa Indep. Sch. Dist. No. I-011 v. Falvo, 534 U.S. 426 (2002).

[600] 429 U.S. 589 (1977).

[601] *Id.* at 606.

[602] *Id.* at 601–04.

[603] *See* Francis S. Chlapowski, *The Constitutional Protection of Informational Privacy*, 71 B.U.L. Rev. 133 (1991).

[604] 15 F.3d 264 (2d Cir. 1994).

[605] *Id.* at 268.

information was "substantial" and balanced against the individual's right to privacy.[606]

Another example of balancing may be found in *United States v. Westinghouse Electric Corp.*[607] In this case, the Third Circuit decided whether disclosure of employees' medical records was allowed to facilitate a statutorily approved occupational health and safety evaluation.[608] The court noted that the employees' medical records in this case were more revealing than the information sought in *Whalen* and therefore were entitled to privacy protection.[609] However, upon balancing the concerns presented,[610] the court determined that the public need for research and safety outweighed the employees' general interests in privacy.[611]

Additionally, *Plante v. Gonzales* supported *Whalen's* distinction between informational privacy and decisional privacy.[612] The court analyzed Florida's "Sunshine Amendment"[613] requiring elected officials to publicly disclose personal financial information.[614] Because disclosure of financial information was deemed an "information" issue rather than an issue affecting an autonomy right, the court applied the balancing test.[615] Ultimately, the court determined that the public interests supporting disclosure of its elected officials' financial information was stronger than the officials' privacy interests in nondisclosure and therefore held constitutional the amendments requiring mandatory disclosure.[616]

Another constitutional protection of private information can be based on the freedom of association. These cases recognize the liberty interest of individuals to associate with others without fear of disclosure of that information to government.[617] In *NAACP v. Alabama*, the Supreme

---

[606] *Id.* at 269.

[607] 638 F.2d 570 (3d Cir. 1980).

[608] *Id. See* 29 U.S.C. §§ 651–678 (2000).

[609] *Westinghouse*, 638 F.2d at 577.

[610] The court enunciated factors to aid in its analysis of whether an intrusion into an individual's privacy is justified: the type of record requested; the information it does or might contain; the potential for harm in any subsequent nonconsensual disclosure; the injury from disclosure to the relationship in which the record was generated; the adequacy of safeguards to prevent unauthorized disclosure; the degree of need for access; and whether there is an express statutory mandate, articulated public policy, or other recognizable public interest militating toward access. *Id.* at 578.

[611] *Id.* at 580.

[612] 575 F.2d 1119 (5th Cir. 1978).

[613] FLA. CONST. art. II, § 8.

[614] *Plante*, 575 F.2d at 1122.

[615] *Id.* at 1134.

[616] *Id.* at 1136.

[617] NAACP v. Alabama, 357 U.S. 449 (1958).

Court held that the government could not intrude upon the privacy right of freedom of association to belong to the NAACP. This reasoning relies on the support of the constitutional rationale of freedom of association to protect against the release of information to the government.

Whereas some federal courts, as noted above, interpret *Whalen* to provide only minimal constitutional protection of informational privacy, other federal courts harshly refuse to recognize *any* constitutional protection for informational privacy. For instance, the Sixth Circuit held in *J.P. v. DeSanti* that although the Constitution protects fundamental rights and autonomy, it does not protect informational privacy.[618] Likewise, in *Doe v. Wigginton*, thirteen years after *DeSanti*, the same court found no general constitutional right to nondisclosure of private information.[619] Federal constitutional law, like tort law, will go only as far as a court's interpretation in a particular circumstance.

The following are examples of informational intrusions held constitutional:

- Employee drug testing[620]
- Compelled disclosure of psychiatric care[621]
- Compelled disclosure of health information[622]
- Compelled public disclosure of criminal records[623]
- Compelled disclosure of group affiliations[624]
- Disclosure of financial transactions[625]

---

[618] 653 F.2d. 1080, 1087–90 (6th Cir. 1981).

[619] 21 F.3d 733, 740 (6th Cir. 1994) (holding that inmate did not have a constitutional right of nondisclosure of his status as HIV positive by prison officials to corrections officer).

[620] *See, e.g.*, Stanziale v. County of Monmouth, 884 F. Supp. 140 (D.N.J. 1995) (noting that the permissibility of a particular drug-testing program was to be determined by balancing the government's interest against the intrusion upon the employee's privacy right).

[621] Strickland v. Linahan, 72 F.3d 1531 (11th Cir. 1996) (holding that the Fifth Amendment was not violated when a court permitted the prosecution to cross-examine a psychiatrist about information revealed by the defendant to the psychiatrist but not discussed by the psychiatrist on direct examination).

[622] Amente v. Newman, 653 So. 2d 1030 (Fla. 1995) (holding that the medical records of patients other than the plaintiff were discoverable if identifying information within the records was redacted).

[623] *See, e.g.*, Emmanouil v. Roggio, No. CIV.A.06-1068, 2007 WL 1174876 (D.N.J. April 19, 2007) (recognizing that New Jersey specifically guaranteed public access to criminal records).

[624] *See, e.g.*, Society of Jesus of New England v. Commonwealth, 808 N.E.2d 272 (Mass. 2004) (observing that the compelled disclosure of religious membership violated the right of free association only if it brought adverse consequences on members of the church).

[625] United States v. Richter, 610 F. Supp. 480 (N.D. Ill. 1985) (holding that the currency transaction reporting requirements of the Bank Secrecy Act were not unconstitutional), *aff'd sub nom.* United States v. Mangovski, 785 F.2d 312 (7th Cir. 1986).

These examples demonstrate that when the government wants to compel disclosure of information, it can usually justify such disclosure because of the lower threshold the government must meet.

4. The Supreme Court and Privacy

The U.S. Supreme Court is often the decision maker that leads the way in sensitive and important decisions that balance constitutional principles and social change. In cases such as *Brown v. Board of Education* and *Roe v. Wade*, the Court made major changes in direction in national policy. Since privacy is subject to interpretation of social forces, the Court is a focal point in the development of privacy law. A book by Alice Bartee tracks the evolution of privacy, looking at a series of major issues including reproductive rights, abortion rights, the right to privacy in sexual activity, and the right to refuse medical treatment.[626] The lesson of the evolution of these causes through the last century is that the definition of privacy changes with the passage of time. A lost case dealing with contraceptives is later won. Some courts and individual justices have extremely differing views on evolving social values. There are "originalists" and those who believe that the Constitution changes with time.

One type of constitutional analysis recognizes that changing social forces can grant a greater degree of individual privacy, especially in the area of decisional privacy. For example, in *Lawrence v. Texas*,[627] the Supreme Court overruled *Bowers v. Hardwick*,[628] holding a Texas sodomy statute unconstitutional as "seeking to control a personal relationship that . . . is within the liberty of persons to choose."[629] This case was based on a narrow opinion that overruled the previous narrow decision of *Bowers*. Justice Anthony Kennedy found that there was a due process right to private consensual sexual relations. He did not find a "fundamental right

---

[626] ALICE FLEETWOOD BARTEE, PRIVACY RIGHTS: CASES LOST AND CAUSES WON BEFORE THE SUPREME COURT (2006).

[627] 539 U.S. 558 (2003).

[628] 478 U.S. 186 (1986).

[629] *Lawrence*, 539 U.S. at 567. However, in a lengthy dissent, Justice Antonin Scalia argued that the majority "has taken sides in the culture war," departing from its role of neutral observer. *Id.* at 602. Justice Clarence Thomas also dissented, stating that he could "find [neither in the Bill of Rights nor any other part of the Constitution a] general right of privacy." *Id.* at 605-06. Following a textual method of constitutional analysis, Justice Thomas and others holding similar views are unlikely to grant stronger constitutional protection to privacy rights.

to homosexual relations,"[630] but he did find the state statute overreaching. The Court cited the line of privacy cases protecting decisional privacy under the due process clause of the Fourteenth Amendment.[631] As this case shows, the Court has been willing to change its position over time, and it is reasonable to assume that it may change in the future.

The Court's interpretation of decisional privacy rights does not directly relate to informational privacy rights. Cases supporting decisional privacy rights often involve declaring a statute unconstitutional as infringing upon substantive due process rights. Expanding these rights is not supported by justices who advocate federalism or favor a textual constitutional analysis.[632] In sharp contrast, however, these same justices who dissented in *Lawrence* are more willing to embrace the right of privacy with respect to personal information.[633] This fact may be the result of two factors. First, protecting against the disclosure of information does not require a liberal construction of the Constitution. The justices' interpretation is that the protection of freedom of expression emanates from the earliest principles and should be protected. Second, protecting against the disclosure of sensitive information does not pose the challenge to "morals," "traditional values," or "originalism" that a proposed fundamental right like the right to homosexual activity would pose.

Constitutional protections for liberty and privacy have never been static. The courts have been willing to shift the boundaries of protection from state action, recognizing that with new technology comes new ways to violate protected liberty interests. In a Fourth Amendment context, the Court specifically recognized that modern technology could intrude in

---

[630] Opponents offered a parade of horribles and "slippery slope" arguments that this case would lead to legal protection of prostitution, polygamy, and incest. *See* BARTEE, *supra* note 626, at 222-25.

[631] *Lawrence*, 539 U.S. at 564–67.

[632] *See, e.g.*, Roe v. Wade, 410 U.S. 113, 171 (1973) (Rehnquist, C.J., dissenting); *see also* John H. Ely, *The Wages of Crying Wolf: A Comment on Roe v. Wade*, 82 YALE L.J. 920, 935–36 (1973) ("What is frightening about *Roe* is that this super-protected right is not inferable from the language of the Constitution, the framers' thinking respecting the specific problem in issue, any general value derivable from the provisions they included, or the nation's governmental structure.").

[633] *See, e.g.*, Bartnicki v. Vopper, 532 U.S. 514, 556 (2001) (Rehnquist, C.J., dissenting). Chief Justice Rehnquist, joined in dissent by Justices Scalia and Thomas, opposed the majority's holding that the First Amendment protected a radio station's broadcast of illegally obtained cell-phone conversations. The statutes proscribing this behavior, the dissent argued, "protect the important interests of deterring clandestine invasions of privacy and preventing the involuntary broadcast of private communications." *Id.* at 553.

new ways without physically intruding. In *Kyllo v. United States*, the Supreme Court wrote, "It would be foolish to contend that the degree of privacy secured by the Fourth Amendment has been entirely unaffected by the advance of technology. For example . . . the technology enabling human flight has exposed to public view (and hence, we have said, to official observation) uncovered portions of the house and its curtilage that once were private."[634] In *Kyllo*, the Court found the use of a heat sensor in an investigation to be a search in the sense of requiring a warrant.[635] Here, the Court seems to embrace the notion that protection of basic rights and liberties must respond to technological changes. In the Fourth Amendment context, the Court must strike new balances between the state's interests in recovering relevant evidence and a citizen's right to be secure in his or her house, papers, and effects. Logically, informational privacy should also be accorded more protection than before because of advancing technological intrusions.

So perhaps a Supreme Court that has been reluctant to expand privacy in the sensitive areas such as sexual autonomy and the right to die may be more flexible in protecting informational privacy in the future. In other words, the Court might be more open to the impact of evolving technology than to evolving social norms. In sum, privacy has an uncertain future in the Court, both in the decisional and informational realms.

C. Federal Statutory and Regulatory Protections and State Protections for Privacy

The extensive policy efforts by federal and state governments represent attempts to fill gaps in common-law, tort, and constitutional remedies. There are more than forty federal statutes, multiple regulations, several state constitutions, and hundreds of state statutes tackling specific types of intrusions.

This issue-by-issue approach is different from the approach of the European Union and other governments that have created comprehensive citizen privacy rights. There are logical reasons for the incremental approach. Any sweeping privacy policy would confront free-press issues,

---

[634]   533 U.S. 27, 2043 (2001).
[635]   *Id.* at 2046.

national-security issues, and opposition from the data industry. So with the exception of some broad state constitutional rights to privacy,[636] protections have been created through specific measures rather than a comprehensive right.

Protections are enacted when new intrusions occur or new ways to intrude are invented. The legislative process reacts to crisis and political pressure. The analogy is that we build stoplights at the intersection after fatal accidents occur—but not before. Topics of focus for privacy policy have included Social Security numbers, library records, credit-card information, banking records, medical information, video voyeurism, autopsy photos, video-rental records, and so on. Usually abuses or visible cases have driven the reforms. For example, the use of video-rental records in Judge Bork's Supreme Court confirmation hearings drove the legislation making those records confidential.[637]

The circumstances of an intrusion and the gaps in existing remedies help explain why a particular policy was created. Take stalking statutes, for example. They establish a policy to protect against an emotional intrusion upon a person who is followed or harassed by another.[638] Neither the Constitution, tort law, nor the common law protect against that intrusion: being followed closely by a private person is not a constitutional violation; it is probably not intrusion upon seclusion; it is not trespass; it is not false imprisonment; a picture taken in public by paparazzi and published is probably not public disclosure of private facts. A new remedy was created to fill a gap. If that same type of harassment occurs on the Internet, there is a federal stature addressing "cyberstalking."[639]

Another example is the disclosure of personal medical information. Policymakers have sought to protect sensitive medical records because

---

[636] ALASKA CONST. art. I, § 22; ARIZ. CONST. art. II, § 8; CAL. CONST. art. I, § 1; FLA. CONST. art. I, § 24; HAW. CONST. art. I, §§ 6, 7; ILL. CONST. art. I, §§ 6, 12; LA. CONST. art. I, § 5; MONT. CONST. art. II, § 10; S.C. CONST. art. I, § 10; WASH. CONST. art. I, § 7.

[637] See Video Privacy Protection Act of 1988, 18 U.S.C. § 2710 (2000); see also infra Appendix I, section 4(m).

[638] For a list of all state stalking statutes, see Internet Safety, Stalking Laws, www.wiredsafety.org/cyberstalking_harassment/us_states/us_stalkinglaws_list.html (last visited May 16, 2008).

[639] Under 18 U.S.C. § 875(c), it is a federal crime, punishable by up to five years in prison and a fine of up to $250,000, to transmit any communication in interstate or foreign commerce containing a threat to injure the person of another. Section 875(c) applies to any communication actually transmitted in interstate or foreign commerce—thus it includes threats transmitted in interstate or foreign commerce via the telephone, e-mail, beepers, or the Internet.

they believe that disclosure of the information would be intrusive to the reasonable person. Yet without specific policies, constitutional, tort-law, and common-law remedies may not work. Consider how much information is collected by doctors, hospitals, health-care providers, and the government. For example, it is clear that the government can collect information for public-health purposes or even detain patients if a compelling public-health interest is demonstrated. Such records may well be public and available to newspapers, relatives, and insurance companies if there is no policy to protect them or make them confidential.

Federal and state statutes focus on protecting citizens from intrusions or information disclosures our society deems harmful. So, statutes may deal with issues ranging from stalking to disclosures of rape victims names. These legislative efforts fall into a series of categories that help us make sense of hundreds of enactments and help us analyze the basic reasons and background that generated the legislation. It is important to understand that the two general goals of legislation are to keep private entities from violating privacy and to keep public entities from violating privacy. For example, a restriction on the release of personal banking information regulates a private entity. A restriction on the release of Internal Revenue Service ("IRS") information regulates a public entity. Both policies protect financial information.

Among privacy issues are a series of intrusions that are unequivocally bad, and there will be no controversy in outlawing such practices and providing criminal remedies—examples include identity theft,[640] video voyeurism, stalking, and hacking into secure systems. The issue is not regulation but rather prevention and punishment. The offenders are criminals. The difficulty comes in detection and enforcement.

There are a substantial number of other privacy issues that require monitoring and regulation because the information is sensitive but the exchange and use of that information has been deemed to have value in our society. For example, the creation of health, education, credit, and financial information is inevitable and an important part of our society.

---

[640] Identity theft continues to be an issue because of the difficulty of enforcement among the multiple entities with information. The Federal Trade Commission reported that 10 million Americans were victims of identity theft in 2003, with an average financial impact of more than $10,000. That year's identity theft losses to businesses and financial institutions totaled nearly $48 billion and consumer victims reported $5 billion in out-of-pocket expenses. www.ftc.gov/opa/2003/09/idtheft.shtm (last visited May 17, 2008). *See also* FEDERAL TRADE COMMISSION, IDENTITY THEFT SURVEY REPORT 4–6 (2003), *available at* http://www.ftc.gov/os/2003/09/synovatereport.pdf.

A set of questions must be answered when defining an approach to a legislative remedy for a privacy intrusion:

1. How is the intrusion defined?[641]
2. How much information should be collected by governmental or private entities?[642]
3. Who should be allowed access to information? For example, medical information is limited to use by medical personnel.
4. Should the information be destroyed after a period of time? To limit continued possibilities of disclosure, some statues require the destruction of records after a designated period of time.[643]
5. What standard of accuracy should the distributor of information have? Should distributors be liable for inaccuracies of public records they copy?
6. Should an individual be given notice of the collection of information and a chance to correct errors? Several consumer and credit statutes require notice and the opportunity to correct mistakes.
7. What remedy should be available for violations? Depending on the severity of the intrusion, remedies may include damages, fines, and criminal penalties.
8. How is the policy to be enforced? Are there agencies with investigatory powers, or is enforcement available in the courts?

Many of these issues parallel principles of privacy articulated by the European Union and by privacy advocates.[644]

---

[641] This task may be complicated. For example, in defining video voyeurism, a drafter of legislation needs to avoid criminalizing a mother taking a picture of her baby on a blanket.

[642] If the amount of information collected is minimized, breaches of privacy can be avoided. If information is not collected, it cannot be negligently released or released by a later change in policy. Minimization also avoids conflicts with public-records laws. Information need not be kept secret if it is never collected. An example of avoiding information collection is not requiring disclosure of Social Security numbers to obtain a professional license. *See* Children's Online Protection Act, 15 U.S.C. §§ 6501–6506 (2000); *id.* § 6502(b)(1)(A)(i) (limiting the collection of information about children and providing that notice must be given on the Web site and specify what information is collected, how it is used, and the site's disclosure policy).

[643] One example is the Video Privacy Protection Act, 18 U.S.C. § 2710 (2000). Section 2710(e) provides that "[a] person subject to this section shall destroy personally identifiable information as soon as practicable, but no later than one year from the date the information is no longer necessary for the purpose for which it was collected and there are no pending requests or orders for access to such information under subsection (b)(2) or (c)(2) or pursuant to a court order." *Id.* § 2710(e).

[644] *See* discussion *supra* Chapter III, § C-2.

Another broad set of issues focuses on the increasingly important role of national security and surveillance. Those issues are discussed in other sections of this book. In this chapter, however, it is critical to identify the role of government in the large array of privacy-protection statutes. In virtually all statutes dealing with information concerning education, health, credit, finance, personal communications, computer use, or even library use, the government is treated differently and has greater access to this information than anyone else.[645]

There are exceptions within the various statutes granting government access, but there are also general statutes dealing with government access for security purposes, such as the Patriot Act and the Communications Assistance for Law Enforcement Act of 1994.[646]

Privacy policies can be organized into ten categories (see below). Do certain statutes overlap categories? Yes. For example, controlling IRS data is both a regulation of public data and a restriction on the release of financial information. These categories are not perfect, but they help in analyzing the policies involved.

Some categories cover relatively narrow topics such as video rentals or direct intrusions such as stalking or video voyeurism. The more difficult and comprehensive categories involve consumer protection, credit protections, financing institutions, and health care. Health care is a defined, albeit broad, area. Consumer issues may involve everything from the collection and cataloging of information to the dissemination of information. Credit information, itself a broad category, has received special attention in the form of distribution limitations and other requirements.

The laws and policies in these categories are applied to several *types* of entities that handle information. For example, some groups such as credit-card companies and banks collect information in the course of their business. Another group, termed "data brokers,"[647] gathers information from many different data gatherers and then sells that information for different purposes and to different entities. Data brokers gather information for security checks, background checks, credit checks, marketing lists, and so on. They sell this information to private entities, the government,

---

[645] *See* discussion *infra* Chapter IV, § D-1.

[646] The stated purpose of the Communications Assistance for Law Enforcement Act ("CALEA"), 47 U.S.C. § 1001 (2000), is "to make clear a telecommunications carrier's duty to cooperate in the interception of communications for Law Enforcement purposes, and for other purposes."

[647] *See* discussion *supra* Chapter III, § B-1.

and individuals. The complex matrix of policies depends on who gathers the information, the type of information, and who is buying or obtaining the information. For example, the National Security Agency will be able to obtain information that Macy's (seeking marketing information) will not be able to obtain.

As will be discussed, some states have their own policies and protections as well. Affected industries have expressed concern about the possibility of fifty different state policies impairing their efficiency. They have therefore sought nationwide uniformity through federal preemption. In some cases they have been successful;[648] in others the states may have more stringent approaches.[649]

The modes of protection for those policies guarding against physical intrusions are different. For example, policies dealing with stalking and video voyeurism punish the intrusions either criminally or by civil penalty. The difference in treatment reflects the value guarded. In other words, protecting information is the aim in dealing with consumer records. By comparison, stalking statutes and the like aim to punish an intrusive act.

The categories and their goals are as follows:[650]

1. **Medical records:** Statutes in this category restrict the release of sensitive personal medical information (e.g., the Health Insurance Portability and Accountability Act of 1996).

2. **Financial, credit, and consumer records:** Statutes in this category protect personal-finance-related information as well as information on consumer purchases and credit information.

3. **Educational records:** Because of the broad range of data collected, statutes in this category protect information accumulated by schools.

4. **Personal identity information and personally sensitive information:** Statutes in this category protect information that

---

[648] The Fair Credit Reporting Act, 15 U.S.C. §§ 1681–1681u (2000), virtually bars states from adopting stronger laws. For other examples, see Electronic Privacy Information Center, http://www.epic.org (last visited May 13, 2008).

[649] *See* David Silverman, *Data Security Breaches: The State of Notification Laws*, 19 Intel. Prop. & Tech. L.J. 5 (2007). Consider, for example, California's Security Breach Information Act, Cal. Civ. Code §§ 1798.80, 1798.81.5, 1798.82, 1798.84 (2002). California's was the first state legislation in this field, with thirty-four states following suit. In 2006, Congress debated many breach-notification bills, all of which "would have established weaker notice requirements than most of the existing state laws, which would have been preempted by the federal legislation." Silverman, *supra*, note 649 at 10.

[650] A more complete list of statutes is provided in Appendix I.

identifies a person and could facilitate identity theft (e.g., Social Security numbers, driver's license information, credit-card numbers) as well as particular types of records containing highly intrusive, offensive, or sensitive content (e.g., autopsy photos, video-rental records, library records, parental records, adoption records, juvenile records, names of abortion patients).

5. **Personal communications:** Statutes in this category protect information about private communications by individuals (e.g., phone, cell phone, e-mail communications).

6. **Computer use or computer-generated information:** Statutes in this category protect against abuses of data compilations, focusing on abuses in the collection, retention, and distribution of mass amounts of information.

7. **Business information:** Statutes in this category protect trade secrets and proprietary information.

8. **Exemptions from public records and protection against public intrusions:** Statutes in this category protect particular types of publicly held information and exempt from disclosure materials deemed confidential or intrusive, such as social security numbers and personnel files. These types of files may contain sensitive information that would be publicly available if not protected. This information may have been voluntarily or involuntarily obtained. These policies also protect against intrusions by the government that are not necessarily the result of the release of information (e.g., 42 U.S.C. § 1983 punishes misconduct relating to privacy rights, illegal surveillance, and the availability of information generated in the justice system).

9. **Statutes protecting against private intrusions:** These statutes protect against particular actions relating to privacy of the person but not the release or misuse of information (e.g., stalking, video voyeurism, cyberstalking, telephone solicitation).

10. **Statutes authorizing governmental intrusions:** These statutes authorize intrusions for public purposes or national-security purposes (e.g., the Patriot Act authorizes intrusions for security purposes).

State and federal governments have enacted numerous laws in furtherance of these principles. These principles involve the content and use of information, as well as protection against intrusive actions. So a protection could prohibit financial information, in the possession of the federal government, from being made available to a bank without permission. Or a policy could prohibit adoption information in the possession of a local court from being posted on its Web site. The type of information, the use of the information, and the party to whom the information is disclosed all matter. For example, even if the federal government could not disclose financial information to a bank without permission, it might be able to disclose such information to the FBI without permission. And in some states, adoption information may be available in the court files but not on the court Web site.

1. Federal Privacy Protections

a. Federal Statutes

This section discusses some of the federal privacy statutes and the rationales and policies underlying them. In addition, because of the breadth and number of statutes, Appendix I contains a more comprehensive treatment of the federal statutes.

One of the first statutory efforts to protect privacy was legislation regulating communications through the Federal Communications Commission ("FCC").[651] Additional efforts appeared concerning the 1954 census. Congress also recognized the need to include privacy exceptions to the Freedom of Information Act.[652]

Since these earlier policy changes, public concerns about privacy have accelerated, as has the pace of legislative activity. Although these efforts can be viewed as valiant attempts to enhance privacy protections, the overall landscape for remedies still is not comprehensive for several reasons. First, many of the privacy protections in the multiple statutes are overridden by security policies in the Patriot Act and the Foreign Intelligence

---

[651] *See* Communications Act of 1934, 48 Stat. 1064 (codified at 47 U.S.C. § 605 (2000)).

[652] The Freedom of Information Act, 5 U.S.C. § 552 (2000), provides exceptions for "trade secrets and commercial or financial information obtained from a person and privileged or confidential," *id.* § 552(b)(4), for "personnel and medical files and similar files the disclosure of which would constitute a clearly unwarranted invasion of personal privacy," *id.* § 552(b)(6), and for "records or information compiled for law enforcement purposes, but only to the extent that the production of such law enforcement records or information . . . could reasonably be expected to constitute an unwarranted invasion of personal privacy," *id.* § 552(b)(7).

Surveillance Act of 1978, for example.[653] Not surprisingly, national safety
and security override privacy interests, and the courts generally uphold
that conclusion. Second, the statutes cannot impair publication of information protected by the First Amendment.[654] Last, the accumulation and
sale of information from public sites is not prohibited by these acts.[655]
These statutes, however, do offer some protections in terms of notifying
citizens and providing opportunities for correcting mistakes. Overall,
despite the numerous enactments, the individual remains at risk.

Federal protections have been more successful in some areas than in
others. And given the reach of federal jurisdiction, in some instances only
federal policy changes will be effective on national and international
privacy issues because of the need for uniformity or broad coverage. For
example, a state-by-state approach to the privacy of Internet communications would be ineffective. But it should be noted that some state policies can be harbingers of broader changes or can provide the opportunity
to view policy efforts before they are attempted on a national scale.[656]
First, federal policy efforts are described below.

1. MEDICAL RECORDS

These policies protect against disclosure of health, medical, and genetic
information. Statutory protections are provided in the Health Insurance
Portability and Accountability Act, the Substance Abuse Privacy Act, and
the Veterans Health Administration Privacy Policy. The Health Insurance
Portability and Accountability Act of 1996 ("HIPAA")[657] contains its own
"privacy rule," issued by the Department of Health and Human Services.[658]
The privacy rule protects an individual's privacy in individually identifiable
health information, which HIPAA defines as any information, "whether
oral or recorded in any form or medium." In other words, the rule protects
all private health information, whether in spoken words or in electronic

---

[653] *See* discussion *infra* Chapter V, § A-2.
[654] Some statutes, such as the Video Voyeurism Act successfully restrict intrusion and
avoid the First Amendment problem by defining the unlawful acts as willful and intentional. *See* discussion *infra* Chapter IV, § C-1(a)(ix).
[655] It is not prohibited, but it can be restricted.
[656] Thirty-four states have passed genetic-nondiscrimination legislation, before Congress
passed legislation in 2008. *See* discussion *supra* Chapter III, § B-3(c).
[657] *See* Chapter IV, § D-1.
[658] 45 C.F.R. pts. 160, 164 (2007). Congress's right to direct the Department of Health and
Human Services to issue these rules was upheld by the Fourth Circuit in South Carolina
Medical Ass'n v. Thompson, 327 F.3d 346 (4th Cir. 2003).

or written form. The rule provides protection for individuals from disclosure of information relating to a "past, present or future physical or mental health or condition" that can be used to identify the individual, or reasonably could be used to do so.[659] HIPAA protects against disclosure of a broad range of medical information, whereas some statutes protect a narrower privacy interest. In the 1970s, Congress enacted 42 U.S.C. § 290dd-2, which makes confidential "records of the identity, diagnosis, prognosis, or treatment of any patient" that is treated in a drug- or alcohol-abuse facility directly or indirectly assisted by the federal government.[660] The statute recognizes a fairly narrow set of circumstances allowing disclosure, including consent by the patient. So for three decades Congress has recognized a privacy interest in information relating to an individual's treatment for alcohol and substance abuse.

There are some exceptions to HIPAA for public-health purposes or security purposes.[661] Nonetheless, health-care records are now among the better-protected types of private information.

II. FINANCIAL, CREDIT, AND CONSUMER RECORDS

Business and financial information have received significant federal attention. Acts protecting this area of privacy include the Economic Espionage Act of 1996, the Gramm-Leach-Bliley Act of 1999, the Fair Credit Reporting Act of 1970, and the Fair and Accurate Credit Transactions Act of 2003.

The Gramm-Leach-Bliley Act ("GLBA"),[662] among other provisions, allows individuals to prevent financial institutions from sharing their "nonpublic personal information" with third parties. The term "financial institution" includes a variety of institutions from banks and credit-reporting agencies to mortgage lenders and financial advisers.[663] The GLBA, like the Fair and Accurate Credit Transactions Act, requires financial

---

[659] 42 U.S.C.A. § 1320d(6)(b) (West 2001). Some health care records are now available on the Internet. With little trouble CNN reporter Elizabeth Cohen found her history of mammograms and the birth control she uses as she wrote a story about accessibility of medical records online. *See* Elizabeth Cohen, *Your private health details may already be online*, CNN, June 5, 2008, *available at* http://www.cnn.com/2008/HEALTH/06/05/ep.online.records/index.html (last visited June 12, 2008).

[660] 42 U.S.C.A. § 290dd-2(a) (West 1998).

[661] Under HIPAA's privacy rule, 45 C.F.R. § 164.528, individuals have a right to an accounting of the disclosures of their protected health information by a covered entity or the covered entity's business associates. However, no accounting is required for disclosures made for national-security or intelligence purposes.

[662] 15 U.S.C. §§ 6801–6809 (2000); *see also supra* Chapter III § B-5c, *see also infra* Appendix I.

[663] *See* 15 U.S.C. § 6809; *see also* Trans Union LLC v. FTC, 295 F.3d 42 (D.C. Cir. 2002).

institutions to notify consumers of the institutions' data-sharing policies and allow individuals to opt out of many types of disclosures and information sharing.[664] The GLBA limits the circumstances under which a financial institution can disclose a consumer's nonpublic personal information to a third party that is not affiliated with the financial institution or consumer.[665] A financial institution is inclusively defined as one "significantly engaged" in financial activities.[666] Generally, the GLBA requires that financial institutions notify the individual of the disclosure and provide an opportunity for them to opt out of the disclosure.

However, the extent to which these protections apply depends on the relationship between the financial institution and the consumer. According to the Federal Trade Commission ("FTC"), which is in charge of promulgating the privacy rules under the GLBA, individuals are divided into two categories: consumers and customers.[667] A consumer is "someone who obtains or has obtained a financial product or service from a financial institution used primarily for personal, family, or household purposes."[668] A customer, on the other hand, is someone with an ongoing relationship with the financial institution.[669] The requirements differ for consumers and customers. If the information concerns a *consumer* and is disclosed to a nonaffiliated third party, the financial institution must provide the consumer with a privacy notice, including an opt-out notice.[670] However, if the information either is not disclosed or meets an exception, no notice is required. The exceptions relate mainly to information shared in "processing and administering a financial transaction requested or authorized by a consumer."[671] Consumers may not opt out of these disclosures. If the disclosure relates to information concerning a *customer*, the notice requirements are more demanding. An initial notice is always

---

[664] 15 U.S.C. § 6802(a), (b).

[665] *See* How to Comply with the Privacy of Consumer Financial Rule of the Gramm-Leach-Bliley Act: A Guide for Small Businesses from the Federal Trade Commission 5 (2002), *available at* http://www.ftc.gov/bcp/conline/pubs/bus-pubs/glblong.pdf.[hereinafter GLBA Guide].

[666] *Id.* at 6–7. Among the examples given by the FTC are an entity that lends, transfers, or safeguards money for another; check cashiers; and sellers of wire transfers or money orders. Also, providing financial-investment or economic advice makes an entity a financial institution. Brokering loans, servicing loans, collecting debts, and providing career counseling qualify as well.

[667] *Id.* at 7.

[668] *Id.*

[669] *Id.*

[670] *See infra* Appendix III.

[671] GLBA Guide, *supra* note 665, at 15.

required for customers, regardless of whether information is disclosed. For example, Macy's can disclose consumer information to other affiliate stores without notice. However, for broader disclosures, the financial institution must provide an opt-out notice, give a reasonable amount of time for the consumer to opt out of the disclosure before it occurs, and provide an annual notice.

Consumer v. Customer Notice

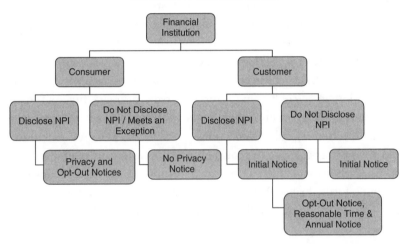

Although at first glance these requirements may seem stringent, they leave a wide array of information unregulated. Significantly, an entity must fall into the category of financial institution in order to be governed by the GLBA. Indeed, banks and credit-card companies clearly provide the types of services that qualify them as financial institutions. Less clear is whether retailers, who have access to a vast amount of consumer information, qualify as well. According to the FTC, a retailer that offers credit directly to consumers by issuing its own credit card is governed.[672] So retailers like Best Buy that offer a credit card to their customers would likely fall into the category of "financial institution" and would therefore be covered by the GLBA.

Would the grocery store with whom an individual has a discount card qualify? Likely not, since the dividing line is whether financial services are provided. Recall that information on tens of millions of households is shared by way of consumer discount cards offered by grocery stores and other retailers.[673] This vast area of consumer information remains unregulated. Since grocery stores and retailers that do not extend

---

[672] *Id.* at 6–7.
[673] *See supra* text accompanying notes 288–89.

credit to their customers are not financial institutions, they may share nonpublic information with nonaffiliated third parties without disclosure. A moment's reflection should produce a long list of items that individuals purchase, but do so under a false impression of privacy. For instance, adult diapers, condoms, many nonprescription medications, and other products can tell a great deal about a person when combined with a Social Security number, an address, an e-mail address, a name, or other personal information.[674] Complete strangers are able to obtain information about an individual's purchases of products that one would keep hidden from view if company came over.

The Fair Credit Reporting Act ("FCRA") regulates the sale and exchange of credit reports.[675] Credit agencies are prohibited from using or selling the information in a credit report for noncredit or marketing purposes. Congress expanded the protections in the FCRA in 2003, when it passed the Fair and Accurate Credit Transactions Act ("FACTA").[676] FACTA requires credit-reporting agencies to provide consumers with privacy notifications and the option to opt out of information disclosures. Credit-reporting laws are quite focused since there are only three major credit-reporting agencies—Experian, Equifax, and TransUnion—and specifically address those agencies' practices as well as the accuracy and security of information.

Credit-reporting agencies have a responsibility under the law to make an effort to be accurate. In one case Experian was found to be negligent because the company reported that a Mr. Dennis had a judgment for delinquent rent entered against him in Los Angeles Superior Court. That report was mistaken, but Experian used it in its credit report on Mr. Dennis. The court said: "This case illustrates how important it is for Experian, a company that traffics in the reputations of ordinary people, to train its employees to understand the legal significance of the documents they rely on."[677] This case shows that with the right facts, the privacy protections on credit reporting can be effective.

Overall, information about credit is substantially regulated. Less regulated, however, is information derived from consumer activities not directly related to credit activity.

---

[674] *See* Katherine Albrecht, *Supermarket Cards: The Tip of the Retail Surveillance Iceberg*, 79 Denv. U. L. Rev. 534 (2002).

[675] 15 U.S.C. §§ 1681–1681u (2000). *See* Chapter IV, § E-2; *see also infra* Appendix I.

[676] Pub. L. No. 91-508, 84 Stat. 1114 (1970) (codified as amended in scattered sections of 15 U.S.C.).

[677] Dennis v. BEH-1, LLC, 520 F.3d 1066, 1071 (2008).

iii. Educational Records

Privacy in educational records has been addressed with acts like the Family Educational Rights and Privacy Act of 1974 ("FERPA"), which protects the privacy of student records.[678] The act prevents the release of a student's records absent permission, except under certain circumstances, such as the release to the student's new school or to state and local juvenile authorities.[679] Schools may not deny students access to their educational records.[680] FERPA also allows students over eighteen as well as the parents of minor students to view the student's educational records and request changes to false or misleading information.[681] If the minor student's parents feel that the information is incorrect, they are to be provided with a hearing to contest the information in the record.[682]

The contours of FERPA have been tested in the courts with interesting results. In one case, the parents of a student brought an action under 42 U.S.C. § 1983, which provides a private right of action to redress deprivations under color of state law of any federal rights, privileges, or immunities. They claimed that the school violated FERPA by allowing "peer grading."[683] The practice is a common one, whereby teachers allow students to trade their assignments with other students in the class, who then grade the assignments while the teacher provides the answers to the problems. The parents claimed that the practice amounted to the release of sensitive information about students without parental consent, in violation of FERPA.[684] The Supreme Court held that the practice did not violate FERPA, as the student papers were not "maintained" by the school at the point when they were located in the hands of another student.[685] Furthermore, the Court explained, the students were not a "person acting for" an educational institution within the meaning of FERPA.[686]

FERPA, some have argued, does not go far enough to protect student privacy, particularly at the university and college level.[687] For instance,

---

[678] 20 U.S.C. § 1232g (2000); *see also infra* Appendix I.
[679] *Id.* § 1232g(a)(1)(A).
[680] *Id.* § 1232g(a)(1)(A)–(B).
[681] *See* http://www.ed.gov/policy/gen/guid/fpco/ferpa/index.html (last visited May 17, 2008).
[682] *Id.* § 1232g(a)(2).
[683] Owassa Indep. Sch. Dist. No. I-011 v. Falvo, 534 U.S. 426 (2002).
[684] *Id.* at 428.
[685] *Id.* at 432–33.
[686] *Id.* at 433.
[687] Jennifer C. Wasson, *FERPA in the Age of Computer Logging: School Discretion at the Cost of Student Privacy?*, 81 N.C. L. Rev. 1348, 1349 (2003) ("At colleges and universities across the country, students may not realize the extent to which information regarding

when students use a computer on the school's network or in a school computer lab, information about their practices is often logged.[688] Likewise, when students make use of their standard-issue identification cards, schools log information about the uses of the cards.[689]

IV. PERSONAL IDENTITY INFORMATION AND PERSONALLY SENSITIVE INFORMATION

This is a broad category that covers information of a highly personal nature, whether because it could identify an individual, disclose something highly sensitive and private about an individual, or both. Threats to privacy that involve the appropriation of identity, name, or likeness are addressed in the False Identification Crime Control Act of 1982,[690] the Identity Theft and Assumption Deterrence Act of 1998,[691] the Identity Theft Penalty Enhancement Act,[692] and the Internet False Identification Act of 2000.[693] Other acts relating to identity protection include the Brady Handgun Violence Prevention Act,[694] the Cable Communications Policy Act of 1984,[695] the Census Confidentiality Statute of 1954,[696] the Children's Online Privacy Protection Act of 1998,[697] the Driver's Privacy Protection Act of 1994,[698] the Fair Credit Reporting Act of 1970,[699] and the Fair and Accurate Credit Transactions Act of 2003.[700]

Some federal statutes aim to protect an individual's privacy interest in information that could disclose an individual's identity. The need for the protection of personally identifiable information is illustrated by a recent case. In 2007, Florida citizens brought a section 1983 action against high-level members of the Department of Highway Safety and Motor

---

their computer use, daily activities and whereabouts may be appropriated without their knowledge or consent.").

[688] *Id.* at 1349–53.

[689] *Id.* at 1350–51.

[690] Pub. L. No. 97-398, 96 Stat. 2009 (1982) (codified as amended in 18 U.S.C. § 1028).

[691] Pub. L. No. 105-318, 112 Stat. 3007 (1998) (codified as amended in 18 U.S.C. § 1028).

[692] Pub. L. No. 108-275, 118 Stat. (2004) (codified as amended 18 U.S.C. § 1028A).

[693] Pub. L. No. 106-578, 114 Stat. 3075 (2000) (codified as amended at 18 U.S.C. § 1028).

[694] Pub. L. No. 103-159, 107 Stat. 1536 (1993) (codified at 18 U.S.C. §§ 921–922).

[695] Pub. L. No. 98-549, 98 Stat. 2794 (1984) (codified as amended at 45 U.S.C. § 551).

[696] Pub. L. No. 98-497, 98 Stat. 2287 (1984) (codified as amended at 44 U.S.C. §§ 2201–2207).

[697] Pub. L. No. 105-227, 112 Stat. 2681 (1998) (codified as amended at 47 U.S.C. §231).

[698] 18 U.S.C. 2721 (1994 & Supp. II 1997).

[699] Pub. L. No. 91-508, 84 Stat. 1114 (1970) (codified as amended in scattered sections of 15 U.S.C.).

[700] Pub. L. No. 108-159, 117 Stat. 1952 (2003) (amending 15 U.S.C. §§ 1681–1681u).

Vehicles for selling their personal information[701] to mass marketers.[702] The personal-identity information was disclosed by the individuals in order to obtain their driver's licenses and vehicle registrations. The plaintiffs alleged that the officials violated their right to privacy under the Driver's Privacy Protection Act ("DPPA").[703] The motor-vehicles officials claimed qualified immunity, but the Eleventh Circuit found that the claims overrode the officials' qualified immunity.[704] The court held that the DPPA creates a clear and unambiguous right to privacy in personal driver information.[705] The court also held that the privacy right created under the DPPA could be separately enforced via a section 1983 action.[706] This case represents a clear invasion of personal-identity privacy (by a governmental entity entrusted with the information) and the success of a federal statute in protecting against such invasions.

Federal policies protecting identity have been a focus for several years. Regulations are more stringent, but identity theft is a continuing problem that statutes alone cannot solve.

In addition to statutes protecting personally identifiable information, there are also statutes protecting information that is highly sensitive to an individual. Some of these statutes encompass both concepts.[707] In other words, they protect against the disclosure of highly sensitive and personally identifiable information. These statutes generally either set forth restrictions on the distribution of information or prohibit the collection of certain information.

The exemptions in the Freedom of Information Act discussed below have been interpreted to protect information such as voice recordings of accident victims prior to death, photographs of a suicide scene, and an FBI background sheet. All these sets of information fall within the category of highly sensitive information, and although the Freedom of Information Act is not a specific statutory protection of privacy, the statute's

---

[701] "Personal information" was defined as "information which identifies an individual, including an individual's photograph, social security number, driver identification number, name, address (but not the 5-digit zip code), telephone number, and medical or disability information, but does not include information on vehicular accidents, driving violations, and driver's status." 18 U.S.C. § 2725 (2000).

[702] *Collier v. Dickinson*, 477 F.3d 1306 (11th Cir. 2007).

[703] 18 U.S.C. §§ 2721–2725 (2000).

[704] *Collier*, 477 F.3d at 1312.

[705] *Id.* at 1309–10.

[706] *Id.*

[707] Examples include the Video Privacy Protection Act, the Cable Communications Policy Act, and the Social Security Act.

exemptions have proved valuable in protecting the private nature of highly sensitive information by preventing its disclosure.

There are particular statutes protecting information that arises from certain specific consumer transactions that themselves reveal sensitive information.[708] Some examples are the Telephone Consumer Protection Act of 1991, the Video Privacy Protection Act of 1998, and the Cable Communications Policy Act of 1984.

The Video Privacy Protection Act ("VPPA") protects an individual's personal information by prohibiting videotape providers from knowingly disclosing personal information, such as titles of rented videos, without the written authorization of the consumer.[709] Similarly, the Cable Communications Policy Act ("Cable Act")[710] protects consumers' personally identifiable information, including the types of programming they purchase, from disclosure by the cable companies.[711]

As a further safeguard under the Cable Act, cable operators are required to destroy personally identifiable information when it is no longer necessary for the purpose for which it was collected, provided that there is no pending request by the consumer for that information.[712]

The Cable Act itself faces new challenges not foreseeable at the time of its signing. The Patriot Act and the needs of law enforcement necessitate and authorize more disclosure of information of cable-related information.[713] Additionally, the involvement of cable companies as Internet providers and the advent of Internet video raise new questions about the privacy of an individual's viewing selections.[714]

Whereas these statutes protect privacy interests by restricting the distribution of information, others restrict or prohibit the collection of information. The Children's Online Privacy Protection Act

---

[708] Other sensitive purchase information may be protected under other protected categories that have sensitive content. For example, purchases of medicine or medical supplies may be protected information under HIPAA.

[709] 18 U.S.C. § 2710 (2000); see also infra Appendix I.

[710] 47 U.S.C. § 521 (2000).

[711] Id. § 551(c).

[712] Id. § 551(e).

[713] See generally Gabe Rottman, Who Watches the Watchers (as They Watch You, Watching Television)? Law Enforcement Access to Cable Records at the Dawn of IP-Based TV, 95 GEO. L.J. 1671, 1705 (2007) ("Fortunately, from a privacy perspective, it appears that records revealing viewing habits of cable and [internet television] subscribers will be protected under the privacy laws—at least for now. Unfortunately, video delivered over the public Internet will almost certainly lack any such protection.").

[714] Id.

("COPPA")[715] prohibits the collection of personal information about children under the age of thirteen unless notice[716] is provided and the collector obtains "verifiable parental consent."[717] COPPA arose to combat the reality that "the Internet can pose a threat to children, exploit them, and compromise their privacy," by protecting children's personal information.[718] COPPA represents a policy decision that children's privacy rights were of a highly sensitive nature and in need of added protection.

One example of a ban on the collection of a certain type of information is the Employee Polygraph Protection Act ("EPPA").[719] The EPPA makes it illegal, with limited exceptions, for private employers to use lie-detector tests either in the hiring process or during employment. Although it was Congress's concern about the misuse and unreliability of information elicited via polygraph that led to the adoption of the EPPA,[720] the statute's effect is to protect a privacy interest in those applying for jobs in the private sector. In short, employees need not worry about being exposed to the intrusive polygraph test, as the collection of information via polygraph is prohibited.

The very fact that there are so many statutes in this category demonstrates the specific and incremental approach this country has chosen to take.[721] Clearly, more types of intrusions will be invented or discovered in the future, and more statutes will be passed.

v. Personal Communications

When we communicate with others we frequently expect that communication to be personal and private. With the advent of various types of modern communications, the law has tried to adapt and to protect those communications when they are made by artificial means such as through telephones, e-mail, and cell phones.

---

[715] 15 U.S.C. §§ 6501–6506 (2000).
[716] Under 15 U.S.C. § 6502(b)(1)(A)(i), the notice must be on the Web site and include what information is collected, how it is used, and the site's disclosure policy.
[717] *Id.* § 6502(b)(1)(A)(ii).
[718] Danielle Garber, *COPPA: Protecting Children's Personal Information on the Internet*, 10 J.L. & Pol'y 129 (2001).
[719] 29 U.S.C. §§ 2001–2009 (2000).
[720] Veazey v. Commc'ns & Cable of Chicago, Inc., 194 F.3d 850, 858 (7th Cir. 1999).
[721] The U.S. approach is different from that of the European Union, which establishes broader basic privacy rights. *See* discussion *supra* Chapter III, § C-2 and *infra* Chapter VII, § A-1.

One of the longest-standing areas of federal privacy legislation is communications. Federal statutes in this sector include the Electronic Communications Privacy Act of 1986, and the Telecommunications Act of 1996.[722]

Section 222 of the Telecommunications Act of 1996, entitled "Privacy of Customer Information," places a duty on telecommunications companies to protect the confidentiality of customer information.[723] Congress desired to protect, "among other things, [information regarding] to whom, where, and when a customer places a call."[724] The FCC issued a regulation in 1998 requiring that customers opt in before companies could use customer data to market services to which the customers did not already subscribe. This opt-in provision would ostensibly provide an added layer of privacy protection for consumers. However, the Tenth Circuit Court of Appeals held that the FCC regulation violated the First Amendment as an impermissible regulation of commercial speech.[725]

Recent legislation on cell-phone communications actually includes provisions that facilitate identifying and locating individuals. Cell phones are required to contain components that allow their location to be traced.[726] This feature has benefits for law enforcement, and there are examples of how it has worked to locate criminals and to help with 911 emergencies.[727] Also, Verizon offers parents a "Chaperone" service that allows them to set up a "geofence" around a certain area. Verizon will send a text message to the parent if the child holding the cell phone leaves that area.[728] So people are carrying federally mandated tracking devices in

---

[722] Other examples include: Communication Act of 1934, the Telephone Consumer Protection Act of 1991, the Wireless Communications and Public Safety Act of 1999.

[723] Pub. L. No. 104-104, 110 Stat. 56 (1996) (codified as amended in scattered sections of 47 U.S.C.).

[724] Brian A. Kelly, U.S West, Inc. v. FCC: *Exposing the Deficiencies in Government Attempts to Protect Customer Privacy*, 52 ADMIN. L. REV. 1055, 1056 (2000).

[725] U.S. West, Inc. v. FCC, 182 F.3d 1224 (10th Cir. 1999), *cert. denied*, 530 U.S. 1213 (2000).

[726] The Wireless Communications and Public Safety Act of 1999 (911 Act), 47 U.S.C. § 615a (2000), encourages the prompt deployment of a nationwide seamless communications infrastructure for emergency services. The FCC responded to the 911 Act by enacting the enhanced 911 system. The enhanced 911 system requires cell-phone carriers to provide the specific location of a cell phone to public-safety answering points. *See generally E911 Roundtable*, GPS WORLD, Mar. 1, 2002, *available at* http://www.gpsworld.com/gpsworld/article/articleDetail.jsp?id=12235&pageID=1.

[727] Ellen Nakashima, *Cellphone Tracking Powers on Request*, WASH. POST, Nov. 23, 2007, at A1.

[728] *Id.*

their pockets. The issue is whether the government will exercise restraint in using this tool.

The Electronic Communications Privacy Act[729] protects the exchange of wire, oral, and electronic communications. Most notably, it includes the Stored Communications Act ("SCA"), which prohibits the unauthorized accessing of stored wire or electronic communications.[730] Professor Orin S. Kerr explains that the SCA is "dense and confusing, and few cases exist explaining how the statute works," and that it "freeze[s] into law the under-standings of computer network use as of 1986."[731] In very basic terms, the SCA "creates a set of Fourth Amendment–like rules in light of the uncertain application of Fourth Amendment protections to stored Internet files."[732] The SCA creates rules regarding when disclosure of electronic communica-tions (typically e-mail) may be compelled[733] or be made voluntarily.[734]

The modern world of e-mail communication is fraught with risks of disclosing personal information. Contents of traditional mail are consid-ered confidential.[735] With e-mail, it depends. E-mail abandoned on the server of a provider for six months has no expectation of privacy.[736] While individuals have a reasonable expectation of privacy to information stored on their home computer,[737] the same is not true if it is a shared computer where multiple persons have the password.[738] Expectations of privacy decrease if there are multiple recipients of an e-mail. In any case the date, time, user and Internet addresses accessed by the user may be released to the government without a warrant. Finally, Internet sites visited (IP addresses) are not private but specific pages with the Web site (URLs) are not.[739]

---

[729] Pub. L. No. 99-508, 100 Stat. 1848 (1986) (codified at 18 U.S.C.).
[730] 18 U.S.C. §§ 2701–2711 (2000). These sections have been given several different names by commentators, including the "Electronic Communications Privacy Act" because they were enacted as a part of that law in 1986. See Orin S. Kerr, A User's Guide to the Stored Communications Act, and a Legislator's Guide to Amending It, 72 Geo. Wash. L. Rev. 1208, 1208 n.1 (2004).
[731] Kerr, supra note 730, at 1208; id. at 1214.
[732] Id.
[733] 18 U.S.C. § 2703 (2000).
[734] Id. § 2702.
[735] Ex Parte Jackson, 96 U.S. 727 (1877) (General expectation of privacy in mailed item).
[736] 18 U.S.C. § 2703(a) (2000).
[737] U.S. v. Lifshitz, 369 F.3d 173, 190 (2d Cir. 2004).
[738] White v. White, 781 A.2d 85, 90 (N.J. Super Ct. Family Div. 2001) (interpreting statute drafted to match the ECPA, found the statutory protections are only meant to protect unauthorized interceptions and because the wife had the password, the interception was authorized).
[739] United States v. Forrester, 512 F.3d 500, 510 (9th Cir. 2008).

VI. COMPUTER USE OR COMPUTER-GENERATED INFORMATION

This category covers information that is generated by computer. Today, computers assemble data that is used by individuals, governments, and businesses. At issue is the massive amount of information accumulated by the government, how such information may be obtained and used, and how it should be secured.

Protections in this category are a response to the aggregation phenomenon discussed earlier and the large amount of information collected and maintained by the government.[740] Aggregation is the assembly and organization of otherwise diffuse and remote information by computer. The issues involved include the accuracy of data collected and the appropriate use of that data.

The Privacy Act of 1974[741] prohibits the government from collecting information for one purpose and then using it for another.[742] The government, of course, collects information about individuals, and the Privacy Act was an early attempt to regulate the manner in which that data could be used. The government began Project Match in 1977 in an effort to detect fraud by applicants to federal aid programs.[743] The government considered this activity legal under the "routine use"[744] exception to the Privacy Act.[745]

The Privacy Act was amended in 1988 by the Computer Matching and Privacy Protection Act ("CMPPA").[746] The CMPPA prohibits the disclosure of any record in a system to any recipient or nonfederal agency for use in a matching program unless a written matching agreement is entered into with the recipient.[747] The agreements must meet several quite specific requirements pertaining to the purpose, procedure, notice, and justification for the matching.[748] Though the CMPPA provides a rigorous set of procedural protections and formalities, some have pointed out that it also allows the sharing of information between governmental agencies.[749]

---

[740] *See* discussion *supra* Chapter III, § B-4(a).

[741] 5 U.S.C. § 552a (2000).

[742] 62 AM. JUR. 2D *Privacy* § 12 (2007).

[743] SOLOVE, *supra* note 3, at 599.

[744] "Routine use" is defined as being a use compatible with the purpose for which the information was collected. 5 U.S.C. § 552a(a)(7) (2000).

[745] SOLOVE, *supra* note 3, at 599.

[746] 5 U.S.C. § 552a(o) (2000).

[747] *Id.*

[748] *Id.* The requirements are found in § 552a(o)(A)–(K).

[749] *See* Privacilla.org, The Computer Matching and Privacy Protection Act, http://www.privacilla.org/government/cmppa.html (last visited May 8, 2008).

Additionally, the CMPPA allows one governmental agency to use the information for a purpose that differs from that of the agency from which it received the information.[750]

The E-Government Act of 2002[751] requires that governmental agencies that accumulate information conduct privacy impact assessments. Agencies must assess the reasons for holding the information as well as actions that directly or indirectly affect an individual's privacy.[752] Under the act all agencies and contractors that run a public Web site must have an electronic privacy policy.[753] The policy must set forth what information is collected, why it is collected, how the information will be used, with whom it will be shared, notice and consent opportunities, and how the information will be secured.[754]

VII. Business or Trade Information

The Economic Espionage Act is one example of Congress protecting a business's right to privacy in the confidential information relating to its research and development.[755] The act criminalizes the theft of trade secrets. Section 1831 of the act concerns "economic espionage," penalizing the theft of trade secrets to benefit a foreign government.[756] Section 1832 of the act penalizes the theft of trade secrets to benefit anyone other than the owner of the trade secret.[757] Likewise, the Uniform Trade Secrets Act provides civil penalties for the theft of trade secrets.[758] Like almost all information, trade secrets have become more vulnerable because the Internet allows for rapid and easy dissemination of information.[759] Another statute that protects copyrights on the Internet is the Digital Millennium Copyright Act.[760] That act implements two World Intellectual

---

[750] *Id.*

[751] 44 U.S.C. §§ 3501–3521 (Supp. 2005).

[752] Kenneth P. Mortensen & Nuala O'Connor Kelly, *The Privacy Act of 1974 and Its Progeny, in* Proskauer on Privacy, *supra* note 123, § 12:1, § 12:4.

[753] 44 U.S.C. § 3501(c)(2) (Supp. 2005).

[754] *See* Corey A. Ciochetti, *E-Commerce and Information Privacy: Privacy Policies as Personal Information Protectors,* 44 Am. Bus. L.J. 55 (2007).

[755] Pub. L. No. 104-294, 110 Stat. 3488 (1996) (codified as amended 18 U.S.C. 1831).

[756] 18 U.S.C. § 1831 (2000).

[757] *Id.* § 1832.

[758] Unif. Trade Secrets Act, 14 U.L.A. 437, *et seq.* (1985).

[759] For an analysis of the Internet's impact on trade secrets, see Elizabeth Rowe, *Saving Trade Secret Disclosures on the Internet Through Sequential Preservation,* 42 Wake Forest L. Rev. 1 (2007).

[760] *See supra* note 361–62.

Property Organization treaties and seeks to prevent copyright invasions particularly over the Internet.[761] Interestingly, the act does limit liability for ISPs by amending sec. 512 of the Copyright Act.[762]

The Freedom of Information Act ("FOIA")[763] exempts from disclosure "trade secrets and commercial or financial information obtained from a person and privileged or confidential."[764] As Judge Bazelon from the D.C. Circuit Court of Appeals explained, "[t]his provision serves the important function of protecting the privacy and the competitive position of the citizen who offers information to assist government policy makers."[765] FOIA also exempts "inter-agency or intra-agency memorandums or letters which would not be available by law to a party other than an agency in litigation with the agency."[766] These provisions, as previously discussed, are exemptions from the general rule of disclosure. Courts, therefore, are careful when applying them. Given FOIA's overall policy of disclosure, the exemptions are "narrowly construed."[767]

VIII. Exemptions from Public Records and Protections Against Public Intrusions

Acts in this category include the Computer Security Act of 1987, the Census Confidentiality Statute of 1954, the CMPPA, the E-Government Act of 2002, FOIA, the Paperwork Reduction Act of 1995, the Privacy Act of 1974, the Privacy Protection Act of 1980, and the Social Security Number Confidentiality Act of 2000. This category is closely related to the sixth category, which covers information collected by the government and computer information.

The federal FOIA provides for the disclosure of certain information, but the act also lists exceptions, such as one for personnel, medical, and "similar" files, "the disclosure of which would constitute a clearly unwarranted invasion of privacy."[768] In *New York Times Co. v. NASA*, the court analyzed whether disclosure of a recording of the Challenger astronauts' voices before the space shuttle exploded would constitute a "clearly

---

[761] *See* www.copyright.gov/legislation/dmca.pdf (last visited May 17, 2008).
[762] *Id.*
[763] 5 U.S.C. § 552 (2000).
[764] *Id.* § 552(b)(4).
[765] Bristol-Myers Co. v. FTC, 424 F.2d 935, 938 (D.C. Cir. 1970).
[766] 5 U.S.C. § 552(b)(5)(2000).
[767] 37A Am. Jur. 2d *Freedom of Information Acts* § 131 (2007); *see also* Fisher v. Renegotiation Bd., 473 F.2d 109, 112 (D.C. Cir. 1972); *Bristol-Meyers*, 424 F.2d at 938.
[768] 5 U.S.C. § 552(b)(6) (2000).

unwarranted" invasion of personal privacy, pursuant to the statutory exemption.[769] The court held that, on balance, the family members' privacy interests outweighed the public's right to know and that the disclosure would constitute a clearly unwarranted invasion of the family members' privacy under the FOIA provision.[770]

FOIA also includes an exemption for records or information compiled for law-enforcement purposes, "but only to the extent that the production of such (materials) ... could reasonably be expected to constitute an unwarranted invasion of personal privacy."[771] Exemption 7(c) is broader than the exemption discussed in New York Times v. NASA, as the Supreme Court explained in a 1989 case involving a criminal defendant's rap sheet.[772] Whereas exemption 6, relating to personnel, medical, and similar files, requires a "clearly unwarranted" invasion of privacy, records and information collected for law-enforcement purposes can be excluded from responses to FOIA requests if disclosure of the information is reasonably expected to lead to an invasion of privacy.[773] The Court in Reporters Committee stated that "the privacy interest in a rap sheet is substantial. . . . [I]n today's society the computer can accumulate and store information that would otherwise have surely been forgotten long before a person attains age 80, when the FBI's rap sheets are discarded."[774]

The Supreme Court held that exemption 7(c) applied to the photographs of the scene of a public official's suicide.[775] The Court held that FOIA recognized the privacy rights of surviving family members and that those privacy interests outweighed the public interest in disclosure.[776]

The case of Wen Ho Lee illustrates the potential effectiveness of the Privacy Act when it applies. Under the act, there is a private right of action against a governmental agency when records pertaining to an individual have been improperly disclosed by that agency.[777] Mr. Lee, a former nuclear-weapons scientist accused of spying, sued the Departments of Energy and Justice for leaking information to the Associated Press and

---

[769] 782 F. Supp. 628, 630 (D.D.C. 1991).
[770] Id.
[771] 5 U.S.C. § 552(b)(7)(c) (2000).
[772] U.S. Dep't of Justice v. Reporters Comm. for Freedom of Press, 489 U.S. 749 (1989).
[773] Id. at 756.
[774] Id. at 771.
[775] Nat'l Archives & Records Admin. v. Favish, 541 U.S. 157 (2004).
[776] Id.
[777] 5 U.S.C. § 552a (2000).

several newspapers. Mr. Lee was able to maintain a cause of action long enough to settle for $1.6 million.[778]

Public intrusions are protected under 42 U.S.C. § 1983. This civil-rights statute has been used as a remedy when a public officer or employee is a party to an invasion of privacy.[779] For example, a decedent's surviving siblings had a protected interest for purposes of a section 1983 claim against a county and a private photographer taking pictures of the deceased for commercial purposes. The court found section 1983 liability under a "shocks the conscience" analysis.[780]

This remedy also may apply to misconduct by law enforcement. For example, a court found section 1983 liability where a Secret Service agent brought a CBS news crew into a home.[781] Section 1983 provides a remedy against public conduct that is not reachable through other remedies.

IX. STATUTES PROTECTING AGAINST PRIVATE INTRUSIONS

These statutes focus on private intrusions into private spaces of individuals. These intrusions are not based on disclosure of information. Examples of statutes in this category include the Video Voyeurism Prevention Act of 2004[782] and stalking statutes. Stalking statutes represent a well-established statutory remedy for intrusions caused by someone following or harassing another person. There are stalking statutes throughout the United States.[783] They overwhelmingly have been upheld against constitutional challenges such as those based on claims of infringement of freedom of association or vagueness. Terms such as "repeatedly," "willful," and "malicious"

---

[778] See *Ex-weapons Scientist Settles Privacy Suit for $1.6 Million*, BRECHNER REP., Aug. 2006, at 1, *available at* http://brechner.org/reports/2006/08aug2006.pdf; *see also* Lee v. Dep't of Justice, 413 F.2d 53, 55–56 (2005).

[779] *See* Sheetz v. The Morning Call, Inc. 747 F. Supp 1515 (E.D. Pa. 1990) (discussing a newspaper reporter who conspired with a state actor for purposes of § 1983 to publish private facts).

[780] Melton v. Bd. of Comm'rs, 267 F. Supp 859 (S.D. Ohio 2003).

[781] Ayeni v. Mottola, 35 F.3d 680 (2d Cir. 1984).

[782] 18 U.S.C. § 1801 (Supp. 2004) (amending the federal criminal code to prohibit knowing videotaping, photographing, filming, or recording by any means, or broadcasting an image of a private area of an individual, without that individual's consent, under circumstances in which that individual has a reasonable expectation of privacy, and defining a "private area" as the naked or undergarment-clad genitals, pubic area, buttocks, or female breast of an individual).

[783] For a state-by-state database of state stalking statutes, see Stalking Resource Center, http://www.ncvc.org/src/main.aspx?dbID=DB_State-byState_Statutes117 (last visited May 8, 2008).

that characterize the unwelcome conduct as criminal have facilitated holdings that the statutes are constitutional.[784]

In fact, a federal statute prohibiting "cyberstalking,"[785] has been upheld.[786] In that case, the stalker had continually e-mailed threats and obscene comments to a television reporter. Harassment by electronic means, as well as physical harassment, can be attacked. In several factual situations these statutes can operate as a statutory option to what might be an intrusion-upon-seclusion tort and make the conduct criminal. However, not all tort intrusions meet the statutory requirements. For example, a single instance of a video intrusion into someone's bedroom would not fit the requirement of repeated intrusions in stalking statutes.

X. STATUTES AUTHORIZING GOVERNMENTAL INTRUSIONS

Government investigations and national security represent perhaps the most troubling category of federal enactments. These statutes give the federal government the authority to collect information and to override various other privacy acts in the name of security. Examples include the Bank Secrecy Act, the Communications Assistance for Law Enforcement Act of 1994, the Computer Fraud and Abuse Act, the Omnibus Crime Control and Safe Streets Act of 1968, and the Patriot Act.

The Patriot Act has been discussed elsewhere in this book. In sum, the act allows governmental investigations to acquire information otherwise deemed private by other statutes.[787]

An easily understood example of the interplay between federal statutes authorizing governmental intrusions and the privacy of Americans is the Bank Secrecy Act.[788] Under this legislation, financial institutions[789] must monitor customers, maintain records, and file "suspicious activity reports" when they suspect that a transaction may be illegal.[790] They also must report credit extensions over $10,000 not secured by real property

[784] *See* Robert P. Faulkner & Douglas H. Hsiao, *And Where You Go I'll Follow: The Constitutionality of Antistalking Laws and Proposed Model Legislation*, 31 HARV. J. ON LEGIS. 1 (1994).
[785] 18 U.S.C. § 2261A(2) (2000).
[786] United States v. Bowker, 372 F.3d 365 (6th Cir. 2004).
[787] *See* Chapter IV, § A-2.
[788] 31 U.S.C. §§ 5311–5330 (2000).
[789] 31 C.F.R. § 103.11 (2007) includes, among others, in the definition of "financial institutions" banks, securities brokers, telegraph companies, and some casinos.
[790] *See* Privacilla.org, The Bank Secrecy Act, http://www.privacilla.org/government/bank-secrecyact.html (last visited May 8, 2008); *see also* COMPTROLLER OF THE CURRENCY ADM'R OF NAT'L BANKS, BANK SECRECY ACT / MONEY LAUNDERING ACT: COMPTROLLER'S

and all transactions involving the exchange of foreign currency. Suspicious activity reports must disclose the transacting individual's name, a description of the transaction, the existence of the institution's suspicions, and the basis for those suspicions.[791] In the post-9/11 environment, suspicious activity reports have "risen exponentially" because of heightened concerns and expanded requirements under the Patriot Act.[792] These reports are available to a wide variety of law-enforcement agencies, but plaintiffs have historically met with little luck when attempting to gain access to them via discovery.[793]

A comprehensive analysis of all these statutes is a book-long enterprise that is beyond the scope of this book. A review of the statutes indicates that some areas seem far better protected than others. For example, HIPAA may be complex, but it seems to provide a strong policy basis for privacy in health-care records. The effectiveness of some of the other federal statutes in protecting the privacy of American citizens is limited. The press's freedom to feed the public with gossip and scandal, national-security concerns, and a thriving information industry illustrate the challenges to the piecemeal approach of federal privacy legislation. This collection of statutes has evolved over time, growing to address numerous different categories, but it leaves citizens a step behind in confronting the newest and latest threats to privacy. The public is also ill informed about many types of contemporary intrusions, so individuals have not spoken with a loud or demanding voice on some issues that appear important to individuals when they are surveyed.[794] Several surveys have been conducted to determine what individuals feel is most intrusive to them personally. For example, one survey showed that individuals felt

HANDBOOK (2000), *available at* http://www.occ.treas.gov/handbook/bsa.pdf#search=%22bank%20secrecy%20act%22.

[791] *See* Alex C. Lakatos & Mark G. Hanchet, *Confidentiality of Suspicious Activity Reports*, 124 BANKING L.J. 794 (2007).

[792] *Id.*

[793] *Id.* (noting, however, that the Fifth Circuit's recent decision in *BizCapital Bus. & Indus. Dev. Corp. v. OCC*, 467 F.3d 871 (5th Cir. 2006), may change this trend).

[794] A 2005 survey revealed that 73 percent of respondents believed falsely that banks are barred by law from sharing information with other companies and affiliates and 75 percent of respondents believed falsely that the presence of a privacy policy on a Web site means that the company cannot sell customers' information to others. *See* JOSEPH TUROW, LAUREN FELDMAN & KIMBERLY MELTZER, ANNENBERG PUB. POL'Y CTR. OF THE UNIV. OF PA., OPEN TO EXPLOITATION: AMERICAN SHOPPERS ONLINE AND OFFLINE (2005), *available at* http://www.annenbergpublicpolicycenter.org/Downloads/Information_And_Society/Turow_APPC_Report_WEB_FINAL.pdf.

that monitoring e-mail was highly intrusive, yet such surveillance is allowed with relative ease. As public awareness is heightened, more statutory responses are likely.

b. Regulatory Protections

In addition to federal statutory protections there are regulatory efforts aimed at protecting citizens' privacy. Agencies like the FCC and the FTC have broad regulatory powers that can be effective in addressing some privacy concerns.

For the purposes of this book, I will use the FTC as an example of the ways in which the federal government may use regulatory action to protect citizens' privacy. The power of the FTC comes from the Federal Trade Commission Act of 1914.[795] The act states that "unfair methods of competition in or affecting commerce, and unfair or deceptive acts or practices in or affecting commerce, are hereby declared unlawful."[796] Additionally, the act empowers and directs the FTC to "prevent persons, partnerships, or corporations . . . from using unfair methods of competition in or affecting commerce and unfair or deceptive acts or practices in or affecting commerce."[797] The act precludes the FTC from regulating certain entities, such as financial institutions and commercial carriers, and from regulating certain foreign transactions.[798] Under the act, the FTC has the power to obtain injunctive remedies and to bring civil actions for penalties of up to $10,000 per violation.[799]

The FTC's involvement in the protection of consumer privacy is relatively recent. In 1995, Congress and leading privacy experts asked the FTC to become active in these matters.[800] Since 1998, the FTC has brought a number of actions aimed at protecting consumer privacy, and many of these actions have been settled.[801] These actions include:

1. GeoCities, in which the FTC required the company to post a privacy notice on its Web site to inform consumers how information collected its Web site would be used;[802]

---

[795] 38 Stat. 717 (1914) (codified as amended in scattered sections of 15 U.S.C.).
[796] 15 U.S.C. § 45(a)(1) (2000).
[797] Id. § 45(a)(2).
[798] Id. § 45(a)(2), (3).
[799] Id. § 45(m)(1)(A); see also SOLOVE, supra note 3, at 750.
[800] Id.
[801] Id.
[802] Id.

2. ReverseAuction, in which the FTC took action against the company for improperly obtaining the personal information of other businesses' customers and making misrepresentations;[803] and

3. Eli Lilly, in which the FTC addressed the use of inadequate information-security procedures.[804]

The 2006 settlement of ChoicePoint's case involving a data-security breach provides an excellent detailed example of FTC enforcement. ChoicePoint, an Atlanta-based publicly traded company, obtained and sold the personal information of consumers, including names, Social Security numbers, birth dates, employment information, and credit histories.[805] ChoicePoint acknowledged that in 2005 the personal financial records of more than 163,000 consumers in its database had been compromised.[806] At least eight hundred cases of identity theft arose from the company's data breach.[807]

The FTC charged that ChoicePoint's security and record-handling procedures violated consumers' privacy rights and federal laws. The FTC alleged that ChoicePoint did not have reasonable procedures to screen prospective subscribers, and that ChoicePoint turned over consumers' sensitive personal information to subscribers whose applications raised serious authenticity concerns.[808] The FTC alleged that ChoicePoint approved as customers individuals who lied about their credentials and used commercial mail drops and public fax machines for business contact information.[809] According to the FTC, ChoicePoint failed to improve its application-approval procedures or monitor its subscribers, even after receiving notification from law-enforcement authorities of fraudulent activity going back to 2001.[810] The FTC charged that ChoicePoint violated the Fair Credit Reporting Act ("FCRA") by providing consumer credit histories to subscribers who did not have a permissible purpose to obtain them and by failing to maintain reasonable procedures to verify its subscribers'

---

[803] *Id.* at 752.
[804] *Id.* at 753.
[805] Press Release, FTC, ChoicePoint Settles Data Security Breach Charges; to Pay $10 Million in Civil Penalties, $5 Million for Consumer Redress (Jan. 26, 2006), *available at* http://www.ftc.gov/opa/2006/01/choicepoint.htm (last visited May 8, 2008).
[806] *Id.*
[807] *Id.*
[808] *Id.*
[809] *Id.*
[810] *Id.*

identities and the intended use of the information.[811] The FTC also charged that ChoicePoint violated the Federal Trade Commission Act by making false and misleading statements about the company's privacy policies, confidentiality protocols, and security practices relating to the personal information that it collected and maintained.[812] ChoicePoint made statements such as, "ChoicePoint allows access to . . . consumer reports only by those authorized under the FCRA. . . ." and "Every ChoicePoint customer must successfully complete a rigorous credentialing process. ChoicePoint does not distribute information to the general public and monitors the use of its public record information to ensure appropriate use."[813]

Faced with FTC action, ChoicePoint settled. The final judgment and order required ChoicePoint to:

1. pay $10 million in civil penalties—as of 2006, the largest civil penalty in FTC history—and provide $5 million for consumer redress;
2. establish and maintain reasonable procedures to ensure that consumer reports are provided only to those with a permissible purpose;
3. verify the identity of businesses that apply to receive consumer reports, including making site visits to certain business premises and auditing subscribers' use of consumer reports;
4. establish, implement, and maintain a comprehensive information-security program designed to protect the security, confidentiality, and integrity of the personal information it collects from or about consumers;
5. obtain, every two years until 2026, an audit from a qualified independent third-party professional to ensure that its security program meets the standards of the order;
6. be subject to standard record-keeping and reporting provisions to allow the FTC to monitor compliance; and
7. prevent future violations of the FCRA and the Federal Trade Commission Act.[814]

---

[811] *Id.*
[812] *Id.*
[813] *Id.*
[814] *Id.*

Regulatory efforts, like those of the FTC, have the potential to address some major privacy concerns. An example of a successful action in which tort remedies failed is the case brought by the FTC against the *Girls Gone Wild* video company. Two cases are discussed in the section below on torts.[815] One of them had no remedy in tort. However, a court found that the company had violated the FTC by trafficking in obscene videos.[816]

Another example of FTC involvement in privacy policy is the agency's determination that companies must comply with their published privacy policies.[817] This action is important to assure customers that lofty claims made on Web sites and in other publications are in fact followed. The FTC says that a company that collects and uses personal identifying information in violation of its own privacy policy has committed unfair or deceptive practices in violation of 15 U.S.C. § 45.

The combination of federal statutes and regulations provides a complex and substantial set of remedies. Beyond federal laws are even more laws among the fifty states targeted at privacy issues. In some cases, the states have gone further with protections than the federal government.

2. State Privacy Protections

In light of the failures of federal constitutional law and common-law torts to protect certain privacy rights, many states have created remedies to protect their citizens' privacy rights. These statutes have been enacted

---

[815] *See* discussion *infra* Chapter IV, § D-5.

[816] Press Release, Dep't of Justice, "Girls Gone Wild" Company Sentenced to Pay $1.6 Million in Fines in Sexual Exploitation Case (Dec. 13, 2006), *available at* http://www. usdoj.gov/opa/pr/2006/December/06_crt_831.html.

[817] For example, in response to data breaches in cases where the company promised that individuals' personal information would be protected, the FTC has asserted jurisdiction over retail stores in order to protect consumers, treating lax computer security measures as an unfair trade practice. In out-of-court settlement agreements, the FTC has required merchants to comply with the "safeguards rule" of the Gramm-Leach-Bliley Act, which was created to regulate financial institutions. Some commentators question whether the FTC's jurisdiction and assertions would be upheld in court. *See* Benita A. Kahn & Heather J. Enlow, *The Federal Trade Commison's Expansion of the Safeguards Rule*, FED. LAW., Sept. 2007, at 39. The safeguards rule requires financial institutions to "develop, implement, and maintain a comprehensive information security program that is written in one or more readily accessible parts and contains administrative, technical, and physical safeguards that are appropriate to [the institution's] size and complexity, the nature and scope of [its] activities, and the sensitivity of any customer information at issue." 16 C.F.R. § 314.3 (2007).

in response to specific problems such as the publication of autopsy photos or the appropriation of name or likeness.[818] State policymakers operate in the same ten areas discussed above under the section on federal privacy protections. However, unlike the federal government, some states have adopted constitutional provisions giving citizens a greater right to privacy than that granted by the federal Constitution.[819]

a. State Constitutional Privacy Provisions

State constitutions have been found to give more extensive rights in a number of controversial cases. The Kentucky Supreme Court held that the state constitution offered greater protection than the U.S. Constitution and struck down a state law against homosexual sodomy.[820] This case preceded the Supreme Court's decision in *Lawrence v. Texas*,[821] and the Kentucky court was more explicit in citing the right to privacy as the basis for its decision.

The Florida Supreme Court found the Parental Notice of Abortion Act,[822] which requires a minor to notify her parent, or to explain to a court that she is mature enough to make the decision herself, prior to receiving an abortion, unconstitutional under the Florida Constitution.[823] The court applied strict scrutiny, noting that in Florida, the right to privacy is fundamental and thus requires a compelling state interest to be furthered through the least intrusive means.[824] However, in November 2004, citizens of Florida passed a constitutional amendment allowing parental notification of abortion, essentially overruling the *North Florida* decision.[825]

State constitutions have been the basis for protecting the right to die,[826] protecting the right to refuse medical treatment,[827] protecting the right to

---

[818] For example, New York, Florida, and California each have statutes that go beyond the common-law tort of appropriation of name or likeness, providing the victims of appropriation with greater remedies by providing relatives with the right to inherit the cause of action. *See* Cal. Civ. Code §§ 3344–3344.1 (1984); Fla. Stat. § 540.08 (1998); N.Y. Civ. Rights Law §§ 50, 51 (2000).

[819] *See infra* Appendix II.

[820] Commonwealth v. Wasson, 842 S.W.2d 487 (Ky. 1982); *see also* Powell v. State, 510 S.E.2d 18 (Ga. 1998).

[821] 539 U.S. 558 (2003).

[822] Fla. Stat. § 390.01115 (1999).

[823] N. Fla. Women's Health Counseling Servs. Inc. v. State, 28 Fla. L. Weekly S549 (Fla. 2003).

[824] *Id.*

[825] *See* Fla. Const. art. X, § 22.

[826] Oregon, People v. Seven Thirty-Five East Colfax, Inc. (Colo. Sup. St., 1985, Kan. Sup. Ct. 1990).

[827] Schloendorff v. Soc'y of N.Y. Hosp., 211 N.Y. 125 (N.Y. 1914).Benjamen Cardozo said that "[e]very human being of adult years and sound mind has a right to determine

use sexually stimulating devices,[828] invalidating a criminal sodomy statute,[829] upholding the issuance of same sex marriage licenses,[830] permitting the personal use of marijuana in the home,[831] and invalidating an antisodomy statute as applied to heterosexual consenting adults.[832] In other words, states as diverse as Colorado, New York, Kansas, Georgia, Hawaii, New Jersey, Alaska, Kentucky, and Florida have used constitutional privacy provisions and other parts of their constitutions to protect controversial privacy rights. States can provide leadership in the privacy area because of the constitutional options available.

b. Protecting Private Information in Court Records

One of the greatest sources of personal information is court records. The amount of information collected during criminal or civil proceedings in the courts of the United States is staggering. The court system runs on information; some of the information is accurate and some is not. A large portion of that data involves the most sensitive of information derived from divorce proceedings, adoptions, juvenile proceedings, criminal investigations, and estate proceedings. Court documents were buried in file cabinets for decades, but now modern computers have made the data available and easily manageable. Courts have addressed directly the need to maintain the privacy of the willing and unwilling subjects of the court system while maintaining the American tradition of open proceedings. Court rules have existed for some time that allow judges to redact sensitive information on motion of counsel.[833] Also, litigation has sought to keep court records secret on the basis of constitutional protections.[834]

---

what shall be done with his own body." *Id.* at 129. This is said to be the beginning of "informed consent" needed for medical procedures.

[828] *In re* Quinlan, 355 A.2d 647 (N.J. 1976).

[829] *See* discussion *infra* Chapter V, § A-2.

[830] Baehr v. Lewin 852 P.2d 44 (Haw. 1993) (subsequently overruled by state constitutional amendment). In 1999, the Vermont Supreme Court ruled that state laws denying benefits to same-sex partners violated equal protection. Baker v. State, 744 A.2d 864 (Vt. 1999).

[831] Ravin v. State, 537 P.2d 494 (Alaska 1975).

[832] State v. Pilcher, 242 N.W.2d 348 (Iowa 1976).

[833] *See* State v. Rolling, No. 91-3832, 1994 WL 722891, at *5 (Fla.Cir.Ct. July 27 1994) ("The public's right to information which permits the public to evaluate the operations of government must be balanced against the intrusion on the right to privacy").

[834] *See* Barron v. Florida Freedom Newspapers, 531 So. 2d 133, 116 (Fla. 1988); *see also* Post-Newsweek Stations, Florida, Inc. v. Doe, 612 So. 2d 549, 552 (Fla. 1992).

Several states have created commissions to address the issue of privacy in court records in the computer age.[835] This issue will not go away soon. There are strong advocates for opening up the process and posting virtually all information online. The press is of course interested in access to the myriad newsworthy cases in the courts at any time. They are also interested, as are scholars, in researching such topics as the number of school-bus drivers who have previously been convicted of a felony.

There is currently no uniform policy across the country; nor is one likely. The Florida committee made the following recommendations:

1.   Reduce the gathering of unnecessary information
2.   Educate attorneys and parties on the importance and enforcement of privacy policies
3.   Identify certain categories that will be redacted and held private, such as adoption proceedings and certain family-law proceedings
4.   Adopt a process for reviewing data before it is made public or placed on the court's Web site

The ultimate goal of the report was to allow information to be placed online but to provide protections adequate to ensure that information that should be private is not disclosed either in hard copy or electronic copy.

The handling of data in the court system will become more sensitive as e-filing becomes more of a reality. The federal courts already take or require many filings electronically. It is certain that paper will become less and less a part of court proceedings. But the data involved will become no less sensitive. The challenge is to balance the need for open court proceedings and personal privacy in an increasingly electronic environment. All the potential solutions to this challenge are expensive and complex.

c. State Statutory Protections

States have enacted statutes to protect privacy interests, ranging from protections against data brokers to protection against the dissemination of autopsy photos. For instance, at least nineteen states provide some form of *statutory* recognition of the right to publicity that augments the privacy tort of appropriation of personality and right to publicity.[836]

---

[835] *See* COMM. ON PRIVACY & COURT RECORDS, *supra* note 234. The author chaired this Florida Supreme Court committee.
[836] *See* CAL. CIV. CODE §§ 3344–3344.1 (Deering 2008); FLA. STAT. § 540.08 (2007); 765 ILL. COMP. STAT. § 1075/1 (West 2008); IND. CODE § 32-36 (2008); KY. REV. STAT.

Florida law provides that a decedent's spouse or children may bring an action on behalf of the deceased for the unauthorized publication of his or her name or likeness.[837] Florida also allows an action where one's "name, portrait, photograph, or other likeness" is used for "any commercial or advertising purpose."[838] The Florida statute was derived from New York's privacy statute, which does not allow the right of privacy to extend beyond one's death but does allow an action when the name, portrait, or picture of a living person is used for advertising or trade purposes.[839] Although Florida and New York limit statutory protection to name and likeness, other states go further and protect identifying personal traits such as signature,[840] voice,[841] gestures and mannerisms,[842] or "any aspect of an individual's 'persona.'"[843]

Another area where states have acted to protect privacy is video intrusion. A federal law makes video voyeurism a crime when conducted in a place where the person being recorded has a reasonable expectation of privacy.[844] A total of forty-seven states also have enacted legislation that

---

§ 391.170 (West 2007); Mass. Gen. Laws Ann. ch. 214, § 3A (West 2008); Neb. Rev. Stat. § 20-202 (LexisNexis 2008); Nev. Rev. Stat. §§ 597.770–.810 (LexisNexis 2007); N.Y. Civ. Rights Law §§ 50, 51 (Consol. 2008); Ohio Rev. Code Ann. § 2741.01 (LexisNexis 2008); 42 Pa. Cons. Stat. § 8316 (West 2007); R.I. Gen Laws §§ 9-1-28, 9-1-28.1(a)(2) (2008); Tenn. Code Ann. § 47-25-110 (2008); Tex. Prop. Code Ann. § 26.001(Vernon 2007); Utah Code Ann. § 45-3-1 (2008); Va. Code Ann. § 8.01-40 (2008); Wash. Rev. Code § 63.60.010 (LexisNexis 2008); Wis. Stat. § 895.50(2)(b) (West 2008).

[837] Fla. Stat. § 540.08(1)(c); *see also* Campus Commc'ns, Inc. v. Earnhardt, 821 So. 2d 388 (Fla. Dist. Ct. App. 2002).

[838] Fla. Stat. § 540.08(1).

[839] N.Y. Civ. Rights Law § 50 (Consol. 2008).

[840] *See, e.g.,* Wash. Rev. Code §§ 63.60.010.

[841] *See, e.g.,* Cal. Civ. Code §§ 3344–3344.1.

[842] Ind. Code § 32–36.

[843] Ohio Rev. Code Ann. § 2741.01; *see, e.g.,* White v. Samsung Elec. Am., Inc., 971 F.2d 1395, 1399 (9th Cir. 1992), *reh'g denied,* 989 F.2d 1512 (9th Cir. 1993), *cert. denied,* 508 U.S. 951 (1993) (company's advertisement used a robot dressed like game show hostess Vanna White and placed next to game board similar to Wheel of Fortune set. The court held that White had a cause of action and said: "[t]elevision and other media create marketable celebrity identity value. Considerable energy and ingenuity are expended by those who have achieved celebrity value to exploit it for profit. The law protects the celebrity's sole right to exploit this value whether the celebrity has achieved her fame out of rare ability, dumb luck, or a combination thereof."

[844] *See* Video Voyeurism Prevention Act of 2004, 18 U.S.C. § 1801 (Supp. 2004) (amending the federal criminal code to prohibit the knowing videotaping, photographing, filming, recording by any means, or broadcasting of an image of a private area of an individual, without that individual's consent, under circumstances in which that individual has a reasonable expectation of privacy, and defining a "private area" as the naked or under-garment clad genitals, pubic area, buttocks, or female breast of an individual).

prohibits nonconsensual photographic or video recording of persons in a state of undress or nudity, provided that the individual is recorded while in a location where he or she has a reasonable expectation of privacy.[845] So if a person took an intrusive picture of a woman's or a man's private parts, an aggrieved person might have a federal criminal action, a state statutory action that might include an action for dissemination of the information, or a tort action for intrusion upon seclusion. The real-world challenge is that the facts may make one or more of the remedies unavailable.[846]

Like the federal government, states also have exceptions to public-records acts.[847] Virtually all states have numerous exceptions to public-record laws to protect sensitive information such as financial, medical, or credit data.

An important example of a state court using court rules, the state constitution, and common sense to find in favor of a privacy right when balanced against public records was the case of *State v. Rolling*.[848] At issue in that case was whether to allow disclosure of crime-scene and autopsy photographs of five victims of brutal murders.[849] The court described the test as one of balancing the public's right to know against the residual

---

[845] National Center for Victims of Crime, Video Voyeurism Laws, http://www.ncvc.org/ src/AGP.Net/Components/DocumentViewer/Download.aspxnz?DocumentID=37716 (last visited May 8, 2008). For examples of such forms of state legislation, see FLA. STAT. §§ 810.14, 810.145 (2004), (prohibiting the secret recording of a person who has a reasonable expectation of privacy and prohibiting commercial dissemination of video voyeurism products); LA. REV. STAT. ANN. § 14:283 (2000]) (comprehensive video voyeurism statute drafted to cover "up-skirt" and "down-blouse" photography); MISS. CODE § 97-29-63 (1999) (prohibiting videotaping in public and private places where persons have a legitimate expectation of privacy, expressly covering dressing rooms, locker rooms, tanning salons, bedrooms, and bathrooms); OHIO REV. CODE § 2907.08 (2001) (prohibiting the use of a camera to record images through or underneath clothing); WASH. REV. CODE § 9A.44.115 (2003) (creating felony criminal liability for those who record others under circumstances in which they have a legitimate expectation of privacy); WIS. STAT. § 942.08 (1998) (prohibiting the placement of secret surveillance devices in places where individuals enjoy a reasonable expectation of privacy, and prohibiting nonconsensual, nude photography of persons in such private places).

[846] For example, in State v. Glas, 147 Wash. 2d 410, 414 (2002), a Washington court held that a state voyeurism statute failed to cover intrusions of privacy in public places and thus failed to prohibit "up-skirt" photography in a public location because the statute only covered locations where a victim would have an expectation of privacy. Although the subject of the photograph was a "private part," because the woman was physically located in a public place, she was not protected under the statute.

[847] *See* FIRST AMENDMENT FOUND., FLORIDA'S GOVERNMENT-IN-THE-SUNSHINE MANUAL AND PUBLIC RECORDS LAW MANUAL (2007), *available at* http://myfloridalegal.com/ webfiles.nsf/WF/MRAY-6Y8SEM/$file/2007Sunshine.pdf (last visited May 8, 2008).

[848] 22 Med. L. Rep. 2264 (Fla. Cir. Ct. 1994).

[849] *Id.*

privacy interests of the victims' relatives.[850] The court considered four factors[851] in its analysis and determined that the photographs could be made available for public viewing, but could not be reproduced or removed from the possession of the records custodian.[852] This case provides an example of how state courts can analyze and balance the conflicting rights of public access and privacy. The analysis was based on court rules, constitutional principles, and judicial interpretation. The long-term result was the legislature's reliance on this analysis when it ultimately passed a statute protecting autopsy photos a decade later.[853]

Like federals statutes, state statutes also provide privacy protection with regard to the collection of personal information by data brokers. The data-broker industry is a fast-growing, largely self-regulating industry that sells personal information about millions of individuals.[854] The largest data brokers, corporations such as ChoicePoint, Acxiom, and the LexisNexis subsidiary Seisint, maintain billions of records on almost every citizen in the nation.[855] However, most individuals are unaware that their personal information is being collected by data brokers and sold to third parties.[856] The widely reported security breach at ChoicePoint in February 2005 significantly raised public awareness about the existence of data brokers and the extensive quantities of personal information contained in their databases.[857] In addition, the ChoicePoint security breach stirred state legislatures into action to further protect the informational privacy rights of individuals.

---

[850] *Id.* at 2269.

[851] The court described the four factors as follows: (1) the relevance of disclosure of the material to furthering public evaluation of governmental accountability; (2) the seriousness of the intrusion into the close relatives' right to privacy that disclosure of the material would cause; (3) the availability, from other sources—including other public records—of material that is equally relevant to the evaluation of the same governmental action but is less intrusive on the right to privacy; and (4) the availability of alternatives other than full disclosure that might serve to protect both the interests of the public and the interests of the victims. *Id.*

[852] *Id.* at 2271.

[853] *See* Family Protection Act, FLA. STAT. § 406.135 (2003).

[854] *Personal Information: Data Brokers: Hearing on S.B. 550 Before the Senate Judiciary Comm.*, 2005-2006 Leg., Regular Sess. 11 (Cal. 2005) [hereinafter *California Hearings*] (statement of Sen. Speier, bill author).

[855] *Id.*

[856] Data files may be acquired for consumer marketing or employment screening and may contain personally identifiable information such as Social Security numbers, account numbers, and driver's license numbers.

[857] *California Hearings, supra* note 854, at 2 (statement of Sen. Speier); *see also* discussion *supra* Chapter IV § C-1(b).

State legislative responses have focused primarily on (1) improving security measures for the systems that store personal information; (2) requiring notification to individuals in the event of a security breach; and (3) enabling individuals to place security alerts or freezes on their credit reports. These are all helpful steps in preventing identity thieves from using the personal information held by data brokers to their advantage. However, because of the high value placed on personal information, individuals also expect to have control over access or the right to obtain disclosure of information held by data brokers.[858] In California, businesses currently are required to disclose to customers, upon request, the categories of personal information shared with third parties for marketing purposes.[859]

Finally, in addition to allowing individuals access to their personal information, state legislatures are evaluating mechanisms to ensure the accuracy of the data that is held. At present, individuals lack the ability to check for inaccuracies and correct errors.[860] The ability to verify is a critical right because some inaccurate information that is collected and disclosed to third parties, such as whether one is a convicted felon,[861] is highly harmful.

In 2002, California, the state trendsetter with regard to privacy laws, enacted a security-breach notification statute[862] requiring data brokers to notify California residents whenever the data broker has a reasonable belief that unencrypted personal information has been acquired by an unauthorized person.[863] At the time of the ChoicePoint security breach in February 2005, California was the only state to require data brokers to notify individuals when their information had been compromised. Indeed, the ChoicePoint breach became known to the public only because the company was required to follow California law. Since the highly publicized breach, at least thirty-five state legislatures have introduced legislation modeled on California's security-breach notification law. Currently, at least nineteen states have signed into law a requirement

---

[858] *California Hearings, supra* note 854, at 11 (statement of Sen. Speier).

[859] CAL. CIV. CODE § 1798.83 (2005).

[860] *California Hearings, supra* note 854, at 12 (statement of Sen. Speier).

[861] For example, in the 2000 presidential election approximately 2000 Florida voters whose voting rights had been automatically restored in other states were kept off the rolls and, "in many cases, denied the right to vote." Robert E. Pierre, *Botched Name Purge Denied Some the Right to Vote*, WASH. POST, May 31, 2001, at A01.

[862] CAL. CIV. CODE § 1798.29 (2003); CAL. CIV. CODE § 1798.82–.84 (2005).

[863] Personal information triggering the notice requirement is the individual's name plus one or more of the following: Social Security number, driver's license or state ID card number, or financial account numbers.

that data gatherers notify residents of a security breach in their personal information.[864]

According to Timothy Skinner,[865] security-breach notification laws serve a twofold purpose. First, notification enables affected individuals to take steps, such as canceling credit cards and contacting credit bureaus, to prevent misuse of their personal information.[866] The sooner individuals are notified of a security breach, the more likely it is that the damage can be averted.[867] Second, security-breach notification laws help ensure that data brokers put in place reasonable security measures for personal information.[868] There is a strong incentive to secure the systems that store personal information because "[c]ompanies do not want to get to the point of notification."[869] Notification of a security breach is not only bad for business and embarrassing, but it forces data brokers to inform individuals that they are collecting their personal information. Nevertheless, notice should not occur only when there has been a security problem; all individuals should have access to all information about themselves held by data brokers.

In May 2005, the California Senate passed legislation that provides guidance for the regulation of data brokers. Significantly, the California Data Brokers Access and Accuracy Act[870] requires data brokers to allow individuals the right to request disclosure of all their personal information compiled and maintained by the data broker. Further, the data broker must provide disclosure of the specific sources of the data about the individual.[871] Much like the federal Fair and Accurate Credit Transactions Act,[872] which entitles consumer to obtain one free credit report annually, the California

---

[864] 2005 Ark. Acts 1167; 2005 Conn. Pub. Acts 148; DEL. CODE ANN. Tit. 6, § 12B-101-06 (2008); FLA. STAT. § 817.5681 (2005); S.B. 230, 148th Gen. Assem., Reg. Sess. (Ga. 2005); 2005 Ill. Laws 36; 2005 Ind. Acts 503; 2005 La. Acts 499; 2005 Me. Acts 379; 2005 Mont. Laws 518; 2005 Nev. Stat. 485; 2005 N.D. Laws 447; R.I. Gen. Laws § 11-49.2-7 (2008); 2005 Tenn. Pub. Acts 473; TEXAS BUS. & COM. CODE § 48.103 (2005); WASH. REV. CODE § 19-42.17 (2005).

[865] See Timothy H. Skinner, *California's Database Breach Notification Security Act: The First State Breach Notification Law Is Not Yet a Suitable Template for National Identity Theft Legislation*, 10 RICH. J.L. & TECH 1 (2003).

[866] *Id.* at 21.

[867] *Id.*

[868] *Id.* at 24.

[869] *Id.*

[870] S.B. 550, 2005-2006 Leg., Reg. Sess. (Cal. 2005) (enacted).

[871] *Id.*

[872] PUB. L. No. 108-159, 117 Stat. 1952 (2003) (amending 15 U.S.C. §§ 1681–1681u).

law requires data brokers are to disclose, free of charge, a single document containing the requested information once a year.[873] Although California proposes to limit the type of information that must be disclosed as well as the categories of entities to which it applies,[874] the Data Brokers Access and Accuracy Act may become a model for both federal and state legislation, as well as the de facto standard for the data-broker industry.

The second major element of the act focuses on the accuracy of the information maintained by data brokers. As discussed earlier, when individuals are notified and obtain access to their personal information, they may find that the information is "riddled with errors."[875] Inaccurate information may or may not be harmful, and it may not have been disclosed to a third party. Nevertheless, individuals lack the ability to correct errors contained in the report. Opponents of a provision that would have enabled individuals to request and remove inaccuracies held by data brokers successfully argued that it is unreasonable to require data brokers to make corrections when the source information is a public record.[876] Data brokers argue that they cannot make changes to the information held in their databases unless they determine that it is inconsistent with the source.[877] Still, state legislatures may look to the federal Fair Credit Reporting Act[878] to address the issue of inaccurate information held by data brokers. The act allows individuals to dispute information contained in their credit reports and lays out a process that credit-reporting agencies must follow to verify the accuracy of the disputed information.[879]

---

[873] Cal. S.B. 550.

[874] For example, personal information that must be disclosed does not include information derived from the media or other public sources, used for processing a financial service requested by the individual, or used solely for fraud prevention or to comply with the Patriot Act. Moreover, the term "data broker" is narrowly defined to exclude governmental entities, financial institutions regularly engaged in an activity regulated by the Fair Credit Reporting Act, certain health insurers, and Internet service providers not regularly engaged in the compilation of consumer data.

[875] STAFF, ANALYSIS OF S.B. 550, 2005-2006 Leg., Reg. Sess., at 2 (Cal. 2005).

[876] Id.

[877] For example, Acxiom's privacy policy states that "[i]f an individual wants to change or correct inaccurate information or have that information removed . . . he or she should contact the source of the information. These sources include telephone companies and county clerks' offices. Since Acxiom is not the original source, we do not alter the information in our databases unless we discover it is inconsistent with the source." Acxiom, http://www.acxiom.com (last visited May 16, 2008).

[878] 15 U.S.C. §§ 1681–1681u (2000).

[879] Id.

States provide a separate and distinct source of policies for addressing privacy invasions. With explicit conditional protections and varied statutory remedies, state policies accord an important option for protecting privacy and operate as important laboratories for privacy policy.

D. Tort Protections

Beyond constitutional and statutory remedies are the privacy torts that are the progeny of Warren and Brandeis and further described by Prosser.[880] Where the intruder is a private entity, tort law may provide a remedy against an invasion of privacy. The courts began to accept the concept as early as 1905.[881]

Prior to Warren and Brandeis's landmark law-review article, privacy had some protections under early common law. Trespass law protected individuals from physical invasion of their property by others.[882] Criminal law protected individuals from personal assault and from eavesdropping. Libel law was available to protect individuals against damage to their reputation caused by untruths, although truth was a defense to any libel action. The Fourth Amendment protected the privacy of the home and led to legislation protecting messages sent by telegraph, but both applied only to governmental intrusions. Injunctions were available to prevent the publication of private letters, but such injunctions were based on the property right the owner had in the physical object of the letter itself, rather than its contents.[883]

Historical circumstances may have fostered public support for distinct privacy rights because of the cultural and social changes brought about by industrialization and urbanization.[884] The Industrial Revolution caused many people to live in overcrowded conditions, thereby reducing individual privacy.[885] As Warren and Brandeis pointed out in "The Right to Privacy," previous common-law actions used to safeguard privacy, such as criminal law protecting individuals from personal assault and trespass

---

[880] See Prosser, *supra* note 31; *see* Warren & Brandeis, *supra* note 22.
[881] See Pavesich v. New England Life Ins. Co., 50 S.E. 68 (1905) (holding that the unauthorized use of an individual's picture in an insurance company's advertisement was a violation of privacy protected by tort law but emanating from natural law).
[882] Ken Gormley, *One Hundred Years of Privacy*, 1992 Wis. L. Rev. 1335, 1343.
[883] Benjamin C. Bratman, *Brandeis and Warren's* The Right to Privacy *and the Birth of the Right to Privacy*, 69 Tenn. L. Rev. 623, 634 (2002).
[884] *Id.* at 644.
[885] *See id.*

law protecting individuals from physical invasion of their property by others, were unable to fully guard against invasions of privacy rights in an increasingly urban society.[886]

All tort remedies face hurdles similar to those faced by other privacy protections, including challenges raised by freedom of speech and press[887] and a shifting definition of "reasonableness" as it is applied in privacy torts. This reasonableness standard is contingent upon the unpredictable and ever-changing cultural standards of the community.[888] For example, Alaska considers itself to have a populace who expect more privacy then citizens of other states. Reasonableness may be set by a judge or a jury, depending on the situation.[889] The actual test of reasonableness is applied in slightly different ways in each type of tort.[890] One's "reasonable expectation" may be directly affected by one's personal conduct.[891] If particular

---

[886] Gormley, *supra* note 882, at 1352.

[887] *Id.* at 1374–91.

[888] *See* Ravin v. State, 537 P.2d 494, 503–04 (Alaska 1975) ("In Alaska we have also recognized the distinctive nature of the home as a place where the individual's privacy receives special protection. This court has consistently recognized that the home is constitutionally protected from unreasonable searches and seizures, reasoning that the home itself retains a protected status under the Fourth Amendment and Alaska's constitution distinct from that of the occupant's person. The privacy amendment to the Alaska Constitution was intended to give recognition and protection to the home. Such a reading is consonant with the character of life in Alaska. *Our territory and now state has traditionally been the home of people who prize their individuality and who have chosen to settle or to continue living here in order to achieve a measure of control over their own lifestyles which is now virtually unattainable in many of our sister states*.").

[889] For example, in City of North Miami v. Kurtz, 653 So. 2d 1025, 1029 (Fla. 1995), the Florida Supreme Court held that, as a matter of law, "Florida's constitutional privacy provision does not afford the applicant . . . [a] . . . reasonable expectation of privacy." In Diaz v. Oakland Trib. Inc., 139 Cal. App. 3d 118 (Ct. App. 1983), in contrast, reasonableness was decided by the jury. By comparison, juries routinely determine whether defendants in negligence claims acted reasonably under the circumstances. *See, e.g.,* Southern Ry. Co. v. Mann, 108 So. 889, 891 (Fla. 1926) ("The question of whether or not the agents of the company (defendant) exercised all ordinary and reasonable care and diligence in approaching the crossing was one of fact to be determined by the weight and probative force of the evidence as other questions of fact are determined.").

[890] The reasonable-expectation question related to torts is presented in different forms for different torts: (1) an intrusion upon solitude or seclusion must be "highly offensive to a reasonable person," RESTATEMENT (SECOND) OF TORTS, § 652(b) (1977); (2) false light requires that the impression created be "offensive to a reasonable person," *id.* § 652E; and (3) public disclosure of private facts is defined as publicizing a matter that would be "highly offensive to a reasonable person," *id.* § 652D.

[891] *See* discussion *infra* note 1028–34 referencing the first *Girls Gone Wild* case (plaintiff had knowingly exposed herself in a public place, so she did not have a reasonable expectation of privacy); *see also* Post-Newsweek Stations v. Doe, 612 So. 2d 549 (Fla. 1993). In a case dealing with the release of information as opposed to a tort action for damages, the court said, "Because the Does' privacy rights are not implicated when

conduct is viewed by society as immoral, then it is likely that the privacy of that conduct will not be protected.[892] But definitions of "reasonable expectation" are unpredictable. In one outrageous result, the Supreme Court of Mississippi found that a video made by a husband of his wife's homosexual encounter, through the window of a bedroom, did not invade a reasonable expectation of privacy, because the husband was in a child-custody battle.[893] It should be said that the dissent in this case was strong,[894] and no other courts have reached a remotely similar result.

Freedom of the press is one of the biggest barriers to tort remedies.[895] Ironically, the growth of journalism and photography in the late nineteenth century, and the abuse of the press in disseminating information, was one of the principal reasons Warren and Brandeis published "The Right to Privacy."[896] Nevertheless, as will be seen in the discussion of each tort, protecting free speech remains a priority.

It is important to understand that the tort remedies are pursued for damages incurred by the release of information, with the exception of the intrusion-upon-seclusion tort, in which the wrong is the intrusion rather than the release of information. In the context of seeking damages for publication, it is critical to understand that once information is released, if the information is newsworthy, it can be published and will be protected speech that will not support liability. There are examples in which a court may preclude the public release of information for privacy purposes, but if that same information is already available to a press source, publication of the information would not result in damages. These cases are two examples:

- *State v. Rolling.* A court refused to release crime-scene photos because of the horrific impact the release would have on relatives.[897]
- *New York Times Co. v. NASA.* A court refused to release an audio tape from the crash of the space shuttle Challenger under the privacy exception to the Freedom of Information Act.[898]

---

they participate in a crime, we find that closure is not justified." *Id.* at 552. This conclusion was criticized strongly by the dissent, since the parties' names had only been in a prostitute's book of "Johns" and they had not even been charged with a crime.

[892] *See* discussion *supra* Chapter IV, § B-2.

[893] Plaxico v. Michael, 735 So. 2d 1036, 1039–40 (Miss. 1999).

[894] *Id.* at 1040–41.

[895] *See* discussion *supra* Chapter IV, § A.

[896] *See* Gormley, *supra* note 882, at 1352.

[897] 22 Media L. Rep. (BNA) 2264 (Fla. Cir. Ct. 1994).

[898] 782 F. Supp. 628 (D.D.C. 1991).

In each of these cases, had the information been released, it could have been published under First Amendment protections and very likely not punishable under tort law. If a newspaper photographer had taken a crime-scene picture in a public place, that picture could be publishable as newsworthy. Defining "newsworthy" is a difficult task, but if an event occurs in a public place and is of interest to the public, the courts will usually defer to the First Amendment.[899] The moral of these stories is that if information is in the possession of a public body and has not yet been released, there may be a better chance of stopping its release than punishing its publication. In more than one case involving the publication of sensitive information, the U.S. Supreme Court has barred states from punishing the press for publishing accurate information available in the public record.[900] These publications were protected, even in the case of the publication of such sensitive information as the name of a rape victim[901] and the names of juvenile offenders.[902]

There are four categories of privacy invasions recognized in tort law: appropriation of name or likeness, intrusion upon seclusion, false light, and public disclosure of private facts.[903]

1. Appropriation of Name or Likeness and "Right of Publicity"

"Appropriation" and "right of publicity" have been treated as slightly different means to protect the unauthorized use of a person's name or likeness. Two different restatements describe these remedies.[904] A commentator suggests that "appropriation" is a remedy for harms to dignity and "right of publicity" is a remedy for harms to the pocketbook.[905]

---

[899] *See* discussion *infra* Chapter VII, § B-4.
[900] *See* Cox Broadcasting Corp. v. Cohn, 420 U.S. 469, 496–97 (1975).
[901] *See id.* at 491; *see also* Florida Star v. B.J.F., 491 U.S. 524 (1989).
[902] *See* Oklahoma Publ'g Co. v. Dist. Court, 430 U.S. 308 (1977).
[903] *See* Prosser, *supra* note 31, at 383.
[904] RESTATEMENT (SECOND) OF TORTS § 652C (1977); RESTATEMENT (THIRD) OF UNFAIR COMPETITION § 46 (1995).
[905] 1 J. THOMAS McCARTHY, THE RIGHTS OF PUBLICITY AND PRIVACY § 5:64 (2d ed. 2006).

	Appropriation	Right of publicity
Infringing act	unpermitted use of identity	unpermitted use of identity
Impact	on personal dignity	on property right in persona
Measure of damage	mental/physical injury	damage to the value of identity/persona

The tort of appropriation of name or likeness is the unauthorized use of another's name or likeness for a commercial advantage.[906] Truth of the depiction is not a defense or an issue, as it is in false light, and there is no need to show that the information is sensitive, as in public disclosure of private facts. Although defendants often raise the argument that celebrity status "waives" any right of publicity, the right of publicity actually protects the proprietary commercial value of identity, regardless of celebrity status.[907] This right is protected as a common-law right and has also been protected by statutes.[908]

There is some developing federal case law suggesting that state-law remedies for the tort of misappropriation or the right of publicity are preempted by federal copyright laws.[909] However, in *Toney v. L'Oreal*, the Seventh Circuit revisited an earlier decision[910] and held that the right of publicity claim was not preempted by the federal copyright laws.[911] The court reasoned that the right of publicity is a broader right that encompasses not just copyrightable material but a person's intangible identity.[912] Therefore, it is possible that a person could sue for both copyright infringement and "appropriation" or "right of publicity."

Even though this privacy tort can be split into "appropriation of personality" and "right of publicity," with "publicity" protecting property rights and "appropriation" protecting personal dignity,[913] the Eleventh Circuit in *Alloson v. Vintage Sports Plaques* concluded that they represent the

---

[906] RESTATEMENT (SECOND) OF TORTS § 652C (1977) ("One who appropriates to his own use or benefit the name or likeness of another is subject to liability to the other for invasion of his privacy.").

[907] 1 McCARTHY, *supra* note 905, § 5:65; *see also* Carson v. Here's Johnny Portable Toilets, Inc., 698 F.2d 831, 834 (6th Cir. 1983) ("[T]he right of privacy and the right of publicity protect fundamentally different interests and must be analyzed separately.").

[908] *See* Prosser, *supra* note 31; CAL. CIV. CODE § 3344 (Deering 2008); FLA. STAT. § 540.08 (2007); N.Y. CIV. RIGHTS LAW § 51 (Consol. 2008).

[909] *See* Toney v. L'Oreal USA, 384 F.3d 486 (7th Cir. 2004).

[910] *Id.*

[911] Toney v. L'Oreal, 406 F.3d 905, 910 (7th Cir. 2005). In *Toney*, a model contracted with a company to use her likeness for the packaging and advertising of a hair product. A subsequent assignee of the contract used the model's likeness past the date set in the contract, and the model was found to have the right to sue under the Illinois Right of Publicity Act.

[912] *Id.*

[913] *See* 1 McCARTHY, *supra* note 905, § 5:64; Robert C. Post, *Rereading Warren and Brandeis: Privacy, Property and Appropriation*, 41 CASE W. RES. L. REV. 647, 677–79 (1991) ("It is not enough, therefore, simply to split the contemporary appropriation tort into two, half protecting dignity and half property, and leave the election to the plaintiffs. In the end, there will be times when we will be forced to choose the circumstances in which we will protect one aspect of personality or the other.").

same interests. In that case the court stated, "We read Alabama's commercial appropriation privacy right, however, to represent the same interests and address the same harms as does the right of publicity as customarily defined."[914] But there may well be circumstances that compel a choice of one remedy or the other.

Appropriation typically applies when an individual's picture or name is used in connection with the promotion of a product or service.[915] The privacy interest protected by the appropriation tort is the individual's interest in the exclusive use of his or her identity, as it is represented by his or her name or likeness, to the extent that it might benefit that individual or others.[916] A simple example would be a cereal company using an unauthorized photograph of a celebrity on its boxes as an endorsement of its product. A more complicated example might be an advertisement featuring a recognizable trait of a celebrity or celebrity persona, without the actual use of a name or photograph.[917] This component of the tort acknowledges that "likeness" can be something identifiable other than simply a name or a face.[918]

A victim of appropriation may suffer distinct losses, both financial and to one's dignity.[919] The plaintiff may be successful (even if the plaintiff is a public figure and the information conveyed is newsworthy) as long as there is the requisite commercial intrusion.[920] Nonetheless, in some situations a claim may be barred if the intrusion is newsworthy or protected by freedom of expression.[921] In other words, it depends on the circumstances. There is no bright-line test.

---

[914] Alloson v. Vintage Sports Plaques, 136 F.3d 1443 (11th Cir. 1998) (concluding that "there was no significant difference between Alabama's commercial appropriations privacy tort and the right of publicity").

[915] See Pavesich v. New England Life Ins. Co., 50 S.E. 68 (1905); see also RESTATEMENT (SECOND) OF TORTS § 652C cmt. b (1977).

[916] RESTATEMENT (SECOND) OF TORTS § 652C cmt. a (1977).

[917] See, e.g., White v. Samsung Elec. Am., Inc., 971 F.2d 1395, 1399 (9th Cir. 1992), reh'g denied, 989 F.2d 1512 (9th Cir. 1993), cert. denied, 508 U.S. 951 (Cal. 1991) (company's advertisement used a robot dressed like game show hostess Vanna White and placed next to a game board similar to Wheel of Fortune set was held to be a sufficient "likeness" to support a right of publicity action).

[918] Carson v. Here's Johnny Portable Toilets, Inc., 698 F.2d 831 (1983) (holding that use of the phrase "Here's Johnny" was enough to support a claim).

[919] See Theodore F. Haas, Storehouse of Starlight: The First Amendment Privilege to Use Names and Likenesses in Commercial Advertising, 19 U.C. DAVIS L. REV. 539 (1986).

[920] See Grant v. Esquire, Inc., 367 F. Supp. 876 (S.D.N.Y. 1973); Zacchini v. Scripps-Howard Broadcasting Co., 433 U.S. 562 (1977).

[921] See, e.g., Montgomery v. Montgomery, 60 S.W.3d 524 (Ky. 2001) (holding that a son's use of his deceased father's voice and likeness in a music video did not violate the right of publicity because it was protected by freedom of expression).

In a right-of-publicity case involving pure commercial speech (an advertisement that does no more than propose a commercial transaction), a plaintiff need not show intent to identify the plaintiff.[922] However, when the use occurs in noncommercial speech, the First Amendment's protections apply, and intent must be proved. Actual malice is required for a public figure to recover damages,[923] and intent is required for a non-public figure. Again, the results are driven by the facts. A magazine's publication of a photograph of Dustin Hoffman in the film *Tootsie* was deemed protected speech.[924] The results would be different if the same picture were used in a commercial advertisement.

Similarly, statutes can create causes of action for appropriation of name or likeness.[925] An example of how statutory interpretation can limit this remedy is *Tyne v. Time Warner Entertainment Co.*[926] In *Tyne*, the family of the lead character portrayed in the novel and film *The Perfect Storm* brought an appropriation claim against the makers of the film.[927] The family claimed that the film misappropriated their father's personality by modeling the main character on his life for commercial benefit without the family's permission and mischaracterizing Mr. Tyne and portraying the story as true.[928] The plaintiffs also had to demonstrate that Time Warner knowingly disregarded the truth for the publication not to be protected speech.[929] Again, newsworthiness is not a defense in appropriation cases involving advertising.[930] The Eleventh Circuit did not find that Tyne's portrayal in this movie was protected speech, so the action was not limited by the First Amendment.[931] The circuit court certified the question to the Florida Supreme Court of whether the statute covered a

---

[922] *See* RESTATEMENT (THIRD) OF UNFAIR COMPETITION § 46 cmt. e (1995).

[923] *See* Hoffman v. Capital Cities/ABC, Inc., 255 F.3d 1180, 1186 (9th Cir. 2001). In this case, the Ninth Circuit held that a magazine's use of altered photographs of Dustin Hoffman in the film *Tootsie* was protected speech. The photographs were not part of an advertisement, and the fact that they may have helped sell copies of the magazine was not enough to qualify them as commercial speech. Therefore, Hoffman, a public figure, had to prove actual malice by clear and convincing evidence.

[924] *Id.*

[925] *See* CAL. CIV. CODE § 3344 (Deering 2008); FLA. STAT. § 540.08 (2007); N.Y. CIV. RIGHTS LAW § 51 (Consol. 2008).

[926] 336 F.3d 1286 (11th Cir. 2003).

[927] *Id.* at 1288.

[928] *Id.*

[929] *Id.* at 1290.

[930] FLA. STAT. § 540.08(4). Under the Florida statute a true protrayal in advertising would support liability but the same portrayal in a "bona fide news report" would not.

[931] *Tyne*, 336 F.3d at 1292–93.

movie as a commercial activity.[932] In Florida, appropriation of name or likeness is a statutory claim, and an individual whose name is misappropriated must prove that the depiction was egregiously false.[933] The Tynes ultimately were denied recovery because the statute was interpreted by the Florida Supreme Court to apply to misappropriation of personality only in an advertising context and not to other commercial activities such as a movie.[934] This restrictive interpretation ends up severely limiting the statutory right. Under this interpretation, it seems that relief will be available only to celebrities because advertisers are unlikely to use images of regular people.[935]

This remedy is important in dealing with certain types of abuses because of its characterization as protecting a property interest. But the practical utility of this remedy is curtailed by the pervasive limitation of the remedy to the use of information in advertising only.[936]

2. Intrusion upon Seclusion

The tort of intrusion upon seclusion involves the act of prying or intruding into an individual's affairs. This remedy, in effect, provides us spatial privacy. This tort is distinct from the other three because no publication of the private intrusion is necessary—the intrusion itself is the tort.[937]

---

[932] *Id.* at 1293.

[933] FLA. STAT. § 540.08(1)(c).

[934] *Tyne*, 336 F.3d at 1292–93.

[935] *But see* Gritzke v. MRA Holdings, LLC, No. 4:01CV495-RH, 2002 WL 32107540 (N.D. Fla. Mar. 15, 2002) (holding that where a young woman was used in advertising for *Girls Gone Wild* videos without her permission, recovery under this statute was possible because the representation was used in advertising). (This case is discussed *infra* in text accompanying notes 1018–27).

[936] The remedy is further limited in some states that only extend a right of publicity to living persons. *See* Shaw Family Archives, Ltd. v. CMG Worldwide, Inc., 486 F. Supp. 2d 309 (S.D.N.Y. 2007) (holding that under both New York and California laws at the time of her death, Marilyn Monroe's right of publicity of her image—including the iconic photograph of the star standing on a subway gate—died with her and was not descendible). California has since adopted a postmortem property right. *See* CAL. CIV. CODE § 3344.1(Deering 2008); *see also* N.Y. CIV. RIGHTS LAW § 50 (CONSOL. 2008) (no descendible right of publicity).

[937] *See* RESTATEMENT (SECOND) OF TORTS § 652B cmt. b (1977) ("The invasion may be by physical intrusion into a place in which the plaintiff has secluded himself, as when the defendant forces his way into the plaintiff's *room in a hotel* or insists over the plaintiff's objection in entering his home.... It may be by *some other form of investigation or examination into his private concerns,* as by opening his private and personal mail, searching his safe or his wallet, examining his private bank account, or compelling him by a

This tort requires that the intruder pry into something private and that a reasonable person would find the intrusion objectionable.[938] For example, when someone eavesdrops on another's private conversation through electronic means, a court is likely to find that an intrusion of privacy has occurred.[939]

Courts generally do not extend the privacy-intrusion tort to news-gathering activities conducted in a public place, because there is no reasonable expectation of privacy,[940] or to private activities once they are deemed newsworthy.[941] Ultimately, a plaintiff's ability to recover under this tort is directly related to potentially varying interpretations of the definition of "seclusion" and "newsworthiness."

Intrusions can be into physical locations, such as a home or hotel, or personal "spaces," such as a bank account. A direct physical intrusion on one's body also has been held to be an intrusion within the scope of this tort.

The case of *Allstate Insurance v. Ginsberg* is an example of a case in which the court rejected an intrusion-upon-seclusion case when personal sexual harassment was alleged.[942] The court held that the remedy for intrusion is limited to a "'place' in which there is a reasonable expectation of privacy . . . not a body part."[943] Pointing out that the Supreme Court of Alabama had expanded the tort of invasion of privacy to include a sexual-harassment claim,[944] the *Ginsberg* court expressly declined to recognize the definition of actionable intrusion in section 867 of the *Restatement of Torts*, which includes "the wrongful intrusion into one's private activities

---

forged court order to permit an inspection of his personal documents. The *intrusion itself* makes the defendant subject to liability, even though there is no publication or other use of any kind of the photograph or information outlined.").

[938] *See id.* § 652B (1977) ("One who intentionally intrudes, physically or otherwise, upon the solitude or seclusion of another or his private affairs or concerns, is subject to liability to the other for invasion of his privacy, if the intrusion would be highly offensive to a reasonable person.").

[939] *See* Nader v. General Motors Corp., 255 N.E.2d 765 (1970) (holding that no invasion of privacy occurs when information known about an individual is discovered, but recognizing an invasion where defendant eavesdropped on plaintiff's private conversations and where plaintiff proved that defendant "overzealously" kept him under surveillance).

[940] Ethan E. Litwin, *The Investigative Reporter's Freedom and Responsibility: Reconciling Freedom of the Press with Privacy Rights*, 86 GEO. L.J. 1093, 1095 (1998).

[941] *See* Bartnicki v. Vopper, 532 U.S. 514 (2001).

[942] 863 So. 2d 156 (Fla. 2003).

[943] *Id.* at 162.

[944] *Id.* at n.3 (citing Phillips v. Smalley Maintenance Servs., Inc., 435 So. 2d 705, 711 (Ala. 1983)).

in such manner as to outrage or cause mental suffering, shame, or humiliation to a person of ordinary sensibilities."[945]

Under section 652B of the *Restatement (Second) of Torts*, discussing intrusion upon seclusion, the definition of "intrusion" is extended to include any invasion of the solitude or private affairs of another—an alternate act apart from one involving an intrusion into a physical place.[946] Thus, the *Second Restatement* definition focuses on the conduct of the intruder, not merely the place of the intrusion.

The chief justice of Florida, Harry Lee Anstead, joined by Justices Pariente and Quince, dissented, stating that "[h]ere, the alleged victim was obviously not 'left alone' and her privacy was violated in the most personal and intimate way."[947] Citing numerous cases recognizing an actionable invasion-of-privacy claim for unreasonable touching or comments, Chief Justice Anstead concluded that the unwelcome sexual touching of a person's body intrudes upon a person's physical solitude and seclusion and thus that "allegations of such intrusions do state a cause of action for invasion of privacy as a physical intrusion into one's personal and private quarters."[948]

A successful claim alleging invasion of privacy relating to sexual harassment under the definitions of intrusion articulated by the *Second Restatement* and the Alabama court would stand in sharp contrast to the *Ginsberg* rule, requiring a plaintiff to show that "the matters intruded into are of a private nature and that the intrusion would be so offensive or objectionable that a reasonable person subjected to it would experience

---

[945] RESTATEMENT OF TORTS § 867 (1939).

[946] RESTATEMENT (SECOND) OF TORTS § 652B (1977).

[947] *Ginsberg*, 863 So. 2d at 165 (Anstead, C.J., concurring in part and dissenting in part).

[948] *Id.; see also* Kelley v. Worley, 29 F. Supp. 2d 1304, 1311 (M.D. Ala. 1998) (asserting that plaintiff's invasion-of-privacy claim based on defendant's sexually harassing acts of physical contact at work should have survived defendant's summary-judgment motion); Vernon v. Med. Mgmt. Assoc. of Margate, Inc., 912 F. Supp. 1549, 1561 (S.D. Fla. 1996) (holding that the plaintiff's invasion-of-privacy claim showing "a pattern of persistent touching, squeezing, fondling, hugging, blowing and tickling, along with the repetition of lewd and vulgar sexual remarks" should have survived a motion to dismiss); Stockett v. Tolin, 791 F. Supp. 1536, 1556 (S.D. Fla. 1992) ("[T]he repeated and offensive touching of the most private parts of Plaintiff's body . . . constitutes an intrusion into [the plaintiff's] physical solitude amounting to an invasion of privacy under Florida law."); Rogers v. Loews L'Enfant Plaza Hotel, 526 F. Supp. 523, 528 (D.D.C. 1981) (holding that plaintiff stated a claim for invasion of privacy where she alleged that her supervisor repeatedly called her at home and at work to make lewd comments about her sex life).

outrage, mental suffering, shame, or humiliation."[949] This requirement replaces the *Ginsberg* mandate that the intrusion be into a "place" where one has a reasonable expectation of privacy with a more practical threshold, calling for a reasonably offensive act and extending the potential for recovery to acts that occur in public places, like the workplace. This expanded definition of the intrusion tort would arguably allow a plaintiff to recover damages from another who uses a secret camera to record images from underneath one's skirt or down one's blouse, regardless of the fact that the recording occurred in the middle of a busy public sidewalk or shopping mall and not in a restroom stall or dressing room.

When a plaintiff claims intrusion upon seclusion based on the defendant's actions toward the plaintiff's deceased relative, the claim may be struck down if the plaintiff cannot show that the defendant invaded the plaintiff's privacy as well. In *Rothstein v. Montefiore Home*,[950] a nursing-home applicant's estate and widow sued the nursing home for invasion of privacy, alleging that the nursing home disclosed the applicant's financial information.[951] The court stated that liability for intrusion upon seclusion occurs when a person "intentionally intrudes, physically or otherwise, upon the solitude or seclusion of another or his private affairs or concerns, . . . if the intrusion would be highly offensive to a reasonable person."[952] Deciding that the estate could not bring a claim for invasion of privacy because the right is personal, the court then analyzed whether the trial court was correct in granting summary judgment to the nursing home.[953]

Reviewing the nursing home's actions de novo, the court stated that for the applicant's privacy to be invaded, the nursing home's conduct in releasing the application to her stepdaughter must be "highly offensive to the reasonable person."[954] Noting that the information was not disclosed to the public, but rather to a family member, the court stated that it could not find the nursing home's conduct highly offensive to a reasonable person.[955] Thus, the court upheld the district court's grant of summary

---

[949] 62A Am. Jur. 2d *Privacy* § 65 (2005) (citing *Ex parte* Atmore Cmty. Hosp., 719 So. 2d 1190 (Ala. 1998)).

[950] 689 N.E.2d 108 (Ohio Ct. App. 1996).

[951] *Id.* at 109. The information was allegedly disclosed to the applicant's stepdaughter. *Id.* The financial information disclosed included the applicant's tax returns and a listing of assets. *Id.* at 111.

[952] *Id.* at 110 (quoting Restatement (Second) of Torts § 652B (1977)).

[953] *Id.* at 111.

[954] *Id.* (citing Sustin v. Fee, 431 N.E.2d 992, 993–94 (Ohio 1982)).

[955] *Id.* at 112.

judgment, finding that the plaintiff could not establish a prima facie case to maintain her invasion-of-privacy claim.[956]

Recovery results are inconsistent to say the least. In one case a newspaper was liable for printing the picture of a woman whose skirt had been blown up over her head.[957] In another case, a newspaper was not liable for printing the picture of a boy playing soccer that showed his genitalia.[958]

Finally, this tort may be of great long-term value because courts may chose to define "intrusion" more broadly in the future. Further, because this tort is not always negated by First Amendment protections, because it is focused on the intrusion not its publication, this tort can avoid one of the primary barriers to privacy remedies.

3. False Light

The tort of false light involves the publishing of facts presenting an individual in a manner inconsistent with his or her attributes.[959] Therefore, unlike intrusion upon seclusion, or the right of publicity and public disclosure of private facts, false light requires that the defendant covey an untruth. For example, individuals may claim false light when a reporter or newspaper writes an untrue or defamatory story about them.[960] The use of truthful information also can give rise to a false-light claim when the information is used in a way that portrays a person in a manner that amounts

---

[956] *Id.*

[957] Daily Times Democrat v. Graham, 162 So. 2d 474 (Ala. 1964).

[958] *See* McNamara v. Freedom Newspapers, Inc., 802 S.W.2d 901 (Tex. App. 1991).

[959] *See* RESTATEMENT (SECOND) OF TORTS § 652E (1977). Section 652E provides:
One who gives publicity to a matter concerning another that places the other before the public in a false light is subject to liability to the other for invasion of his privacy, if:
(a) the false light in which the other was placed would be highly offensive to a reasonable person, and
(b) the actor had knowledge of or acted in reckless disregard as to the falsity of the publicized matter and the false light in which the other would be placed.

[960] *See, e.g.,* Cantrell v. Forest City Publ'g Co., 419 U.S. 245 (1974) (finding that an article published in the respondent's newspaper placed the petitioner in a false light because of significant misrepresentations). In *Cantrell*, the petitioner's husband and forty-three other people died in an Ohio bridge collapse in 1967. One year after the collapse, a reporter did a follow-up story to show the impact of the collapse on the petitioner's family. The reporter interviewed the petitioner's children and took fifty pictures while the petitioner was away. The article depicted the family's abject poverty with photographs and a description of the children's old, ill-fitting clothes and the deteriorating condition of their home. The petitioner claimed that the article portrayed her family incorrectly and that the false story made them the objects of pity and ridicule.

to a distortion of his or her true attributes.[961] False light differs from defamation in that defamation requires harm to an individual's reputation in the community, whereas false light requires that the conduct be highly offensive to a reasonable person, without requiring damage to the individual's reputation.[962] In other words, defamation is an intrusion on status, and false light is a injury to dignity. False light, therefore, is potentially more expansive. Furthermore, in contrast to defamation, false light applies only to information alleged to be factual or true that portrays the plaintiff inaccurately; it does *not* apply to opinions.

Tort law analyzes a claim for false light differently depending on whether the matter disclosed is of public interest and whether the individual is a public or private figure. In cases involving public figures where the matter is of public interest, the court may require a showing of actual malice to find that the defendant committed a wrong.[963] However, when a private individual is involved, the court may not require proof of actual malice, but instead may require a showing of negligence.[964] So a newspaper that acts reasonably will not be liable for mistaken inaccuracies that are newsworthy. Libel law also gives the news entity a path to rectify the mistake.[965]

---

[961] *See, e.g.,* Heekin v. CBS Broadcasting, Inc., 789 So. 2d 355 (Fla. Dist. Ct. App. 2001) (reversing summary judgment in favor of broadcaster that aired an interview containing true facts about plaintiff in connection with stories about domestic violence). However, after remand and another appeal, the Second District Court of Appeals dismissed as a matter of law the same complaint upheld in *Heekin I* because, after actually viewing the allegedly false-light piece, the trial court ruled that it created no false impression. *Heekin v. CBS Broadcasting, Inc.,* 892 So. 2d 1027 (Fla. Dist. Ct. App. 2004).

[962] *See* Denver Publ'g Co. v. Bueno, 54 P.3d 893 (Colo. 2002) (discussing the differences and similarities between defamation and false light and ultimately deciding that Colorado will not recognize the tort of false light, because of its extensive overlap with the tort of defamation and its potential to chill speech protected by the First Amendment); *see also* Diane L. Zimmerman, *False Light Invasion of Privacy: The Light That Failed,* 64 N.Y.U. L. Rev. 364 (1989) (critiquing the false-light tort); *cf.* Bryan R. Lasswell, *In Defense of False Light: Why False Light Must Remain a Viable Cause of Action,* 34 S. Tex. L. Rev. 149 (1993) (defending the existence of the false-light tort). For example, a pilot was portrayed as praying to Jesus when he was actually Jewish; the action is not detrimental in society but is harmful to him.

[963] *See* New York Times Co. v. Sullivan, 376 U.S. 254 (1964).

[964] *See* West v. Media Gen. Convergence, Inc., 53 S.W. 3d 640, 648 (Tenn. 2001).

[965] State libel laws may allow for retractions and corrections to avoid liability. For example, Florida law provides that if it appears that libelous statements were made in good faith, criminal proceedings will be discontinued and barred if "a full and fair correction, apology, and retraction was published in the same editions or corresponding issues of the newspaper or periodical in which said article appeared, and in as conspicuous place and type as was said original article." Fla. Stat. § 836.08 (1980). Additionally, some statutes eliminate the recovery of damages when the retraction or correction meets certain criteria. *See* Twin Coast Newspapers, Inc. v. Superior Court, 208 Cal. App. 3d 656, 658 (Ct. App. 1989) (find-

Stories about individuals who are not public figures may be declared newsworthy even if they are highly offensive. Frequently, stories about victims of crimes or their relatives may be offensive but newsworthy. In *Romaine v. Kallinge*, individuals who had been held hostage by a psychotic killer sued the author and publisher of a book detailing the ordeal, claiming false light and public disclosure of private facts.[966] The plaintiffs alleged that a statement in the book falsely implied criminal conduct or associated them with drug users, thus casting them in a false light.[967] The court stated that liability for false light would be found when "[o]ne ... gives publicity to a matter concerning another that places the other before the public in a false light [and]; (a) the false light in which the other was placed would be highly offensive to a reasonable person, and (b) the actor had knowledge of or acted in reckless disregard as to the falsity of the publicized matter and the false light in which the other would be placed."[968] The court found that the statement in the book could not reasonably be interpreted as associating the plaintiffs with illegal drug activity.[969] Furthermore, the court noted that the sentence was only a minor or insubstantial portion of the overall text, and therefore, any inaccuracies or false statements could not "fairly be regarded as highly offensive to a reasonable person as a matter of law."[970]

The court also addressed a claim of public disclosure of private facts. The court stated that an invasion of privacy occurs "when it is shown that the matters revealed were actually private, that dissemination of such facts would be offensive to a reasonable person, and that there is no legitimate interest of the public in being apprised of the facts publicized."[971] Although the court noted that the facts disclosed in the book "would be highly offensive to a reasonable person," the court held that *the newsworthiness exception applied because the facts were of legitimate concern to the public*

---

ing a newspaper immune from liability for general or punitive damages when the retraction appears in as conspicuous a manner as the statements claimed to be libelous appeared).

[966] 537 A.2d 284 (N.J. 1988). A statement in the book that the victims were meeting to relate news "about a junkie they both knew who was doing time in prison" was the basis for the false-light claim. *Id.* at 288–89. The public-disclosure claim was based on a chapter's narration of the events. *Id.* at 289.

[967] *Id.* at 293.

[968] *Id.* at 294 (citing RESTATEMENT (SECOND) OF TORTS § 652E (1977)).

[969] *Id.* at 295–96.

[970] *Id.* at 296.

[971] *Id.* at 297 (citing Bisbee v. John C. Conner Agency, 186 N.J. Super. 340 (A.D. 1982); RESTATEMENT (SECOND) OF TORTS § 652D (1977)).

and were a part of the public court record.[972] The court also stated that the intense publicity at the time of the event described in the book strongly indicated that the material was newsworthy.[973] Thus, the court held that the information contained in the book was entitled to protection, and the plaintiffs' privacy was not.[974]

It is possible for publication of *truthful* information to result in false-light liability. For example, publishers might choose to print truthful information but not all the information, and thereby convey a false impression. What if a newspaper published a story saying that "Mrs. Smith had sex with a man who was not her husband" and did not disclose the fact that she had been raped? That text is a truthful statement that places Mrs. Smith in a false light and implies a falsehood.

To sustain a false-light claim based on truthful information, the plaintiff must meet a higher standard. The plaintiff must prove that the publicized information was, as *perceived* by the public, false, that it placed the plaintiff in a false light, and that the defendant knew or should have known of its falsity.[975] When seeking a remedy for publication of true information, the plaintiff must prove intent and establish that intent by clear and convincing evidence.[976] This is a high standard but a necessary hurdle for a plaintiff to clear in order to bring a false-light invasion-of-privacy claim based on publication of truthful information. As the Supreme Court has stated, the risk of abuse to one's name from publication of truthful information is an "essential incident of life in a society which places a primary value on freedom of speech and of press."[977]

It is also possible that a claim for false light could exist where there is no defamation. A situation in which a false-light action might be available but a defamation action might not was presented by the case involving Jews for Jesus. A newsletter for the organization reported that the plaintiff had converted to Christianity.[978] That was not the plaintiff's recollection

---

[972] *Id.* at 298–99 (emphasis added); *see also* Cox Broadcasting Corp. v. Cohn, 420 U.S. 469, 494–95 (1975).

[973] *Romaine*, 537 A.2d at 302–03; *see also* RESTATEMENT (SECOND) OF TORTS § 652D cmt. f (1977) ("Those who are the victims of crime or are so unfortunate as to be present when it is committed . . . are regarded as properly subject to the public interest.").

[974] *Romaine*, 537 A.2d at 305.

[975] *See* Cantrell v. Forrest City Publ'g Co., 419 U.S. 245 (1974); Time, Inc. v. Hill, 385 U.S. 374, 387–88 (1967).

[976] Machleder v. Diaz, 801 F.2d 46, 56 (2d Cir. 1986); Peoples Bank & Trust Co. v. Globe, 978 F.2d 1065, 1068 n.2 (8th Cir. 1992); Ashby v. Hustler Mag., 802 F.2d 856, 860 (6th Cir. 1986); Stanley v. General Media Com., 149 F. Supp. 2d 701, 707 (W.D. Ark. 2001).

[977] *Hill*, 385 U.S. at 388.

[978] Rapp v. Jews for Jesus, 944 So. 2d 460, 462 (Fla. Dist. Ct. App. 2006).

and she sued.[979] The appellate court held that no defamation existed because the statements did not harm her reputation in the larger community.[980] But, the court said, under the *Restatement* it was possible that she had been portrayed in a false light that was highly offensive to a reasonable person and that hurt and damaged her.[981] The fact that a false-light case could exist without defamation is one of the reasons false light is controversial to some commentators.[982]

False light is an asset to privacy remedies because it is more expansive than defamation. However, it is still limited by the requirement of falsity and the fact that, even in the case of falsity, if there is not negligence or knowledge of falsity, the First Amendment will likely prevent liability of a publisher.

4. Public Disclosure of Private Facts

The tort of public disclosure of private facts is defined as the publication or public disclosure of private information about an individual, such that a reasonable person would object to the matter being made public.[983] Public disclosure of private facts differs from false light because the information disclosed may be true, but it must be of such a sensitive or personal nature that an individual of reasonable sensitivity would find its publication offensive. For instance, abortion-clinic protesters holding signs that reveal the names of women about to receive abortions could be considered highly offensive to a reasonable person and of little concern to the public.[984] However, when the information is truthful and part of a public record, courts are not likely to find an invasion of privacy.[985] There are exceptions

---

[979] *Id.*

[980] *Id.* at 465.

[981] *Id.* at 465–66.

[982] *See, e.g.*, Gannett Co., Inc. v. Anderson, 947 So. 2d 1 (Fla. Dist. Ct. App. 2006).

[983] RESTATEMENT (SECOND) OF TORTS § 652D (1977) ("One who gives publicity to a matter concerning the private life of another is subject to liability to the other for invasion of his privacy, if the matter publicized is of a kind that (a) would be highly offensive to a reasonable person, and (b) is not of legitimate concern to the public."). The *Restatement* further explains that enforcement of public disclosure may be limited by free-speech and free-press provisions of the First Amendment. *See* New York Times Co. v. Sullivan, 376 U.S. 254 (1964).

[984] *See* Doe v. Mills, 536 N.W.2d 824, 829 (Mich. Ct. App. 1995) (holding that the defendant-protesters' actions, alleged by the plaintiffs to be highly offensive and calculated to embarrass and offend plaintiffs, were "sufficient to constitute a question for the jury regarding whether embarrassing private facts were involved in a public disclosure").

[985] *See, e.g.*, Cox Broadcasting Corp. v. Cohn, 420 U.S. 469 (1975) (holding that accurate publication of the name of a rape victim obtained from publicly available official court

to this rule. For example, in *Melvin v. Reid* (also known as the *Red Kimono* case), a film company was held liable for telling a true story, from public records, of a former prostitute.[986] This exception, a California case, tends to prove the rule that most courts and now the U.S. Supreme Court hold that when information is open to the public, the press cannot be punished for publishing it.[987] This rule clearly makes a great deal of sensitive information available to the press for publication. Another threshold question for this tort is what constitutes "public disclosure." Interestingly, disclosure to other individuals does not always constitute "public" disclosure.[988]

Courts have held that no showing of intent is necessary for a plaintiff to recover under the tort of public disclosure of private facts. For instance, in *Cason v. Baskin*, the famous author Marjorie Kinnan Rawlings was sued for invasion of privacy for publishing private facts in her novel *Cross Creek*.[989] The lower court ruled that Ms. Rawlings had not invaded the plaintiff's privacy. The Florida Supreme Court reversed and stated that malice was not required for the tort of public disclosure of private facts.[990] Ultimately, the case was a landmark for privacy law, but the actual recovery of damages was very small.[991]

If facts are newsworthy, their publication will be protected, even if the facts are personal and sensitive. If a person is a public figure, or even if an individual is a private person involved in a newsworthy event, what would normally be private can be published without liability.[992]

---

records did not violate the plaintiff's right of privacy because the events reported were of legitimate public concern).

[986] 297 P. 91 (Cal. Dist. Ct. App. 1931); *see also* Briscoe v. Reader's Digest Ass'n, 483 P.2d 34 (Cal. 1971).

[987] *Cox Broadcasting*, 420 U.S. at 469.

[988] RESTATEMENT (SECOND) OF TORTS § 652D cmt. b (1977)("[I]t is not an invasion of the right to privacy . . . to communicate a fact concerning the plaintiff's life to a single person or even a small group of persons."). This portion of the *Restatement* has come under serious criticism. Jonathan B. Mintz, *The Remains of Privacy's Disclosure Tort: An Exploration of the Private Domain*, 55 MD. L. REV. 425, 438 (1996).

[989] 20 So. 2d 243 (Fla. 1945).

[990] *Id.* at 246.

[991] After four years of litigation, the plaintiff was awarded only one dollar and court costs because she "[did] not show that [she] ha[d] thereby sustained any actual or compensatory damage as a result of the publication by the defendant." Cason v. Baskin, 30 So. 2d 635, 640 (Fla. 1947).

[992] *See* Shulman v. Group W. Productions, Inc., 955 P.2d 469 (Cal. 1988). In *Shulman*, a cameraman for a television show accompanied a rescue helicopter to an accident scene. Once there, the cameraman filmed the rescue workers' extrication efforts, as well as treatment efforts and transport in the rescue helicopter. The footage was later broadcast

In *Diaz v. Oakland Tribune, Inc.*, the court recognized that malicious intent was not one of the four elements required to find liability for public disclosure.[993] Intent or malice was only necessary for determining punitive damages.[994]

In an action for public disclosure of private facts, newsworthiness and First Amendment protections are consistent barriers because many courts define newsworthiness expansively. It seems that the courts are hesitant to find liability in the disclosure of truthful information even when it is gossip, hurtful, and not part of public debate.[995]

The fact is that current society defines less and less to be private. People are putting personal information on Web sites, such as MySpace and YouTube, that would be unthinkable even thirty years ago. Those disclosures are obviously not private facts. Further, if sensitive facts that we do not wish to disclose are newsworthy, they can be published.

5. Privacy Torts Generally

Although tort law may provide some protection for privacy rights, there are substantial limits. Each of the torts has its distinct elements of proof. But all have some similar limits. The right does not survive the death of an individual[996] and is not assignable.[997] It is recognized as a personal right and does not extend to family members.[998] Also, First Amendment

---

on a television show. The segment included the plaintiff telling rescue workers that "I just want to die. I don't want to go through this." The plaintiff, who consented to none of the filming or recording of the events that left her a paraplegic, sued for public disclosure of private facts. The California Supreme Court found that the story was of a legitimate public interest (newsworthy), as were the plaintiff's words, and therefore that the plaintiff could not meet the elements of the private-facts tort.

[993]   139 Cal. App. 3d 118, 126–27 (Ct. App. 1983).

[994]   *Id.* at 135–36.

[995]   *See* discussion *infra* Chapter VII § B-4; *see also* Zimmerman, *supra* note 35, at 295 n.11.

[996]   *See* RESTATEMENT (SECOND) OF TORTS § 652I cmt. b (1977). But some appropriation-of-personality statutes grant surviving relatives a right to protect the deceased's rights. *See* CAL. CIV. CODE § 33441.1 (2000); FLA. STAT. 496 § 540.08 (1997); N.Y. CIV. RIGHTS LAW §§ 50, 51 (2000).

[997]   *See* RESTATEMENT (SECOND) OF TORTS § 652I cmt. a (1977). *But see id.* § 652C cmt. a (analogizing an individual's right against appropriation of name or likeness to a property right, the use of which may be assigned to a third person).

[998]   *See* discussion of relational privacy *infra* Chapter IV, § E-5.

rights can preclude any of the tort actions if the disclosure of information is deemed newsworthy or protected speech.[999]

One example of tort law's deficiency in protecting informational privacy rights is a case involving the unauthorized publication of a family member's autopsy photographs. In *Williams v. City of Minneola*, police officers gratuitously disclosed photographs and a videotape of an autopsy.[1000] The appellants, the mother and sister of the victim, sued the police officers for invasion of privacy and then appealed the trial court's grant of summary judgment in favor of the police officers.[1001] A Florida appellate court noted that although there is no general prohibition against a family member claiming invasion of privacy when a deceased relative's autopsy photographs are revealed, "such relatives must shoulder a heavy burden in establishing a cause of action."[1002] The court went on to state that in unusual circumstances, a defendant's conduct toward a decedent may be "sufficiently egregious" to justify a separate cause of action brought by the immediate family members.[1003] It is interesting to note that the court discussed *Loft v. Fuller*,[1004] which suggested that grotesque pictures of a deceased relative's body may be of a nature sufficiently egregious to allow a family member to bring a separate invasion of privacy claim.[1005] Indeed, manipulation of lighting or the positioning of a body for the purpose of enhancing the shocking appearance may be sufficient to allow for tort recovery.[1006] Nevertheless, the *Williams* court held that because only a few people viewed the videotapes and photographs, the trial court did not commit a reversible error in granting summary judgment to the defendants.

Although tort law may not assist family members wishing to keep autopsy records confidential, state statutes may provide the means to do so. In *Campus Communications, Inc. v. Earnhardt*, the same court that decided *Williams* analyzed a claim for injunctive relief brought by the widow of racecar driver Dale Earnhardt against a newspaper publishing

---

[999] *See* discussion of newsworthiness *infra* Chapter VII, § B-4 and discussion of disclosure of public documents *supra* Chapter III, § B-4.

[1000] 575 So. 2d 683 (Fla. Dist. Ct. App. 1991), *rev. denied*, 589 So. 2d 289 (Fla. 1991).

[1001] *Id.* at 686.

[1002] *Id.* at 689–90 (citing Loft v. Fuller, 408 So. 2d 619 (Fla. Dist. Ct. App. 1981), *rev. denied*, 419 So. 2d 1198 (Fla. 1982)).

[1003] *Id.* at 690.

[1004] 408 So. 2d 619 (Fla. Dist. Ct. App. 1981), *rev. denied*, 419 So. 2d 1198 (Fla. 1982).

[1005] *See Williams*, 575 So. 2d at 690.

[1006] *Id.*

company to prevent disclosure of the deceased's autopsy photographs.[1007] The court analyzed the claim under section 406.135 of the Florida Statutes and held that the newspaper publishing company did not show good cause[1008] to overcome the statutory mandate of nondisclosure of autopsy photographs.[1009] Notably, the Family Protection Act was passed after Mr. Earnhardt's death and was designed to be applied retroactively. The court quoted the trial court's opinion, noting that publication of the autopsy photographs would cause the decedent's family members "deep and serious emotional pain, embarrassment, humiliation, and sadness."[1010] The death of Dale Earnhardt revealed the need for privacy protection beyond tort law when there is a strong public interest in personal information that should be kept confidential.

Often, multiple privacy torts are brought together in actions for violation of several distinct rights. For example, facts may support a suit for public disclosure of private facts and intrusion upon seclusion as well. In *Ledbetter v. Ross*, a social worker called a former patient's wife and told her that he (the social worker) had received confidential information during sessions with her husband concerning therapy she had undergone with a psychologist.[1011] The social worker then told her the details of the information.[1012] The woman sued for invasion of privacy, asserting claims for public disclosure of private facts and intrusion upon seclusion.[1013] The court found no

---

[1007] 821 So. 2d 388, 391–92 (Fla. Dist. Ct. App. 2002).

[1008] *See* FLA. STAT. § 406.135(2)(a) (2001) (stating that "upon a showing of good cause, [a court] may issue an order authorizing any person to view or copy a photograph or video recording of an autopsy or to listen to or copy an audio recording of an autopsy and may prescribe any restrictions or stipulations that the court deems appropriate. In determining good cause, the court shall consider whether such disclosure is necessary for the public evaluation of governmental performance; the seriousness of the intrusion into the family's right to privacy and whether such disclosure is the least intrusive means available; and the availability of similar information in other public records, regardless of form. In all cases, the viewing, copying, listening to or other handling of a photograph or video or audio recording of an autopsy must be under the direct supervision of the custodian of the record or his or her designee.").

[1009] *See id.* § 406.135(1) ("A photograph or video or audio recording of an autopsy in the custody of a medical examiner is confidential and exempt from the requirements of s. 119.07(1) and s. 24(a), Art. I of the State Constitution, except that a surviving spouse may view and copy a photograph or video or listen to or copy an audio recording of the deceased spouse's autopsy. . . . The custodian of the record, or his or her designee, may not permit any other person to view or copy such photograph or video recording or listen to or copy an audio recording without a court order. . . .").

[1010] *Earnhardt*, 821 So. 2d at 402.

[1011] 725 N.E.2d 120, 122 (2000).

[1012] *Id.*

[1013] *Id.*

public-disclosure invasion because the caller did not publicly divulge or disclose the information to anyone but Mrs. Ledbetter—and she already was aware of the fact she had received therapy.[1014] The court concluded that there was no public disclosure under these facts.

Addressing the intrusion-upon-seclusion claim, the court stated that the plaintiff must "demonstrate that there was an 'intrusion upon the plaintiff's physical solitude or seclusion, as by invading his home or other quarters'" and that "[t]o rise to the level of tortious conduct, 'the intrusion must be something which would be offensive or objectionable to a reasonable person.'"[1015] Following this standard, the court found that the defendant's phone call was not physically intrusive.[1016] Furthermore, the court held that the defendant's conduct was not "unreasonable," because there was only a single phone call with no threats or abusive language.[1017]

Another use of privacy torts that is evolving over time is the notion of privacy in public places. The intrusion might be couched in terms of an intrusion upon seclusion, public disclosure of private facts, false light, or even appropriation of personality. But there are multiple barriers to recovering for disclosure or recording something done in public.

Recent claims in the arena of tabloid news productions, an industry that typically relies on First Amendment protection for product marketing, raise new concerns about an individual's right to enjoy some level of privacy while in public view. In a controversial video and DVD series called *Girls Gone Wild*, young women have been filmed, in public, in various states of undress. These images, which typically portray college-aged women publicly exposing their breasts, buttocks, and genitalia at Mardi Gras and spring-break activities, have been amassed into *Girls Gone Wild* products and commercially marketed as *Girls Gone Wild* videos. These videos often depict young women who are intoxicated and coaxed by cameramen into undressing in public. Producers argue that they are merely documenting newsworthy celebration events and are thus entitled to First Amendment protection. Videos of the *Girls Gone Wild* genre fall into the general category of video voyeurism and raise questions about an individual's right to privacy in public places as well as issues involving knowledge and consent. Can a person protect against the dissemination of a recording of herself when

---

[1014] *Id.* at 123.
[1015] *Id.* (quoting W. PAGE KEETON ET AL., PROSSER AND KEETON ON THE LAW OF TORTS § 117, at 854–55 (5th ed. 1984)).
[1016] *Ledbetter*, 725 N.E.2d at 124.
[1017] *Id.*

such recording was made in a public place where no person would have a reasonable expectation of privacy? Can an intoxicated person legally consent to such a recording? Does a person who exposes parts of his or her body in public consent to being videotaped? Does that consent extend to viewing by the crowd, or does it extend to all persons in the future who may purchase a video of the act? And does public curiosity, in and of itself, amount to newsworthiness?

Becky Lynn Gritzke, a business major at Florida State University, was videotaped topless at a Mardi Gras celebration in New Orleans in 2001, but was never asked to sign a release. She was smiling, cupping her breasts, and looking into the camera, obviously aware that she was being recorded. Soon afterward, her friends reported seeing her in television ads for the *Girls Gone Wild* videos and DVDs. Her topless image also was depicted on the cover of the video she was in and on the Internet site associated with the video. Topless images of Ms. Gritzke even appeared on billboards in Europe with the caption "American Girls."

Ms. Gritzke brought suit against MRA Holdings, Inc. LLC, the company that produces and markets the *Girls Gone Wild* videos, which often appear on late-night television commercials, alleging that the use of her image on videotape covers and billboards violated both her privacy rights and statutory law.[1018] Florida law makes it a crime to "publish, print, display or otherwise publicly use for purposes of trade or for any commercial or advertising purpose the name, portrait, photograph, or other likeness of any natural person."[1019] Florida common law also recognizes tort claims for misappropriation of a person's likeness and portrayal of a person in a false light.[1020]

Ms. Gritzke eventually settled her claim against MRA, but only after the U.S. District Court for the Northern District of Florida denied MRA's motion to dismiss.[1021] Addressing Ms. Gritzke's common-law invasion-of-privacy claims, the court held that she was entitled to recover, provided that she could make an adequate factual showing in support of her claims at trial.[1022] In denying MRA's motion to dismiss, the court recognized the potential for recovery under Ms. Gritzke's claims that MRA misappropriated

---

[1018] Gritzke v. MRA Holdings, LLC, No. 4:01CV495-RH, 2002 WL 32107540 (N.D. Fla., Mar. 15, 2002).

[1019] FLA. STAT. § 540.08 (1998).

[1020] *See* Tyne v. Time Warner Entm't Co., 901 So. 2d 802 (Fla. 2005).

[1021] *See Gritzke*, 2002 WL 32107540.

[1022] *Id.* at *2.

her likeness "by commercial exploitation of her photograph without her consent" and portrayed her in a false light "by falsely suggesting [that she] willingly participated in and endorsed defendant's videotape."[1023] The court also held that she had a valid cause of action under section 540.08 of the Florida Statutes, Florida's "right to publicity" statute, because of MRA's publication of her photograph in Florida on *Girls Gone Wild* videotape covers and advertisements without her permission.[1024] Finally, the court held that she could potentially recover under Florida's Deceptive and Unfair Trade Practices Act,[1025] which makes unlawful "[u]nfair methods of competition, unconscionable acts or practices, and unfair or deceptive acts or practices in the conduct of any trade or commerce,"[1026] because MRA "used her photograph without her permission, in a manner falsely suggesting that [she had] endorsed defendant's product."[1027] Ultimately, the plaintiff did not recover under public disclosure of private facts or intrusion upon seclusion, because the circumstances did not support those remedies. But she was able to recover for the use of her image in advertising.

In a subsequent case brought by Veronica Lane, another Florida resident featured in a *Girls Gone Wild* video, Ms. Lane sued *Girls Gone Wild* producers in the U.S. District Court for the Middle District of Florida.[1028] That court held that Ms. Lane's claim under section 540.08 of the Florida Statutes was insufficient.[1029] The court, citing *Tyne v. Time Warner Entertainment Co.*,[1030] refused to allow her to recover because she failed to show that her name or likeness was used in advertising to directly promote a service or product.[1031] The court rejected Ms. Lane's arguments that she was either too intoxicated or too young to consent to the recording.[1032] Using the *Gritzke* analysis, the court granted summary judgment against Ms. Lane for her common-law claim for misappropriation of name or likeness, holding that appropriation was covered statutorily under section

---

[1023] *Id.*
[1024] *Id.*
[1025] FLA. STAT. §§ 501.201–.213 (2001).
[1026] *Id.* § 501.204(1).
[1027] *Gritzke*, 2002 WL 32107540, at *2.
[1028] Lane v. MRA Holdings, LLC, 242 F. Supp. 2d 1205 (M.D. Fla. 2002).
[1029] *Id.* at 1215.
[1030] 204 F. Supp. 2d 1338 (M.D. Fla. 2002).
[1031] *Lane*, 242 F. Supp. 2d at 1215.
[1032] *Id.*

540.08 of the Florida Statutes, which trumps any such common-law claim.[1033] The court also granted summary judgment against Ms. Lane for her false-light claim, holding that "[i]f the publicity is an accurate portrayal of the public display, [and] if the publicity is not unreasonable and false, then [a] plaintiff has no actionable privacy interest, even if the publicity has caused embarrassment, offense, or damage."[1034]

The *Lane* court was completely unsympathetic to Ms. Lane's privacy claims and distinguished her case from Ms. Gritzke's, noting that Ms. Lane's image was never used in any form of advertising. Perhaps the court found an inherent contradiction in a person who exposed herself to a complete stranger with a camera and then claimed infringement upon her right to privacy. Once Ms. Lane's age-based and intoxication-based claims of incapacity to consent to being recorded were rejected, the only necessary analysis was the extent to which an individual's reasonable expectation of privacy would preclude subsequent dissemination of the recording. The court ruled that there is no such reasonable expectation, limiting recovery to instances in which such a recording is directly used for the purpose of commercial advertising.

Interestingly, the *Girls Gone Wild* company was fined for failure to comply with a federal statute designed to protect against the use of underage persons in videos.[1035] So, in this case, the company was punished under a statute rather than held liable under a tort.[1036]

6. Conclusion

The traditional torts are important tools in seeking remedies to intrusions, but they have significant limitations. Because of the overlay of the

---

[1033] *Id.* at 1221–22 (citing FLA. STAT. § 540.08 (1998)).

[1034] *Id.* at 1222 (citing Easter Seal Soc. for Crippled Children & Adults v. Playboy Enters., Inc., 530 So. 2d 643, 647 (La. Ct. App. 1988)).

[1035] *See* Press Release, Dep't of Justice, *supra* note 816.

[1036] *Id.* "The entertainment company that produces the 'Girls Gone Wild' films and its founder pleaded guilty Tuesday to charges they failed to document the ages of female performers in sexually oriented productions. Mantra Films of Santa Monica, California, entered a plea agreement in a federal court in Panama City, Florida, the Justice Department said. Authorities said Joseph Francis, founder of Mantra Films and a related company, MRA Holdings, also agreed to plead guilty to charges to be filed later in Los Angeles, and to pay fines and restitution totaling $2.1 million." Terry Frieden, *'Girls Gone Wild' Producers Fined $2.1 Million*, CNN.COM, Sept. 12, 2006, http://www.cnn.com/2006/LAW/09/12/ggw.plea/index.html.

First Amendment, the torts are limited when the damage is caused by a disclosure that is "newsworthy." That determination depends directly on the facts in each case. For example, the disclosure of facts concerning an affair of the president of the United States would be newsworthy, whereas the same information about a private party could be an intrusion. As discussed above, an embarrassing picture of a young woman in a *Girls Gone Wild* video has no remedy, but the use of that same image in an advertisement is subject to liability under appropriation of personality. In some circumstances, the traditional torts of intrusion upon seclusion and appropriation of personality are not precluded by "newsworthiness" defenses. Is there a need for a new privacy tort or, can a broader interpretation provide better protection? These options will be discussed more fully in the remedies section of this book.[1037]

Because the goal is to achieve a remedy for intrusions, any injured person must look at all options for relief. In addition to traditional privacy torts and federal and state privacy policies, there are some specialized and targeted legal remedies for certain types of intrusions.

E. Other Legal Tools Used to Protect Privacy

Aside from the traditional privacy torts and federal and state constitutional protections, several other remedies protect the four spheres of privacy: autonomy, information, property, and personal physical space.[1038] Some tools relate to treating information as property and will be discussed more extensively in the next section. Others are suggested as new reforms. Those ideas will be discussed in the section on potential new remedies for the future.

Some of these remedies, such as intentional infliction of emotional distress, implied contract, trespassing, false imprisonment, and defamation, are rooted in the common law. These remedies protect information, property, and physical space. Relational privacy is not actually a distinct remedy, but rather a judicial doctrine that treats harm to a close relative as a harmful intrusion to the individual. This remedy is employed through court interpretation and through statutes.

[1037] *See* discussion *infra* Chapter VII, § B-4.
[1038] *See* discussion *supra* Chapter III, § A.

1. Intentional Infliction of Emotional Distress or Outrageous Conduct

This tort of intentional infliction of emotional distress or outrageous conduct ("IIED") protects against intrusions based on the malicious conduct of a defendant. One who by extreme and outrageous conduct intentionally or recklessly causes severe emotional distress to another is liable for such emotional distress.[1039] Additionally, if a member of the victim's immediate family is present during the intentional or reckless tortious act and suffers severe emotional distress as a result, the actor is liable for IIED regardless of whether the distress results in bodily harm.[1040] The actor also is liable to any other nonimmediate family member who is present and suffers bodily harm as a result of the severe distress caused by the actor's tort.[1041]

The IIED tort has been used as a remedy for the disclosure of harmful information about an individual.[1042] The law is still in a stage of development, and the ultimate limits of this tort have not yet been determined.[1043] It is not one of the four classic privacy torts, and it has limited utility because of the requirement of outrageous conduct on the part of the defendant. Although some courts have found liability, application is not uniform across jurisdictions. For example, one court considered the act of police officers showing a young boy an autopsy video not sufficiently outrageous to sustain the action.[1044]

It is not enough that a defendant acts with tortious, criminal, or even malicious intent.[1045] The court must first determine "whether the defendant's conduct may reasonably be regarded as so extreme and outrageous as to

---

[1039] RESTATEMENT (SECOND) OF TORTS § 46 (1977).

[1040] A proposed draft of section 45 of the *Third Restatement of Torts* may alter the analysis. In the draft version, comment l suggests that it would not suffice for the immediate family member to be merely "present" at the time of the outrageous conduct. The draft version would require the family member to have "contemporaneous perception of the event." RESTATEMENT (THIRD) OF TORTS: LIABILITY FOR PHYSICAL HARM § 45 (Tentative Draft No. 5, 2007).

[1041] *Id.* The proposed draft would expand on the treatment in section 46(2) of the *Second Restatement* of conduct "directed at" a third party by specifically stating that the claimant's emotional harm results from bodily or emotional harm to another.

[1042] RESTATEMENT (SECOND) OF TORTS § 46, cmt. c (1977).

[1043] *Id.*

[1044] *See* Williams v. City of Minneola, 575 So. 2d 683 (Fla. Dist. Ct. App. 1991); *see also* Hustler v. Falwell, 485 U.S. 46 (1988) (applying the First Amendment to this tort and finding sovereign immunity for actions of public employees).

[1045] RESTATEMENT (SECOND) OF TORTS § 46, cmt. d (1977).

permit recovery."[1046] If the judge believes it is reasonable, the question is then submitted to the jury to determine whether the facts justify recovery.[1047]

2. False Imprisonment: Trapping Schwarzenegger

The tort of false imprisonment arises if the personal liberty of a person is violated without lawful authority.[1048] For example, when the conduct of a photographer invades the privacy of an individual in such a way as to limit the individual's liberty, the tort of false imprisonment may apply. Such was the case in 1998 when photographers surrounded Governor Arnold Schwarzenegger's vehicle as he and his wife, Maria Shriver, picked up one of their children from day care.[1049] The event happened just one week after Governor Schwarzenegger underwent open-heart surgery, and Governor Schwarzenegger later testified that he thought it was a kidnapping attempt.[1050] The actions of the photographers caused Governor Schwarzenegger to get into an accident.[1051] Both photographers were convicted of misdemeanor false imprisonment and one was convicted of reckless driving.[1052]

In addition to proving confinement in a false-imprisonment action, a plaintiff must prove that the defendant intended a confinement, an assault, or a battery of the plaintiff or a third person.[1053] As illustrated by Governor Schwarzenegger's experience, the paparazzi, in their relentless pursuit of celebrity snapshots, sometimes cause harm to their targets. In April 2005, Reese Witherspoon had a similar altercation. When she exited her gym, paparazzi surrounded Ms. Witherspoon and besieged her car.[1054] The crowd became so thick and unwilling to move that Ms. Witherspoon could not leave the parking lot.[1055] When she was finally able to leave, the

[1046] Id cmt. h.
[1047] Id. (determining whether defendant's acts are "outrageous in character and extreme in degree").
[1048] Hamburg v. Wal-Mart Stores, Inc., 116 Cal. App. 4th 497 (Ct. App. 2004).
[1049] Pamela McClintock, Gubernator Snaps Back at Paparazzi, VARIETY, Oct. 2, 2005, available at http://www.variety.com/article/VR1117930079.html?cs=1&s=h&p=0.
[1050] Id.
[1051] Id.
[1052] Id.
[1053] RESTATEMENT (SECOND) OF TORTS § 35 (1965).
[1054] Wenn, Witherspoon in Paparazzi Attack, HOLLYWOOD.COM, Sept. 7, 2005, http://www.hollywood.com/news/Reese_Witherspoon_in_Paparazzi_Attack/2444751.
[1055] Id.

group followed her to her Los Angeles home, where they again surrounded her car and blocked her entrance to her own home.[1056] Ms. Witherspoon filed a (criminal) false-imprisonment claim against the reporters, but the district attorney's office dismissed the charges when it was unable to corroborate the facts as Ms. Witherspoon described them.[1057] If Ms. Witherspoon had pursued a false-imprisonment tort claim, she would have been required to prove intent on the part of the group to assault or imprison her. The individuals in the crowd of photographers may well have intended to prevent her movement in order to secure a prize photograph. That certainly would seem to be the case if they blocked her entrance into her home. However, the circumstances also may have been that the group formed no intent, but rather simply found themselves in a large, competitive crowd, pushing and shoving to get close to Ms. Witherspoon, with resulting confusion and inconvenience.

The privacy interest protected in these circumstances is the right to personal physical space. By impairing an individual's ability to move freely, the "imprisoners" have directly constrained the physical independence and personal privacy of the individual. These cases are not limited to paparazzi and celebrities. A private individual, if wrongly detained, has had his or her privacy rights violated and is entitled to compensation. For example, false imprisonment also encompasses the narrower tort of false arrest. An action for false arrest is predicated upon the lack of legal authority to arrest and detain an individual. This action requires either that the process used for the arrest was void on its face or that the issuing tribunal was without jurisdiction; it is not sufficient that the charges were unjustified.[1058] In some states, a claim for false arrest due to prolonged detention arises if the person is deprived of his or her liberty after the period of the arrest expires.[1059] Even absent probable cause, however, police officers have qualified immunity from criminal and civil liability for false imprisonment. If a police officer believed in good faith that probable cause existed, that officer is immune.

In *City of St. Petersburg v. Austrino*, a man was arrested at his house at 5 a.m. for allegedly altering a prescription for painkillers to include

---

[1056] D.A.: *Papparazzi Didn't Attack Witherspoon*, PEOPLE, Aug. 10, 2005, *available at* http://www.people.com/people/article/0,1092133,00.html.

[1057] *Id.*

[1058] Strickland v. Univ. of Scranton, 700 A.2d. 979 (Pa. Sup. Ct. 1997).

[1059] Martinez v. City of Los Angeles, 141 F.3d. 1373 (9th Cir. 1998).

a refill.[1060] An emergency-room physician prescribed the medicine, including a refill, because the plaintiff was in great pain and about to leave town.[1061] The inclusion of refills by emergency-room doctors was uncommon at this hospital.[1062] The arresting officer relied on hearsay from a night pharmacist, who had spoken to a nurse at the hospital uninvolved in treating the plaintiff.[1063] The officer never contacted the doctor who prescribed the refill or reviewed hospital documents before making the arrest.[1064] The court upheld the jury's finding for the plaintiff, which held the city 90 percent liable for the arrest.[1065] The court stated that "in the context of an arrest which requires probable cause, it is incumbent upon a police officer to make a 'thorough investigation and exercise reasonable judgment before invoking the awesome power of arrest and detention.'"[1066]

The remedy of false imprisonment is useful in specific circumstances of physical invasions. It provides a useful tool to protect against public or private types of intrusions that involve physical restraint.

3. Trespass

Trespass is another common-law remedy to redress an intrusion. The law of trespass is based on a person's unauthorized physical presence on the property of another and can protect one of the spheres of privacy: property. One incurs trespass liability by intentionally (a) entering the land in the possession of the other, or causing a thing or a third person to do so; (b) remaining on the land; or (c) failing to remove from the land a thing that one is under a duty to remove.[1067] Trespass liability is incurred regardless of whether the trespass causes any harm to a legally protected interest of another.[1068]

There is a strong need to protect people from intrusions made possible by technological advancements, such as zoom lenses and parabolic microphones.[1069] The principle of trespass can be expanded to protect against

---

[1060] 898 So. 2d 955 (Fla. Dist. Ct. App. 2005).
[1061] *Id.* at 957.
[1062] *Id.*
[1063] *Id.*
[1064] *Id.*
[1065] *Id.*
[1066] *Id.* at 959 (citing Mahon v. City of Largo, 829 F. Supp. 377, 386 (M.D.Fla.1993).
[1067] RESTATEMENT (SECOND) OF TORTS § 158 (1965).
[1068] *Id.*
[1069] Erwin Chemerinsky, *Protecting Privacy from New Technologies: The California Privacy Protection Act of 1998*, HUM. RTS., Fall 1999, at 13, *available at* www.abanet.org/irr/hr/fall99humanrights/chemerinsky.html.

electronic intrusions.[1070] Imagine an aggressive photographer—whether a fan, a paparazzo, or even a stalker—who stands on a ten-foot ladder on a public sidewalk to see over an eight-foot wall and take pictures with a zoom lens of a person's acts in that person's home.[1071] No trespass has occurred, but this behavior is exactly the kind of intrusion that the law of trespass aims to redress.[1072]

Further, taking, misusing, or intruding upon personal information is an intrusion that violates trespass principles just as an intrusion on property does. This idea is examined more in the section on property theory and in the section on remedies.[1073]

4. Contract Theory

Breach of contract is another possible remedy for protecting privacy. When companies post privacy policies on their Web sites or provide printed privacy policies to their customers, the companies are obligating themselves to adhere to certain terms. A violation of these terms potentially gives rise to claim by those affected. A company that communicates to its clients that personal information will be kept confidential and not be shared with third parties could face a breach-of-contract claim from clients if such information was divulged to a third party. In addition, the FTC may enforce a company's privacy policy.[1074] Examples of company privacy policies can be found in Appendix III.

Other potential uses of contract theory are the expansion of implied contract to deal with intrusive information disclosures and utilization of "unjust enrichment." These ideas will be examined in the remedies section.[1075]

[1070] This remedy may parallel the tort of intrusion upon seclusion.

[1071] Chemerinsky, *supra* note 1069.

[1072] *Id.*

[1073] See discussion *infra* Chapter IV, § F and Chapter VII, § B-5.

[1074] For example, the now-defunct online retailer Toysmart.com represented to consumers that personal information would never be shared with third parties. During its bankruptcy proceedings, the company sought to auction off its customer data to the highest bidder. The FTC intervened and prohibited this practice under its section 5 authority. *See* Press Release, FTC, FTC Announces Settlement with Bankrupt Website, Toysmart.com, Regarding Alleged Privacy Policy Violations (July 21, 2000), *available at* http://www.ftc.gov/opa/2000/07/toysmart2.shtm; *see also* discussion *supra* Chapter IV, § C-1(b).

[1075] *See* discussion *infra* Chapter VII, § B-8.

5. Relational Privacy: Protecting Families from Invasions

"Relational privacy" is not an actual common-law remedy as much as it is an approach to protect intrusions that occur to relatives of a deceased person. Privacy is generally considered a personal right that is held by an individual. That right expires with the individual's death and cannot be claimed by others. However, developing law and public policy have recognized the interests of parents, siblings, and spouses. These interests relate to the disclosure of information about a close relative and are protected either through the prevention of the publication of information or through recovery for damages from the release of the information.

The form and effect of these remedies is important. Preventing the release of sensitive information is a critical threshold. Section 7(c) of the Freedom of Information Act acknowledges the need to keep potentially harmful and intrusive information private. As discussed below, that act has been used to protect relatives. Courts also have chosen to restrict or deny access to sensitive information upon requests by relatives to protect their privacy.

Preventing the release of information is critical because once information has become public, disclosure by the press will almost always be protected speech and relatives will be unable to recover damages. Once information is public, the reproduction of that information in the press is almost universally protected. If the information involved is about a newsworthy event, such as the murder or suicide of a noteworthy person, the publication will certainly be protected speech. Consequently, when possible, preempting the release of information is an important strategy for relatives.

a. Legislation and Policy

Some legislatures have recognized the rights of relatives to prevent the public distribution of autopsy photographs, on the theory that public disclosure will harm close relatives.[1076] This logic has been applied at the federal level in a series of Freedom of Information Act cases that found the release of photos or other harmful information to be an unwarranted invasion of a relative's privacy.[1077]

[1076] *See* discussion *supra* Chapter IV, § D-5.

[1077] Nat'l Archives & Records Admin. v. Favish, 541 U.S. 157 (2004); Badhwar v. U.S. Dep't of Air Force, 829 F.2d 182 (D.C. Cir. 1987); New York Times Co. v. NASA, 782 F. Supp. 628, 631 (D.D.C. 1991).

There are some cases, including *Rolling v. State*,[1078] that examined the rights of parents and siblings to be protected from the public release of crime-scene and autopsy photos that would otherwise have been made public. The argument made[1079] and accepted by the court was that these close relatives had privacy rights of their own, separate and distinct from those of their deceased loved ones. This distinction is the principal point. Accepting this argument does not require the privacy right of a deceased to survive. There is a separate right attributed to the relatives. In *Reid v. Pierce County*, for example, the court held that "the immediate relatives of a decedent have a protectable privacy interest in the autopsy records of the decedent."[1080]

Another case in which relatives sought to protect the release of information that would otherwise become public was *Versace v. State Attorney of Florida (Dade County)*.[1081] The Versace family asked the Miami-Dade circuit court to close the extensive investigative files related to Gianni Versace's murder. One strong argument the family had was that since the killer, Andrew Cunanan, had committed suicide, no murder trial would occur. Therefore, the justification for closing the file was even stronger than in the *Rolling* case, in which there was in fact a penalty phase of the trial that used the evidence in question to impose the death penalty.

These issues are all about protection and preventing harm. None of these cases and statutes above provided economic relief to harmed relatives.

b. Torts and Economic Recovery

Economic and tort recoveries usually are not available to relatives. But there have been some examples. In the 1912 case of *Douglas v. Stokes*, parents hired a photographer to take only twelve pictures of their conjoined twins who had died.[1082] The photographer instead took thirteen pictures,

---

[1078] 22 Media L. Rep. (BNA) 2264 (Fla. Cir. Ct. 1994).
[1079] I made this argument on behalf of the families.
[1080] Reid v. Pierce County, 136 Wash. 2d 195, 212 (1998). In *Reid*, a number of families claimed that employees of the medical examiner's office in Pierce County, Washington, kept scrapbooks of autopsy photographs and displayed them at parties and road-safety classes without asking permission of the decedents' families.
[1081] *See* Complaint of Plaintiff, Versace v. State Attorney of Florida (Dade County), No. 97-29417 CA 32 (Fla. Cir. Ct. filed Dec. 30, 1997), *available at* http://www.courttv.com/archive/legaldocs/newsmakers/versace.html.
[1082] 149 Ky. 506, 509 (1912). " The most tender affections of the human heart cluster about the body of one's dead child. A man may recover for injury or indignity done the body

made copies from the negatives, and obtained a copyright for the thirteenth picture. He published the picture and was sued by the parents for publication of private facts. The court allowed recovery for the invasion of the parents' memory of their late children. In a later case, the Kentucky court clarified that the basis for recovery was not a property right but an intrusion upon a privacy right.[1083] There do not appear to be any modern cases that replicate these decisions.[1084] However, the circumstances in the *Stokes* case could well generate recovery today under the theory that the photographer had wrongly appropriated the personality of the children and profited from his action.

Because the tort of right of publicity is property-based, a relative may be able to recover for the illegal use of a person's identity after that person has died. There are several examples where relatives have recovered for appropriation of personality of a well-known relative after his or her death.[1085]

There are some torts that are in fact a proxy for a claim of invasion of privacy that are based on the conduct of a defendant, such as the intentional infliction of emotional distress.[1086] In *Williams v. City of Minneola*, a Florida court found that the family of a deceased fourteen-year-old boy had standing to bring a claim for intentional infliction of emotional distress after local law-enforcement officers played the boy's autopsy video at a party.[1087] The court held that a spouse, child, sibling, or parent could bring the action regardless of whether there was any physical harm.[1088] Further, a person may cause intentional infliction of emotional distress to a third party if the person's outrageous acts will reasonably cause severe emotional distress to that third party.[1089]

Some statutes allow economic and financial recovery for violations that occurred to a deceased relative. One example is section 1983 of the Civil Rights Act, which applies when the violation is by a public employee. Section 1983 is discussed elsewhere in this book.[1090]

---

and it would be a reproach to the law if physical injuries might be recovered for and not those incorporal injuries which would cause much greater suffering and humiliation."
[1083] Brents v. Morgan, 299 S.W. 967 (1927).
[1084] *See, e.g.*, Bazemore v. Savannah Hosp., 155 S.E. 194 (Ga. 1930). Georgia allowed parents to recover for the publication of private facts in a case involving a malformed child.
[1085] *See* discussion *supra* Chapter IV, § D-1.
[1086] *See* RESTATEMENT (SECOND) OF TORTS § 46 (1977).
[1087] 575 So. 2d 683, 690 (Fla. Dist. Ct. App. 1991), *rev. denied*, 589 So. 2d 289 (Fla. 1991).
[1088] *Id.* It should be noted that, ultimately, the family did not recover.
[1089] RESTATEMENT (SECOND) OF TORTS § 46 cmt. 1 (1965).
[1090] *See* discussion *supra* Chapter IV, § C-1(a)(iv) and *infra* Appendix I.

Perkins v. Principal Media Group, a case involving the broadcasting of an autopsy on the television show *True Stories from the Morgue*, provides an example of the panoply of options that can be sought by relatives.[1091] The attorney in that case believed that the relatives would be able to recover under several theories, including under section 1983 and for intentional infliction of emotional distress.[1092]

Nonetheless, it seems that there are major hurdles to seeking damages for an invasion of privacy to a deceased relative. Courts have been reluctant to extend the theories used to protect relatives from public releases of harmful images or of information about a deceased in order to allow a financial recovery after the release occurs.

6. Defamation

A defamation suit provides a remedy for harmful false statements made about an individual. Traditional common-law rules in the case of both libel and slander required the plaintiff to prove (1) defendant's publication to a third person (2) of defamatory material (3) concerning the plaintiff.[1093] Defamation law aims to protect a plaintiff's reputation. A defamatory statement is one that tends to lower the esteem with which the plaintiff is held in the community or to deter others from associating with the plaintiff.[1094] As explained above, defamation often overlaps with, though it differs from, the tort of false light.[1095] Although defamation is not normally defined as a privacy protection, as a remedy it acts to compensate a person who has been harmed by a disclosure. This harm is certainly related to privacy interests, and this remedy can be used to vindicate a harm to personal reputation and dignity associated with what we think of as privacy rights. The tort often does deal with the manner in which a person is presented to others and may sometimes concern private information. Defamation often is used to seek compensation for statements made by the press. Consequently, the First Amendment protections for such

---

[1091] Plaintiff's Memorandum in Opposition to Media Defendants' Motion to Dismiss at 16-20, Perkins v. Principal Media Group, No. 3:03-CV-00578 (M.D. Tenn., May 12, 2005). *See* discussion *infra* Chapter VI, § K.

[1092] Telephone Interview with David Smith, Law Offices of David Randolph Smith & Edmund J. Schmidt III, in Nashville, Tenn. (Dec. 20, 2006).

[1093] 2 DOBBS ON TORTS § 401 (2001).

[1094] RESTATEMENT (SECOND) OF TORTS § 559 (1965).

[1095] *See* discussion *supra* Chapter IV § D-3.

statements are in full force. If the disclosure is newsworthy, a remedy for defamation is unlikely.

For example, the bar is high for a public figure who wishes to pursue a claim of defamation. A public-figure plaintiff must prove actual malice by clear and convincing evidence in order to recover for defamation.[1096] Private persons enjoy a higher degree of protection, however, particularly when the matter is of a purely private concern. Therefore, private information may be protected through the use of defamation, provided that its revelation is harmful to the plaintiff's reputation.

In *Dunn & Bradstreet, Inc. v. Greenmoss Builders, Inc.*,[1097] the plaintiff sued a credit-reporting agency for distributing a false report to its subscribers that stated that the plaintiff had filed for bankruptcy. The information exchanged was confidential, and pursuant to the subscription agreement, subscribers were not permitted to share it with anyone else. The report injured the plaintiff, who sought compensatory and punitive damages.

The Supreme Court found that the speech in *Dunn & Bradstreet* involved a private figure and a matter of purely private concern.[1098] Therefore, the First Amendment did not serve as an obstacle to the punishment of the speech in question. Accordingly, the Court held that in matters involving private figures and matters of purely private concern, actual and punitive damages may be awarded without a showing of actual malice by clear and convincing evidence. The decision in *Dunn & Bradstreet* does not address this remedy in privacy terms. However, it is important for its recognition that disclosure of harmful information can be outside the First Amendment protection. Also important to note is the varying characteristics of defamation in different countries. As discussed elsewhere in this book, an action that would be protected speech in the United States may well constitute defamation in another country.[1099]

F. The Property-Theory Alternative: Protecting Privacy as Property

Because there are limitations to constitutional and tort remedies, property theory has been suggested as a means of securing privacy interests.

[1096] *See* New York Times Co. v. Sullivan, 376 U.S. 254 (1964).
[1097] 472 U.S. 749 (1985).
[1098] *Id.* at 762.
[1099] *See infra* note 1422.

In fact, property theory is already a fundamental part of the privacy-rights theory, particularly in actions for right of publicity and appropriation of personality.[1100] So if the thing we are trying to protect can be described as some type of property interest, then perhaps property-type remedies can augment the arsenal of privacy protections.

1. The Theory of Property Protection

Private property rights evolved from an individual's right to assert ownership derived from the value placed on production and labor.[1101] Property rights are often based on a theory of production and labor associated most frequently with John Locke—the right that every man has to the exclusive possession and control of the products of his own labor.[1102] The backbone of intellectual-property law is based on Locke's conception of property as the fruits of one's labor and as an extension of oneself. Under this theory, we gain a property right in something when it emanates from ourselves.

Modern courts still look to this production-and-labor theory of property to determine whether someone has a legally recognizable property interest in certain kinds of information. For example, confidential business information has long been recognized as property.[1103] One reason cited for extending property protection to business information is that "confidential information acquired or compiled by a corporation in the course and conduct of its business is a species of property to which the corporation has the exclusive right and benefit."[1104] Because the confidential information is generated from the business, the business has a right to decide how to use it.

The production-and-labor theory of property can be extended to include the protection of one's personality and personal information. In "The Right to Privacy," Warren and Brandeis pointed to the expenditure of thought and time necessitated by living life itself. For instance, they wrote:

> If the amount of labor involved be adopted as the test, we might well find that the effort to conduct one's self properly in business

---

[1100] *See* discussion *supra* note 143.
[1101] *See, e.g.,* Jefferys v. Boosey, (1854) 4 H.L. Cas. 815.
[1102] John Locke, Second Treatise on Civil Government: Two Treatises of Government (1690).
[1103] Carpenter v. United States, 484 U.S. 19, 26 (1987).
[1104] *Id.*

and in domestic relations had been far greater than that involved in painting a picture or writing a book; one would find it far easier to express lofty sentiments in a diary than in the conduct of a noble life.[1105]

Scholars have suggested the production-and-labor theory of property as a means to protect intimate details about a person's past. For instance, Edward Shils declares that the growth of individualism spawned the belief that "one's actions and their history 'belonged' to the self which generated them and were to be shared only with those with whom one wished to share them."[1106]

Another theory looks to originality and uniqueness as grounds for property rights.[1107] It is argued that the uniqueness of certain kinds of information and ideas are the true characteristics that tend to invoke property protection.[1108] Illustrating a key distinction between the production-and-labor theory of property and the originality theory of property, Warren and Brandeis note that intellectual property, unlike physical property, protects the *expression* of ideas, not necessarily the ideas themselves. Even though ideas were obviously the result of intellectual labor, the common law protected only the original expression of ideas. In other words, originality and uniqueness were more important under the common law than production and labor. Justice Holmes also emphasized the importance of originality in protecting a property right.[1109] In explaining the extent of copyright protection, Justice Holmes wrote, "Personality always contains something unique. It expresses its singularity even in handwriting, and a very modest grade of art has in it something irreducible, which is one man's alone. . . . That something he may copyright."[1110]

More-recent writers suggest that individuality, freedom, and privacy are intertwined with property and affect how people perceive themselves. In discussing the genesis of the Western philosophy that people are independent and free to pursue their own ends, Mona Amer notes the cultural

---

[1105]   Warren & Brandeis, *supra* note 22, at 206–07.
[1106]   Edward Shils, *Privacy: Its Constitution and Vicissitudes*, 31 LAW & CONTEMP. PROBS. 281 (1966).
[1107]   *See, e.g.*, Moore v. Regents of Univ. of Cal., 51 Cal. 3d 120 (1990).
[1108]   *See* Warren & Brandeis, *supra* note 22, at 206–07; *see also* Cabaniss v. Hipsey, 151 S.E.2d 496 (Ga. Ct. App. 1966).
[1109]   Bleistein v. Donaldson Lithographing Co., 188 U.S. 239 (1903).
[1110]   *Id.* at 250.

changes that have affected how individuals perceive themselves.[1111] She asserts that the concepts of private ownership and individuality developed concurrently, and that this concurrence "is likely more than coincidence—the sense of individuality can be said to arise from the private ownership of property."[1112] She further states that "[p]roperty, or rather the ability to acquire property, may even create the individual's sense of self. The right to own property separate and different from anyone else's is as fundamental to individuality as is the distinctness of the genetic code."[1113]

When lawyers discuss property, it is termed a bundle of rights. The legal definition of "property" most often refers not to the particular physical object, but rather to the legal bundle of rights recognized in that object. The "bundle of rights" that is associated with property includes the rights to possess, to use, to exclude, to profit, and to transfer.[1114] As courts have continually noted, "[o]wnership is not a single concrete entity but a bundle of rights and privileges as well as of obligations."[1115]

Rights within this "bundle" may be conferred, but they may be limited. The dissent in *Moore v. Regents of University of California* illustrates this proposition with a series of examples in which a property interest is found even though a law has limited some of the rights conferred on property.[1116]

The dissent stated that "both law and contract may limit the right of an owner of real property to use his parcel as he sees fit [citing zoning and nuisance laws]. Owners of various forms of personal property may

---

[1111]   Mona S. Amer, *Breaking the Mold: Human Embryo Cloning and Its Implications for a Right to Individuality*, 43 UCLA L. Rev. 1659, 1677 (1996).

[1112]   *Id.* at 1678.

[1113]   *Id.*; *see also* Margaret Jane Radin, *Property and Personhood*, 34 Stan. L. Rev. 957, 1004 (1982) ("A person cannot be fully a person without a sense of continuity of self over time. To maintain that sense of continuity over time and to exercise one's liberty or autonomy, one must have an ongoing relationship with the external environment, consisting of both things, and other people. . . . One's expectations crystallize around certain things, the loss of which causes more disruption and disorientation than does a simple decrease in aggregate wealth. For example, if someone returns home to find her sofa has disappeared, that is more disorienting than to discover that her house has decreased in market value by 5%.").

[1114]   *See* 63C Am. Jur. 2d *Property* § 1 (2007) ("As a matter of legal definition, 'property' refers not to a particular material object but to the right and interest in an object. 'Property' in a thing does not consist merely in its ownership or possession, but also in the lawful, unrestricted right of its use, enjoyment, and disposal. In its precise legal sense, property is nothing more than a collection of rights.").

[1115]   Union Oil Co. v. State Bd. of Equal., 60 Cal. 2d 441, 447 (1963).

[1116]   51 Cal. 3d 120, 165–66 (1990) (Mosk, J., dissenting).

likewise be subject to restrictions on the time, place, and manner of their use [citing public health and safety laws that restrict in various ways the manufacture and use of such property as food and drugs]."[1117] The dissent also noted that "some types of personal property may be sold but not given away, while others may be given away but not sold,"[1118] and that "others may neither be given away nor sold."[1119] The dissent explained that "the limitation or prohibition diminishes the bundle of rights that would otherwise attach to the property, yet what remains is still deemed in law to be a protectable property interest."[1120]

In other words, because property or title is a complex bundle of rights, duties, powers, and immunities, the pruning away of some or a great many of these rights does not entirely destroy the title or the label as property.

2. Using Property Theory in Privacy Protections

Courts have been willing to use property theory to protect what most would term typical personal privacy interests. A property interest may be recognized even though the law does not specifically label an object as property. In other words, when the law confers rights over a particular object, tangible or intangible, courts may find that such rights give rise to a protected property interest because they closely correspond to the bundle of rights by which property has traditionally been defined. For example, one state court recognized an individual's property interest in the deceased body of a loved one.[1121] Although state law did not label the relatives' right to the deceased body as a property interest, the court reasoned that regardless "of the legal label the State places on the rights in a dead body, . . . these rights nevertheless exist . . . [and] closely correspond

---

[1117]   *Id.* at 165.

[1118]   *Id.* at 166. For instance, a person contemplating bankruptcy may sell his or her property at its "reasonably equivalent value" but may not make a gift of the same property. *See* 11 U.S.C. § 548(a) (Supp. 2005). One may give away wild fish or game that he or she has caught or killed pursuant to a license but may not sell it. FISH & GAME CODE §§ 3039, 7121 (1984 & West Supp. 1993).

[1119]   *Moore*, 51 Cal. 3d at 166 (Mosk, J., dissenting). For example, a license to practice a profession, or a prescription drug in the hands of the person for whom it is prescribed.

[1120]   *Id.* at 165.

[1121]   Whaley v. County of Tuscola, 58 F.3d 1111 (6th Cir. 1995), *cert. denied*, 516 U.S. 975 (1995).

with the 'bundle of rights' by which property has been traditionally defined."[1122]

In *Arnaud v. Odom*, several parents brought suit in federal court contending that the Deputy Coroner had performed experiments on the bodies of their dead babies by dropping them onto a concrete floor in violation of their constitutional privacy and property rights.[1123] The court refused to invoke the federal constitutional right to privacy. Instead, the court suggested that state tort law sufficed to protect parents' privacy interests in their child's corpse, explaining that "by creating a quasi-property right of survivors in the body of a deceased relative and providing state tort claims to protect that right, the [state] . . . has recognized the intimacy and sanctity of that right."[1124] The court thus acknowledged the kinship between the common-law privacy tort and state property rights.

Additionally, in *Whaley v. County of Tuscola*, the court declined to dismiss a section 1983 suit alleging that the extraction of the corneas and eyeballs of deceased persons without obtaining their close relatives' consent deprived the relatives of constitutionally protected property without due process, in violation of the Fourteenth Amendment.[1125] Observing that traditionally, "property" has been conceptualized as a bundle of rights that includes the right to possess, to use, to exclude, to profit, and to dispose, the court found that Michigan law provided the next of kin with a constitutionally protected property interest in a deceased relative's body by protecting the right to possess the body for burial, to prevent its mutilation, and to dispose of it by gift.[1126] The court explained that "the existence of a constitutionally protected property interest [does] not rest on the label attached to a right granted by the state but rather on the substance of the right."[1127] Furthermore, the court disregarded the fact that Michigan courts remedy violations of such rights under the category of tort law rather than property law. Instead, the court concluded that these rights over the body rise to the level of constitutionally protected property rights because they closely correspond to the bundle of rights by which property has traditionally been defined. As the court said, "For this reason . . . we conclude that Michigan . . . provides the next of kin

[1122] *Id.* at 1117.
[1123] 870 F.2d 304 (5th Cir. 1989).
[1124] *Id.* at 311.
[1125] 58 F.3d 1111.
[1126] *Id.* at 1114.
[1127] *Id.*

with . . . a property interest in a dead relative's body, including the eyes. Accord-ingly, the next of kin may bring a constitutional claim under the Due Process Clause."[1128]

Interestingly, we may not own exclusive property rights to some components of our bodies. In deciding whether a plaintiff had a property right in his spleen cells, the Supreme Court of California, in *Moore v. Regents of University of California*, emphasized the importance of origi-nality and uniqueness in recognizing a property right.[1129] The court held that a patient did not have a conversion cause of action against his physi-cian for use of his spleen cells to patent a cell line, because the patient did not have a property interest in his cells.[1130] One reason offered for this determination was that the patient's cells were common to all men. The court explained:

> Lymphokines, unlike a name or a face, have the same molecular structure in every human being and the same, important functions in every human being's immune system. Moreover, the particular genetic material which is responsible for the natural production of lymphokines, and which defendants use to manufacture lym-phokines in the laboratory, is also the same in every person; it is no more unique to [the plaintiff] than the number of vertebrae in the spine or the chemical formula of hemoglobin.[1131]

The issue of ownership of cells or genetic material is a developing area that affects privacy and property rights.[1132]

As mentioned above, the right to exclude is an element of property rights. A good example of distinguishing a purely personal right from a property interest is Madhavi Sunder's analysis of the U.S. Supreme Court's decision to allow the exclusion of an openly gay and lesbian group from an Irish parade in South Boston.[1133] She argues that the Court constructed a property right out of the parade organizers' purely personal right to

---

[1128] *Id.* at 1117. *But see* Florida v. Powell, 497 So. 2d 1188, 1191 (Fla. 1986) (finding that a Florida statute authorizing the medical examiner to extract corneas from decedents during autopsies did not constitute a taking of the relatives' private property, because the next of kin possess no property right in the decedent's body).

[1129] 51 Cal. 3d 120 (Cal. 1990).

[1130] *Id.* at 138–39.

[1131] *Id.*

[1132] *See* ROBIN COOK, CHROMOSOME 6 (1997); Priscilla Wald, *What's in a Cell? Jon Moore's spleen and the Language of Bioslavery*, 36 NEW LITERARY HIST. 205 (2005).

[1133] Sunder, *supra* note 98.

freedom of expression.[1134] In *Hurley v. Irish-American Gay, Lesbian and Bisexual Group of Boston*, the Court held that the parade organizers had the right to exclude others so that communication produced by private organizers would not be shaped by all those who wished to join in with some expressive demonstration of their own.[1135] However, Sunder notes that although the Court protected a personal right to freedom of expression, the interest protected by the Court was akin to a property right. In supporting this proposition, she notes that the Court emphasized the organizer's previous conduct in relation to the parade.[1136] Because the members of the parade had *previously excluded* others from the parade, they subsequently gained the right to use the parade to express their own message.[1137] Therefore, the organizers' right to exclude and use the parade as they wished was based on its exercise of these rights in the past. Sunder argues:

> [A] property owner enjoys property rights of absolute use and exclusion only to the extent that she has already exercised such rights in the process of creating her property. This means that property rights are created when an author works through a process of creative use and exclusion to define her work and her relationship to it. The ensuing property right in law, granted as both reward and incentive for her labor, guarantees her continued right to absolute use and exclusion in the name of preserving her property.[1138]

This idea of being able to control a parade because it is "property" is analytically interesting and may provide another theory to argue that the exercise of autonomy or expression is an aspect of property rights.

The property approach to private interests contrasts with purely personal rights such as decisional privacy rights. Decisional privacy is afforded strong protection because of the importance placed on one's autonomy to make certain decisions rather than the tangible value of a created property right. Autonomous decisions theoretically do not rise to the level of a property right, because no thing has been "created." In the case of the Boston parade, a thing had been created. Ultimately, property

---

[1134] *Id.* at 151 ("By agreeing with the Council's characterization of speech as something privately owned, the Court created an intellectual property right in the parade.").

[1135] 515 U.S. 557, 569–70 (1995).

[1136] Sunder, *supra* note 98, at 152–53.

[1137] *Id.*

[1138] *Id.* at 152.

theory is available to protect some "privacy interests" that are difficult to classify, such as protecting body parts or the right to exclude a group from a parade.

3. Information as Property

The right to control and to exclude others, as previously described, is part of the bundle of property rights. A central part of informational privacy is the ability to control information, to make it secret, or to exclude selected individuals from access to information. "Appropriation of personality" is based directly on the theory of taking value from someone's personality. The property-right theory can operate well with respect to certain types of data. Currently, much personal information cannot reasonably be expected to be private.[1139] Can endowing accessible information with property aspects help protect it? Property theory clearly is used to control and protect the use of publicly available information through copyrights.

Both federal and state governments protect intellectual property, ostensibly because it generally fits under the philosophical rubric of property. If that is true, then information about oneself should, in theory, also be afforded protection. First, traditional property theory is based on the principle that property is rivalrous. For example, if one consumes an apple, it no longer exists for someone else to consume, at least not in the form of an "apple" proper. If one mixes his or her labor with unowned land, then that land is his or hers and no one else's, because one person cannot enjoy using a piece of land for farming while another simultaneously enjoys using the same piece of land for a mutually exclusive purpose. The same is true of informational property, in that one cannot enjoy the value of one's secret while another simultaneously enjoys the value of disclosing it. However, because intellectual property is nonrivalrous, this principle does not apply there. Songs are copyrighted, for instance, with only the "author" enjoying full legal ownership of the song. But nothing prevents the song from being simultaneously performed, recorded, or listened to, as long as the ownership rights are honored. Theory aside, federal courts usually look to state law to determine whether a property interest exists.[1140] As a consequence, several federal courts have

---

[1139]   Daniel J. Solove, *Conceptualizing Privacy*, 90 CAL. L. REV. 1087, 1111 (2002).
[1140]   Brown v. Trench, 787 F.2d 167, 170 (3d Cir. 1986).

protected an individual's right to privacy on the basis of state property law.[1141]

Warren and Brandeis concluded that an individual's intention to market or sell his or her information is not dispositive in protecting the right to privacy.[1142] To illustrate this concept, they note that the protection afforded by common-law copyright to an unpublished writing is "entirely independent of its pecuniary value, its intrinsic merits, or of any intention to publish the same."[1143] A tort claim based on intrusion upon seclusion protects an individual's right to use his or her own personality and personal information independent of any intent to sell or profit. A tort claim asserting public disclosure of private facts protects an individual's right to pass his or her personal history and information on to another without fear of distortion from any third party. Indeed, the right to "keep" a secret implies the right to use your own personal information as you see fit.

The right to privacy has been characterized as the right to be let alone,[1144] the right of limited access to self,[1145] the right to secrecy,[1146] and the right to intimacy.[1147] Although these characterizations may differ somewhat in form, one common theme that runs throughout is that the right to privacy depends on the right to exclude others from one's private life. For instance, the torts of intrusion upon seclusion and public disclosure of private facts require an invasion of something secret, secluded, or private pertaining to the plaintiff.[1148] The tort of appropriation of name or likeness grants the individual the right to exclude others from the use of such characteristics without the individual's approval or license. Clearly, a basic attribute of an effective right to privacy is the individual's ability to control the circulation of personal information.

[1141] *See, e.g.,* Bd. of Regents of State Colls. v. Roth, 408 U.S. 564, 577 (1972) ("Property interests, of course, are not created by the Constitution. Rather they are created and their dimensions are defined by existing rules or understandings that stem from an independent source such as state law—rules or understandings that secure certain benefits and that support claims of entitlement to those benefits.").

[1142] Warren & Brandeis, *supra* note 22, at 207.

[1143] *Id.*

[1144] *See* Warren & Brandeis, *supra* note 22, at 193.

[1145] *See, e.g.,* E.L. Godkin, *Libel and Its Legal Remedy*, 12 J. Soc. Sci. 69, 80 (1880) ("Nothing is better worthy of legal protection than private life, or, in other words, the right of every man to keep his affairs to himself, and to decide for himself to what extent they shall be the subject of public observation and discussion.").

[1146] *See* discussion *supra* Chapter IV, § F-2.

[1147] *Id.* at 1121–24.

[1148] Nelson v. Maine Times, 373 A.2d 1221 (Me. 1977).

The U.S. Supreme Court has said that informational privacy is "control over information concerning his or her person."[1149] However, one difficulty with assigning property ownership to information is the shared nature of some personal information.[1150] For instance, personal information is often formed in *relationships* with others, with all parties to that relationship having some claim to that information. If an individual wished to control the dissemination of information about his abusive past with his wife, the wife also would seem to have a right to control her own history and decide whether her story should be told. Intimate relationships demonstrate the extremes of the problem of shared ownership of information. For example, a woman chose to reveal intimate and embarrassing details about a congressional aide with whom she had had a relationship.[1151] Although property theory may provide a better alternative in some circumstances, in this case perhaps the tort theory of public disclosure of private facts could be a cause of action. This case will be discussed more fully later in this book.[1152]

The most prominent privacy remedy based on property is the right of publicity. It most obviously confers the property-like right of an individual to sell or transfer his or her personality, name, and likeness,[1153] such as the exclusive right to use one's own identity and personality for one's own benefit. The individual's interest in keeping this information private may stem from a desire to use the information for personal benefit and to prevent others from using it for their benefit. The property characteristics of the tort of the right of publicity make it distinguishable from other privacy torts, not because there is a greater property interest in publicity, but because the measurable value of the injury is different. Whereas the value of the injury for an invasion of privacy such as public disclosure of private facts is intrinsic to the individual, the market confers the value of the injury for an invasion of the right of publicity. In other words, the key feature distinguishing the right of publicity from the personal right of privacy is the measure of damages. The former focuses on the commercial injury to the plaintiff, whereas the latter focuses on the personal harm to the plaintiff.

[1149] U.S. Dep't of Justice v. Reporters Comm. for Freedom of Press, 489 U.S. 749, 763 (1989).
[1150] *See* ARTHUR MILLER, THE ASSAULT ON PRIVACY: COMPUTERS, DATA BANKS, AND DOSSIERS 25 (1971).
[1151] *See* Steinbuch v. Cutler, 463 F. Supp. 2d 4 (D.D.C. 2006); *see also* Dahlia Lithwick, *Is Anything Private Anymore?*, WASH. POST, Jul. 30, 2006, at B2.
[1152] *See* discussion *infra* Chapter VI, § I.
[1153] RESTATEMENT (SECOND) OF TORTS § 652(c) (1977).

Most cases analyzing the various aspects of privacy, including the right to publicity, define the right as a personal one that is not transferable and does not survive the death of an individual.[1154] However, statutes have allowed individuals with relatives to inherit the rights of the deceased under actions relating to right to publicity.[1155] Therefore persons with commercial value in their persona have the right to control the conditions under which that persona may be used—even after death.[1156]

Some aspects of the actions relating to the protection of one's persona have a property basis; some aspects may be more related to tort. In an article discussing Warren and Brandeis's "The Right to Privacy," Robert Post posits that the *tort of appropriation*, unlike the *tort of publicity*, should not be considered a property right, because appropriation of one's personality is an offense to a reasonable person's sensibilities, not an injury to property.[1157] On the other hand, the right to publicity recognizes the commercial value of the picture or representation of an individual or performer.[1158]

Property theory has been used to protect private information in other situations beyond the right of publicity:

- Pictures or images have been protected. As a Missouri court asserted, "one has an exclusive right to his picture, on the score of its being a property right of material profit."[1159]
- Under Florida law, the results of genetic tests "are the exclusive property of the person tested, are confidential, and may not be

---

[1154] *See, e.g.,* Brinkley v. Casablancas, 438 N.Y.S.2d 1004, 1010 (App. Div. 1981) (stating that although other courts applying New York law have found the right of publicity to be a valid transferable property right, New York courts have found the statutory right of privacy to be neither descendible nor assignable); Antonetty v. Cuomo, 502 N. Y.S.2d 902, 906 (Sup. Ct. 1986). For instance, comment g to section 46 of the *Restatement (Second) of Torts* states that "the personal interests protected under the right of privacy are not transferable," However, 652 C(a) even though comment a to section expressly permits transferability for appropriation privacy by stating ". the right created by it is in the nature of a property right, for the exercise of which an exclusive license may be given to a third person, which will entitle the licensee to maintain an action to protect it."
[1155] Statute allowing inheritances, *see supra* note 818.
[1156] *See* Chapter IV § D-1 for a discussion of laws allowing succession of right to publicity.
[1157] Post, *supra* note 913 at 674–75.
[1158] *Id.* at 666.
[1159] Munden v. Harris, 153 Mo. App. 652, 660 (Ct. App. 1911). The court analyzed the value one has in the exclusive right to his or her picture, not just in terms of potential material profit from it, but as "a property right of value, in that it is one of the modes of securing to a person the enjoyment of life and the exercise of liberty." *Id.*

disclosed without . . . consent."[1160] Similarly, the Georgia legislature declared that genetic information is the "unique property of the individual tested" and that it is "appropriate to limit the use and availability of genetic information" to "protect individual privacy and . . . preserve individual autonomy."[1161]

- A personal letter has been protected as property on the basis of the value of the tangible object.
- Confidential business information has long been recognized as property.[1162]
- In *Pfeiffer v. CIA*, the court held that an investigative report prepared by a CIA agent was indisputably the property of the CIA, although the report could not be copyrighted.[1163] The court reasoned that the report belonged to the CIA because "it was created at government expense, with government materials and on government time."[1164]

Information has been protected under property theory in a wide range of circumstances and is a viable option for protecting some types of information.

4. Remedies and Damages

Damages, when related to property, generally relate to determining the monetary value of a "thing." For example, courts have distinguished the right of publicity from other privacy rights because the loss of the right of publicity constitutes an economic injury to the individual.[1165] But a

---

[1160] FLA. STAT. § 760.40 (1994).

[1161] GA. STAT. § 33-54-1 (1995).

[1162] Carpenter v. United States, 484 U.S. 19, 26 (1987). Even if confidential information holds no commercial value for a business organization, courts still have recognized a property interest in the information under the labor theory of property.

[1163] 60 F.3d 861 (D.C. Cir. 1995); *see also* United States v. Elliot, 711 F. Supp. 425 (N.D. Ill. 1989). In *Elliot*, the defendant, accused of wire fraud, argued that the confidential client information he appropriated for profit was not the "property" of the law firm. *Id.* The defendant argued that an essential ingredient of property is the ability to exploit it. *Id.* Therefore, because the law firm was precluded from using the confidential client information for personal gain, it followed that the law firm had no "property interest" in the confidential client information. *Id.* The court rejected this assertion and held that all confidential information does not have to be of the same nature to be considered property. *Id.* The court reasoned, therefore, that the law firm had the right to possess the confidential information.

[1164] *Pfeiffer*, 60 F.3d at 864.

[1165] *See, e.g.,* Lugosi v. Universal Pictures, 25 Cal. 3d 813 (1979).

privacy-related injury may generate a different kind of damage beyond the value of the property. Additionally, some remedies in property-related privacy actions relate to exclusion from access rather than monetary damage.[1166] In these cases, the property theory is protecting "interests" that do not fit neatly into the categories of decisional privacy or informational privacy. For example, protecting access to the Boston parade or a CIA report may represent interests that are not financial.

In property-related actions regarding information protection, other damages may be possible. If privacy rights are attached to a property interest in personality, why did Warren and Brandeis attempt to distinguish the right to privacy as a personal invasion to sensibilities and separate it from a property-interest analysis? Warren and Brandeis possibly were concerned with distinguishing privacy rights from the common law's protection of property rights because of the assessment of damages. At the time of their article, damages available to a plaintiff for invasions of personality, analyzed under property rights and common-law copyright, were "measured by market tests of unjust enrichment or lost profits."[1167] They thus stated, "[O]ur law recognizes no principle upon which compensation can be granted for mere injury to the feelings."[1168] Robert Post argues that "[b]y reconceptualizing personality in terms of emotional integrity, Warren and Brandeis desired to make damages available instead for distress and anguish. They thus advocated that damages be seen as compensation for 'the value of mental suffering.'"[1169]

Harold Gordon argues that although Warren and Brandeis's concept of the right to privacy was premised on previously recognized property rights, Warren and Brandeis nevertheless felt a need to recognize a distinct right of privacy independent of property rights, especially since absent such rights, the basic injury was a violation of the individual's right "to be let alone," and the essential injury was to one's feelings with consequent mental anguish.[1170] However, the right of privacy is not necessarily "independent" of the property interest, but more "independent" of an injury commonly recognized for harm to property, loss of profits, and monetary value. What Warren and Brandeis possibly were searching for

---

[1166] Warren & Brandeis, *supra* note 22, at 207.

[1167] Post, *supra* note 913, at 665.

[1168] Warren & Brandeis, *supra* note 22, at 197.

[1169] Post, *supra* note 913, at 666.

[1170] Harold Gordon, *Right of Property in Name, Likeness, Personality and History*, 55 Nw. U. L. Rev. 553 (1960).

was a means of protection for the distinct injury that resulted from an invasion of privacy independent from loss of profits.

Thus, Warren and Brandeis did not reject the property aspects of the interest involved, but instead advocated recognition of a distinct injury to personal sensibilities, independent of the common-law rights of property protection. Consequently, they asserted that the "obligation is simply to observe the legal right of the sender of the letter whatever it may be, and whether it be called, his right of property in the contents of the letter, or his right to privacy."[1171]

To determine the amount of injury to an individual's property interest, one must analyze the specific property right that is invaded. One right in this bundle of property rights is the right to profit from property, and the market will measure the value of this particular right. However, property ownership also confers upon the individual the right to exclude others and the right to use the property as the owner wishes, even absent a desire to use the property for economic benefit. The value to the property owner of the right to exclude and use the property is the privacy value inherent in property ownership. It is intrinsic and personal to the owner. The privacy value of property ownership is not separate from the property interest but originates from the ownership of property itself.

The combination of a property and privacy right may generate damages beyond mere property damages. In *Canessa v. J.I. Kislak*,[1172] the court allowed mental suffering damages for the violation of a property right in personality, citing the 1894 case *Corliss v. E.W. Walker Co.*:[1173]

Robert Post also argues that a court justifies liability in terms associated with the ownership of property, as opposed to the property in and of itself.[1174] The "ascertainable" harm to the property should not be measured solely by the potential for profit and monetary gain.[1175] The rights attributable to property ownership also include the right to exclude others from the property and the right to use the property as the individual sees fit. When these property rights are violated, compensation based solely on the loss of potential profit does not correspond with the invaded property right. Instead, damages for injury to personal integrity and sensibility are more consistent with the loss of the individual's

---

[1171]   Warren & Brandeis, *supra* note 22, at 212.
[1172]   97 N.J. Super. 327 (Sup. Ct. Law Div. 1967); 235 A. 2d 62 (N.J. Super 1967).
[1173]   64 F. 280, 282–85 (C.C.D. Mass. 1894).
[1174]   Post, *supra* note 913, at 674.
[1175]   *Id.*

property rights to use and exclude others from their personality, name, likeness, or intimate details. The owner's personal sensibilities are injured because he or she has lost a personal right that attaches to a property interest. The distinction, therefore, between loss of profits and injury to sensibilities is relevant only to the question of damages.

In fact, some courts implicitly have recognized such a damages-based proposition. In *Waits v. Frito-Lay, Inc.*, the court rejected the notion that damages available in a right-of-publicity action are limited to economic injury.[1176] In this case, a prominent singer, Tom Waits, philosophically opposed the use of his voice in commercial advertising because he believed it compromised his artistic integrity.[1177] Knowing that Waits would not consent to the use of his voice in advertising, Frito-Lay hired a singer to copy Waits's voice and singing style for a Frito-Lay commercial. The *Waits* court acknowledged that the plaintiff's claim for appropriation of name or likeness was based on a property right to the exclusive use of his voice; still, the court upheld not only the jury's award to the plaintiff of compensatory damages for voice misappropriation of $100,000 for the fair market value of his services, but also a $200,000 award for injury to his peace, happiness, and feelings caused by the unauthorized use of his voice. In an example of how tort damages can be applied to a property theory, the court reasoned:

> The defendants argue that in right of publicity actions, only damages to compensate for economic injury are available. We disagree. Although the injury stemming from violation of the right of publicity "may be largely, or even wholly, of an economic or material nature," we have recognized that "it is quite possible that the appropriation of the identity of a celebrity may induce humiliation, embarrassment, and mental distress."[1178]

The *Waits* court also cited *Grant v. Esquire, Inc.*[1179] in recognizing two distinguishable values involved in the right to publicity. The *Grant* case

---

[1176] 978 F.2d 1093, 1103 (9th Cir. 1992).
[1177] Waits's opposition to using his voice in commercial advertising could be considered an example of lexical ordering. *See* JOHN RAWLS, A THEORY OF JUSTICE 37–38 (rev. ed. 1999). Lexical ordering exists when values are ranked in such a way that they are not interchangeable with values that exist on a different level. *See* JEFFREY L. HARRISON, LAW AND ECONOMICS IN A NUTSHELL 49–52 (1995). Lexical ordering is relevant here because in cases such as *Waits*, it may not be possible to fully compensate a plaintiff for certain misappropriations.
[1178] *Waits*, 978 F.2d at 1103.
[1179] 367 F. Supp. 876 (S.D.N.Y. 1973).

involved a suit by the actor Cary Grant against *Esquire* magazine for publishing a photograph of his head superimposed on a model's torso.[1180] Grant, like Waits, had taken a public position against reaping commercial profits from the publicity value of his identity.

The court, after finding that Grant had a protectable right of publicity, noted that "[i]f the jury decides in plaintiff Grant's favor he will of course be entitled to recover for any lacerations to his feelings that he may be able to establish," in addition to the fair market value of use of his identity.[1181] Thus, the courts in both *Grant* and *Waits* recognized that the value an individual places on his or her identity may involve more than an economic value. The integrity and autonomy value placed on likeness was heightened by the fact that both celebrities philosophically opposed the commercial use of their identities. In other words, the value conferred by Grant's and Waits's rights to exclude others from the use of their identities was elevated.

For instance, celebrities who sue under the right of publicity solely or mainly because they did not profit from the unauthorized use of their identities may not place as high a value on the right to exclude or the right to use their names, likenesses, or personalities as they place on the right to profit from such use. However, a private individual who does not wish to profit from his or her identity at all, but solely wishes to exclude others from its use, may place a much higher value on the right to exclude. In the latter instance, a court might award nominal compensatory damages for the fair market value of the individual's identity but higher damages for the injury to the person's integrity and sensibilities, which have been violated through the unauthorized use.

Either way, whether the individual wishes to profit from his or her private information or wishes simply to exclude others from its use, the factors that initially constitute a property interest are the same. These factors include the individual's distinct and unique personality, as well as the creative effort and labor that goes into the conduct of one's life. Because of these property attributes, a celebrity has a property interest in his or her personality and consequently the exclusive right to profit from it or assign it to others. This right derives from the fact that an individual owns his or her personality and consequently enjoys, under the bundle of property rights, the right to profit from it. Nonetheless, the private individual's

---

[1180]   *Id.*
[1181]   *Id.* at 881.

lack of intent to profit from his or her private life should not affect the nature of personality as a property interest. Instead, it should affect how and what type of damages are sought as a remedy.

As discussed above, property ownership is not absolute; rather, it is subject to regulation and limits on its use. Ownership of intellectual property is not absolute either. For instance, trade secrets are subject to reverse engineering, and copyright,[1182] patent,[1183] and trademark[1184] law allow for the "fair use" of each, respectively. When personal information is recognized as a property right, one implication is that exclusive ownership of such information likely will be subject to limitations similar to those found in intellectual-property law. Indeed, at least one court has already recognized that some privacy issues, most notably the right of publicity, "*[do] not differ in kind from copyright.*"[1185] However, personal information also may be analogized to trade secrets. One requirement for protection of a trade secret is that the secret's value flows from its being kept secret. Similarly, the privacy value of an individual's personal information flows from its being kept secret as well.

If we extend the analogy between privacy in personal information and intellectual-property law, the possibility for "fair use" of such information emerges. For instance, section 107 of the 1976 Copyright Act protects the "fair use" of copyrighted material.[1186] The factors to be considered in a fair-use case are:

1. the purpose and character of the use, including whether such use is of a commercial nature or is for nonprofit educational purposes;
2. the nature of the copyrighted work;
3. the amount and substantiality of the portion used in relation to the copyrighted work as a whole; and
4. the effect of the use upon the potential market for or value of the copyrighted work.[1187]

Using similar factors, a court could determine whether the unauthorized use of personal information was either a violation of an individual's

---

[1182] 17 U.S.C. § 107 (2000).
[1183] 15 U.S.C. § 1115(b)(4) (2000).
[1184] 35 U.S.C. § 271(e) (2000).
[1185] Baltimore Orioles, Inc. v. Major League Baseball Players Ass'n, 805 F.2d 663, 679 (7th Cir. 1986) (emphasis added).
[1186] 17 U.S.C. § 107.
[1187] *Id.*

right to control information about himself or herself or a legitimate addition to the public domain. Indeed, one benefit of applying the copyright fair-use doctrine to the privacy realm is the large body of case law that can be analogized when lawsuits based on a property right in privacy begin to emerge. For instance, a large body of copyright case law exists on the issue of parody. Using those precedents as a frame of reference, a court would be equipped to decide issues based on the right to control information about oneself in the same way that courts decide issues about the right to control creative expressions.

One can see the implication of applying the fair-use doctrine to personal information when the idea is discussed in the context of a real case. For instance, take the facts of the *True Stories from the Morgue* case mentioned earlier.[1188] Recall that broadcasters wanted to televise an autopsy. If a property right in one's image was protected, and if that right could be transferred, sold, or bequeathed to an heir, then an heir of the subject of the broadcast autopsy would argue that the use was commercial, that the image was of a particularly private nature, and that such use should be presumptively unfair. The defendant would argue that the use was educational and that the nature of the image was a necessary part of the program's overall educational benefit.

With a property theory of informational privacy, tort theory may be used to garner some form of compensation for families such as the one in the *True Stories from the Morgue* case. Although the First Amendment may allow one to publicize such private information, it would cost the disseminator if such information were viewed as property.

Property theory provides a range of damage remedies and exclusion remedies. In the quest to protect privacy interests, property theory is an important option.

[1188]   Perkins v. Principal Media Group, No. 3:03-CV-00578 (M.D. Tenn., May 12, 2005).

CHAPTER V

Why Legal Tools Are Failing

Even with all the available legal tools discussed, huge gaps remain in the ability to protect an individual's privacy. The deficiency is most visible in the protection of information, or "disclosural privacy." The deficiencies are attributable to gaps in legal doctrine that cannot adapt to modern society or technology, basic values such as free speech and national security, and the fragmented approach of state and national legislation.

A. Public Safety, Security, and Health Versus Privacy

As a matter of policy and as a matter of law, privacy is consciously and directly sacrificed for a perceived greater public good. Public security and public health are two of the most substantial justifications. These purposes often are found to be compelling interests that justify intrusions.[1189] From quarantining public-health risks to publishing lists of sex offenders,

---

[1189] There are examples of legal health quarantines where individuals can be detained against their will. Quarantines for communicable diseases such as cholera, diphtheria, infectious tuberculosis, plague, smallpox, yellow fever, viral hemorrhagic fevers, and severe acute respiratory syndrome ("SARS") may be authorized by federal executive orders. *See* Centers for Disease Control & Prevention, Dep't of Health & Human Services, Fact Sheet on Legal Authorities for Isolation/Quarantine (May 3, 2005), http://www.cdc.gov/ncidod/sars/factsheetlegal.htm.

legislators and courts have intentionally and directly overridden privacy interests to advance the public interest. Public opinion generally supports these interests. For example, intrusions targeted to protect against terrorism are supported, even if they are invasive and there are no judicial standards for review. There are other bases for public intrusions, such as policies supporting public morality,[1190] but policies based on public health and safety are the strongest justifications for intrusions.

When the publication of private information will increase public safety, courts have held that the informational privacy interest does not stand in the way. For instance, in Wisconsin, private medical records of mental patients may be released by the state to local law-enforcement officials and the media in order to apprehend an escaped patient.[1191] Texas courts also have held that protecting the public from crime can, in certain circumstances, outweigh personal privacy.[1192] Further, information regarding sexual predators or child molesters is often posted on the Internet.[1193] Although some may consider it a privacy violation to publicize criminals' names, others certainly see this as necessary for the safety of children and the neighbors of such convicted criminals. In addition, information regarding individuals infected with contagious diseases may be reported to protect others against potential health risks.[1194] Thus, when public-health, safety, or national-security interests are implicated, courts will likely hold that privacy interests do not bar to publication.[1195]

[1190] *See, e.g.,* Loving v. Virginia, 388 U.S. 1 (1967). Miscegenation statutes of the past are one example of prohibitions that can only be based on a moral reason rather than other public purposes.

[1191] Wis. Stat. § 51.30(4)(b) (2003).

[1192] *See* Knapp v. State, 942 S.W.2d 176, 179 (Tex. Crim. App. 1997) ("Society can afford the physician-patient privilege in certain civil cases in order to protect personal privacy, but the need to protect the public from crime requires disclosure of the same information in criminal cases.").

[1193] *See, e.g.,* http://offender.fdle.state.fl.us/offender/homepage.do (last visited May 9, 2008) Florida Department of Law Enforcement, http://www3.fdle.state.fl.us/ (last visited May 9, 2008) (providing access to database of registered sexual offenders).

[1194] *See, e.g.,* Fla. Stat. § 381.0031(4) (2002) (allowing medical practitioners to release medical information regarding communicable diseases when necessary to protect public health); Fla. Stat. § 384.25(1)–(2) (requiring the reporting of individuals testing positive for sexually transmitted diseases, but requiring that individual confidentiality be maintained).

[1195] These public-purpose justifications do not even have to meet compelling-interest tests, except in some states (e.g., Florida). These justifications are used to justify a range of intrusions from drug testing and locker inspections at school to employer monitoring (also by consent) of e-mails and phones.

1. Public Health

The interests of public health have long been given primacy over individual rights. So personal freedom is overridden when inoculations are required in public school[1196] or even when detention is required for a person diagnosed with a contagious disease.[1197] Protecting public health can impinge on private autonomy rights as well as otherwise private information. Information regarding health and safety that includes other personal information also may be published to aid research in the fields of health and medicine.[1198]

Increasing amounts of medical information are now available from genetic research. Information on individuals' personal medical risks are being accumulated. On one hand, such need for medical-information disclosure seems desirable. Yet on the other hand, any disclosure of health-related information poses a real threat to the vitality of the insurance principle, which is based on the law of averages and requires that certain health details remain undisclosed in order to protect a large number of

---

[1196] See Farina v. Bd. of Educ., 116 F. Supp. 2d 503, 513 (S.D.N.Y. 2000). In Farina, the parents of a minor child objected to an inoculation requirement established in New York. The federal district court denied the parents' request for a preliminary injunction because the parents failed to show that their inoculation objection stemmed from "genuine and sincere religious beliefs."

[1197] For example, the federal government detained a man for two weeks after it was discovered that he had traveled throughout the United States, Canada, and Europe with an extremely contagious and drug-resistant form of tuberculosis. See David Brown, Man with Rare TB Detained, Isolated, WASH. POST, May 30, 2007, at A3.

[1198] See, e.g., FLA. STAT. § 405.01 (2002) (exempting from liability medical information released to research groups, governmental health agencies, medical associations and societies, and in-hospital medical staff committees "to advance medical research and medical education"). Florida law also limits the publication of this research, emphasizing that it must advance medical research or education in the interest of reducing morbidity or mortality. Id. § 405.02. In addition, any published information must keep any individual's name confidential. Id. § 405.03. California's Confidentiality of Medical Information Act, CAL. CIV. CODE § 56.10 (West 2007), requires health-care providers, employers, and insurers to obtain written authorization from patients prior to disclosing identifiable information. In Minnesota, it was permissible to release medical information to state and private research groups prior to 1997 under certain circumstances. Minnesota changed its law in 1997 to allow the release of medical information for research purposes to external research groups only with the written consent of the patient. MINN. STAT. § 144.335 (1997). Additionally, the HIPAA privacy rule establishes the conditions under which protected health information may be used or disclosed by covered entities for research purposes. "Research" is defined in the privacy rule as "a systematic investigation, including research development, testing, and evaluation, designed to develop or contribute to generalizable knowledge." 45 C.F.R. § 164.501 (2007).

individuals against overwhelming medical costs. Thus, health-care costs are subsidized through a pool of insurance premiums as a result of individual uncertainty and fortuitous loss.[1199]

2. Public Security: Protecting Against Crime and Terrorism

Courts tend to view public safety and security as an overriding, "compelling" public interest when balanced against personal privacy rights.[1200] Courts will uphold what would generally be considered a substantial invasion of privacy if, for example, the policy protects individuals against sex offenders.[1201]

The recent escalation in terrorism globally has reinforced governments' desires to fight terrorism at almost any cost. There is clearly a willingness to sacrifice aspects of personal privacy in return for homeland security and a perceived protection from domestic terrorism. Nowhere is this trend better illustrated than in the Patriot Act.[1202] For example, Title II of the act allows the attorney general to intercept wire, oral, and electronic communications relating to terrorism, and Title III permits the secretary of the treasury and the attorney general to subpoena or summon records of any foreign bank that maintains a correspondent account in the United States.[1203] Although these provisions may raise privacy concerns regarding

---

[1199] See Compagnie des Bauxites v. Insurance Co. of N. Am., 724 F.2d 369 (3d Cir. 1983) (quoting RESTATEMENT OF CONTRACTS § 291 cmt. a (1932) and defining a fortuitous event as "an event which *so far as the parties to the contract are aware,* is dependent on chance").

[1200] See United States v. Salerno 481 U.S. 739, 750–51 (1987) (holding that pretrial detention based on fear of future criminal acts was valid because an individual's liberty interests may, "in circumstances where the government's interest is sufficiently weighty, be subordinated").

[1201] See E.B. v. Verniero, 119 F.3d 1077 (3d Cir. 1997) In *E.B.,* sex offenders brought an action challenging the constitutionality of community-notification provisions in New Jersey's "Megan's Law." The court upheld the statute and stated that the effects of notification on sex offenders' reputational interests and safety were not unduly burdensome when evaluated in light of the state's interest in protecting the public. *Id.* at 1096–97.

[1202] Uniting and Strengthening America by Providing Appropriate Tools Required to Intercept and Obstruct Terrorism (USA PATRIOT) Act of 2001, Pub. L. No. 107-56, 115 Stat. 272. *See generally* Fletcher N. Baldwin, Jr. & Robert B. Shaw, *Down to the Wire: Assessing the Constitutionality of the National Security Agency's Warrantless Wiretapping Program: Exit the Rule of Law,* 17 U. FLA. J.L. & PUB. POL'Y 429 (2006).

[1203] See J.J. Norton & H. Shams, *Money Laundering Law and Terrorist Financing: Post September 11 Responses—Let Us Step Back and Take a Deep Breath?,* 36 INT'L LAW. 108 (2002).

the collection of individuals' financial information, financial institutions are protected from liability by the act's safe-harbor provisions if the information is collected after the financial institution learns of suspected terrorist activity.[1204]

In particular, section 215 of the Patriot Act greatly expands the authority of the FBI under the Foreign Intelligence Surveillance Act of 1978 ("FISA") to search private "tangible things," such as books, records, papers, documents, and other items, in order to "obtain foreign intelligence information . . . or to protect against international terrorism or clandestine intelligence activities."[1205] Before the Patriot Act was enacted, FBI agents only had FISA access to private information of business records in the possession of a common carrier. In addition, the FBI had to show "specific and articulable facts giving reason to believe that the entity to which the records pertain is a foreign power or an agent of a foreign power."[1206] Today, the Patriot Act requires the FBI to show only that the "records concerned are sought for an authorized investigation consistent with the purposes of section 215" in order to receive court permission for a FISA search.[1207] Therefore, the FBI now has easier access to an individual's tangible things, which, in turn, diminishes informational privacy.[1208]

The Patriot Act and FISA support what has been termed "transaction surveillance," which was discussed previously.[1209] Although this technique can be very intrusive, because of overriding concerns of security, courts and legislatures will continue to support these intrusions.

In sum, the overriding public interests in health and security will almost always override even the most sensitive privacy interests, including those relating to family and the home.

[1204] *See, e.g.,* R.S. Pasley, *Privacy Rights v. Anti-Money Laundering Enforcement,* 36 N.C. BANKING INST. 121 (2002) (discussing section 314 of the Patriot Act, which provides a safe harbor for financial institutions that transmit, receive, or share information for the purposes of identifying and reporting terrorist or money-laundering activities).

[1205] 50 U.S.C. § 1861(a)(1) (Supp. 2001).

[1206] Intelligence Authorization Act of 1999, PUB. L. No. 105-272, 112 Stat. 2396 (1998).

[1207] 50 U.S.C. § 1861(b).

[1208] *See* ACLU v. Dep't of Justice, 321 F. Supp. 2d 24, 35–38 (D.C. Cir. 2004) (holding that despite privacy interests, the ACLU could not gain access to the number and type of requests and records of searches performed by the FBI, because such searches fall under the "national security" exception to the Freedom of Information Act).

[1209] *See* discussion *supra* Chapter III, § B-4(a).

B. The First Amendment, Newsworthiness, and the Modern Press

A major reason for the failures of privacy remedies are our First Amendment protections. Statutes protecting private cell-phone communications[1210] and state statutes protecting against the disclosure of personal information[1211] are unconstitutional as impairing the First Amendment. Tort actions against the press for false light[1212] and public disclosure of private facts[1213] almost always fail because the disclosures are newsworthy.

The First Amendment represents a firm barrier to any state or federal legislation that substantially restricts the news media; therefore, it provides a constitutional limit as well as a political force described later.[1214] The other broad impact is the protection of newsworthy disclosures against any cause of action in the United States. As mentioned previously, this broad protection is not granted in many other countries.[1215]

The importance of newsworthiness is undisputed, but it is a slippery concept in the courts. The courts labor to balance the public interest in access to information and the private right to be protected from intrusions. Courts usually have protected the media's right to invade individual privacy under the notion that the community interest in knowledge outweighs the individual interest in privacy.[1216] A newsworthy story that is true will virtually always fall under the First Amendment's protection of free speech, even if the story is private and offensive.[1217] The First Amendment also will protect a newsworthy story that turns out to be unintentionally false.[1218] The U.S. Supreme Court, in *Time, Inc. v. Hill*, said that sanctions against innocent or even negligent misstatements by the press would "present a grave hazard of discouraging the press from

---

[1210]   Bartnicki v. Vopper, 532 U.S. 514 (2001).

[1211]   Smith v. Daily Mail Publ'g Co., 443 U.S. 97, 105–06 (1979) (holding unconstitutional a statute punishing the truthful publication of an alleged juvenile delinquent's name lawfully obtained by a newspaper by monitoring the police band radio frequency and interviewing eyewitnesses).

[1212]   *See* Time, Inc. v. Hill, 385 U.S. 374, 386 (1967).

[1213]   *See* Florida Star v. B.J.F., 491 U.S. 524 (1989) (extending the newsworthiness doctrine to the publication of a rape victim's name legally obtained from a publicly released police report).

[1214]   See discussion *infra* Chapter V, § C.

[1215]   *See* discussion *supra* Chapter III, § C-6(e).

[1216]   *Hill*, 385 U.S. at 386.

[1217]   *See* Edwards v. Nat'l Audubon Soc'y, Inc., 556 F.2d 113, 120 (2d Cir. 1977).

[1218]   *See Hill*, 385 U.S. at 388.

exercising the constitutional guarantees." Although emphasizing the importance of the First Amendment's right of free speech, the Court reaffirmed prior decisions rendering calculated, knowing falsehoods and statements made with reckless disregard for the truth outside of the realm of First Amendment protection. A newsworthy story that is intentionally falsified will fall beyond the scope of the First Amendment's protection.[1219] Also, a person will not be able to recover damages for the disclosure of an intrusive fact, such as the fact that she was sterilized, even though these facts emerge as untargeted collateral damage from a "newsworthy" investigation of a medical facility.[1220]

The more assertive First Amendment advocates believe that the proper process is "let the press decide." This "test" would require courts to find anything that has been published to be newsworthy. This self-regulating approach has serious flaws in the new world of paparazzi, bloggers, and Internet news sources that exist without standards. This problem is evident from the breadth and practices in modern American media. The media is often deliberately intrusive and sensationalistic—for example, the tabloid media.[1221] Before the Internet, information in the form of rumor and conjecture was mitigated by the fact that by the time such information was disseminated throughout the country, its falsity was already known. Today, such information is instantly disseminated without an accuracy check performed by more-responsible media.[1222] The ability of the Internet to set loose unsubstantiated rumor, which often destroys individual informational privacy, is often protected under the First Amendment because the issues may be determined to be "newsworthy" and involve matters of public concern.[1223] The tabloids argue that their product is of public consequence and public interest, pointing to the fact that the public buys tabloids.[1224] This argument means that anything that

---

[1219]   *See* Mohanv. M.M. Corp., No. 02A01-9608-CV00182, 1997 WL 167210 (Tenn. Ct. App. Apr. 10, 1997) (holding that an industry magazine disregarded the truth or falsity of an article on a record producer's departure from Memphis and, despite the article's newsworthy character, genuine issue of material fact existed as to the magazine's liability).

[1220]   Des Moines v. Howard 283 N.W.2d 289, 302 (Iowa 1979), *cert. denied*, 445 U.S. 904 (1980) (discussing an individual who was sterilized in a program that was being attacked by the newspaper).

[1221]   Witness such Web sites as Death.com, which features celebrity autopsies.

[1222]   *See* Rodney A. Smolla, *Will Tabloid Journalism Ruin the First Amendment for All of Us?*, 9 DePaul-LCA J. Art & Ent. L. 1, 9–10 (1998).

[1223]   *See id.* at 15–16.

[1224]   *See id.* at 16 (stating that "such topics [sex and scandal] must be on matters of public concern or there would be no way to explain all the concern that is paid to them");

sells is protected speech. In other words, newsworthiness is equated to all public curiosity.

A Supreme Court case that puts press privilege in perspective is the case of the human cannonball Hugo Zacchini. Mr. Zacchini sued a news station for filming and airing his entire fifteen-second act.[1225] A freelance reporter taped the show without permission. The trial court granted summary judgment to the news station, but the state court of appeals reversed. The state supreme court found that that the television station was privileged to report on matters of legitimate public interest, even if the subject matter would ordinarily be protected by the right of publicity, unless the information was used for private gain or intended to injure the plaintiff.[1226] In a surprising rejection of the newsworthiness defense, the U.S. Supreme Court, in a 5–4 decision, held that the First Amendment did not privilege the broadcast of a performer's entire act as news.[1227] The opinion made clear that the press could report on the act, but, in an opinion reflecting some aspects of property theory, the Court found that the press could not broadcast the entire performance without compensating the performer. The reasoning was that by presenting the entire perform-ance, the press had thereby made it less likely that people would pay for the performance.

The dissent by Justice Lewis Powell expressed concern about chilling reporting on events, suggesting that that the media might be compelled to opt for verbal reporting rather than filming the entire act. Powell sug-gested that the station should not be liable absent a strong showing "that the news broadcast was a subterfuge or cover for private or commercial exploitation."[1228] This case focused on the commercial nature of the damage to the performer. The *Zacchini* case does not address the usual deference to newsworthiness, since the opinions try to avoid that issue. A broader question is, When can newsworthiness be a defense, and when does the court find particular facts newsworthy?

Have the courts specifically found any disclosures *not* to be newsworthy? Yes. There are a few cases in which courts have determined that there is

C. Calvert, *Revisiting the Voyeurism Value in the First Amendment: From the Sexually Sordid to the Details of Death*, 27 SEATTLE U. L. REV. 721 (2004).
[1225] Zacchini v. Scripps-Howard Broadcasting, 433 U.S. 562 (1977).
[1226] *Id.* at 562.
[1227] *Id.* at 575.
[1228] *Id.* at 581 (Powell, J., dissenting).

no "legitimate" purpose of disseminating information. In *McCabe v. Village Voice, Inc.*, the court found the publication, in the *Village Voice*, of a nude photograph of the plaintiff in a bathtub to be a needless intrusion into her private life.[1229] But republishing previously published, uncopyrighted photographs of a celebrity is newsworthy.[1230]

Courts differ as to the test that should be employed to determine whether something is "newsworthy" or of "legitimate public concern."[1231] Courts have considered factors such as (1) whether the action occurred in public; (2) whether the information is public; (3) whether the disclosure is intrusive and violates community standards; (4) whether the person is a public figure; and (5) whether the information is relevant to the public. In evaluating newsworthiness and considering these factors, the courts appear to have taken one of four approaches: (1) the restatement approach; (2) the California approach; (3) the nexus approach; or (4) the "let the press decide" approach.[1232]

1. The Restatement Approach

Section 652D of the *Restatement (Second) of Torts* states: "In determining what a matter of legitimate public interest is, account must be taken of the customs and conventions of the community; and in the last analysis what is proper becomes a matter of the community mores."[1233]

Surely, the press must be able to publish information that is consistent with the First Amendment's goal of ensuring an informed citizenry. According to comment h of section 652D, account must be taken as to the morals and values of the community when determining legitimate public interest.[1234]

[1229] McCabe v. Village Voice, Inc., 550 F. Supp. 525, 530 (E.D. Pa. 1982). Although McCabe consented to the nude photograph that might have been published in a book, she did not consent to publication in a newspaper.

[1230] Margaret v. High Soc'y Mag., Inc., 498 F. Supp. 401, 406–07 (S.D.N.Y. 1980).

[1231] Many courts use the terms "newsworthy" and "of legitimate public interest or public concern" interchangeably. Examples of public interest and concern? A least one commentator, however, has noted that "the definition of what is newsworthy—containing that 'indefinable quality of information that arouses the public's interest and attention'—is, in some respects, somewhat broader than the exceedingly difficult to define notion of what is of legitimate concern to the public." DAVID A. ELDER, THE LAW OF PRIVACY § 3:12 (1991).

[1232] *See* Geoff Dendy, *The Newsworthiness Defense to the Public Disclosure Tort*, 85 KY. L.J. 147, 157–63 (1996-97).

[1233] RESTATEMENT (SECOND) OF TORTS § 652D (1977), *see also* Virgil v. Time, Inc., 527 F.2d 1122 (9th Cir. 1975), *cert. denied*, 428 U.S. 998 (1976).

[1234] RESTATEMENT (SECOND) OF TORTS § 652D cmt. h (1977).

According to the *Second Restatement,* "[t]he line is to be drawn when the publicity ceases to be the giving of information to which the public is entitled, and becomes a morbid and sensational prying into private lives for its own sake, with which a reasonable member of the public, with decent standards, would say that he had no concern."[1235]

One of the goals of the First Amendment is to allow the press to publish information that "is needed or appropriate to enable the members of society to cope with the exigencies of their period."[1236] However, as contemplated in the *Restatement* excerpt above, the press should not be able to create newsworthiness simply by revealing a story to the public, regardless of the fact that some interest inevitably will be stimulated. Furthermore, when deciding where to draw the line between what is newsworthy and what should be kept private, the courts should bear in mind that the First Amendment also protects individual expression. One approach is to hold that once a favorable determination of newsworthiness is made, the court must then consider whether, despite the newsworthiness, the matter reveals facts so offensive as to shock the community's notions of decency.[1237] In determining newsworthiness and whether the individual's right to privacy and freedom of expression outweighs such newsworthy elements of the information, the courts rely on community standards. In practice, however, there are few findings that a newsworthy disclosure violates community standards. The determination that information is newsworthy is the determinative factor.

There are two potential problems with such reliance on community standards. First, an expansive use of community standards flies in the face of James Madison's assertion that some rights, such as freedom of speech, are so fundamental that they should not be stamped out by majority will. Alexander Hamilton believed that the inclusion of a bill of rights in the U.S. Constitution was unnecessary because the protection of speech must depend on public opinion and on the general spirit of the people and of the government.[1238] In Hamilton's view, because the Constitution promised a representative government, if the people want freedom of the press and freedom of speech, they will have them.[1239] James Madison rejected this

---

[1235] *Id.*
[1236] Time, Inc. v. Hill, 385 U.S. 374, 386 (1967).
[1237] Baugh v. CBS, Inc., 828 F. Supp. 745, 755 (N.D. Cal. 1993).
[1238] Hentoff, *supra* note 104.
[1239] *Id.*

idea on the basis that the Bill of Rights represented a check on the power of the majority to control the views and thoughts of the minority.[1240] Such fundamental rights as freedom of religion or freedom of expression should be protected even against the will of the majority. However, if courts rely solely on community standards and opinion to determine the newsworthiness of private details, Hamilton's vision prevails. In these circumstances, the protection of speech depends on public opinion as expressed in community standards.[1241] Second, community standards do not remain constant. As the dissent recognized in *Bartnicki v. Vopper*, a "matter of 'public concern'" exemption is "an amorphous concept that the Court does not even attempt to define."[1242] For instance, a close examination of the *Restatement (Second) of Torts* test for newsworthiness reveals the vague and indistinct nature of the newsworthiness doctrine. The *Restatement* draws a line between information to which the "public is entitled" and information with which a "reasonable person with decent standards" would say he had no concern.[1243] The reasoning is circular. The reasonable person, assumedly the jury, must decide to which information the public is entitled, but what the public is entitled to depends on community standards. It appears that the "community standard" test is narrower than the "reasonable person" test used in other privacy contexts. Thus, the individual's right to privacy and the individual's right to free expression may depend on the community's opinion. The scope of the term "community" is undefined. Indeed, if the community is defined to be as small as one local county, legal predictability becomes almost impossible. Jurors are then able to impose their own ultraconservative or ultraliberal opinions, without regard for common notions of decency held just one county away. The drafters of the Bill of Rights clearly did not envision such ambiguous dependence, but instead advocated individual freedoms apart from the state, arguably requiring a national standard. Another problem with the community-standards approach is that modern society may have widely "desensitized" community standards. What was shocking once may now be viewed as a routine disclose of intimate details.

[1240] *Id.*

[1241] *See id.*

[1242] Bartnicki v. Vopper, 532 U.S. 514, 553 (2001) (Rehnquist, C.J., dissenting).

[1243] Restatement (Second) of Torts § 652D (1977).

2. The California Approach

The California approach is best demonstrated in *Diaz v. Oakland Tribune, Inc.*[1244] The *Diaz* case stemmed from a newspaper column that disclosed that the female president of a college's student association was actually a man.[1245] The student body president, Toni Diaz, was born a man, but three years before the publication of the column, Diaz underwent "gender corrective surgery."[1246] Ms. Diaz took care to keep her prior sex a secret, even going so far as to change her school and Social Security records and her driver's license. She disclosed the surgery only to her family and close friends.[1247]

Ms. Diaz was elected student body president for the 1977–1978 academic year and was billed as the first woman to hold that position.[1248] She was later selected as the student representative to the college's board of trustees.[1249] At no time did she reveal any information concerning her surgery.[1250] News of her election and her appointment to the board did, however, appear in the college newspaper.[1251]

The column in question appeared after an area newspaper published articles mentioning Ms. Diaz and the misuse of student funds.[1252] During the student-funds controversy, the columnist was informed by confidential sources that Ms. Diaz was previously a man. The columnist then searched police records and found that Diaz, as a man, had an arrest record. The actual column, however, had nothing to do with this arrest or the student-funds controversy.[1253] Instead, the column was a compilation of notes from the education beat mixed with a small amount of commentary.[1254] Ms. Diaz sued for invasion of privacy by public disclosure of private facts.[1255] The newspaper argued that the publication was newsworthy and

---

[1244] 139 Cal. App. 3d 118 (Ct. App. 1983).
[1245] *Id.* at 124. The column read: "The students at the College of Alameda will be surprised to learn their student body president, Toni Diaz, is no lady, but is in fact a man whose real name is Antonio.... Now I realize, that in these times, such a matter is no big deal, but I suspect his female classmates in P.E. 97 may wish to make other showering arrangements." *Id.* at 139.
[1246] *Id.* at 123.
[1247] *Id.*
[1248] *Id.*
[1249] *Id.*
[1250] *Id.*
[1251] *Id.* at 123–24.
[1252] *Id.* at 124.
[1253] *Id.*
[1254] *Id.* at 139.
[1255] *Id.* at 125.

therefore protected by the First Amendment.[1256] The jury found for Ms. Diaz.[1257]

On appeal, the newspaper argued that the lower court erred in the instructions provided to the jury concerning the right to privacy and who has the burden of proving or disproving newsworthiness.[1258] The lower court instructed the jury that the right to privacy is only to be abridged "when there is a compelling public need."[1259] The court of appeals found that requiring a compelling public need would infringe on the rights of freedom of speech and freedom of the press.[1260] Accordingly, the court found that the jury instruction misstated the law and reversed the judgment.[1261]

The lower court also instructed the jury as to plaintiff's burden in showing an invasion of privacy. Instead of instructing the jury that the plaintiff had the burden of proving that the publication was not privileged, the lower court explained that the defendant had the burden of proving newsworthiness.[1262] The court of appeals found that placing this burden on the defendant would have a chilling effect on the right to free speech.[1263] Accordingly, the court of appeals held that the plaintiff, Ms. Diaz, had the burden of proving that the article was not newsworthy.[1264] But, importantly, the court held that in this case, newsworthiness was a question of fact to be decided by the jury, rather than a matter of law.

In finding that Ms. Diaz had the burden of proving that the article was not newsworthy, the court of appeals discussed California's settled three-part test for newsworthiness: "the social value of the facts published, the depth of the article's intrusion into ostensibly private affairs, and the extent to which the party voluntarily acceded to a position of notoriety."[1265] The court ruled that a jury should decide the newsworthiness question.[1266]

As part of the newspaper's contention that the disclosure was newsworthy, the newspaper asserted that because Ms. Diaz was a public figure,

---

[1256] *Id.*
[1257] *Id.*
[1258] *Id.* at 127.
[1259] *Id.*
[1260] *Id.*
[1261] *Id.*
[1262] *Id.*
[1263] *Id.* at 130.
[1264] *Id.*
[1265] *Id.* at 132 (citing Briscoe v. Reader's Digest Ass'n, 483 P.2d 34 (Cal. 1971)).
[1266] *Id.* at 133.

her real sexual identity was important.[1267] The court disagreed and found that Ms. Diaz was a limited public figure; as such, the public only needed to know about her fitness for the office of student body president.[1268] The court ruled that Ms. Diaz's gender was not *per se newsworthy* under the three-part test, but that it was a question for a jury to decide.[1269] Nevertheless, the court stated that even public figures are entitled to keep certain information concerning their home and sex lives private.[1270]

Therefore, under this test, a jury may determine that a major intrusion was not justified by the "social value of the facts published." This, however, is a minority position nationwide. The fact that this test allows a jury to evaluate the content of an article to determine what is newsworthy most certainly makes First Amendment advocates nervous.

3. The Nexus Approach

Under the nexus test used by the Fifth and Tenth Circuits, there must be "a logical nexus (or relationship) . . . between the complaining individual and the matter of legitimate public interest."[1271] The Tenth Circuit uses the term "substantial relevance" in place of "logical relationship."[1272] Under this test, one must first determine whether the publication was a matter of legitimate public interest. In *Campbell v. Seabury Press*, the Fifth Circuit case that announced the nexus test, the court found that matters of legitimate public interest include "information concerning interesting phases of human activity and embrace[] all issues about which information is needed or appropriate so that individuals may cope with the exigencies of their period."[1273] Further, the court found that such information could be disclosed even when involving persons who have not sought publicity.[1274] This test is considerably different from the three-part California test, since there need not be "social value" derived from the information.

[1267] *Id.* at 134.

[1268] *Id.*

[1269] *Id.*

[1270] *Id.*

[1271] *Id.* at 162 (quoting Campbell v. Seabury Press, 614 F.2d 395, 397 (5th Cir. 1980)).

[1272] *Id.* at 163 (quoting Gilbert v. Medical Economics Co., 665 F.2d 305, 308 (10th Cir. 1981)).

[1273] 614 F.2d 395, 397 (5th Cir. 1980).

[1274] *Id.*

If the facts of the *Diaz* case were evaluated under the Nexus test, it would appear from the *Campbell* opinion that Ms. Diaz would not prevail. The newspaper could argue that Ms. Diaz's sex change was a matter of public interest because it concerned an "interesting phase of human activity." Further, the fact that Ms. Diaz was student body president and billed as the first woman to hold that position may make the publication even more newsworthy.

4. The "Let the Press Decide" Approach

Another approach is called the "leave it to the press" model. This model, noted also by Professor Diane Zimmerman,[1275] is a "*Tornillo*-type"[1276] approach to analyzing newsworthiness. That is, the judiciary defers to the judgment of the editorial department.[1277] If this approach were used in *Diaz*, a court would obviously find no liability on the part of the defendant newspaper.

Under the broad "leave it to the press" option, there are several areas that have received de facto newsworthiness protection that clearly allows the press to decide. Public records are one example. The Supreme Court allowed the publication of a rape and murder victim's name because it was in public court records.[1278] Another example is that if truthful information is lawfully obtained, it will be protected as in *The Florida Star v. B.J.F.* [1279] At issue in *B.J.F.* was the disclosure of information regarding the identity of a rape victim.[1280] In upholding the newspaper's First Amendment right to release the name of the victim, the Supreme Court noted that an individual's right to privacy must be balanced against the interest of newspapers to publish lawfully obtained material.[1281] The Court stopped

---

[1275] Zimmerman, *supra* note 35, at 353.

[1276] *See* Miami Herald Publ'g Co. v. Tornillo, 418 U.S. 241 (1974). In *Tornillo*, a newspaper criticized a political candidate and refused to print the candidate's response. Tornillo argued that the newspaper violated a state "right of reply" statute granting a political candidate a right to equal space to answer criticism and attacks on his or her record by a newspaper and making it a misdemeanor for the newspaper to fail to comply. The U.S. Supreme Court held that the state statute was unconstitutional and that the treatment of public issues and public officials are at the discretion of the newspaper's editors. *Id*. at 258.

[1277] Dendy, *supra* note 1232, at 159.

[1278] *See* Cox Broadcasting Corp. v. Cohn, 420 U.S. 469, 496–97 (1975).

[1279] 491 U.S. 524 (1989).

[1280] *Id*. at 527–28.

[1281] *Id*. at 530.

short of saying that printed truthful, lawfully-obtained material is always protected against an individual's privacy interest.[1282] The Court did, however, hold that "where a newspaper publishes truthful information which it has lawfully obtained, punishment may lawfully be imposed, if at all, only when narrowly tailored to a state interest of the highest order."[1283]

Although courts are inconsistent, most take a narrow view when determining that something is not newsworthy. In other words, most often courts find published information to be newsworthy or protected speech. The *Diaz* case and the *Red Kimono*[1284] case are two isolated examples in which a court found the defendant liable for disclosing true and not misleading facts. Other cases such as *McCabe v. Village Voice*,[1285] in which the court found a photograph of a nude woman in a bathtub not to be newsworthy, *Daily Times Democrat v. Graham*,[1286] in which the court found the newspaper liable for publishing a picture of a woman whose skirt had blown over her had, and *Vassiliades v. Garfinckel's*,[1287] in which the court found for a plaintiff whose before and after plastic-surgery photos were published without her consent, addressed the offensive use of photographs. It appears that courts may be more inclined to protect against intrusive images than intrusive words. In the cases dealing with

---

[1282]   *Id.* at 541.

[1283]   *Id.*

[1284]   Melvin v. Reid, 297 P. 91 (Cal. Ct. App. 1931). In *Melvin*, a female prostitute named Gabrielle Darby was tried and acquitted of murder charges. She turned from her past, married Bernard Melvin, and "lived an exemplary, virtuous, honorable, and righteous life" while keeping her previous life hidden from her friends and her community. *Id.* at 286–87. Without her knowledge or consent, the defendants released a film entitled *The Red Kimono*" and advertised the film as a real-life story, using Ms. Darby's maiden and married names. Ms. Darby claimed that the film caused her friends and community to scorn her and caused her mental anguish and damages in excess of $50,000. A California court held that "the publication by respondents of the unsavory incidents in the past life of appellant after she had reformed, coupled with her true name, was not justified by any standard of morals or ethics known to us, and was a direct invasion of her inalienable right guaranteed to her by our Constitution, to pursue and obtain happiness." *Id.* at 93.

[1285]   550 F. Supp. 525 (E.D. Pa. 1982).

[1286]   162 So. 2d 474 (Ala. 1964). *But see* Neff v. Time, Inc., 406 F. Supp. 858 (D.C. Pa. 1976) (upholding a publishers right to publish a photograph of a man with his fly down at a sporting event against a tortuous claims of commercial appropriation and various punitive damages); McNamara v. Freedom Newspapers, Inc. 802 S.W.2d 901 (Tex. App. 1991) (involving a picture of the exposed genitals of a boy at a soccer game). Interestingly, the *McNamara* court concluded that the disclosure was innocent, but the *Graham* court concluded that the picture was not related to the story and perhaps not newsworthy.

[1287]   492 A.2d 580 (D.C. Ct. App. 1985).

the plastic surgery and the bathtub photographs, the courts focused on the plaintiffs' expectations regarding the use of these sensitive images.[1288] The rarity of cases proves that a finding that a publication is not newsworthy is a rare occurrence indeed. The contemporary state of the law of "newsworthiness" is quite close to a doctrine of "let the press decide."

In addition to being disclosed by the press, personal information is sometimes fictionalized to create an entertaining or profitable work. Although fiction is certainly an acceptable form of entertainment when presented as fiction,[1289] it may fall outside of First Amendment protection when presented as truth.[1290] Use of one's name or likeness for entertainment purposes, such as in a book or movie, would hardly seem to fit within the newsworthiness exception. However, the fact that a movie is typically made for profit does not remove it from constitutional protection. In *Joseph Burstyn, Inc. v. Wilson*, the U.S. Supreme Court stated that expression by means of motion picture is included within the free-speech and free-press guarantees of the First Amendment.[1291] However, the Court also noted that movies are not necessarily subject to the precise rules governing other means of expression, because each method of communication presents its own distinct set of issues and challenges.[1292]

When dramatic license is at work, it may be difficult to distinguish between truth and fiction, or between negligence in reporting and knowing falsity or reckless disregard of the truth. Whether the information depicted is true or false, a movie company still may find shelter under the First Amendment. Hence, an individual whose name or likeness is

---

[1288] In both instances, a primary issue was whether the subject of the photographs consented to the particular use of the photographs. For example, the court in the plastic surgery case held that the plaintiff "was entitled to expect photographs of her surgery would not be publicized without her consent." *Id.* at 586–87.

[1289] *See* Hicks v. Casablanca Records, 464 F. Supp. 426, 433 (S.D.N.Y. 1978) (holding that the right of publicity does not apply where a fictionalized account of an event in a public figure's life is portrayed in a book or movie and it is evident to the public that the events portrayed are fictitious); *cf.* Pring v. Penthouse Int'l Ltd., 695 F.2d 438, 442 (10th Cir. 1982) (stating the test for a false-light claim not as whether the work is classified as fiction or humor, but whether the portions in context could reasonably be understood as describing actual facts about the plaintiff).

[1290] *See* Harte-Hanks Comnc'ns, Inc. v. Connaughton, 491 U.S. 657, 692 (1989) (stating that failure to investigate the factual basis of a newspaper story alone will not support a finding of actual malice, but purposeful avoidance of the truth will); People's Bank & Trust Co. v. Globe Int'l Publ'g, Inc., 978 F.2d 1065, 1069–70 (8th Cir. 1992) (holding that defendant newspaper depicted plaintiff in a false light by purposely avoiding discovering the truth about her yet holding its stories out as factual or true).

[1291] 343 U.S. 495, 502 (1952).

[1292] *Id.* at 502–03.

dramatized in a book or movie may nevertheless fail on a claim of appropriation of name or likeness. If the individual's name or likeness is not used directly to promote the work, but rather as part of the work, a court may find that no invasion of privacy has occurred.[1293] Further, if the individual depicted in the book or movie is no longer living, courts also may find a lack of standing to make a claim.[1294] However, an actor's heirs may have a claim under copyright law.

The First Amendment provides broad protection for the disclosure of information, often at the expense of privacy rights and individuals' control over personal information. The courts have been unable to create a stable or predictable test to determine whether information is "newsworthy." In Chapter VII, I analyze how reforming the newsworthiness test could help better protect privacy. The evolution of modern intrusive news and Internet dissemination requires rethinking the nature of information that is of "legitimate public concern" under the true meaning of the First Amendment.

C. The Politics of Privacy

Privacy in its various forms is controversial. One can find commentators writing on the politics of privacy as it relates to abortion, homosexuality, and women's rights.[1295] But citizens are also concerned about the privacy of their personal information. In April 2006, the Center for American

---

[1293] *See* Tyne v. Time Warner Entertainment Co., L.P., 336 F.3d 1286, 1290 (11th Cir. 2003) (certifying question to the Florida Supreme Court as to whether the defendant's admittedly unauthorized use of the plaintiffs' and their relatives' names and likenesses was "for trade, commercial, or advertising purposes," as that phrase is used in section 540.08 of the Florida Statutes (quoting FLA. STAT. § 540.08 (1998)); *see also* FLA. STAT. § 540.08 (1998).

[1294] For example, in *Tyne*, the lower court found that the plaintiffs, children of a deceased boat captain who was erroneously and negatively depicted in the defendant's motion picture, could prevail in their claim only if they could show that they experienced an independent violation of their own personal privacy rights. *See* Tyne ex rel. Tyne v. Time Warner Entertainment, 204 F. Supp. 2d 1338, 1343 (M.D. Fla. 2002). Although the children themselves were depicted in the film, the court held that the film's portrayal of them was not so egregious as to justify a separate invasion-of-privacy claim. *Id.* The appellate court affirmed this portion of the lower court's ruling, stating that Florida's "relational" right to privacy does not extend to "depictions that are merely inaccurate or dramatized." Tyne, 336 F.3d at 1293.

[1295] *See e.g.*, Danaya C. Wright, *The Logic and Experience of Law:* Lawrence v. Texas *and the Politics of Privacy*, 15 FLA. J.L. & PUB. POL'Y 423–41 (2004).

Progress conducted a poll and found that 69 percent of respondents were very or somewhat worried about having their identities stolen.[1296] A greater percentage of respondents cited identity theft as a concern than cited any other concern in the survey, including getting cancer, being victimized by violent crime, or being hurt or killed in a terrorist attack.[1297] Further, consumers are bombarded with news reports of informational privacy breaches and studies by organizations such as the FTC in early 2000, which indicated that only 20 percent of Web sites complied with the FTC standards for adequate privacy.[1298] Nonetheless, there are strong forces that obstruct substantial reforms. First, there is the commitment to free speech. Reforms must honor the First Amendment. Second, the commitment to public records means that keeping information in public possession confidential is more difficult. Third, the sale and distribution of information is a big business that does not want to be overregulated. And fourth, some information gathering is justified by the need to protect the public from criminal or foreign attacks.

1. Public Records

Public records are a source of information for the press and for the data industry. Further, public policy supports open records to ensure accountability and to foster public debate. There are limits to the openness of public records, as demonstrated by the exceptions to public-records laws across the country.[1299] When the debate over public records becomes a very public debate, sometimes privacy wins.

One of the successes for privacy protection was Florida's passage of legislation protecting family members against the disclosure of autopsy pictures. However, the extraordinary and tragic circumstances surrounding the passage of that bill must be considered very unusual.

[1296] Poll conducted April 13–20, 2006, by Greenberg Quinlan Rosner Research for the Center for American Progress, the Center for Responsible Lending, the National Military Family Association, and AARP.

[1297] Id.

[1298] FTC, PRIVACY ONLINE: FAIR INFORMATION PRACTICES IN THE ELECTRONIC MARKETPLACE: A REPORT TO CONGRESS ii–iii (2000), available at http://www.ftc.gov/reports/privacy2000/privacy2000.pdf.

[1299] For example, there are over a thousand exceptions to Florida's open government laws that are identified in the Florida Sunshine Manual, See generally 2008 GOVERNMENT IN THE SUNSHINE MANUAL (Office of the Attorney General of Florida, 2008).

Dale Earnhardt died in a crash on the last lap of the 2001 Daytona 500 race. Under Florida law, an autopsy was required. Media representatives sought access to the autopsy photos, and a preliminary court action blocked release. At that point, the Florida legislature took up and passed the Family Protection Act, which required persons seeking access to autopsy photographs to show a reason to grant access. The passage of the statute created the classic confrontation between public-disclosure advocates, including the media, and privacy advocates.

The statute was opposed by most media and was challenged in court under Florida's unique open-records constitutional provision.[1300] The provision passed the legislature overwhelmingly and survived the court challenge. The unique and tragic death of such a popular public figure and the active advocacy of his widow, Teresa Earnhardt, made the difference in passage. An attorney and principal lobbyist for the bill, Thom Rumberger, described the opposition to the bill: "Virtually every news organization in Florida, and beyond, opposed it because it was an exception to open records."[1301] Arguments by the media included the statement that no member of the mainstream media would ever publish an autopsy photo. But there are other forms of media beyond the mainstream media. In fact, one of the media outlets involved in the Earnhardt trial,[1302] had published an autopsy photograph of another racecar driver, Neil Bonnett, who had been killed at Daytona in the early 1990s.[1303]

A number of other states have similar protections for the privacy of victims' families.[1304] In specific instances, privacy can prevail. Access to public records, particularly with regard to the conduct of public business, is good public policy. However, there should be limits to intrusions into the lives of regular citizens.

[1300] *See* Campus Commc'ns v. Earnhardt, 821 So. 2d 388 (Fla. Dist. Ct. App. 2002).

[1301] Telephone Interview with Thom Rumberger, partner at Rumberger, Kirk & Caldwell, in Tallahassee, Fla. (Mar. 24, 2008).

[1302] Michael Uribe was a plaintiff and owner of Web site city.com. *See also* findadeath.com and celebritymorgue.com (last visited June 22, 2008).

[1303] Transcript at 11, Earnhardt v. Volusia County, Office of the Med. Exam'r, No. 2001-30373-CICI (Fla. Cir. Ct. July 10, 2001). One of the most dramatic moments of the trial was the testimony of Neil Bonnett's daughter when she described the trauma of seeing her father on the Internet site "gutted like a deer."

[1304] Anaklara Hering, *No two states alike: A statutory analysis of survivor privacy rights*, presented to the Law Division of the national convention of the Association for Education in Journalism and Mass Communications, 2008. A comparison of the state laws controlling access to autopsy records is available in the Marion Brechner Citizen Access Project database at www.citizenaccess.org.

2. The Data Industry

The political issues for federal reforms in the information industry are accuracy of the information; notification of citizens; and accountability for errors.[1305] As described in earlier sections, the federal laws fall short. Why? Members of the industry have pointed out that the information they acquire is usually from public sources and have argued that they cannot be held accountable for the public errors. Notification every time information is requested about a person is said to be impractical. Notably, states have made significant policies in this arena, particularly California.

Early privacy legislation focused on finding an appropriate definition for the public problem. Politicians and scholars debated whether it was a problem of civil liberties and constitutional rights, one of controlling or managing technological change, or one of bureaucratic or organizational accountability.[1306] For the industry, the value of access to informational databases is enormous, as indicated by the chief economist at Dunn & Bradstreet: "It's so inexpensive to redistribute data that public data has in effect become a commodity with very low overhead."[1307] On the other hand, policy communities[1308] fighting for informational privacy often lack the political power to defeat the industry by themselves. For example, when a 1994 amendment to the Fair Credit Reporting Act ("FCRA") was being proposed, one Congressman, Al McCandless (R-Cal.), said that "he was sympathetic to the consumer groups' but argued that their requests would raise costs or be cumbersome or impossible to implement."[1309] Further, since technology advances faster than Congress can pass legislation, congressional policy generally does not focus on technological change, but rather articulates a privacy value that should govern the use of advancing technology in an organizational setting.[1310]

[1305] An example of federal legislation is the Fair and Accurate Credit Transactions Act of 2003, Pub. L. No. 108-159, 117 Stat. 1952 (2003) (amending 15 U.S.C. §§ 1681–1681u). *See* Terrance J. Keenan, *The FACT Act of 2003: Securing Personal Information in an Age of Identity Theft*, 2 SHIDLER J.L. COM. & TECH. 5 (2005).

[1306] *See* PRISCILLA REGAN, LEGISLATING PRIVACY: TECHNOLOGY, SOCIAL VALUES, AND PUBLIC POLICY 20 (1995).

[1307] *Sellers of Government Data Thrive*, N.Y. TIMES, Dec. 26, 1991, at D2.

[1308] Policy communities are specialists in a given policy area, including researchers, congressional staff, interest-group advocates, academics, and government analysts who seek to balance the interests of the industry and the consumer. *See* JOHN KINGDON, AGENDAS, ALTERNATIVES, AND PUBLIC POLICIES 122–28 (2003).

[1309] *Credit Reform Dies in House, in* 1992 CONGRESSIONAL QUARTERLY ALMANAC 119 (1993).

[1310] Regan, *supra* note 1306, at 70.

The end result weighs heavily in favor of allowing the industry to self-regulate because of implementation costs and efficiency.

Today, advocates increasingly are reaching beyond their policy communities and forming coalitions with larger interest groups such as the ACLU to achieve policy legislation.[1311] There are numerous interest groups such as the Privacy Rights Clearinghouse[1312] and the Cyber Security Industry Alliance[1313] that represent a voice in Washington to protect informational privacy but still require coalitions with larger groups to succeed. However, there is yet to be a broad awakening and advocacy from most citizens. There may be substantial interest, but there is little focused citizen advocacy.

3. The First Amendment

There is a strong and effective lobby on issues that affect the ability of the press to publish. Further, constitutional protections can overturn privacy legislation. Even a statute focused on Internet child pornography failed because it was overbroad and limited free speech.[1314]

Under the First Amendment, any reform that affects the freedom to publish on the basis of content is suspect. Therefore, legislation such as the Video Voyeurism Prevention Act[1315] focuses on the conduct of the photographer rather than the content of the video. Under the act, a person must have the intent to capture an image of a "private area" of an individual without consent, and must do so under circumstances in which the individual has a reasonable expectation of privacy. The statute defines "reasonable expectation" as existing under those circumstances in which a person could disrobe in privacy or in which a reasonable person would believe that the private area would not be visible in public. The act is an example of a statute that has a narrow impact. For example, this statute would not provide relief in the case of a *Girls Gone Wild* video filmed in public places and with the acquiescence of the subjects.

[1311]   *Id.* at 210. This was the case with the passage of the Electronic Communications Privacy Act (1986) and the Employee Polygraph Protection Act (1988).

[1312]   *See* Privacy Rights Clearinghouse, http://www.privacyrights.org (last visited May 19, 2008).

[1313]   *See* Cyber Security Industry Alliance, http://www.csialliance.org/home (last visited May 19, 2008).

[1314]   Ashcroft v. ACLU, 542 U.S. 656 (2004) (finding the statute too vague and therefore an impairment to communication).

[1315]   18 U.S.C. § 1801 (Supp. 2004).

The First Amendment does well in contests with privacy, and it appears that that will continue to be the case.

4. National Security and Public Safety

Even when the privacy right is at its strongest, as with the protection of decisional privacy, national-security or public-safety concerns will prevail as a compelling public interest. When the interest is in privacy of personal information, these public purposes are even more likely to prevail. With the substantial concerns about national security as a backdrop, there has been an increase in the authorization and use of surveillance, such as through wiretaps and the interception of e-mail messages. Compelling public interest arguments citing security usually prevail, as political arguments are in favor of national security. The Patriot Act and other national-security legislation have tested the outside edges of governmental authority but generally have received strong public support.[1316]

At least with regard to the security and safety area, the direction of public policy in the last few years clearly has been toward more intervention and intrusion rather than less.

5. Public Referenda

To date, eleven states have enacted constitutional privacy provisions.[1317] In 1978, Florida's freestanding privacy provision was introduced.[1318] It received active support from officials in both parties and from House and Senate members who were considered liberal and from some who were classified as conservative.[1319] It was debated and advocated as a measure to keep big government away from the individual—an argument that worked with liberals, conservatives, and libertarians. Some opponents expressed concern that the provision would provide a separate basis for

---

[1316] Baldwin & Shaw, *supra* note 1202.

[1317] *See infra* Appendix II.

[1318] *See* Ben F. Overton & Katherine E. Giddings, *The Right of Privacy in Florida in the Age of Technology and the Twenty First Century: A Need for Protection from Private and Commercial Intrusion*, 25 Fla. St. U. L. Rev. 25, 34–40 (1997).

[1319] Senate cosponsors included Senator Jack Gordon, considered a liberal from Miami, and Senator Dempsy Barron, considered a conservative from Florida's panhandle. The author was the principal House sponsor.

supporting abortion rights. Also, some media organizations opposed the provision, expressing concern that it would hamper access to public records. Ultimately, the voters approved the provision by over 60 percent.[1320] Privacy as a general concept is politically popular.[1321] The specific impacts relating to volatile issues such as abortion are more controversial. For example, Florida passed a constitutional amendment specifically designed to authorize the legislature to enact parental notification policies for abortion after a previous statute had been struck down under the basic privacy provision.[1322]

[1320] The provision received 60.6% of the vote. *See* http://election.dos.state.fl.us/elections/resultsarchive.index.asp?=11/4/1980&DATAMODE= (last visited June 20, 2008).
[1321] For example the vote on the Florida resolution in the legislature was, in the House 98 Yeas and 4 Nays and in the Senate 34 Yeas and 2 Nays. *See*, Mills, supra note 73 at 827–28. *See generally* Ballot Measures Database compiled by the National Conference on State Legislatures, *available at* http://www.ncsl.org/programs/legismgt/elect/dbintro.htm (last visited May 20, 2008) (providing a database with results of all state legislative and constitutional referenda since 1989).
[1322] FLA.CONST Art X § 22. *See* In Re TW, 551 So.2d 1186 (Fla. 1989) and North Florida Women's Health and Counseling Services, Inc. v. State, 866 So.2d 612 (Fla. 2003).

CHAPTER VI

How Privacy Works in Real Cases:

The Worst-Case Scenarios

The review of legal tools and why those tools often fail shows the complexity and difficulty of navigating privacy claims. A review of a cross section of actual circumstances demonstrates how all these remedies and defenses create a tangled web for citizens and advocates. A particular factual circumstance may simultaneously raise issues in under tort law and common law and affect statutory remedies. Listed below are some disturbing intrusions and how the law reacted to each.

A. *Rolling v. State*: Tragedy and Intrusion

In the middle of August 1990, the college town of Gainesville, Florida, became a focus of world attention for a series of acts of primeval savagery.[1323] Six college students were impaled, beheaded, eviscerated, raped, and murdered. The petite brunette women were attacked in their apartments. A male student was also killed. Press came from around the globe. One after another the murders came and rumors flowered. "Fifteen are dead but the police don't want to tell us." The truth was worse than the rumors.

[1323] A concise and provocative description of the facts surrounding these murders can be found in the opinion of the Florida Supreme Court in State v. Rolling, 695 So. 2d 278 (Fla. 1997).

Six were dead, and there were no suspects. Law enforcement scoured the area, checking all motels, hotels, vacant lots, and boarding houses.

Finally, a suspect was arrested. It was the wrong person. Several weeks later, Danny Harold Rolling was apprehended in nearby Ocala, Florida, on another charge, and the facts began to fall into place. A drifter with delusions of poetic and musical talent was the killer. Forensic and other evidence identified his DNA and demonstrated that he was the monster. Ultimately, he confessed and gave horrifying details of the murders. A jury considered the death penalty. Part of the evidence they reviewed consisted of crime-scene photos of the grotesque atrocities. They rendered a decision in favor of the death penalty, and in 2006 that penalty was carried out.

The photos of the crime scene had been a point of interest for some of the press. The press generally claimed access to the photos, but most professed that they would never publish such horrible material. The state attorney, Rod Smith, asked that I represent the state in a proceeding to prevent the release of the photos to the public.

In one meeting that I will remember for the rest of my life, I met with parents and siblings of the victims. They had already been horribly hurt and could not imagine having their loved ones displayed to the world, naked and broken. Our discussions focused on how to protect the dignity of their loved ones after their passing.

We faced some significant legal hurdles in trying to prevent the disclosure of these photographs by the state. First, as a matter of law, a deceased person has no privacy right. However, anyone who doubts the potential harm to the parents and loved ones of the release of photographs of these brutal murders need only look into their eyes. The harm was, and the right most certainly should be, theirs. Therefore, the focus of our legal argument was the actual intrusion on the relatives rather than an intrusion on the deceased.

Another legal difficulty we faced concerned the nature of the photographs. Floridians have a statutory right of access to public records. The purpose of this statute is to ensure transparency and accountability in the work done by officers of the state. The photographs involved in this case were taken by officers of the state in their official duties.[1324] Furthermore, criminal trials in Florida are to remain open to the public pursuant to

---

[1324]   Florida v. Rolling, 22 Media L. Rep. (BNA) 2264 (Fla. Cir. Ct. 1994).

Florida's rules of criminal procedure, unless a significant basis for closure is shown.

The judge was presented with a difficult set of issues to balance and the horrifying reality of the potential public display of the dismembered and tortured young victims.

The court relied on precedent from the Florida Supreme Court holding that the constitutional right of privacy found in article I, section 23 of the Florida Constitution could form a constitutional basis for the closure of criminal proceedings.[1325] Therefore, the photographs would be subject to the right of privacy of the victims, were they still alive. The court looked to a federal court decision holding that the relatives of deceased astronauts had a derivative right of privacy sufficient to deny the disclosure of audio tapes containing the voices of the dead.[1326] The horrible nature of the photographs and the potential harm they posed for survivors of the victims, the court noted, likely was enough to create an independent right of privacy in the family members themselves. The court explained that regardless of the nature of the right, it was "less than that which would inure to the offended individual, if the offended individual had survived."[1327]

Given that a right to privacy existed in the families of the victims, the court balanced this right against the public's right of access to information. The interests on both sides—on one, a right to privacy in a harrowing time; on the other, the need to preserve public oversight of its officials—were weighty, and the court seemed to believe that they were near equipoise.

Ultimately, the court arrived at an innovative remedy that would preserve the interests on both sides. The photographs were made available to members of the public upon reasonable request to the records custodian, subject to restrictions on the copying and removal of the photographs, as well as on the number of individuals allowed to view them at once. That was as far as the disclosure would go. No other disclosures of the photographs were allowed without a court order.

Three very important factors should be considered. First, the photographs at issue were taken by governmental employees. Second, the

---

[1325] *Id.* (relying on Barron v. Florida Freedom Newspapers, 531 So. 2d 116, 133 (Fla. 1988)).

[1326] *Id.* (relying on New York Times Co. v. NASA, 782 F. Supp. 628 (D.D.C. 1991)).

[1327] *Id.*

photographs themselves were in the custody of the court. Third, the remedy sought in this case was an injunction preventing the release of the pictures. The existence of these facts placed the court in the position of weighing privacy against access to public documents.

If the photographs in *Rolling* had been taken by a newspaper of a crime scene in a public place, the court would have faced an entirely different set of issues. If the family in *Rolling* had tried to have the court enjoin pictures taken by the newspapers involved, the issue before the court would have been prior restraint. If the family had sued after publication of the photographs, seeking damages, the court would have considered the newsworthiness of the event.[1328] The intense media coverage and public interest in this case leaves little doubt as to its newsworthiness.

To further illustrate the manner in which timing can affect legal remedies, consider the *True Stories from the Morgue* case (*Perkins v. Principal Media Group*) explored in section K of this chapter. In that case, photographs were taken by a private entity for publication on television. The photographs were published. The plaintiffs in that suit managed to reach a settlement with the defendants. Certain facts may have been working against the defendants. For instance, some of the photographs were taken from within the police tape marking the perimeter around the crime scene, and others were taken in the morgue. It is debatable how the court would have ruled in the case absent the settlement. However, if the photographs represented the public view of the scene of the suicide, it is unlikely that the court would have prevented a news broadcast of the images. Again, the court would have been faced with the publication of pictures taken by a news agency and either prior restraint or newsworthiness concerns.

The *Rolling* case is an example of great intrusions upon the most innocent of people. In this case, the system worked. The end result was a good one. The families of the victims were spared the possibility of being

---

[1328] *See* Shulman v. Group W. Prods., Inc., 955 P.2d 469 (Cal. 1988). In *Shulman*, a cameraman for a television show accompanied a rescue helicopter to an accident scene. Once there, the cameraman filmed the rescue worker's extrication efforts, as well as treatment efforts and transport in the rescue helicopter. The film was later broadcast on a television show. The segment included the plaintiff telling rescue workers, "I just want to die. I don't want to go through this." The plaintiff, who consented to none of the filming or recording of the events that left her a paraplegic, sued for public disclosure of private facts. The California Supreme Court found that the story was of a legitimate public interest (newsworthy), as were the plaintiff's words, and therefore that the plaintiff could not meet the elements of the private-facts tort.

confronted with the images, or some altered version of them, at a super-market or on cable television. What was private remained private, and what was public remained public. This, of course, is not always the case.

Rolling illustrates once again what a powerful tool a state constitutional right of privacy can be. Were this case to have occurred in another jurisdiction, it might not have come out the same way. This case also shows that victims of newsworthy events, no matter how innocent, will always be the subject of intense media and public scrutiny. The families left behind by these events can become involuntary public figures, another unexpected and unwanted event in a series of already difficult circumstances.

B. *The Perfect Storm*: The Imperfect Remedy

The story portrayed in the film *The Perfect Storm* has become well known. A fishing boat from Gloucester, Massachusetts, goes to sea. It is a caught in one of the worst storms in the history of the area, and all hands on the boat, the *Andrea Gale*, are lost at sea.

A dispute arose over the film's depiction of the captain, Billy Tyne. His surviving relatives were deeply hurt because he was depicted as a reckless and desperate person, when in fact he was well known as a careful and successful captain. The issue was whether this intentional and false representation in the movie created liability.[1329]

The first question was whether the film is protected speech under the First Amendment. Films and fictionalized films long have been considered protected speech. Here, however, the fictionalization was knowing and intentional, and the film was represented as a true story. That is an unusual confluence of circumstances. Under these circumstances, the Eleventh Circuit concluded that the film was not protected speech.[1330]

[1329] "This is not a documentary. . . . This is a motion picture, *largely fictionalized*, to tell a story about fishermen in Gloucester, Massachusetts . . . and how their life is, and *not an accurate recreation and retelling of every single element of the story*. Because if you do that—right?—you might have a story that is *accurate but not dramatic*. If you just go with the facts, very often—very, very often, you get a film that doesn't really get into your heart. . . . *Is it correct in every single detail? Of course not, because we had to—made up a lot of things*." Deposition of Wolfgang Peterson (Director), Initial Brief of Plaintiffs/Morants at 8, Tyne v. Time Warner Entm't Co., No. 901 So.2d 802 (Fla. 2005) (No. SC 03-1251) (emphasis added).

[1330] Tyne v. Time Warner Entm't Co., 336 F.3d 1286, 1292–93 (11th Cir. 2003).

Because the film was not considered protected speech and there was an intentional harmful falsehood, justice would seem to support relief for this intrusion.

At the threshold, false light as an action was not available because the would-be plaintiff was deceased. That left the heirs with an action for familial privacy rights or a statutory action in the right of publicity, which has a right of survivorship.

The question of the meaning of Florida's right-of-publicity statute was sent to the Florida Supreme Court. Confronted with statutory language that allowed recovery for the unauthorized use of one's name or likeness for "advertising or other commercial purposes," the Florida Supreme Court took the narrow view that the right to recovery should be permitted only in the case of unauthorized use in an advertising context, not in other commercial activities such as a movie.[1331] That conclusion drastically reduced the viability of the right-of-publicity claim and left the Tyne family without a remedy.

C. *Williams v. City of Minneola*: Police Party with Autopsy Photos

Fourteen-year-old Glenn Williams died in November 1986 of an apparent drug overdose. There was a belief that foul play was involved in Williams's death, so the Minneola police chief instructed a number of police officers to attend the autopsy. The officers took numerous photographs and even an hour-long video of the autopsy.

One of the officers brought the autopsy video home, where it was shown to both law-enforcement personnel and friends of the officer. On February 21, 1987, the *Orlando Sentinel* published an article describing the viewing as a party where the audience joked and laughed. No formal request was made to the police department or to the family to view the tape.

Glenn Williams's mother and sister sued the City of Minneola on various theories in a Florida court, including intentional infliction of emotional distress, invasion of privacy, and tortious interference with a dead body.[1332] The city responded by arguing first, that the photographs and videotape were public records and second, that no recognized tort applied to the facts of the case.

[1331] Tyne v. Time Warner Entm't Co., 901 So. 2d 802, 810 (Fla. 2005).
[1332] Williams v. City of Minneola, 575 So. 2d 683, 686 (Fla. Dist. Ct. App. 1991).

The court first held that although the videotape and photographs may have been public records, that fact does not grant a custodian protection from tort liability "resulting from that person's intentionally communicating public records or their contents to someone outside the agency which is responsible for the records without a bona fide request or official business necessity."[1333] The court, however, concluded that it was a factual question for the jury to determine whether the officers had made a bona fide request or whether it was necessary to the transaction of the agency's business to display such records to the persons to whom they were shown and in the manner in which they were shown.

With respect to intentional infliction of emotional distress, the court held that:

> a cause of action in tort for reckless infliction of emotional distress can lie for outrageous conduct involving pictures of the dead body of a plaintiff's spouse, child, sibling or parent, even though the plaintiff was not present at the display of the pictures and the allegedly tortious conduct did not physically impact the plaintiff, whether or not the emotional distress in turn caused physical harm to the plaintiff.[1334]

This case is critical because it recognizes a privacy right in family members and allows them to bring a claim for reckless or outrageous acts by a third party, even without physical injury. The court remanded the case for a jury to decide whether it was reasonably foreseeable that the Williams family would learn of the events involving the pictures of their dead son.

On remand, the City of Minneola moved for summary judgment, and the trial court granted the motion on the basis of sovereign immunity. The motion for summary judgment was affirmed[1335] because even if the jury found the officers' conduct to be reckless, the City of Minneola was protected by sovereign immunity under Florida law. The family was thus denied any recovery.[1336]

[1333]   *Id.* at 683.

[1334]   *Id.* at 690.

[1335]   Williams v. City of Minneola, 619 So. 2d 983 (Fla. Dist. Ct. App. 1993).

[1336]   Florida law provides, "The state or its subdivisions shall not be liable in tort for the acts . . . of an officer . . . committed in bad faith or with malicious purpose or in a manner exhibiting wanton and willful disregard or human rights, safety, or property." Fla. Stat. § 768.28(9)(a) (2007).

D. The Amy Boyer Case: The Lethal Credit Report

Docusearch, Inc. is an Internet-based investigation and information company operated out of Palm Beach County, Florida. In July 1999, a New Hampshire resident, Liam Youens, placed an online order through Docusearch to obtain the date of birth of Amy Lynn Boyer. In a little over a month, Youens placed six separate orders with Docusearch to locate Boyer. Docusearch obtained Boyer's Social Security number through credit-reporting agencies and provided Youens with Boyer's home and work addresses. On October 15, 1999, Youens used this information to shoot and kill Boyer at her place of work and then turned the gun on himself.

Boyer's estate sought recovery for wrongful death, intrusion upon seclusion, commercial appropriation of private information, violation of the federal Fair Credit Reporting Act, and violation of a New Hampshire consumer-protection act.[1337] The New Hampshire Supreme Court held that Docusearch owed a duty to the plaintiff, asserting that if the disclosure "of information to a client creates a foreseeable risk of criminal misconduct against the third person whose information was disclosed, the investigator owes a duty to exercise reasonable care not to subject the third person to an unreasonable risk of harm."[1338] A party who realizes or should realize that his or her conduct creates a condition involving an unreasonable risk of harm to another has a duty to exercise reasonable care to prevent the risk from occurring. The foreseeable risks under these circumstances are stalking and identity theft.

The court found that Boyer's estate had a cause of action against Docusearch for the release of Boyer's Social Security number, but the court held that a cause of action did not exist for the disclosure of her work address.[1339] Boyer had a reasonable expectation of privacy in her Social Security number, and that privacy was violated when Docusearch obtained and sold Boyer's Social Security number without her knowledge or consent. However, that same expectation of privacy was not found in her work address. The court held that there can be no intrusion upon seclusion where a person's work address is readily observable by members of the public.[1340]

[1337]   Remsburg v. Docusearch, Inc., DNH 90, 2002 WL 844403 (D.N.H. Apr. 25, 2002).
[1338]   Remsburg v. Docusearch, Inc., 149 N.H. 148, 154 (2003).
[1339]   Id. at 156.
[1340]   Id. at 157.

Further, the court granted Docusearch's motion for summary judgment as to Boyer's claim of commercial appropriation. Although the court recognized the availability of the tort, the court asserted that a person whose personal information is sold does not have a cause of action for appropriation against the investigator who sold the information. The court explained that an investigator simply sells the information for the value of the information, distinguishing that action from actually capitalizing on the goodwill associated with the information.[1341]

Thus, it appears that although the consumer data industry has a duty toward third parties when there is a foreseeable risk of criminal harm, the victim's recovery is limited and depends on the nature of the information sold to third parties. Unfortunately, the industry often does not know to whom they are selling personal information, and that can lead to horrific consequences.

E. *New York Times Co. v. NASA* : Broadcasting Final Words

On January 28, 1986, the space shuttle Challenger took off from Cape Canaveral, Florida, and disintegrated seventy-three seconds into flight over the Atlantic Ocean, killing all seven astronauts aboard. The disaster was clearly news in itself, but the Challenger flight was also NASA's first attempt to put a teacher, Christa McAuliffe, in space.

The voice recorder on board the space shuttle was recovered from the floor of the Atlantic Ocean six weeks after the disaster and contained all the conversations and background noises within the shuttle between liftoff and disintegration. In July 1986, a *New York Times* reporter filed a written Freedom of Information Act ("FOIA") request with NASA seeking transcripts as well as a copy of the recovered tapes. NASA provided the reporter with a transcript of the tapes but refused to provide a copy of the tapes, citing an exception to FOIA. FOIA provides that an agency shall not disclose "personnel and medical files and similar files the disclosure of which would constitute a clearly unwarranted invasion of personal privacy."[1342]

Courts have found that the purpose of this privacy provision is to guard against the unnecessary disclosure of files that "contain 'intimate details' of a 'highly personal' nature."[1343] One of the arguments proffered

---

[1341] *Id.* at 158.
[1342] 5 U.S.C. § 552(b)(6) (2000).
[1343] Getman v. NLRB, 450 F.2d 670, 675 (D.C. Cir. 1971).

by the *New York Times* in pursuit of disclosure was that because the transcripts revealed strictly technical conversations, no "intimate details" would be revealed by the disclosure of the voice records. However, the court clarified that the privacy interest of the relatives did not lie in *what* was said on the voice records, but rather in *how* the astronauts said what they did.[1344]

According to the court, this privacy interest was substantial. Besides the trauma experienced by the families every time the tapes were broadcast over the news, the families might be subject to a barrage of mailings and telephone calls from reporters attempting to report the families' state of mind every time a clip of the tape was played.[1345] Although the *New York Times* argued that the public has a strong interest in hearing the various inflections and tenors in the astronauts' voices, the court held that disclosure of the voice recordings would be an unwarranted intrusion of the families' privacy.[1346] Although FOIA favors disclosure, the court held that because the personal privacy interest was substantial, the public interest was uncertain, and the agency had already provided written transcripts, the voice recordings should not be released.

F. *Plaxico v. Michael*: The Reasonable Peeping Father

Glenn Michael and his ex-wife divorced, and a bitter custody battle ensued over their six-year-old daughter. Following the divorce, Mr. Michael's ex-wife had custody of the daughter and moved into a cabin the family used to rent as a vacation home. The ex-wife and daughter were soon sharing the cabin with a roommate, Rita Plaxico.

Mr. Michael was later informed that his ex-wife was having a homosexual relationship with Ms. Plaxico, and as a result, he sought to modify the child-custody arrangement.[1347] Attempting to gather evidence of the homosexual relationship, Mr. Michael slipped up to a window in the cabin and witnessed Plaxico and his ex-wife having sexual relations.[1348] Mr. Michael then retrieved a camera from his vehicle and took three photographs of Ms. Plaxico naked in the bed, covered from the waist

---

[1344]   New York Times Co. v. NASA, 782 F. Supp. 628, 631 (D.D.C. 1991).
[1345]   *Id.* at 632.
[1346]   *Id.* at 633.
[1347]   Plaxico v. Michael, 735 So. 2d 1036, 1038 (Miss. 1999).
[1348]   *Id.*

down with bed sheets. Mr. Michael developed the photographs and delivered them to his attorney, who subsequently used the photographs to help Mr. Michael regain custody of his daughter from his ex-wife.[1349]

Ms. Plaxico learned about the photographs and filed a lawsuit against Mr. Michael for invasion of privacy. Ms. Plaxico claimed that Mr. Michael intentionally intruded upon her seclusion and solitude. Her lawsuit, however, was dismissed by a circuit court in Tippah County, Mississippi, because the trial court found that Mr. Michael had a qualified privilege to obtain the evidence in order to protect his child.[1350]

In a 4–3 decision, the Mississippi Supreme Court stated that in order for a plaintiff to recover for intentional intrusion upon the solitude or seclusion of another, the act must be "a substantial interference with his seclusion of a kind that would be highly offensive to the ordinary, reasonable man, as the result of conduct to which the reasonable man would strongly object."[1351] Applying this test to the facts, the court found that a reasonable person would not feel that Mr. Michael's actions were substantially invasive enough to merit the gross offensiveness required by the test. The fact that his ex-wife was having sexual relations with a woman, rather than a man, was irrelevant to the court, which asserted that any illicit affair would warrant Mr. Michael's actions. The court even stated that "most reasonable people would feel Michael's actions were justified in order to protect the welfare of his minor child."[1352]

In the court's two dissenting opinions, the judges criticized Mr. Michael's actions as an unjustified means to an end. In their view, this was simply a voyeuristic act against a woman, Ms. Plaxico, who was not even a party to the custody proceedings. The dissent claimed that the majority misplaced the qualified privilege and that even if such a privilege existed, it could apply only to the ex-wife, not to Ms. Plaxico.

G. *In re Guardianship of Schiavo*: The Politics of Life Support

Theresa (Terri) and Michael Schiavo were happily married and living in Florida until their lives instantly changed on February 15, 1990. Ms. Schiavo, twenty-seven years old, suffered cardiac arrest as a result of a potassium

---

[1349] *Id.*
[1350] *Id.* at 1037.
[1351] *Id.* at 1039.
[1352] *Id.* at 1040.

imbalance and never regained consciousness.[1353] Following that incident, Ms. Schiavo lived in nursing homes, where she suffered multiple health problems, required the staff to change her diapers regularly, and received her food and hydration by tubes. Michael Schiavo and Terri's family existed amicably for the first three years but soon cut off communication entirely over Ms. Schiavo's future. Mr. Schiavo could discontinue the artificial life support in the absence of an advanced directive ended up as a question in the courts.

The trial and appellate courts found clear and convincing evidence that Theresa was in a persistent vegetative state and that Theresa would elect to cease life-prolonging procedures if she were competent to make her own decision.[1354] After ten years in a persistent vegetative state, Theresa lost most of her cerebral and all but the most instinctive neurological functions, and there was no medical procedure available to repair the harm. Ms. Schiavo's family strenuously appealed in a number of Florida courts, seeking to keep their daughter on artificial life support, but failed.

In their fourth opinion regarding Ms. Schiavo, the Second District Court of Appeals in Florida stated that the case was not about the aspirations of loving parents for their children, but rather "Theresa Schiavo's right to make her own decisions, independent of her parents and independent of her husband," and that unfortunately, the best forum available for such a private matter is a public courtroom consisting of judges "with no prior knowledge of the ward."[1355] Doctors removed Ms. Schiavo's nutrition and hydration tubes on October 15, 2003.

The Florida legislature attempted to intervene and passed an act into law giving the Governor the power to issue a stay to prevent the withholding of nutrition and hydration from a patient under the circumstances surrounding the Schiavo issue. Then governor Jeb Bush issued the executive order, and the nutrition and hydration tubes were reinserted on October 21, 2003.

On the same day, Michael Schiavo brought an action for declaratory judgment, and the trial court found the legislation unconstitutional on its face as an unlawful delegation of legislative authority and as a violation of the right of privacy, and unconstitutional as applied because it allowed the governor to encroach on the judicial power and to retroactively

---

[1353] *In re* Guardianship of Schiavo, 780 So. 2d 176, 177 (Fla. Dist. Ct. App. 2001).
[1354] *Id.* at 177.
[1355] *Id.* at 183.

abolish Ms. Schiavo's vested right to privacy. The Florida Supreme Court agreed and declared the legislation unconstitutional.[1356]

In the absence of an advanced directive, it is clearly problematic for families to make such decisions standing in the shoes of their loved one. Unfortunately, as the court realized, the *Schiavo* litigation quickly moved away from protecting the privacy interests of Terri Schiavo and into a public forum of politics and courtrooms.

H. *Board of Education v. Earls*: On the Road to Random Drug Testing of All Public-School Students

Lindsey Earls, a student in the Tecumseh, Oklahoma, school district, was a member of her school's show choir, the marching band, the Academic Team, and the National Honor Society.[1357] Following the adoption of a new drug-testing policy by her school district in 1998, her membership in these extracurricular activities became dependent on her willingness to consent to random drug tests. In other words, if she remained in the marching band, Lindsey could be summoned at any time to a restroom stall, where she would urinate into a cup. While she urinated, a monitor positioned just outside of the stall listened in.[1358] Lindsey sued the school district, and in 2002, the Supreme Court held that random drug testing of all students who participated in extracurricular activities was permissible under the Constitution.[1359]

In 1995, the Court held random drug testing of all student athletes in a school district to be constitutional.[1360] The Court, relying on precedent that Fourth Amendment protections were less potent in public schools, decided that these protections were even less potent for athletes. The Court discussed the acts of going out for the team and participating in communal undress, as well as the physical dangers inherent in athletics, to emphasize the limited scope of the privacy interest at stake. The Court also determined that the nature of the intrusion upon privacy was, in the case of collecting urine from students for analysis, negligible.[1361] The case tacitly invited further intrusions upon the privacy of public school students,

---

[1356] Schindler v. Schiavo ex rel. Schiavo, 789 So.2d 348 (Fla. 2001).
[1357] Bd. of Educ. v. Earls, 536 U.S. 822, 825 (2002).
[1358] Earls v. Bd. of Educ., 242 F.3d 1264, 1267 (10th Cir. 2001), *overruled by* 536 U.S. 822 (2002).
[1359] *Earls*, 536 U.S. at 825.
[1360] Veronia Sch. Dist. 47J v. Acton, 515 U.S. 646, 655 (1995).
[1361] *Id.* at 658.

and in *Earls*, the Court held constitutional the random drug testing of all students involved in extracurricular activities.

In *Earls*, the Court downplayed the language in *Veronia* about communal undress and athletic injury, relying on the custodial nature of the student-school relationship and its significance for the nature of a student's privacy interest.[1362] Instead of requiring a particularized suspicion before drug testing, the Court focused on the national problem of student drug use and the threat that drug use posed to all students.[1363] Given the limited privacy interest held by students participating in extracurricular activities, the negligible invasiveness of drug testing, and the compelling governmental need to combat student drug use, the Court took another step toward, random drug testing of students for almost any purpose.

The Court in both *Veronia* and in *Earls* "conspicuously omitted discussion as to whether such a policy should apply to all students."[1364] Additionally, the *Earls* Court's recognition of the national nature of the drug problem and the danger posed to all students may signal a willingness to continue the trend toward allowing more extensive random drug testing. Thus, it may only be a matter of time before all public-school students are subject to random tests, simply for going to school.[1365] Indeed, since the *Earls* decision, school districts have seized the opportunity to extend their drug-testing policies. In the town of Katy, Texas, the school district randomly tests all student athletes, students participating in extracurricular activities, and students who drive to school.[1366]

Veronia and *Earls* stand for the proposition that students in public schools have very limited and ever-decreasing privacy rights.[1367] When these rights are violated, there is little recourse for students or parents. Absent egregious violations of protocol, the Fourth Amendment apparently will not help.

[1362] *Earls*, 536 U.S. at 831.

[1363] *Id.* at 834. This is of particular importance, as the school district in *Earls* did not have a drug problem to speak of. In *Veronia*, the drug problem facing the school board was described as "epidemic." 515 U.S. at 662–63.

[1364] John F. Donaldson, *Life, Liberty, and the Pursuit of Urinalysis: The Constitutionality of Random Suspicionless Drug Testing in Public Schools*, 41 VAL. U. L. REV. 815, 848 (2006).

[1365] For a more detailed exploration of this possibility, *see id.*

[1366] *See* NAT'L SCH. BDS. ASS'N, STUDENT DRUG TESTING 11 (2005), *available at* http://www.nsba.org/MainMenu/SchoolBoardPolicies/NSBAFederalGuidanceDocuments/StudentDrugTesting.aspx.

[1367] In Tannahill v. Lockney Independent School District, 133 F. Supp. 2d 919 (N.D. Tex. 2001), a federal court in Texas held unconstitutional a policy that allowed the random drug testing of all students. This case was decided in the interim between *Veronia* and *Earls*, however, and it is unclear whether its analysis would hold post *Earls*.

I. The "Washingtonienne": Kissing and Telling . . . Everyone

Jessica Cutler, a staff member of then senator Mike Dewine of Ohio, led an interesting social life. Unfortunately for at least one man, she decided to write about it. While she was a staffer on the Hill, Ms. Cutler created a blog entitled The Washingtonienne.[1368] In it, she described her thoughts on several matters, but the discussion often centered on her sexual escapades with several men in the Washington, D.C., area. A young man named Robert Steinbuch, who at the time he was described in The Washingtonienne was counsel to the Senate Committee on the Judiciary, sued Ms. Cutler in a federal court in Washington, D.C., for public disclosure of private facts, false-light invasion of privacy, and intentional infliction of emotional distress.

In Mr. Steinbuch's complaint, he alleged that Ms. Cutler referred to him by his initials, Jewish heritage, job title, place of residence, general appearance, and other factors throughout the blog, and ultimately by his full name.[1369] Far from simply musing about their budding relationship, Ms. Cutler discussed in vivid detail aspects of her sexual relationship with "R. S." In his complaint, Mr. Steinbuch alleged that Ms. Cutler disclosed descriptions of his erections and ejaculation, his particular sexual preferences, conversations the two had both in general and during sex, and other intimate details. Mr. Steinbuch claimed to have suffered economic damages, professional and personal harm, severe emotional distress, humiliation, and other damages and asked for $20 million. The very fact that Mr. Steinbuch has initiated litigation, however, exposes him to further public scrutiny.[1370]

This case, unresolved at the time of this writing, raises several important issues. First, it represents a truly vexing factual scenario within the tort of public disclosure of private facts.[1371] Two people have a sexual relationship, and one of them decides to share the details—not at a dinner party, but through media. The tort may not be built to sustain such a scenario. Are the facts truly private if shared by two people?

[1368] On the day Ms. Cutler's identity was discovered, she erased the blog. But archives of the blog were still available to the public at http://www.wonkette.com/archives/the-lost-washingtonienne-wonkette-exclusive-etc-etc-004162.php (last visited May 18, 2008). Ms. Cutler's current Web site is http://www.jessicacutleronline.com (last visited May 18, 2008).

[1369] *See* Complaint of Plaintiff at 3, Steinbuch v. Cutler, No. 05CV00970, 2005 WL 1467405 (D.D.C. May 18, 2005).

[1370] *See*, DANIEL SOLOVE, THE FUTURE OF REPUTATION, GOSSIP, RUMOR AND PRIVACY ON THE INTERNET 120 (2007).

[1371] *See* discussion *supra* Chapter IV, § D-4.

The tort of public disclosure of private facts is meant to punish the truthful disclosure of unnewsworthy matters highly offensive to the reasonable person. However, courts often interpret newsworthiness broadly.[1372] An article by Professor Andrew J. McClurg explains a range of possible newsworthy interpretations of Ms. Cutler's disclosures, including their bearing on women's political theories, D.C. residents' interest in the political implications of the scandal, and the role of women in politics.[1373] If a court agrees that any of these issues are newsworthy and that the blog's content addressed them, Mr. Steinbuch's claim for public disclosure of private facts will fail.

It also should be noted that Mr. Steinbuch has no privacy claim against the Internet service provider ("ISP") through which the blog was disseminated. As previously noted, the Communications Decency Act grants ISPs immunity from liability for information originating from a third party.[1374] Therefore, Mr. Steinbuch's field of potential defendants is limited.[1375]

It appears that the English doctrine of breach of confidence is ill suited to sustain disclosures by former lovers as well. Breach of confidence protects against disclosures made against a confidential relationship or information obtained in breach of confidence. A confidential relationship does not necessarily arise around information regarding an individual's private or sex life.[1376] Although the information shared between two people

---

[1372]   See discussion of newsworthiness *infra* Chapter VII, § B-4. Bonome v. Kaysen, 17 MASS. L. RPTR. 695 (Super. Ct. 2004) is a good example. *Bonome* involved the author of the popular book *Girl Interrupted*. In it, the author described an affair she had with a married man who later became her live-in boyfriend. She discussed their sexual and emotional relationship, explaining one instance in which her boyfriend was physically forceful when trying to initiate sex. He sued for public disclosure of private facts and lost. In gauging newsworthiness, the court used the "nexus" approach of the Fifth and Tenth Circuits and determined that the recurring and seemingly undiagnosable vaginal pain the author suffered and its impact on her relationship with the plaintiff was a topic of legitimate public concern. It was impossible for the author to discuss this matter without discussing the plaintiff. Therefore, the disclosure was protected.

[1373]   Andrew McClurg, *Kiss and Tell: Protecting Intimate Relationship Privacy Through Implied Contracts of Confidentiality*, 74 UNIV. CIN. L. REV. 887, 902 (2006).

[1374]   Under 47 U.S.C. § 230(c)(1), "No provider or user of an interactive computer service shall be treated as the publisher or speaker of any information provided by another information content provider."

[1375]   Steinbuch also filed suit in an Arkansas federal court against Hyperion Books, Disney Publishing Worldwide, Home Box Office, and Time Warner for misappropriation of likeness, intrusion upon seclusion, and false light for a book by Cutler based on the blogs. The complaint was dismissed for lack of personal jurisdiction. *See* Steinbuch v. Cutler, No. 4:06CV00620-WRW, 2007 WL 486626 (E.D. Ark. Feb. 7, 2007).

[1376]   Wacks, *supra* note 428, at 163.

may be private in nature, once one of the parties decides to disclose, the protection wanes.

In *Theakston v. MGN Ltd.*, the host of radio and television shows for the BBC was photographed having sex with a prostitute in a brothel.[1377] He sued to enjoin the publication of the photographs as well as an article about the incident. The court considered the nature of the relationship at hand and determined that transitory relationships are lower on the spectrum of confidentiality than those of a continuing nature.[1378] The nature of the relationship, coupled with the fact that the acts took place in a brothel and the public's interest in the controversy, led the court to refuse to enjoin the news story.[1379] The photographs, on the other hand, were enjoined, as the plaintiff had a reasonable expectation not to be photographed during the incident.[1380]

In *A v. B & C*, a footballer, A, had an affair with C, who in turn decided to disclose the details to newspaper B.[1381] The court explained that if one of the parties to the creation of the confidence decides to publish a story, the protection of the doctrine of breach of confidence gives way to the right of expression.[1382] Emphasizing the sliding scale of confidential personal relationships discussed in *Theakston*, the court also found that transitory sexual relationships do not enjoy the same protections as marriages, and found that B was free to disclose those facts without legal liability.[1383]

Thus, both the American tort of public disclosure of private facts and the English tort of breach of confidence fail to protect information shared in a situation that most people consider very private. Intimate personal relationships, by their nature, expose both parties to the personal details of the other. As a matter of daily life, people confide in their intimate others, whether through conversation, shared experience, or sex. As Professor McClurg explains, romantic partners often know the details of each other's mental and physical health, business affairs, sexual preferences, quirks, eccentricities, and innermost secrets.[1384] This information, which can help to foster and develop a relationship, can also become a

---

[1377] [2002] E.M.L.R. 22.
[1378] *Id.* at 57.
[1379] *Id.* at 69.
[1380] *Id.*
[1381] [2002] EWCA (Civ.) 337 (Eng.).
[1382] *Id.* ¶ 11(x)–(xi).
[1383] *Id.* ¶¶ 45–47.
[1384] McClurg, *supra* note 1373 at 913.

dangerous tool in the hands of a scorned lover. Despite the very personal—and ostensibly private—nature of these relationships, courts have adopted a "caveat emptor" approach to protecting against the disclosure of information in this context. The lesson appears to be: be careful whom you trust with embarrassing information.

J. *Moore v. Regents of the University of California*: Do We Own the "Building Blocks" of Our Lives?

In *Moore v. Regents of the University of California*, doctors guided a patient toward surgery to remove his spleen. Subsequently, Moore's doctors urged that he return several times.[1385] During those visits, doctors removed blood and bone samples. The doctors then used his rare cells for research and the eventual acquisition of a patent.[1386] Moore sued for breach of fiduciary duty and conversion. The California Supreme Court held that he stated a cause of action for breach of fiduciary duty, in that the doctors had a duty to disclose personal interests to the patient, even if unrelated to the patient's health.[1387] Moore failed on the conversion claim, however, because he retained no property interest in his cells after they left his body and the cell line that was the subject of the patent was distinguishable from that which researchers obtained from his body.[1388] This case represents an area of privacy law that is still developing but that has the potential to affect the lives of every person alive.

DNA carries with it a person's genetic and hereditary information. Although it may seem cellular, abstract, and complicated, genetic information is intimately private. In addition to the type of situation presented in *Moore*, where genetic information was taken surreptitiously and under false pretenses and then used for profit, genetic information could be used against its owner in a variety of ways. The obvious risks are loss of employment or health insurance due to a genetic predisposition to a particular disease, a risk addressed by the Genetic Information Nondiscrimination Act.[1389] For instance, DNA houses not only the entire genetic makeup of an individual but information about family members.[1390]

[1385] *See* Moore v. Regents of the Univ. of Calif., 793 P.2d 479 (Cal. 1990).
[1386] *Id.* at 480–82.
[1387] *Id.* at 485.
[1388] *Id.* at 492.
[1389] George J. Annas, *Genetic Privacy: There Ought to Be a Law*, 4 Tex. L. & Pol. 9 (1999).
[1390] *Id.*

Additionally, the collection and retention of genetic information poses privacy and constitutional issues. The DNA Analysis Backlog Elimination Act of 2000, coupled with provisions of the Patriot Act, authorizes the collection and retention of DNA material from individuals convicted of certain crimes, including, among others, murder, assault, sexual and child abuse, kidnapping, robbery, burglary, arson, and acts of terrorism.[1391] The DNA is placed in a database. Five federal circuit courts have upheld these DNA databases as constitutional under the Fourth Amendment.[1392]

There are statutes protecting against discrimination based on genetic information, but they do not address the entire range of issues likely to arise in this context.[1393] A more intimate understanding of the issues surrounding genetic information—starting with the recognition of a privacy interest in it—is required before information containing perhaps the most intimately private facts of a person's existence will be protected.

K. *Perkins v. Principal Media Group*: Broadcasting an Autopsy

On October 5, 2001, Misty Norman and her husband, Torre Norman, checked into the Opryland Hotel in Nashville, Tennessee. Sometime that evening, Misty was thrown from the balcony by her husband, who then fell or jumped. Both died.[1394]

Police came to the scene along with the medical examiner. So too did a film crew from the show *True Stories from the Morgue* on the Learning Channel. This was not an accident but the result of an agreement between the television company and the medical examiner.

Investigators and police secured and sequestered the scene, but permitted the film crew to film the crime scene and the dead body of Misty Norman. The film crew and personnel from the medical examiner's office filmed and narrated an account of the scene, including Mrs. Norman's seminude body and crushed skull.[1395]

[1391]   42 U.S.C. 14135 (2000).

[1392]   *See* United States v. Kincade, 379 F.3d 813 (9th Cir. 2004) (en banc); Roe v. Marcotte, 193 F.3d 72 (2d Cir. 1999); Boling v. Romer, 101 F.3d 1336 (10th Cir. 1996); Jones v. Murray, 962 F.2d 302 (4th Cir. 1992).

[1393]   Janet A. Benton, *Are Your Genes Protected? Federal Legislation and Genetic Discrimination*, 10 J. Gender Race & Just. 285, 287 (2007).

[1394]   Perkins v. Principal Media Group, No. 3:03-CV-00578 (M.D. Tenn., May 12, 2005).

[1395]   *Id.*

The next morning, the medical examiner permitted the film crew to enter his office and photograph the nude bodies of Mr. and Mrs. Norman. He showed the fatal injuries and described wounds that he said indicated "prior suicide attempts."

The parents and sister of Misty Norman sued the Learning Channel, the parties associated with the program, and the medical examiner's office.[1396] The plaintiffs attempted a long list of actions to remedy the invasion, including:

- intrusion upon seclusion;
- public disclosure of private facts;
- invasion of "family privacy";
- invasion of medical records;
- right of publicity;
- violation of a statute preventing involuntary filming;
- an action under 42 U.S.C. § 1983 against the medical examiner;
- intentional infliction of emotional distress;
- negligent infliction of emotional distress;
- statutory misuse of a corpse;
- conversion; and
- deceptive trade practices under state statute.

This case offers an example of the application of numerous remedies. A number of these causes of action failed immediately because they pertain to personal rights held by the individual and do not survive death. The attorney representing the Perkins believed that there was a good chance to prove a family or "relational" right to privacy. In cases relating to freedom of information and the disclosure of autopsy pictures, rights of family members have been recognized, separate and apart from the privacy rights of the deceased.[1397] He also believed that the intentional infliction of emotional distress, and the section 1983 challenge were very viable.

Ultimately, the medical examiner and the television company settled. The television series was cancelled. The settlement suggests that these

---

[1396] The legal authority for the family members to bring an action on behalf of Misty Norman is discussed in Chapter IV, § E-5.

[1397] Telephone Interview with David Smith, *supra* note 1092; *see, e.g.,* New York Times Co. v. NASA, 782 F. Supp. 628 (D.D.C. 1991); Campus Commc'ns, Inc. v. Earnhardt, 821 So. 2d 388 (Fla. Dist. Ct. App. 2002); State v. Rolling, No. 91-3832 CF A, 1994 WL 722891 (Fla.Cir.Ct. July 24, 1994).

outrageous facts provided a good basis for a plaintiff to prevail with a jury. The case also demonstrates that many of the traditional remedies are useless in the face of a terrible intrusion and the need to try multiple and creative approaches to obtain relief.

The lessons learned from these real cases are many. First, intrusions come from all directions: the government, the press, business, and individuals. Even what seem to be obviously bad acts are sometimes not punished—take, for example, the police officers displaying a child's autopsy photos. Second, the First Amendment and free speech are powerful tools. Even the intimate disclosures of the "Washingtonienne" may be newsworthy. Third, the law is lagging behind technology and must struggle mightily to catch up, as is demonstrated by the selling of DNA. Fourth, citizens sacrifice privacy for security, and that trend is unlikely to stop.[1398] Overall, the lesson may be that each circumstance requires a specific a focused assessment of all available remedies and strategies. As mentioned above, had the photographs of the murder victims in *Rolling* been released (or taken by the press), the press' publication of those photos would likely have been protected speech of a newsworthy tragedy. But the photos never were released, so that harm was avoided. With these lessons in mind, the overall strategy for privacy remedies is necessarily complex and extensive.

[1398] *See* discussion *supra* Chapter VI, § H.

CHAPTER VII

Strategies and Remedies to Protect Privacy

The preceding sections of this book compel two conclusions: (1) privacy rights are diminishing in contemporary society; and (2) existing legal tools, which include constitutional protections, tort remedies, statutory protections, and litigation based on property theories, are inadequate to protect privacy in a changing world. This section examines broad policy changes, reinterpretations of existing remedies, the potential for the creation of new theories, and practical options to achieve individual privacy.

In formulating new strategies to protect privacy, one must confront the fact that protecting privacy conflicts with other values, such as public safety and free speech. Furthermore, privacy is subjective to individuals and is a moving target in a quickly evolving society. Perhaps we need a basic shift in the way our society views and values the individual in the privacy context. In both the European Union and Latin America, there is an emphasis on personal dignity, whereas the American philosophy grants primacy to free expression at the expense of personal dignity.

Writers and commentators have taken a range of approaches in suggesting reforms to privacy policies. Some suggest focusing on the issues of data creation and protection rather than rejuvenating old remedies.[1399] This approach often includes establishing a national agency aimed at monitoring, overseeing, and enforcing penalties for abuses of information.[1400]

[1399] Neil M. Richards, *The Information Privacy Law Project*, 94 GEO. L.J. 1087 (2006), *available at* http://ssrn.com/abstract=941181.
[1400] *See id.*

This can be termed the policy approach. Another approach is to enhance and implement legal remedies in courts to make violators of privacy rights pay heavily for mistakes, thereby compelling reform. This could be termed the trial-lawyer approach. A third approach is to let the market drive information-protection reform because consumers will demand more personal privacy.[1401] This is the market approach. There is something to be learned from each of these views and approaches.

Among the various forms of privacy, informational privacy is most in jeopardy when compared with autonomy rights. Constitutional protections of personal autonomy are well developed, and the theories are well established. Personal-autonomy issues, such as abortion rights and the right to die, may face challenges from interpretations of existing law based on evolving Supreme Court positions. The challenge there, however, is not whether a remedy exists but rather how to apply that remedy. If the Supreme Court retreats from previous positions, the application of the remedy will be based on an interpretation of law that no longer recognizes a reasonable expectation of privacy or that finds a compelling governmental interest in regulating conduct. This impact is no less threatening to individual privacy. In fact, one could argue that autonomy issues will be at substantial risk in the years to come. It is not likely, however, that the Court will abolish the privacy right related to autonomy.[1402] In fact, Justice Samuel Alito, a likely swing vote on the issue, has said that a constitutional privacy right exists.[1403] Retreat on issues such as contraception and parental authority in child rearing is unlikely. The issue is defining "family," "marriage," "reproductive rights," and other constitutional catchphrases. But issues of employee and student drug testing, homosexual marriage and adoption, control of genetic material, and other unpredicted issues will test the Court's evaluation of the reasonable expectation of privacy and the compelling interests of the government.

[1401] The Internet service provider America Online announced that it would sell user information, but then quickly stopped such practices upon seeing its stock drop. *See* Malcolm Maclachlan, *Self-Regulation Needed to Ensure Privacy*, TECHWEB, Mar. 13, 1998, http://www.techweb.com/wire/story/TWB19980313S0018.

[1402] *See* Webster v. Reproductive Health Servs., 492 U.S. 490, 536 (1989) (Scalia, J., concurring in part and concurring in judgment) ("[T]he mansion of constitutionalized abortion law, constructed overnight in *Roe v. Wade*, must be disassembled doorjamb by doorjamb, and never entirely brought down, no matter how wrong it may be.").

[1403] *See* Jill Zuckman, *Alito Affirms Right to Privacy*, CHI. TRIB., Jan. 11, 2006, *available at* http://www.chicagotribune.com/news/nationworld/chi-0601110204jan11,1,38263 09.story.

Regardless, with respect to autonomy issues, the argument will be how to apply the right of privacy rather than whether a right to privacy exists.

Among the various forms of privacy, informational privacy is most in jeopardy. Indeed, the more difficult issue is to find an effective remedy for intrusions on personal information. Society has moved too fast for the law to catch up. As e. e. cummings once observed, "progress is a comfortable disease."[1404] Our society has enjoyed its "progress," but are we able to define limits to protect the individual?

In addition to the march of technological progress, rational concerns about national security underpin greater governmental intrusion. The government now has access to many private communications without a search warrant. Further, information and communication systems are more vulnerable to government surveillance and observation, particularly because the predominant modes of communication—e-mail and cellular phones—are insecure by their very nature. The current situation gives the government far more power to scrutinize individuals than ever before, power that is approaching that of Orwell's Big Brother.[1405]

Next, data brokers and other companies that sell information about individuals for marketing and security purposes have the ability to gather personal information without the Fourth Amendment restrictions placed on government. In fact, the information industry works closely and shares information with the government.[1406] In addition to the government, the data brokers sell information to virtually anyone who wants it, including the medical, financial, and insurance industries. The data industry has information on millions of citizens and is proud of it.[1407] Beyond the fact that this information is highly intrusive and generally available without permission, a major concern is that the information industry is quite capable of making mistakes, including the distribution of harmful and inaccurate information[1408] and security breaches that facilitate identity theft.

[1404] E.E. CUMMINGS, 100 SELECTED POEMS 89 (paper ed. Grove Press 1959).

[1405] Congress just recently passed the Protect America Act of 2007, PUB. L. No. 110-55, 121 Stat. 552, amending the Foreign Intelligence Surveillance Act, 50 U.S.C. §§ 1801–1811.

[1406] *See* discussion *infra* Chapter III, § A-2.

[1407] The Acxiom Corporation advertises that its InfoBase List contains the names of 176 million individuals and 111 million households nationwide. Axciom, InfoBase List, http://www.acxiom.com/default.aspx?ID=1758&DisplayID=18 (last visited Aug. 20, 2007).

[1408] For example, the credit-reporting agency Experian relied on public records from a court docket in compiling a man's credit report. The court docket incorrectly stated that a legal judgment had been entered against the man at one point, and correctly noted at another point that the case was settled and dismissed. Experian only reported

Finally, modern media actors—in particular the "stalkarazzi," attack journalists, bloggers, and "bad news" journalists—are more intrusive than ever. Yet, as discussed extensively throughout this book, media actors remain protected by the First Amendment. The "stalkarazzi," the most extreme of these "journalists," make a living by intruding upon individual privacy.[1409] Attack journalists focus on attacking the political class, and "bad news" journalists focus on sensationalism without regard to the impact on innocent third parties. Bloggers simply write whatever they deem interesting and publish it on the Internet. The First Amendment has been strained to its limits to shield actions that were never envisioned by its framers. The media can fulfill their role of informing the public and holding the government accountable without intruding on the most private parts of citizens' lives.

There are multiple sources for remedies, including the U.S. Constitution, state constitutions, federal statutes, multiple state statutes, four historic privacy torts, and other traditional and some novel legal theories. Yet intrusions without recourse abound. Effective remedies for the disclosure of personal information are limited by the myriad accepted justifications for intruding upon privacy. Additionally, there is no overarching textual commitment to privacy in either the Constitution or any federal law. Although there are some broad commitments in places like the European Union, the development of American jurisprudence and policy remains a patchwork. Moreover, whenever broad remedies are sought against privacy intrusions, the specter of lost domestic security or lost freedom of the press are raised. If there are to be solutions, the approach should combine a strengthening of traditional legal theories with a more direct granting of rights and remedies that will address the gaps in privacy protection. When remedies fail to protect basic values, even the most ardent defenders of the common-law precedent recognize the need for change.[1410] In other words, a multifaceted approach, with legal and legislative innovation, is necessary to develop effective privacy protections.

---

the incorrect entry. Bob Egelko, *Court Reverses Itself—Finds Credit Agency Violated Man's Rights*, S.F. CHRON., Sept. 27, 2007, *available at* http://www.sfgate.com/cgi-bin/article.cgi?f=/c/a/2007/09/27/BAJ5SEMHR.DTL.

[1409] *See* John Fuson, *Protecting the Press From Privacy*, 148 U. PA. L. REV. 629, 669 (1999). The publicist Dick Guttman termed this breed of paparazzi the "stalkarazzi." "Paparazzi" literally means "buzzing insects."

[1410] 1 BLACKSTONE, *supra* note 20, at 69–70 ("Yet, this rule admits of exception, where the former determination is most evidently contrary to reason, much more if it be contrary to define law."). Blackstone further said that a manifestly absurd or unjust law is not the law.

A. Implement Basic Policy Changes

1. Create a Right to Informational Privacy Analogous to That of the European Union

If Americans wish to place a higher priority on personal privacy, we should examine the European Union's approach. Even though citizens in the United States revere individuality and the United States was founded on a strong foundation of personal liberties, privacy receives less legal protection here than in the European Union. If the United States was founded, at least partially, to escape hierarchy, royalty, and elitism, why do we not regard privacy more highly than the Europeans?

First, the European Union was founded in the modern era, and its founding documents could include textual regard for privacy in the contemporary context. The United States has been compelled to develop privacy law over two hundred years of court-created precedent in state and federal courts. Second, national security and safety issues have become dominant policies in the United States. This distinction is evidenced by the conflict between U.S. Homeland Security policies and E.U. privacy policies relating to commercial airline travel discussed earlier.[1411] Third, free-speech protections under the First Amendment and the newsworthiness doctrine are more sweeping in the United States. Fourth, the United States has a more open approach to public records.

Although substantial, none of these factors are absolute barriers to enacting a comprehensive privacy policy in the United States. A threshold need is broader recognition of the real and present danger of losing privacy rights in the tidal wave of contemporary society.

In a 2004 *Yale Law Journal* article, James Q. Whitman compares European and American privacy cultures.[1412] According Whitman, the differences between the two ideas are rooted in the concepts of "privacy as an aspect of dignity and privacy as an aspect of liberty."[1413] The American system of privacy protection is oriented toward the concept of privacy as an aspect of liberty.[1414] American privacy law has focused more on intrusions

---

[1411] *See* discussion *supra* Chapter III, § C-6(a).
[1412] James Q. Whitman, *The Two Western Cultures of Privacy: Dignity Versus Liberty*, 113 YALE L.J. 1151 (2004).
[1413] *Id.* at 1161. Robert Post identified these values in 2001. *See* Robert Post, *Three Concepts of Privacy*, 89 GEO. L.J. 2087 (2001).
[1414] Whitman, *supra* note 1412, at 1161.

by the government than on intrusions by the private sector and the media.[1415] The law was created to "maintain a kind of private sovereignty within our own walls."[1416]

In contrast, the European system is based on the concept of privacy as an aspect of dignity.[1417] According to Whitman, the core European privacy rights, that is, the right to control one's image, name, and reputation, as well as "informational self-determination," are all rights intended to allow an individual to shape his or her own public persona.[1418] A main focus of the European laws is protection against the media.[1419] Interestingly, that was a principal focus of Warren and Brandeis's article, which is the basis of tort privacy protections in the United States.

Whitman discusses newsworthiness in the article's section on contemporary European law and free expression.[1420] In contrast to Europe, where personal honor is a constitutional value, the United States views freedom of expression as being paramount.[1421] This explains the broad newsworthiness exception to privacy actions in the United States.[1422] Whitman asserts that European courts would see cases like that involving Oliver Sipple differently from American courts.[1423] The case began on September 22, 1975, when Sara Jane Moore wielded a .38-caliber pistol and attempted to assassinate President Gerald R. Ford while he was visiting San Francisco, California. Oliver Sipple was in the crowd and grabbed or struck Moore's arm as she was about to shoot at the president. The bullet missed Ford by approximately five feet because of Sipple's reaction.

The *San Francisco Chronicle* heralded the act by publishing an article that focused on Sipple's sexual orientation and revealed to the world that Sipple was a homosexual. Sipple filed a lawsuit against the author, the *San Francisco Chronicle*, and a number of other newspapers. Sipple alleged that the papers published private facts about Sipple's life that lead to ridicule, mental anguish, embarrassment, and the disassociation of Sipple from his family.[1424]

[1415] *Id.* at 1162.
[1416] *Id.*
[1417] *Id.* at 1161.
[1418] *Id.*
[1419] *Id.*
[1420] *Id.* at 1196–1202.
[1421] *Id.*
[1422] *Id.* at 1196.
[1423] *Id.* at 1197.
[1424] Sipple v. Chronicle Publ'g Co., 154 Cal. App. 3d 1040, 1044–45 (Ct. App. 1984).

The California court dismissed the out-of-state defendants for lack of personal jurisdiction and granted the California defendants summary judgment because Sipple's sexual orientation was a well-known fact to many people in his local community. Further, the court found Sipple's sexual orientation to be newsworthy since his actions saving the president put him in the public light.[1425]

In Europe, the analysis differs. Freedom of expression is always balanced against personal dignity; and personal dignity often wins.[1426] For example, Whitman cites a French case with facts similar to that of *Sipple*. In 1985, a man attended a gay-pride parade in Paris and dressed as a participant in the parade.[1427] The man's photograph was taken and published. When the man sued, the French court found that he had a right to oppose the photograph's publication.[1428] According to Whitman, the French way of thinking is that "the fact that one has revealed oneself to a restricted public, e.g., the gay community of Paris, does not imply that one has lost all protections before the larger public."[1429]

The United States is not expected to abandon its fundamental commitment to a free press and liberty. But we can consider how to better protect personal individuality and dignity. Further, we should remember how important these rights have been, and will be, to our culture.

2. Expand Statutory Rights

If we cannot create a comprehensive national policy, then we must continue to target abuses and create new remedies. Federal and state governments have made considerable statutory efforts to protect privacy. Clearly, statutory policies are necessary in addition to traditional torts, property, and common-law remedies. Statutes have had an impact on cell-phone privacy, data-broker liability, and the right of citizens to know about the sale of their personal information. Governments could also place more restrictions on their own data collection and provide broader standards for accuracy and accountability.

[1425] *Id.* at 1050. The court also asserted that news of his courageous act was an "attempt to dispel the false public opinion that gays were timid, weak, and unheroic figures." *Id.* at 1049.
[1426] Whitman, *supra* note 1412, at 1197.
[1427] *Id.*
[1428] *Id.*
[1429] *Id.*

Several states have examined privacy rights in the context of public-disclosure policies in court systems. Some common principles for developing remedies have emerged: (1) institute limits on information put into public records; (2) limit access to information to fewer parties; (3) give notice to third parties; and (4) hold parties accountable for accuracy and conduct. Particularly important is the handling of information in public records and held by public entities, since this information is so comprehensive, sensitive, and generally accessible.

Despite the multitude of statutory remedies, a combination of politics and constitutional barriers makes the U.S. laws less comprehensive than those in other jurisdictions. Those barriers are unlikely to be substantially lowered. Nonetheless, interest groups concerned with privacy must target specific abuses and seek limited victories at the state and federal levels. Overall, privacy policies regarding personal decisions, such as the right to die, abortion, and sexual orientation (such as same sex marriage) currently are being argued around state enactments and court interpretations. Ultimately these issues will most likely be resolved in the United States Supreme Court and not in legislative bodies.

There are, however, areas where federal and state legislatures can help greatly to protect against privacy intrusions. There are seven specific areas where statutory reform should be priorities:

1. **Reexamine the extent of immunity of Internet Service Providers**. Currently, the CDA[1430] provides immunity even to ISPs that foster and encourage anonymity for writers of salacious, malicious and slanderous comments.[1431] Congress should review this broad grant of immunity.

2. **Evaluate the coverage of newly passed genetic protection policies**. The newly enacted statute represents tremendous progress.[1432] But genetics is a rapidly changing field. Private agencies are providing DNA tests through the mail.[1433] DNA

[1430] *See*, David L. Hudson, Jr., *Taming the Gossipmongers*, ABA Journal, July 2008, 19. Discussing possible expanded ISP liability.
[1431] *See supra* note 392 regarding juicycampus.com and whosarat.*com*. Plaintiffs continue to lose actions against ISPs based on the expansive interpretation of *Zeran v. America Online*, Inc. 129 F.3d 327 (4th Cir. 1997). Congress should consider at least holding ISPs that foster and protect defamation. Another option may be to provide a remedy for defamatory statements similar to the notice and takedown provision in the Digital Millennium Copyright Act as discussed in Chapter III § B-6 of this book.
[1432] Genetic Information Nondiscrim. Act of 2008, Pub. L. No. 110-233, 122 Stat. 881 (2008).
[1433] *See supra* note 202. An individual may swab the inside of their mouth with a cotton swab and mail the swab to laboratories across the country for various DNA testing.

collection by government is expanding.[1434] Also, evaluations of individuals based on their DNA are becoming more extensive including possible medical, personality and criminal tendencies.[1435] Because of the sensitivity of these issues, they deserve close legislative attention.

3. **Protect personal communications**. Cell phones and e-mail are personal communication modes that were unknown fifty years ago. We cannot know what modes of communication will become available in the next fifty years. Confidentiality of human communications are critical to our culture and to each of us. Statutes have endeavored to protect personal communications. Some have failed.[1436] Holes in protection remain. E-mail left on a server six months is no longer private.[1437] Government monitoring of e-mails is done without warrant.[1438] It is important for policymakers to continue to focus on the importance of private communications.

4. **Stay contemporary with emerging technologies**. Again, we cannot know what the next years will bring in terms of potentially intrusive technology. RFID, ITV, and GPS, among other technologies, offer new ways for individuals and governments to intrude.[1439] More protection is possible. Washington State has acted to prevent data theft from personal RFID equipped cards.[1440] ITV can potentially gather substantial data on individuals but it is not regulated the same way cable television is.[1441] For all these reasons, legislators must be vigilant and privacy advocates must continue to inform policy makers in developing areas of technology still emerging.

5. **Examine controls over company outsourcing of data management**. The practice of outsourcing the management of data to companies in other countries in increasing.[1442] The issue that needs to be

---

[1434] *See supra* note 1447.
[1435] *See supra* note 214. Some tests purport to identify a tendency towards violence.
[1436] *See* Bartnicki v. Vopper, *supra* note 604 and accompanying text.
[1437] *See supra* note 758 and accompanying text.
[1438] See Chapter III, § B-(4)(a).
[1439] *See supra* notes 135–41 and accompanying text for a discussion of these devices and others.
[1440] *See supra* note 383 and accompanying text. Washington state has banned skimmers that can be used to steal personal data from credit cards with RFID chips.
[1441] *See supra* note 153 and accompanying text describing Interactive TV.
[1442] See Chapter III, § C-(6)(c) discussing outsourcing practices.

examined is the availability of remedies to a citizen, for example in the U.S., if the abuse or disclosure of his information occurs in another country by a company that is from the other country.

6. **Protect consumer information.** Increasing electronic sales and marketing will exponentially expand the amount of consumer information available to retailers and marketers. There are substantial statutory protections—both state and federal—expanding protection of consumer information. New marketing and new technology will continue to make this issue difficult. "Cookies" in our computers can and do track our movements on the Internet.[1443] Further, many consumers voluntarily disclose personal information. But innovations such as discount cards[1444] and ITV have substantial amounts individual data and are less regulated than previously known means of collection.

7. **Evaluate data broker practices.** Data brokers are here to stay. There are extensive statutory enactments dealing with data brokers. Still, they are collecting more and more information. Some expansion is the result of increasing amounts of public information of uncertain general value. Other types of information are being marketed that have questionable value. For example, the whosarat.com Web site provides a list of government informants.[1445] The accumulation of information about individuals continues to expand. So should the protections such as notification and liability for inaccuracies and harm to individuals.

Creating statutory privacy protections requires continual diligence at both the state and federal levels. Some issues will be more appropriate for federal policy because of nationwide and global implications. But states have an extremely important role and can augment individual privacy rights in a great number of instances and in emerging issues.

[1443] *See infra* note 1555 and accompanying text for a definition of cookies. Following is Macy's policy on cookies. *See* Appendix III.
"We have carefully selected a company, Coremetrics, to assist us in better understanding how people use our site. macys.com will place cookies on your computer to collect information. The information that is collected through these cookies tells us things like which search engine referred you, how you navigated around our site, what you browsed and purchased and what traffic is driven by banner ads and emails."

[1444] *See supra* note 709 and accompanying text concerning discount cards.

[1445] *See supra* note 392.

3. Establish a New Agency with Oversight on Privacy Issues

One option for improving privacy protection is to create a single governmental agency with the power to set standards for privacy protection, investigate abuses of individual privacy, and enforce privacy policies.[1446] Creating another governmental agency should never be the first option for improving public policy. However, there have been successful examples in other countries in protecting individual privacy.[1447] The closest analogy is that E.U. member states established data protection authorities to enforce each state's data-protection laws.[1448] This model is effective for the European Union partly because a single data-privacy-protection policy applies to both the government and private industry. Indeed, the data-protection laws also created the data-protection authority. Regulatory power still lies in the hands of the legislative authority; the data-protection authority simply has enforcement power.

Creating a similar agency in the United States would be most beneficial if it oversaw both the public and private sectors alike, as in the European Union. Even without a single privacy statute, this outcome would still be possible if Congress enumerated the statutory provisions over which the new agency would have authority. The problem, however, is that unregulated areas would still go uncontrolled. Thus, it would be important for Congress to grant the new agency rule-making power, a

---

[1446] This recommendation has been on the table for many years. For example, the *9/11 Commission Report* alludes to the need for an authority to oversee privacy across the federal government. NAT'L COMM'N ON TERRORIST ATTACKS UPON THE UNITED STATES, THE 9/11 COMMISSION REPORT 395 (2004), *available at* http://www.9-11commission.gov/report/911Report.pdf ("If . . . there is substantial change in the way we collect and share intelligence, there should be a voice within the executive branch for [liberty] concerns. Many agencies have privacy offices, albeit of limited scope."). The report resulted in the creation of the Privacy and Civil Liberties Oversight Board, with no independence from the White House and no clear mandate. Bennie G. Thompson, *The National Counterterrorism Center: Foreign and Domestic Intelligence Fusion and the Potential Threat to Privacy*, 10 U. PITT. J. TECH. L. & POL'Y 3 (2006); *see also* Christopher F. Carlton, *The Right to Privacy in Internet Commerce: A Call for Federal Guidelines and the Creation of an Independent Privacy Commission*, 16 ST. JOHN'S J. LEGAL COMMENT. 393, 426 (2002) ("Congress should create an independent privacy commission to develop privacy legislation and lead the efforts to advance it both in the public and private sector.").

[1447] *See* discussion *supra* Chapter III, § C-2(a).

[1448] Data-protection laws in the European Union originate from a common source, Directive 95/46/EC, which is a binding obligation of member states and served as model legislation for each state. *See* E.U. Directive, *supra* note 366. See *supra* Chapter III, § C-(2)(a) for a discussion of the E.U. data-protection regime.

departure from the E.U. model. Such an agency would still be constrained by other U.S. laws, including the First Amendment, so enforcement would not be directly analogous to enforcement in the European Union. The existence of a privacy agency is not a substitute for better statutory policies.

Although some governmental agencies, such as the FTC, act to protect privacy, they "dabble in privacy when it is a hot political subject."[1449] Currently, the FTC has broad authority over matters of trade and consumer protection. Particularly, the FTC requires financial institutions to implement information-security safeguards, and it has exercised its authority over retailers whose "unfair" practices expose an individual's personal information to hackers and identity thieves.[1450] However, other entities, such as schools or governmental entities that do not engage in trade, are beyond the FTC's jurisdiction. And because the FTC is tasked with many other initiatives, privacy protection may not remain on its agenda forever. A single federal agency that has the power to establish and enforce information-security rules would protect individuals. Such an agency would have limited authority over the protection of personal information and could use the FTC's enforcement regime as a starting point.[1451]

B. Expand Existing Remedies, Reduce Barriers, and Create a New Approach

One of the time-tested advantages of the common law and jurisprudence more generally is the ability to adapt old remedies and principles to new problems. The evolution of constitutional privacy in the autonomy arena over the last fifty years is stunning. The advancement on such issues as race represents a complete shift in positions held merely a century ago. The principles underlying the remedies discussed below are protecting individuals from intrusions into their personal lives and punishing those who intrude. Those simple principles must confront a complex and evolving

---

[1449] Robert Gellman, *Taming the Privacy Monster: A Proposal for a Non-regulatory Privacy Agency*, 17 Gov't Info. Q. 235, 236 (2000).

[1450] *See supra* note 817.

[1451] One commentator argues that regulatory power for a privacy agency is not necessary and that the agency could succeed by assisting the legislature in recommending legislation and reviewing industry's self-regulation of privacy. *See* Gellman, *supra* note 1449.

society. But we should not give up hope that the implementation of the law—and the protections it provides—can catch up to its principles. This section examines how long-standing principles and remedies can be adapted to new realities.

1. Reexamine the "Reasonable Expectation" Doctrine

The first step in evaluating a broad new approach to privacy is to ask whether the "reasonable expectation"[1452] doctrine is working. "Reasonableness" is the threshold for constitutional privacy protections, tort privacy protections, and Fourth Amendment protections against governmental intrusion. We, and other jurisdictions such as Great Britain, do not protect against intrusions that society believes are reasonable and expected. Some of those determinations are easy and intuitive. One's name is not a secret in most contexts. It is less intuitive, however, to find that telephone numbers we have called are not private and that intimate sexual conduct may not reasonably be expected to be private.

The problem with the "reasonable expectation" aspect of the right to privacy is that it is an amorphous threshold, outside of which an individual has no right of privacy. As stated previously, the law does not allow each individual to determine his or her own privacy right; this right must be determined by reference to a reasonable expectation. Who defines "reasonable expectation"? It can be either a judge or a jury depending on the circumstances.[1453] The assessment is not based on a vote or a majoritarian view. Court decisions are comically inconsistent. For example, in Alaska, an individual has a reasonable expectation of privacy to smoke marijuana in his home,[1454] but in Florida, in 1995, information that a person smokes cigarettes was not subject to a reasonable expectation of privacy.[1455] In the first half of the twentieth century, the state could regulate the distribution of contraceptives. In the later part of the century, there was a reasonable expectation of privacy to buy and use contraceptives.[1456]

How do we define what a reasonable expectation is today in an intrusive society? Should juries decide? As in the case of obscenity, should the

---

[1452]   *See* Chapter VII, § B-1.
[1453]   *See, e.g.*, Plaxico v. Michael, 735 So. 2d 1036, 1038 (Miss. 1999). For a discussion of the case, see *supra* Chapter VI § F.
[1454]   Ravin v. State, 537 P.2d 494 (Alaska 1975).
[1455]   City of N. Miami v. Kurtz, 653 So. 2d 1025 (Fla. 1995).
[1456]   Griswold v. Connecticut, 381 U.S. 479 (1965).

local community define the standard? Professors Chris Slobogin and Lior Strahilevitz have suggested using empirical data to determine a society's expectations and social norms.[1457] Professor Post reminds us that commentators have invited the review of social norms.[1458] Even the Supreme Court in *Katz v. United States* suggested that Fourth Amendment jurisprudence ought to recognize society's apparent expectations.[1459] Ultimately, society's willingness to recognize the reasonableness of one's privacy expectation may depend on the intruder. That is, society may be more concerned that the government is obtaining information about us, as compared with a private marketing company that will use the information to sell us books and clothes. There is some evidence that people are more concerned by governmental intrusions, and arguably, the Fourth Amendment holds the government to a higher standard.[1460]

If one accepts that society's expectations should be tested and should be the basis for defining "reasonable expectations" in all its contexts, such a policy could make a major difference. Professor Slobogin's data indicates that some currently unprotected information available both to the government and to private data brokers is viewed as more intrusive than searches that would require Fourth Amendment permission. For example, the disclosure of e-mail addresses to and from which messages were sent and received was deemed more intrusive than the search of a car.[1461]

Perhaps there is a possibility for an evolution of the definition of "reasonable expectation" to reflect the real concerns of citizens today rather than the lowest common denominator of the "YouTube society." Although we should respect sensitivities of the majority, we should remember that some important privacy interests might not garner a majority vote.[1462]

[1457]   Lior Strahilevitz, *A Social Networks Theory of Privacy*, 72 U. CHI. L. REV. 919, 932 (2005); Christopher Slobogin & Joseph E. Schumacher, *Reasonable Expectations of Privacy and Autonomy in Fourth Amendment Cases: An Empirical Look at "Understandings Recognized and Permitted by Society,"* 42 DUKE L.J. 727, 728 (1993).

[1458]   Post, *supra* note 1413, at 2092, 2094 (explaining privacy as a form of dignity that is dependent on everyday social practices).

[1459]   389 U.S. 347 (1967).

[1460]   *See generally* Slobogin, *supra* note 204.

[1461]   *Id.* According to the Ninth Circuit, users have no reasonable "expectation of privacy in the to/from addresses" of their e-mails. *United States v. Forrester*, 512 F.3d 500, 510–11 (9th Cir. 2008).

[1462]   An absolute majoritarian view might not protect socially unpopular privacy interests that courts have protected in the past; e.g., courts have upheld abortion rights and struck down antimiscegenation laws. *See* polls on privacy at http://epic.org/privacy/survey/.

2. Expand Fourth Amendment Protections Against Government Surveillance

The traditional safeguard against governmental searches and seizures is the Fourth Amendment to the U.S. Constitution. The Fourth Amendment protects against unreasonable searches and seizures and requires probable cause for the issuance of warrants. However, these protections apply only if the subject has a reasonable expectation of privacy in the information sought.

As previously discussed, data mining presents a new mode of intrusion that demands a new look at protections. First, the government attains much of its information through private data-mining firms and other institutions, and the so-called third-party rule generally exempts this type of information from the Fourth Amendment's protection.[1463] However, the government's accumulation of this data in today's society is different from obtaining random information from private sources. In effect, the government is obtaining an intimate biography of unprecedented detail, and doing so without showing any reason. Therefore, the current state of Fourth Amendment protections must be expanded to ensure safeguards against governmental intrusions into the private lives of individuals through the practice of data mining.

Fourth Amendment jurisprudence currently states that there is no reasonable expectation of privacy in information knowingly exposed to the public. The issue is, what does "exposed to the public" mean? In *United States v. Miller*, the Supreme Court held that information given to a bank did not enjoy Fourth Amendment protection.[1464] In *Smith v. Maryland*, the Court held that individuals do not have a reasonable expectation of privacy in phone records obtained from phone companies.[1465] E-mail addresses are not protected.[1466] The analysis in these cases points to the individual's act of releasing information with the knowledge that transactional records are routinely kept in these situations. The courts thus concluded information retrieved from third parties does not enjoy Fourth Amendment protection.

[1463] *See* Andrew J. DeFilippis, Note, *Securing Informationships: Recognizing a Right to Privity in Fourth Amendment Jurisprudence*, 115 YALE L.J. 1086, 1097–1102 (2006) (explaining and critiquing the third-party rule).

[1464] 425 U.S. 435, 445 (1976).

[1465] 442 U.S. 735, 745–46 (1979).

[1466] United States v. Forrester, 512 F.3d 500, 510–11 (9th Cir. 2008).

Data mining presents a unique problem. When a large amount of disparate information is gathered, synthesized, and compiled, the resultant picture of an individual is much more specific than that provided by any of the singular components.[1467]

Several legal scholars have argued for overturning *Miller* and *Smith* and have suggested that individuals have a reasonable expectation of privacy in this type of information. Anita Ramasastry attacks the analysis underlying these two decisions.[1468] To consider the act of relinquishing information to third parties a relinquishment of an expectation of privacy in that information to government surveillance is to ignore the reality of modern life. It is almost impossible to function in a modern society without making telephone calls, having a bank account, shopping, or using a credit card. Indeed, Professor Slobogin notes that the type of information obtained from third parties, such as bank and telephone records, is considered by the public to be as private as a person's bedroom, a search of which requires a warrant and probable cause.[1469]

The aftermath of the *Miller* and *Smith* decisions reflects this paradox. The reality today is that an enormous amount of data is mined, collected, distributed, analyzed, and applied without the consent or knowledge of the individual and without constitutional protections.

Professor Slobogin argues that although data mining can be intrusive in some instances, the types of intrusion do not always rise to the level deserving a high degree of justification. Slobogin argues that to properly assess the degree of justification required, we must categorize data-mining methods and weigh the motives and consequences of governmental action. The three major types of data mining are (1) target-driven data

---

[1467] *See* discussion *supra* Chapter III § B-4(c). For instance, the knowledge that someone makes calls to Kiev, as evidenced by phone records, is seemingly innocuous. However, combined with information that the same person was arrested in college at an antidemocratic rally, recently purchased *Das Kapital* at a book store, and flew to Beijing five times in a year paints a different picture. The information, when assembled collectively, transforms a series of random facts into a mosaic of the person's apparent beliefs and conduct. The inference, of course, is that the individual is a Communist, a fact that in the not-so-distant American past could be quite damaging to one's reputation, career, and personal life. Leaving aside the possibility that the information leads to a false positive (one could simply have a particular intellectual interest, rather than a political creed) this information is private in the same sense that one's sexual orientation is private. The intrusion, then, is one into the informational privacy of a person's thoughts and beliefs.

[1468] Anita Ramasastry, *Lost in Translation? Data Mining, National Security and the "Adverse Inference" Problem*, 22 Santa Clara Computer & High Tech. L.J. 757, 764 (2006).

[1469] Slobogin, *supra* note 204.

mining (after a target has been identified, records are searched to obtain information about that person); (2) match-driven data mining (records are searched to match an individual as a person of interest in other databases such as no-fly lists and fingerprint and DNA databases); and (3) event-driven data mining (information from large databases, such as credit-card purchases and travel records, is analyzed in order to discover patterns and predict terrorist or criminal activity). Slobogin recommends specific governmental justifications for each type of data mining, as well as varying justifications within each category. Ultimately, he concludes that private data, sought in connection with an investigation of a single target, deserves a higher degree of justification than impersonal, anonymous records or information sought to identify a perpetrator.

This argument takes into account both the need to protect the privacy of individuals and the countervailing governmental need to investigate criminal activity. Placing different forms of data mining at different points on the spectrum of Fourth Amendment protection would ensure that the government shows probable cause and a legitimate interest in obtaining corporate and public records when obtaining, through target-driven data mining, personal information such as the bank and phone records at issue in *Miller* and *Smith*. Event-driven data mining, on the other hand, as less personal and intrusive, would require only the showing of a legitimate need for the information.

In sum, the current state of Fourth Amendment jurisprudence fails to solve the privacy issues raised by the practice of data mining and electronic surveillance. Although the current state of domestic and geopolitical affairs certainly calls for diligence in the pursuit of criminals and terrorists, the interests of the individual need not yield entirely. The expansion of Fourth Amendment remedies would not necessarily inhibit the government's ability to pursue information, but rather would place limits on that pursuit when it begins to invade the privacy of individuals.

3. Reexamine Intrusion upon Seclusion

Intrusion upon seclusion may provide the most viable tort remedy remaining. A primary strength of the intrusion-upon-seclusion tort is that, at least in some cases, First Amendment rights are not necessarily implicated, because no publication is required for the wrong to be committed. For example, the act of videotaping someone having sex in the privacy of his or her own house is an intrusion in and of itself, whether the images are published or not. The remaining challenge is to develop a consistent definition of "seclusion" and physical solitude. For example, can an individual have a reasonable expectation of seclusion in a public place?

This remedy could have utility for public-space intrusions. A modern concern is intrusion by the government and private parties in public spaces. This phenomenon is described earlier as the panopticon effect.[1470] The interest to be protected is the desire for relative obscurity and perceived obscurity when individuals are generally going about their business in public. For example, an individual might be caught on video by a surveillance camera or by a private individual. If that image is made of someone in a truly public space, like a public square, there is usually no remedy for distributing that image. Either the government or a private party will say that the individual has no reasonable expectation of privacy in a public place. Commentators have been focusing on this issue for years.[1471] There have been court decisions that found intrusions in public spaces. A Pennsylvania court held that "[c]onduct that amounts to a persistent course of hounding, harassment and unreasonable surveillance, even if conducted in a public place or semi-public place, may nevertheless rise to the level of an invasion of privacy based on intrusion upon seclusion."[1472]

Professors Clay Calvert and Justin Brown have urged the expansion of the intrusion-upon-seclusion tort to say that some matters are private even in a public space.[1473] For example, what if a camera positioned in a public square was oriented in such a way as to take pictures of a person's underwear?[1474] Calvert and Brown propose a rule that would protect against an indecent intrusion, without plaintiff's volition, that would be embarrassing to a reasonable person.[1475]

How might this formula work if the intrusion involved photographs taken of a child playing in a park and published on a child-pornography site? The above formula might fail because the photograph itself

---

[1470] *See* discussion *supra* Chapter III § B-6.

[1471] *See, e.g., infra* notes 1410–15.

[1472] Woflson v. Lewis, 924 F. Supp 1413, 1420 (E.D. Pa. 1996).

[1473] Clay Calvert & Justin Brown, *Video Voyeurism, Privacy, and the Internet: Exposing Peeping Toms in Cyberspace*, 18 Cardozo Arts & Ent. L.J. 469 (2000).

[1474] Restatement (Second) of Torts § 652B, cmt. c (1977).

[1475] *See* Calvert & Brown, *supra* note 1473, at 491–93.

might not be "indecent," although it might be utilized for indecent purposes.[1476]

Professor McClurg and others have proposed a multifactor balancing test that considers the motive of the defendant and conduct of the plaintiff.[1477] This test would be a remedy for child pornography. But this test is subject to criticism because it also might support an action based on a picture taken of a person in a skimpy bathing suit at a public beach.

A more limited test could include a defendant's motive, whether a reasonable person would consider the conduct intrusive, and whether the information or image was a matter of public interest. Under this test, the pornographic pictures would be actionable. Also, pictures of well-known people in public would not be actionable, nor would nonoffensive pictures. What about publishing information about a private person entering a strip club from a public street? This is not a matter of public interest, and a reasonable person might consider it intrusive.

A more aggressive application could provide a remedy for several of the intrusions described in this book. For example, a woman was filmed during rescue workers efforts to extricate her from a crash.[1478] She was filmed while in a rescue helicopter receiving emergency treatment and saying "I just want to die." These images were broadcast. She became a paraplegic.[1479] If this is not a public disclosure of private facts because it is newsworthy, could it not be an intrusion upon seclusion? The acts of filming and disclosure could be considered an intrusion upon the seclusion of Ms. Shulman. Of course, the Plaxico[1480] case previously described where a husband films a third party having sex with his wife in her own bedroom is an example of intrusion upon seclusion whether the video is

---

[1476] A photograph of a child playing in a park probably is not embarrassing. The intrusion of taking photographs in a public park probably is not indecent itself; rather, it is the subsequent posting of the photographs on a child-pornography site that elicits moral opprobrium.

[1477] Andrew J. McClurg, *Bringing Privacy Out of the Closet*, 73 N.C. L. Rev. 989, 1057 (1995). The factors to be considered include (1) the defendant's motive; (2) the magnitude of the intrusion; (3) whether the plaintiff could expect to be free from this intrusion because of customs or habits of location; (4) whether the defendant sought the plaintiff's consent; (5) actions by the plaintiff manifesting a desire not to be intruded upon; (6) whether the defendant disseminated the images; and (7) whether the images involve a legitimate public interest.

[1478] *See* Shulman v. Group W. Productions, Inc., 955 P.2d 469 (Cal. 1988) *supra* note 1024.

[1479] The California Supreme Court found that the story was of a legitimate public interest (newsworthy), as were the plaintiff's words, and therefore that the plaintiff could not meet the elements of the private-facts tort.

[1480] See discussion on Plaxico v. Michael at Chapter VI, § F.

ever viewed. The intrusion tort should also be available to close family members based on the nonconsensual filming of a death scene and autopsy of their parents, as occurred in the Perkins case.[1481]

Also, what if a person goes onto an Internet dating Web site and discloses details about another person such as their name, address, e-mail and invites others to call and write that individual?[1482] That individual's actions should be an intrusion upon seclusion.

When private parties are intruding upon the "seclusion" of an individual, this remedy should be an option. Reexamining the basis for intrusion upon seclusion may provide a real and viable remedy to expand privacy protections.

4. Reexamine the Limits of Newsworthiness

Because many current intrusions are said to be cloaked by First Amendment protection, we should ask, what, if any, are the limits of newsworthiness protections? First, we must understand that the new definition of "the press" may include anyone with a Web site and e-mail capability. Claims of coverage of newsworthiness extend to an extraordinary number of entities.

What are the principles and purposes protected by the First Amendment? Today, the First Amendment protects disclosures of what most would consider private matters. If these matters are deemed newsworthy, even if through no fault of the subject, the disclosures are protected. Certainly, analysis, coverage, and information about the government and public figures are at the core of a free and democratic society. But are there limits? There are few cases that have decided that a published item was not newsworthy.

One significant case is the previously discussed *Diaz* case in California.[1483] In this case, a court decided that the fact that an individual had undergone a sex change was not newsworthy and therefore was not

---

[1481] See discussion on Perkins v. Principal Media Group, Chapter VI, § K.
[1482] *See e.g.,* Carafano v. Metrosplash.com, Inc., 339 F. 3d 1119 (9th Cir. 2003) On the dating Web site an individual in Berlin profiled an individual in California and invited others to go to another e-mail address cmla2000@yahoo.com, which, when contacted, produced an automatic e-mail reply stating, "You think you are the right one? Proof it!!" [sic], and providing Carafano's home address and telephone number. The individual was never found and the ISP was held to be immune. *See supra* notes 387–91 and accompanying text.
[1483] *See* Diaz v. Oakland Trib., Inc., 139 Cal. App. 3d 118 (Ct. App. 1983).

protected speech under the First Amendment.[1484] This reasoning might be different if the person involved was a public figure of greater significance than a student body president. In other words, a particular piece of information may be newsworthy in one instance and not newsworthy in another, depending on the individuals involved. An individual's previous drinking habits may become newsworthy following a conviction for driving while intoxicated, even if this behavior would not have been newsworthy previously. The *Diaz* case weighed three factors: (1) the social value of the information; (2) the degree of intrusion; and (3) the extent to which the party consented.[1485] The court said that newsworthiness was to be determined by the jury. Most First Amendment advocates would be troubled by allowing a jury to evaluate the social value of a news story. Usually, the press or news sources are found liable only when their conduct is malicious or grossly negligent. First Amendment rights are also specifically protected in legislative enactments.

Privacy statutes often contain exceptions for information in the public interest. Even if a statute has no specific provision dealing with protected speech, the speech may be protected under the First Amendment. And a court may find such a statute unconstitutional to the extent it prohibits or penalizes speech protected under the First Amendment, as was the case in *Bartnicki v. Vopper.*[1486]

If newsworthiness is not to be a cloak for every abuse, there must be limits. Of course, there currently are limits—First Amendment protections do not apply when one deliberately or maliciously publishes false information.[1487] But these exceptions do not provide comfort to victims of crimes or others who become the subject of media scrutiny through no fault of their own. Television and newspaper stories routinely disclose the names of victims and sometimes their addresses.[1488]

[1484] *Id.* at 134.

[1485] *Id.* at 132 (citing Briscoe v. Reader's Digest Ass'n, 483 P.2d 34 (Cal. 1971)).

[1486] 532 U.S. 514 (2001) (holding that the Wiretap Act prohibitions does not remove the First Amendment shield of freedom of speech when the disclosing party received an illegally intercepted cellular telephone conversation about a public issue, but did not play a part in obtaining the illegal interception).

[1487] New York Times Co. v. Sullivan, 376 U.S. 254 (1964); Time, Inc. v. Hill, 385 U.S. 374 (1967).

[1488] 63.4% of newspaper stories and 42.2% of television stories name crime victims in their stories. 50% of newspaper stories and 34.5% of television stories stated the age of crime victims, while just over 35% of newspaper stories and 29% of television stories named either the victim's or defendant's address, STEVEN M. CHERMAK, VICTIMS IN THE NEWS: CRIME AND THE AMERICAN NEWS MEDIA 126–27 (1995).

What should the limits be? It seems that we have come too far to require that publication of information provide an actual benefit to the public, a consideration that may be a test in other jurisdictions.[1489] So worthless information may still be protected speech. But if that information is highly intrusive, then sometimes privacy prevails.[1490] Further, the Supreme Court has said that "speech involving no matters of public concern" is of "reduced constitutional value."[1491] Therefore, a balancing test may be used to justify protection against intrusive disclosures, at least where the information is worth less to the public.

Some balancing between interests is the basis of the decision in *Diaz* and other cases in which the public benefit is weighed against the degree of intrusion. In other words, to justify an egregiously intrusive disclosure, those courts look for a real public benefit. The formula could include a requirement that a plaintiff show not only a substantial intrusion but also that the information is not newsworthy and does not affect the public interest. If there is a significant intrusion and no public interest, then there should be liability. If the First Amendment is to be protected, the burden to show injury and the absence of "newsworthiness" should be on plaintiff. This type of approach more closely mirrors the test in the European Union and in Great Britain, where a higher value is placed on personal dignity.[1492] We should not expect to abandon the long history of protection for the press, but given the evolving meaning of "press" to include bloggers and paparazzi, there is a need to examine the limits of conduct. The mainstream press has itself recognized the risks that the outrageous conduct of fringe elements pose to the important protections for the press and they should work with privacy advocates to strike a reasonable balance.

[1489] A court in Great Britain held that even when private information relates to a celebrity, there is a prima facie right to keep this information private. *See* Mckennitt v. Ash, [2006] EWCA (Civ) 1714 (Eng.). The *Mckennitt* case represents the British view that "what interests the public is not necessarily in the public interest."

[1490] McCabe v. Village Voice, Inc., 550 F. Supp. 525 (E.D. Pa. 1982) (holding that a photograph of a nude woman in a bathtub was *not* newsworthy. Even though plaintiff impliedly consented to the publication of the nude photograph by a professional photographer in a book, she did not consent to its publication in a weekly newspaper and the photo was not found to be "newsworthy."); Vassiliades v. Garfinckels, 492 A.2d 580 (D.C. 1985) (holding that before and after cosmetic surgery photos were *not* newsworthy).

[1491] Dunn & Bradstreet, Inc. v. Greenmoss Builders, Inc., 472 U.S. 749, 761 (1985).

[1492] *See supra* text accompanying notes 1372–76.

5. Employ Property Theory to Protect Personal Information

In his prescient book on privacy, Arthur Miller said that using property theory to protect personal information was like putting old wine in a new bottle.[1493] Professor Miller did an excellent job of predicting many of our current problems and pointing out that the law was falling behind. The law still is falling behind, and information has become a different commodity since Professor Miller wrote his book in 1971. I wonder how differently he might look at this remedy today.[1494]

Currently, there is an entire industry based on finding and selling information. Data brokers have a broad base of information, and that information has proprietary value. Because of continual breaches,[1495] there is a need for more effective remedies.

Property theory is not an alien concept for protecting information: right of publicity and appropriation of personality are property-based privacy rights. The utility of property theory is that it can achieve results where the tort remedies for privacy breaches fall short. For example, a claim for public disclosure of private facts will fail in cases involving information that is, in fact, not private, whereas the marketing or abuse of that information might be a breach of an individual's property right in the information, providing the basis for a successful action.

One problem is that the accumulation of information has great value to marketers and data gatherers even though data about one individual is not of such great value: the whole is greater than the sum of its parts. What is the damage incurred to an individual whose data is disclosed or even inaccurately disclosed? Unless an individual has been directly harmed, for example, by losing a job, the actual damages associated with the release of information regarding one individual may be so small as to deter litigation. However, class-action suits could bring smaller claims together and make litigation worthwhile. Also, the FTC has remedies focused on the bad conduct of a data gatherer.[1496]

[1493] MILLER, *supra* note 1150, at 211.

[1494] For more recent views, see Paul M. Schwartz, *Privacy Property, and Personal Data*, 117 HARV. L. REV. 2055 (2004); Leslie G. Berkowitz, *Computer Security and Privacy Law: The Third Wave of Property*, 33 COLO. LAW., Feb. 2004, at 57.

[1495] For a chronology of data-security breaches, see Privacy Rights Clearinghouse, http://www.privacyrights.org/ar/chrondatabreaches.htm (last visited May 18, 2008).

[1496] *See* discussion *supra* Chapter IV, § C-1(b).

Property theory may offer remedies that otherwise might not be available, and should be part of the list of options considered by privacy advocates.[1497]

6. Reexamine "Appropriation of Personality" and "Right of Publicity"

The remedies of appropriation of personality and right of publicity are expandable and valuable. First, newsworthiness is not necessarily a defense to these actions. Second, these remedies, more than any other traditional privacy tort action, are based on property theory. In other words, the wrong to be righted is committed by one who appropriates for his or her own benefit another person's name or likeness. This principle has evolved into two separate causes of action: appropriation of personality and right of publicity.

The plaintiff's identity distinguishes these two actions. One tort is an invasion of the psyche, whereas the other is an invasion of the pocketbook.[1498] These are separate torts under section 46 of the *Restatement (Third) of Unfair Competition*[1499] and under section 652C of the *Restatement (Second) of Torts*.[1500] The unfair-competition tort is defined as a right of publicity, whereas the other tort is appropriation of personality. The *Restatement (Second) of Torts* suggests that although the appropriation right acknowledges the importance of dignity, the right is, by nature, a property right. Consequently, each of these torts designed to protect against unauthorized publication is based on property law.

Although newsworthiness is not necessarily a defense, some statutes allow recovery only if a person's identity is used in advertising. Therefore, under those statutes, the use of a person's name in news, art, or literature is not a violation.

This remedy could be expanded by allowing for recovery for any commercial use of a person's identity, as opposed to solely for advertising. In fact, the Florida statute includes such broad language, but the Florida

---

[1497]   For a discussion of these remedies, see *infra* Chapter IV, § F.

[1498]   1 MCCARTHY, *supra* note 905, § 5:61, at 5–110.

[1499]   The *Restatement* states in part, "One who appropriates the commercial value of a person's name, likeness, or other indicia of identity for purposes of trade is subject to liability...." RESTATEMENT (THIRD) OF UNFAIR COMPETITION § 46 (1995).

[1500]   RESTATEMENT (SECOND) OF TORTS § 652C (1977).

Supreme Court has construed the statute only to include advertising, despite the statutory language.[1501] The result of the advertising limitation is that this tort becomes very limited. The remedy should allow recovery against commercial exploitation beyond advertising.

The expansion of this remedy also could allow broader recovery. For example, in *Grant v. Esquire, Inc.*, the court awarded both property-related damages and damages for emotional distress.[1502] The threshold right protected was *Esquire*'s misuse of Mr. Grant's personality. But the court then allowed recovery for emotional distress. Could this formula be used to allow a noncelebrity to gain access to a better remedy? Yes.

7. Use State Constitutional Rights to Blaze a Legal Trail

State constitutions consistently have been interpreted as more stringent and comprehensive than the federal constitution in protecting privacy. Accordingly, some privacy interests may be recognized first in the states. For example, in *State v. Wasson*, the Kentucky Supreme Court found a statute criminalizing homosexual sodomy unconstitutional before the U.S. Supreme Court reached a similar result.[1503]

In the area of decisional privacy, the states often have gone further than the federal government. For example, Oregon has a more far-reaching right-to-die policy than has been allowed nationally by the Supreme Court.[1504] In fact, the federal government unsuccessfully challenged the Oregon policy.[1505]

The fact that a substantial number of states have constitutional privacy provisions gives rise to more opportunities to define the limits of

---

[1501] The Florida statute provides, "No person shall publish, print, display or otherwise publicly use for purposes of trade or for any commercial or advertising purpose the name, portrait, photograph, or other likeness of any natural person without the express written or oral consent to such use. . . ." FLA. STAT. § 540.08 (1998). In Tyne v. Time Warner Entertainment Co., 901 So. 2d 802, 805 (Fla. 2005), the Florida Supreme Court said that "section 540.08, by prohibiting the use of one's name or likeness for trade, commercial or advertising purposes, is designed to prevent the unauthorized use of a name *to directly promote the product or service of the publisher*. Thus, the publication is harmful not simply because it is included in a publication that is sold for a profit, but rather because of the way it associates the individual's name or his personality with something else."

[1502] 367 F. Supp. 876 (S.D.N.Y. 1973).

[1503] *See* 842 S.W.2d 487 (Ky. 1992).

[1504] *See* Oregon Death with Dignity Act, OR. REV. STAT. §§ 127.800–.897 (2007).

[1505] *See* Gonzales v. Oregon, 546 U.S. 243 (2006).

privacy. Although informational privacy is clearly not defined as a fundamental right under the federal Constitution, some states consider informational privacy a fundamental right.[1506]

So the states, as "laboratories of democracy," may be the proving grounds for privacy policy. Individuals injured by intrusions should carefully examine state law and constitutional protections, since there is a real likelihood that the available state protection exceeds federal protections.

For those states without constitutional privacy provisions, the addition of such a right would provide significant and real additional protections. Because most states do not have a constitutional privacy provision, citizens concerned about privacy rights should evaluative how to add that specific right to their constitution.[1507] One need only review the cases implementing state provisions to see the substantial expansion of individual rights.[1508]

8. Expand Common-Law Remedies to Address Current Abuses

a. Conversion[1509]

The tort of conversion is not usually cited as a remedy for enforcing the right to privacy. However, if one accepts the property theory, then one accepts conversion as a remedy.[1510] The tort of conversion arises if there is wrongful interference with one's right of possession. If a person's control or possession of property is denied because of the actions of another, the tort of conversion is a possible tool. Conversion can be applied to either tangible or intangible property. Thus, information, data, images, and other key elements affecting privacy may be protected under a claim for conversion. This action, like trespass to chattels, is based on the acceptance of the property theory[1511] to allow an individual a series of property-related remedies.

[1506] *See* Rasmussen v. South Fla. Blood Servs., 500 So. 2d 533, 534 (Fla. 1987) (ruling that the privacy rights of blood donors (which fostered the ability to obtain more donations) outweighed a blood recipient's right to know if one of the donors from whom he received blood had AIDS).

[1507] *See infra* Appendix II.

[1508] *See* Chapter VII, § B-1. *See, e.g.,* Winfield v. Div. of Pari-Mutuel Wagering, 477 So. 2d 544, 547 (Fla. 1985) (adopting the "compelling state interest" standard to justify an invasion of privacy and shifting the burden to the state to justify an intrusion of privacy).

[1509] Susan E. Gindin, *Lost and Found in Cyberspace*, 34 San Diego L. Rev. 1153 (1997).

[1510] See the discussion on the property theory *supra* Chapter IV, § F.

[1511] *See infra* Chapter III.

b. Trespass to Chattels

Trespass is a remedy to punish intrusion. The challenge is to redefine contemporary intrusions to allow this remedy to be effective in today's world.

Professor Michael Siebecker argues that the common practice of using pieces of data known as cookies[1512] to gather specific consumer information and track an Internet user's browsing habits, which are then used to profile individual Internet visitors, actually represents a common-law trespass to chattels.[1513] According to Siebecker, there has been a dearth of court cases dealing with Internet advertisers' use of cookies to gather information on consumer activity.[1514] Siebecker believes that earlier court precedent regarding the use of the trespass-to-chattels tort to enjoin the use of Internet "spam" advertising means that courts will look favorably on claims that implanting cookies on personal computers could be a trespass to chattels. Using the common-law remedy of trespass to chattels is not a guaranteed remedy, but Siebecker concludes that the likelihood of success of such a strategy is strong.[1515]

How to impose damages is a tough issue. Would damages be only the cost of the minimal memory space used? A better valuation would be an assessment of the value companies would pay to advertise on individual computers. The theory is that they are trespassing on the property of another to advertise. Collectively, that amount would be substantial and could justify a class-type action.

[1512] Cookies are defined by webopedia at http://www.webopedia.com/TERM/c/cookie.htm (last visited May 18, 2008), as "a message given to a web browser by a web server. The browser stores the message in a text file. The message is then sent back to the server each time the browser requests a page from the server. The main purpose of cookies is to identify users and possibly prepare customized Web pages for them. When you enter a Web site using cookies, you may be asked *to* fill out a form providing such information as your name and interests. This information is packaged into a cookie and sent to your Web browser which stores it for later use. The next time you go to the same Web site, your browser will send the cookie to the Web server. The server can use this information to present you with custom Web pages. So, for example, instead of seeing just a generic welcome page you might see a welcome page with your name on it.
The *name cookie* derives from UNIX objects called *magic cookies*. These are tokens that are attached to a user or program and change depending on the areas entered by the user or program.

[1513] *See* Siebecker, *supra* note 113, at 894.

[1514] *Id.* at 900.

[1515] *Id.*

c. Intentional Infliction of Emotional Distress

The tort of intentional infliction of emotional distress is another remedy that may be further expanded to protect privacy. This tort occurs if a person acts intentionally or recklessly in a manner that is extreme and outrageous enough to cause the plaintiff severe emotional distress.[1516] This tort can serve as an effective proxy for public disclosure of private facts, but the plaintiff must show the defendant's intent. Further, because the issue is wrongful conduct, protected speech is not a defense. Therefore, intentionally outrageous conduct will support liability.

One example described in this book could give rise to intentional infliction of emotional distress. The *True Stories from the Morgue* case involved the intentional display on television of an autopsy of a close relative.[1517] If the plaintiff could show the requisite intent, this case would be a perfect example of intentional infliction of emotional distress.

d. Utilize Expanded Contract Theories

As described earlier any direct violation of privacy agreement will be actionable.[1518] A more expansive use of contract theory based on unjust enrichment and implied contract may provide new remedies for intrusion and misuse of information.

i. Unjust Enrichment

As a common-law remedy, unjust enrichment allows for restitution, which is the restoration of the benefit of money, services, or goods that unjustly benefit another.[1519] Unjust enrichment is an equitable remedy that is available when no other remedy at law is applicable. Restitution via unjust enrichment is a remedy designed to prevent a person from retaining property to which the person is not justly entitled.[1520]

To succeed on a claim of unjust enrichment, a plaintiff must prove (1) a benefit conferred on the defendant by the plaintiff; (2) an appreciation

---

[1516]   Williams v. City of Minneola, 575 So. 2d 683, 690 (Fla. Dist. Ct. App. 1991) (recognizing that intentional infliction of emotional distress can occur through the release of information).

[1517]   This case is discussed in Chapter VI, § K.

[1518]   *See* Chapter IV, § E-4.

[1519]   Krug v. Sanzaro, No. CV010454102S, 2004 Conn. Super. LEXIS 966 (Super. Ct. Mar. 30, 2004).

[1520]   Rowland v. Carr, No. CA9727, 1986 Ohio App. LEXIS 9931 (Ct. App. Dec. 24, 1986).

or knowledge by the defendant of the benefit; and (3) the acceptance or retention by the defendant of the benefit under such circumstances as to make it inequitable for the defendant to retain the benefit without payment of its value.[1521]

This remedy could apply as an adjunct to appropriation of name or likeness. However, because it is based in contract principles, a suit on the theory of unjust enrichment may not benefit everyone alike. A person who appropriates the identity of a common person may be less enriched than one who appropriates the identity of a celebrity. Therefore, the common person, although injured, may not collect as much in restitution, because the benefit conferred may be less; the celebrity, however, would likely collect a much greater amount. But the ultimate issue is not how much the wronged persons identity is worth but how much the wrongdoer benefited. So even if an individual's identity were not highly valuable on the market, if someone profited greatly, then they are liable for the degree they benefitted. "Because the basic idea underlying the law of unjust enrichment is that it is inequitable for one party to receive a benefit from another without paying for it, the measure of damages is ordinarily some function of the defendant's gain, rather than the value of what is taken."[1522]

For example, a case was filed by the comedian Rodney Dangerfield's widow to prevent the broadcast of videos of Mr. Dangerfield recorded in his house by his producer, David Permut.[1523] Mr. Permut is said to be planning to edit the material into a film. If Mr. Permut profited from the showing or broadcast of such a film, there would likely be a claim for unjust enrichment. And, as a contract action, it could be brought by Mr. Dangerfield's estate.

Another example involves Virgin Mobile in Australia, which took images from the photograph-sharing Web site Flickr and used them in its advertising campaign. One photograph Virgin Mobile took from Flickr was that of a sixteen-year-old girl, Alison Chang. In the ad, the company printed one of its slogans, "Dump your pen friend," over Chang's picture,

---

[1521] See 26 Williston on Contracts § 68:5 (4th ed.) Chapter 68. Rescission *and* Restitution; Quasi Contractual Recovery.

[1522] Arthur Miller, *Common Law Protection for Products of the Mind: An "Idea" Whose Time Has Come*, 119 Harvard Law Review 703, 773 (2006).

[1523] The Associated Press, *Dangerfield's Widow Sues Over Film*, Sept. 22, 2007, *available at* http://www.washingtonpost.com/wp-dyn/content/article/2007/09/22/AR2007092200801. html (last visited May 9, 2008).

and included another, "Free text virgin to virgin," beneath her photo. Virgin Mobile likely benefited from using the plaintiff's image in its advertising campaign. And because the photograph was chosen to be used in an advertising campaign, it is reasonable to assume that Virgin Mobile appreciated the benefit the use of Chang's likeness would confer. Finally, because Virgin Mobile used Chang's photograph without her consent and ostensibly profited from the use of her photo, it would be inequitable for Virgin Mobile to retain the benefit without payment of its value. However, although there appears to be a cause of action here, the actual value of just compensation for using her image may not be high.

This concept of unjust enrichment requires proof that there has been enrichment, but the remedy has the virtue of being based in property theory and contract theory. Therefore, this type of remedy may avoid First Amendment defenses because recovery is a contract-based equitable remedy to compensate a wrongful taking. The wrong involved is the taking, not the act of communicating information, which might be subject to free-press defenses.

ii. Implied Contract

Another contract-based remedy may be available to protect disclosure of intimate information. Professor Andrew McClurg has proposed that implied contract could be used as a substitute for the tort of public disclosure of private facts.[1524] Indeed, others have argued that recovery through contract theory is the way to protect free speech yet provide a remedy for certain intrusions.[1525] The theory is that there is an implied promise not to reveal certain intimate information. McClurg cites the case of the Washingtonienne, in which a woman posted intimate details about a previous lover on her blog.[1526] Under this theory, the lovers impliedly imposed a restriction on their speech by entering into an intimate relationship, and the court should enforce that contract. To find such a contract, a court must necessarily evaluate the context of the relationship and the information involved to determine the rationality of deeming it a contract.

[1524] McClurg, *supra* note 1373.
[1525] *See* Eugene Volokh, *Freedom of Speech and Information Privacy: The Troubling Implications of a Right to Stop People from Speaking About You*, 52 Stan. L. Rev. 1049 (2000).
[1526] *See* discussion *infra* Chapter VI, § I.

Although the proof may be challenging, this theory is certainly worth exploring in the courts. Further, the idea finds support in the cause of action for breach of confidence, which has essentially become Great Britain's substitute for privacy torts.[1527] In sum, a person faced with the disclosure of intimate details should definitely consider using the implied-contract theory.

9. Evaluate Transnational Remedies

There will be instances when an individual may obtain a remedy and recovery in a foreign jurisdiction that is not available to him or her in the United States. A specific example is the *Gutnick* case discussed previously: the statement made about the Australian businessman would have been protected speech in the United States, but it was not protected speech in Australia and the defendant was held liable.[1528] Some "believe that the U.S. First Amendment reflects universal values and is somehow written into the architecture of the Internet. But the First Amendment does not reflect universal values; to the contrary, no other nation embraces these values, and they are certainly not written in the Internet's architecture."[1529] So we should not be surprised if a person with proper jurisdiction in another country receives relief that would not be available in the United States for the publication of information on the Internet.

Actions by multinational companies may violate an individual's privacy right under the laws of some nations, but not under those of others. Even so, the fact that companies do business worldwide makes them susceptible to public pressure for violating privacy rights.[1530] For example, London-based Privacy International graded the various search engines in a report released on June 9, 2007. The company gave Google its lowest grade out of twenty-two surveyed companies and said that the company had "comprehensive consumer surveillance and entrenched hostility to privacy."[1531] This kind of international scrutiny may provide a path for privacy advocates in various countries.

[1527] *See* Wacks, *supra* note 428 (discussing the theory employed in British courts).
[1528] *See supra* text accompanying note 484.
[1529] GOLDSMITH & WU, *supra* note 484, at 157.
[1530] *See* Skarda-McCann, *supra* note 484.
[1531] Associated Press, *Watchdog Group Slams Google's Privacy Policies*, GAINESVILLE SUN, June 10, 2007, at 7A.

No doubt individuals will look to sympathetic jurisdictions when they have been harmed by international or transborder communications. Given the global nature of communications, more and more individuals may be able to shop for better forums.

American celebrities and foreign public figures have been using the more expansive protections under European law to obtain tort recovery from the media. This tactic has been called "libel tourism." Britney Spears settled a lawsuit against the *National Enquirer* that she filed in Northern Ireland in late summer 2006.[1532] Spears is not the only celebrity to sue in the U.K. courts for libel. Paula Abdul, Whitney Houston, and Jennifer Lopez also have filed suits against American-based publishers in the European courts. But it is not just celebrities who are using the U.K. system to seek vindication for information published about them by the media. According to an article in the *Times*, the latest individuals to use the broad U.K. libel laws are businesspeople, not unlike the Australian businessman's use of the Australian courts in his suit against the *Wall Street Journal*.[1533]

These circumstances indicate that an intrusion that occurs in another jurisdiction may be treated far differently from the same intrusion in the United States and that such alternative remedies may become more popular.

[1532]   Associated Press, *Tabloid Retracts Britney Spears Stories*, USA TODAY, July 18, 2006, *available at* http://www.usatoday.com/life/people/2006-07-18-spears-enquirer_x.htm.

[1533]   *See* Mark Stephens, *New Celebrities of the Libel Courts*, TIMES (U.K.), July 18, 2006, *available at* http://business.timesonline.co.uk/tol/business/law/article687881.ece. It should be noted, however, that an article in the *Wall Street Journal* from late 2006 heralded a judicial decision in the House of Lords that narrowed, albeit only a little, the U.K. libel law. *See* Aaron O. Patrick, *U.K. British Court Ruling Gives Boost to Serious Journalism*, WALL ST. J., Oct. 12, 2006, at B1, *available at* http://online.wsj.com/public/article/SB116055935348389227-uzoY3SuOpLzgmhletBF_w6ghxj8_20061018.html?mod=blogs.

In *Jameel v. Wall Street Journal Europe*, [2006] UKHL 44, Saudi businessmen sued the *Wall Street Journal Europe* for libel because of a 2002 article published by the newspaper detailing investigations into the bank accounts of Saudi businesses suspected of funding terrorism. The *Wall Street Journal* lost the case at trial and was ordered by the jury to pay damages. On appeal, the House of Lords said that the newspaper article may have been privileged under what is called the *Reynolds* defense, which protects matters that are of public interest. (The privilege gets its name from the case *Reynolds v. Times Newspapers Ltd.*, [2001] 2 A.C. 127.) Lord Bingham noted, however, that what engages the interest of the public is not always in the public interest. *Jameel*, [2006] UKHL 44, ¶ 31. (Although traditionally thought of solely as a legislative body, the House of Lords also acts as the highest court for the courts of the United Kingdom. A group called the Lords of Law decides cases appealed to the House of Lords.).

Another variation of this issue is the increased use of "outsourcing" of data compilations. Violations of an American's citizen's privacy may occur in another country, by a company's outsourced provider or by a hacker in another country.[1534] Intrusions are becoming truly global, and remedies must be global as well.

C. Use Personal and Technical Means to Protect Privacy

1. Evaluate Practical and Technological Means to Reduce Loss of Privacy

Although technology is part of the problem in protecting personal privacy, it also can be part of the solution. Citizens can take actions that will limit their exposure to abuse, but ultimately legal protections are still the key to protecting personal privacy.

A key technological strategy in protecting privacy is making communication anonymous. This strategy does not protect the interception of data as much as it hides the source of a signal or the recipient of a message. For example, a political dissident in China can use an anonymizing Web browser to read the news of the Western press or post messages on a blog promoting democracy. Another example is the use of prepaid calling cards or prepaid mobile phones that may leave conversations open to eavesdropping but can make identifying the speakers difficult. Anonymity can protect privacy.

Requiring authentication of identity can also protect privacy in a different context. Authentication may be used as a privacy tool. This method requires users, communicating parties, or persons accessing information to verify their identity.[1535] If authentication is required, only an authorized person should have access to the information sought. The simplest form of authentication is the use of a password or personal identification number ("PIN"). More advanced forms include biometric identification, like iris and fingerprint scans.[1536] Authentication protocols may require verification of multiple pieces of information. The future might even

---

[1534] *See, e.g.,* Brian Krebs, *Shadowy Russian Firm Seen as Conduit for Cybercrime,* Wash. Post, Oct. 13, 2007, at A15 (discussing the "Russian Business Network," an Internet service provider that provides access for a multitude of cybercrimes).

[1535] Westby, *supra* note 414, at 200.

[1536] *Id.* at 202.

bring DNA authentication.[1537] The goal of authentication is to guard against unauthorized access to private information.

Encryption also may be used to protect privacy. Any data, such as e-mails, voice communications, images, or other files, can be scrambled in such a way that the content is meaningless without a decryption key.[1538] In this way, both stored and live communications can remain secure, and unauthorized users can be prevented from gaining access.

After information has already been created and stored, erasing data is another method for protecting privacy.[1539] Although pressing the delete button may appear to eliminate a file or e-mail, traces may still remain on a computer. Specially designed software programs may be able to retrieve information the user thought was deleted. A user may obtain software to securely and permanently delete information, such that all traces of the data are destroyed, by repeatedly writing over the physical areas on the storage medium where that information was once stored. Computer files often contain metadata, information about the data stored, such as the data's creator and editor as well as timestamps. Deleting this information also may serve to protect privacy. Thus, the pool of information available to threaten one's privacy can be minimized and managed.

2. Practical Personal Steps

Protecting one's own privacy is no easy task. Although the previously mentioned technological methods for protecting privacy are useful, the methods are not a panacea. There is little one can do to protect one's privacy from personal blogs with no quality-control editors, from CCTV cameras, or from GPS devices in some cell phones.

[1537] *Id.*

[1538] WESTBY, *supra* note 376, at 197.

[1539] But the erasure must be complete and effective. When a user "deletes" a file, not all traces of that file are removed, and often, the entire file can be recovered using readily available data-recovery tools. For a technical discussion of how computers store and erase files, see ALBERT J. MARCELLA & ROBERT S. GREENFIELD, CYBER FORENSICS: A FIELD MANUAL FOR COLLECTING, EXAMINING, AND PRESERVING EVIDENCE OF COMPUTER CRIMES 48–51 (2002). The practice of selling used cellular phones is a key example of how one's sensitive personal information can be put at risk. Cellular phones use flash memory to store phone numbers and other data. Information presumed to be erased often can be easily accessed using inexpensive software available on the Internet. *See* Ted Bridis, *Cell Phones Spill Secrets*, MSNBC, Aug. 30, 2006, http://www.msnbc.msn.com/id/14588433.

The FTC offers minimal instruction on how to protect one's own privacy.[1540] Some tips offered by the FTC are do not carry any more credit cards or identification cards in your purse or wallet than is necessary, order credit reports from the three credit-reporting agencies once a year, and create difficult passwords for your online information.[1541]

A person may choose to exercise some control over how his or her information is used and stored. For instance, a national "Do Not Call" registry (www.donotcall.gov) allows individuals to stop (most) telemarketers from calling their phones. Individuals may request to stop receiving preapproved credit offers via www.optoutprescreen.com. Also, individuals may contact many of the data brokers, such as Acxiom and Abacus, to remove their names from the mailing lists that they sell to others.

Individuals may obtain information stored about themselves for free, usually annually, to ensure the accuracy of the information. Once a year, an individual can contact the Medical Information Bureau ("MIB") to receive a free copy of his or her MIB report, which contains medical information stored in the insurance industry database. Likewise, one may obtain a free annual credit report via www.annualcreditreport.com. Further, HIPAA gives patients the right to access their medical records at any time to check for discrepancies.

One can be proactive by giving required information only when requested and taking business elsewhere if not satisfied with the manner in which various companies handle personal information. Finally, privacy can be better protected by taking advantage of the opt-out opportunities provided by credit-card companies and others to limit the distribution of personal information.

The bottom line is that many of these tips for privacy protection are limited and do not comprehensively protect against the various potential intrusions by the government, the press, individuals, or data brokers. It is also clear that although following these steps might reduce the number of telemarketers that have your phone number, or reduce the number of mistaken transactions on your credit report, there is no foolproof safeguard against the improper use of personal information, and we must live with and react to this harsh reality.

[1540] FTC, Privacy: Tips for Protecting Your Personal Information, http://www.ftc.gov/bcp/conline/pubs/alerts/privtipsalrt.shtm (last visited May 9, 2008).

[1541] *Id.*

CHAPTER VIII

Conclusion

Privacy, as a central part of personal liberty and individuality, is a touchstone of American democracy and a generally accepted, yet amorphous, global right. A combination of forces from the government, an intrusive society, commercial interests, and segments of the press are, in effect, crushing the individual's right to be let alone. If they were concerned about an intrusive world in 1890, what might Warren and Brandeis think today? In 2008, the law is ill equipped to protect citizens from the private and public assault on their privacy. This onslaught is not the result of some grand conspiracy. No conspiracy could work so well. In fact, the government, the information industry, and the press are, at least on the surface, doing what the public demands: they are providing security, needed information, and the news and gossip that the public wants. The status of our collective privacy is unpredictable, inconsistent,[1542] and changing continually[1543]—a reflection of a society with changing mores and changing technology.

The confluence of technology and the motivations of data brokers are causing the individual to be treated more and more as a statistic. The threshold question is, do we care? Well, we do when we are hurt. We care when the government dictates that a loved one must die painfully.

[1542] In Alaska you have an expectation of privacy for smoking marijuana in your home, but in Florida you do not have an expectation of privacy in smoking tobacco if you want a public job.

[1543] Examples of complete changes in policy in the last century include policies regarding abortion, interracial marriage, and homosexual sex.

We care when we are crime victims scrutinized by the press. We care when we do not get a job because of inaccurate criminal records.

As part of today's culture and society, no individual is immune. As suggested in the introduction, there are very few private aspects of a "day in the life" of a modern citizen. Further, as this book has made clear, the legal solutions are piecemeal and incremental, requiring the public to demand remedies for violations of their right to privacy. The impact is so vast and comprehensive that no one ethnic, religious, or other group is singled out. We are all part of the privacy interest group. So far, most of us are underinformed as to what is happening to us and are largely unaware of any effective legal remedies.

However, there are legal remedies for privacy violations. And, if the privacy right is important, the courts have an obligation to fashion effective options from the myriad remedies. There will be no single sweeping reform that will bestow privacy on each of us. The forces and policies that support intrusions on individual privacy are too substantial and in some cases, are supported by most of the public. For example, most of the public supports warrantless searches and constant camera surveillance to counter violence and terrorism. Likewise, most of the public shows a voyeuristic interest in tabloids and disaster journalism, at least until someone in their own family becomes an unwilling subject. This most individual of rights requires our personal commitment to protect ourselves through our personal choices and actions and our advocacy.

The central lessons of a study of privacy today are as follows:

- No universal agreement exists on the scope of privacy because of inherent moral, political, and perceptual differences.
- Privacy is a broad concept affecting multiple facets of human existence that individuals and governments value as a general principle.
- A single policy is not probable or practical to protect privacy across the globe or even across the county.
- A broader understanding of the scope of privacy (i.e., recognizing which issues are important to individual liberty) is a prerequisite for protecting individual privacy.

The future of individuality and personal autonomy is a cause in need of a constituency. We need to evaluate why we tolerate intrusions on our individual privacy by the government, bloggers, the press, and our fellow citizens. The responsibility is ours. In the immortal words of the cartoon character Pogo, "we have met the enemy . . . and he is us."

ABOUT THE AUTHOR

Dean Emeritus Jon L. Mills is director of the Center for Governmental Responsibility at the University of Florida Levin College of Law. He received his J.D. with honors from the University of Florida College of Law in 1972. In addition to teaching and writing on privacy, Professor Mills has had several direct experiences with the development of public policy and legal advocacy regarding privacy rights, including sponsoring Florida's privacy amendment in the state constitution's Declaration of Rights in 1978; representing the family members of the deceased victims of Gainesville serial murderer Danny Rolling in 1991 to prevent the reproduction of crime-scene photographs; representing the Versace family to close the record—including autopsy and crime-scene photographs—in the murder investigation of Gianni Versace; representing the family of NASCAR driver Dale Earnhardt in 2003 to prevent the release of autopsy photographs; representing the family of Billy Tyne, the sea captain depicted in the motion picture *The Perfect Storm*, in an action for appropriation of name or likeness; representing the First Amendment Foundation in a false-light action against the *Pensacola News Journal*; and most recently, serving as chair of the Florida Supreme Court Committee on Privacy and Court Records in 2006 to formulate recommendations on how to protect privacy while providing access to records on the Internet.

Florida's Constitutional Privacy Amendment. In 1978, Jon Mills, then a Florida state representative, was the lead sponsor of H.J.R. 386, Florida's privacy amendment. The explicit right to privacy was overwhelmingly approved by voters in 1980 and incorporated into the state constitution's Declaration of Rights as article I, section 23 of the Florida Constitution. Interestingly, both liberal and conservative politicians supported this provision,[1544] which was framed as an important amendment intended to keep Florida citizens free from governmental intrusion. The privacy provision passed both houses with few dissenting votes.

Opposition to the privacy amendment came primarily from abortion opponents and the press. The press negotiated for and received a clause stating that the privacy amendment would not apply to public documents, leading to a later debate as to the definition of a public document. Interestingly, some the editorial boards of some newspapers opposed the provision, even though there was a direct reference to preserving public access. A major argument made by opponents to the provision was that a state privacy amendment was unnecessary because there was an existing protection for privacy in *Roe v. Wade*. However, since its adoption, Florida's privacy provision has been interpreted as a fundamental right that is stronger than the federal privacy right, and it has been applied in cases involving both private information and personal decision making.

Rolling v. State. Professor Mills was asked by the state attorney to represent the families of the victims of the serial killer Danny Rolling. The issue was the release of horrific crime-scene photographs to the press and general public. As a special assistant state attorney, Mills viewed the photographs and testified that it would be highly traumatic to the relatives to view the photographs. The court adopted a balancing test and held that the photos could be viewed but not reproduced. The photos were used in the course of a murder trial and the penalty phase (in which prosecutors sought the death penalty), so they were documents of the highest value in a public trial.

Versace v. State Attorney of Florida. Gianni Versace was murdered in Miami Beach, and an intensive manhunt ensued. Andrew Cunanan was identified as the murderer and ultimately killed himself. The investigative documents, crime-scene photos, and autopsy photos were the subject of a disclosure controversy. Parker Thomson and Professor Mills represented the Versace family and its enterprises. Citing *Rolling*, they asked the judge to close the record. They successfully argued that there was even greater justification for closing the records because there had not been, nor would there be, a trial.

[1544]   Although Senator Jack Gordon (D-Miami) and Senator Dempsey Barron (R-Panama City) rarely agreed on any policy decision, they agreed on the necessity of a textual right to privacy.

Campus Communications, Inc. v. Earnhardt. Racecar driver Dale Earnhardt was killed during the last lap of the 2001 Daytona 500. He was autopsied because it was an accidental death. The press sought access to the autopsy photos, and the family hired Professor Mills to help protect the photos. He made the statutory and constitutional arguments in the trial and appellate court. He worked with the trial team of Thom Rhumberger, Parker Thompson, Jud Graves and Dick Lupo. The Florida legislature took up a bill to restrict access to such photos and passed it in the first weeks of the session. The press challenged the bill and litigation ensued. At this point in history, the Internet was fully in use and so were such Web sites as death.com, which specialized in autopsy photos of celebrities. Michael Uribe was one of the media plaintiffs seeking access for his Web site.

The case went first to mediation, where most of the press agreed to an objective review of the autopsy photos by an expert to be chosen by the court from lists submitted by the parties. The expert, a Duke professor, issued an opinion that the photographs were consistent with the written autopsy—the cause of death was "head whip."

Despite the resolution with most parties, the case continued with several of the parties. Testimony was taken on issues including the harm resulting from the public display of autopsy photos on the Internet. One witness was the daughter of Neil Bonnett. Mr. Bonnett had died in a car crash at the Daytona Speedway in the early 1990s. His autopsy photos had been obtained before the effective date of the Florida legislation and were placed on the Internet. His daughter testified about the trauma of seeing the autopsy photos and knowing that they were on the Internet for the world to see. She testified about the horror of seeing pictures of her father, who, as she put it, "was gutted like a deer."

The Perfect Storm. *The Perfect Storm* was a book and a movie. The book was a factual description of the lives of fishermen in New England. The movie, starring George Clooney, was "based on a true story" and was marketed as a factual representation of an incident where extraordinary storm forces conspired to sink the fishing boat the *Andrea Gail*. Professor Mills worked on the constitutional and legal arguments on the 11th Circuit and the Florida Supreme Court. He worked with Tim McLendon, Steve Calvacca and Ned McLeod.

The Captain, Billy Tyne, was portrayed as an unsuccessful captain who was obsessed with catching more fish on this particular expedition at the risk of his men's lives. None of this was true, and the directors and marketers of the movie knew it was not true.

The case was dismissed in federal court after a finding by the Florida Supreme Court that the relevant Florida statute regarding appropriation of personality did not apply, because Billy Tyne was not represented in an advertisement. The court determined that recovery could occur only when a personality was represented in an advertisement.

Anderson v. Pensacola News Journal. This case grew out of a false-light action by Joe Anderson against the *Pensacola News Journal*. The *News Journal* had published a five-part series on Mr. Anderson recounting his various encounters with law enforcement, his indictment, and allegations of bribery and impropriety. The false-light action, however, was focused on the death of his former wife. Years earlier, she was killed by Anderson in what was determined to be a hunting accident. Mr. Anderson claimed that the article describing his wife's death made it appear that he had intentionally shot his wife, thereby portraying him in a false light. Mr. Anderson won a $16 million verdict. Professor Mills has been engaged by the First Amendment Foundation to argue the free-press issues that this case has generated.

Florida Supreme Court Privacy Committee. Professor Mills was asked to chair this committee to sort out the future role of court records on the Internet. Hearings were held across Florida to solicit ideas and viewpoints on Internet and other public access to court records. The choices presented were extremely difficult. At the extremes were put nothing on the Internet, thereby limiting public access, or put everything on the Internet, thereby endangering the privacy of the millions of people with information in court files.

The testimony was intense and predictably contradictory. The committee concluded that court records could be placed on the Internet, but only after significant safeguards were implemented. There are hundreds of exemptions to the disclosure of public records that apply to courts, ranging from protections for victims and children to the protection of trade secrets. A pragmatic concern was that these exemptions were not being effectively implemented, even in the paper world. (Paper files, however, are not as readily accessed because of the "practical obscurity" of paper court records.) Most committee members felt the need to confirm an effective method of protecting exemptions and redacting records before placing such records on the Internet.

APPENDIX I

Privacy in Federal Statutes

This appendix is intended as an aide to the reader in evaluating the full spectrum of federal enactments. These categories are evaluated in the chapter dealing with federal policy (Chapter IV), but not every statute is discussed there. Web sites such as those of Privacilla.org (http://privacilla.org), the Electronic Privacy Information Center (http://epic.org), and the Privacy Rights Clearinghouse (http://privacyrights.org), which have extensive listings of federal policies, may also be a useful reference.

Categories of Federal Legislation Affecting Privacy

These categories are an attempt to organize the vast number of federal enactments. Some statutes appear in more than one category because they affect more than one area of policy. For example, the Bank Secrecy Act appears under the "financial information" category, since banking information is clearly financial. It also appears in the "authorizing governmental intrusions" category, since the act specifically allows the government to collect certain banking data for security purposes.

1. Medical Records

Statutes in this category restrict the release of sensitive personal medical information.

   A. Health Insurance Portability and Accountability Act of 1996

B. Genetic Information Nondiscrimination Act of 2008
C. Substance Abuse Privacy Policies
D. Veterans Administration Privacy Policies

2. Financial, Credit, and Consumer Records

Statutes in this category protect personal-finance-related information as well as information on consumer purchases and credit information.

A. Bank Secrecy Act
B. Fair Credit Reporting Act of 1970
C. Fair and Accurate Credit Transactions Act of 2003
D. Gramm-Leach-Bliley Act of 1999
E. Section 7216 of the Internal Revenue Code
F. Right to Financial Privacy Act of 1978
G. Economic Espionage Act of 1996

3. Educational Records

Statutes in this category protect a broad range of data and information accumulated by schools and other covered educational institutions.

A. Family Educational Rights and Privacy Act of 1974

4. Personal Identity Information and Personally Sensitive Information

Statutes in this category protect information that identifies a person and could facilitate identity theft (e.g., Social Security numbers, driver's license information, credit-card numbers) as well as particular types of records containing highly intrusive, offensive, or sensitive content (e.g., autopsy photos, video-rental records, library records, parental records, adoption records, juvenile records, names of abortion patients).

A. Brady Handgun Violence Prevention Act of 1993
B. Cable Communications Policy Act of 1984
C. Census Confidentiality Statute
D. Children's Online Privacy Protection Act of 1998
E. Driver's Privacy Protection Act of 1994

F. Employee Polygraph Protection Act of 1988
G. Fair Credit Reporting Act of 1970
H. Fair and Accurate Credit Transactions Act of 2003
I. False Identification Crime Control Act of 1982
J. Genetic Information Nondiscrimination Act of 2008
K. Identity Theft and Assumption Deterrence Act of 1998
L. Substance Abuse Privacy
M. Video Privacy Protection Act of 1998
N. Identity Theft Penalty Enhancement Act of 2003
O. Internet False Identification Act of 2000
P. Telephone Consumer Protection Act of 1991

5. Personal Communications

Statutes in this category protect individuals' private communications (e.g., phone, cell-phone, and e-mail communications).

A. Cable Communications Policy Act of 1984
B. Controlling the Assault of Non-Solicited Pornography and Marketing Act of 2003
C. Communications Decency Act of 1996
D. Communications Assistance for Law Enforcement Act of 1994
E. Electronic Communications Privacy Act of 1986
F. Communications Act of 1934
G. Section 222 of the Telecommunications Act of 1996
H. Telephone Consumer Protection Act of 1991
I. Wireless Communications and Public Safety Act of 1999

6. Computer Use or Computer-Generated Information

Statutes in this cateogry protect against abuses of data compilations, focusing on abuses in the collection, retention, and distribution of mass amounts of information.

A. Computer Fraud and Abuse Act of 1984
B. Computer Matching and Privacy Protection Act of 1988
C. E-Government Act of 2002

   D. Freedom of Information Act of 1966

   E. Privacy Act of 1974

   F. Electronic Communications Privacy Act of 1986

   G. Stored Communications Act

7. Business Information

Statutes in this category protect trade secrets and proprietary information, the release of which would cause unreasonable harm to a particular party.

   A. Economic Espionage Act of 1996

   B. Employee Polygraph Protection Act of 1988

   C. Freedom of Information Act of 1966

8. Exemptions from Public Records and Protection Against Public Intrusions

Statutes in this category protect particular types of publicly held information and exempt from disclosure materials deemed confidential or intrusive. These laws also protect against intrusions by the government that are not necessarily the result of the release of information (e.g., 42 U.S.C. § 1983 punishes misconduct relating to privacy rights, illegal surveillance, and the availability of information generated in the justice system). Laws in this category generally protect against intrusions into traditionally protected areas—home, family, and procreation.

   A. Census Confidentiality

   B. Computer Matching and Privacy Protection Act of 1988

   C. Computer Security Act of 1987

   D. E-Government Act of 2002

   E. Freedom of Information Act of 1966

   F. Paperwork Reduction Act of 1995

   G. Privacy Act of 1974

   H. Privacy Protection Act of 1980

   I. Section 1983 of the Civil Rights Act of 1964

   J. Social Security Number Confidentiality Act of 2000

9. *Statutes Protecting Against Private Intrusions*

These statutes protect against particular actions relating to privacy of the person but not release or misuse of information (e.g., stalking, video voyeurism, cyberstalking, telephone solicitation).

A. Controlling the Assault of Non-Solicited Pornography and Marketing Act of 2003
B. False Identification Crime Control Act of 1982
C. Identity Theft and Assumption Deterrence Act of 1998
D. Identity Theft Penalty Enhancement Act of 2003
E. Internal Revenue Code
F. Internet False Identification Act of 2000
G. Paperwork Reduction Act of 1995
H. Privacy Act of 1974
I. Privacy Protection Act of 1980
J. Social Security Number Confidentiality Act of 2000
K. Video Voyeurism Prevention Act of 2004

10. *Statutes Authorizing Governmental Intrusions*

These statutes authorize intrusions for national-security or other public purposes.

A. Bank Secrecy Act of 1970
B. Communications Assistance for Law Enforcement Act of 1994
C. Computer Fraud and Abuse Act of 1984
D. Electronic Communications Privacy Act of 1986
E. Foreign Intelligence Surveillance Act of 1978
F. Omnibus Crime Control and Safe Streets Act of 1968
G. USA PATRIOT Act of 2001
H. Protect America Act of 2007

Summary of Federal Statutes

1. *Medical Records*

1.a. Health Insurance Portability and Accountability Act of 1996 ("HIPAA") Pub. L. No. 104-191, 110 Stat. 1936.

This act mandates procedures to protect the privacy of individuals receiving health-care services. Title I of HIPPA limits restrictions group health plans can place on benefits for preexisting conditions.[1545] Title II of HIPPA mandates the Department of Health and Human Services to promulgate Administrative Simplification rules. The Administrative Simplification rules are designed to increase efficiency in the health care system by creating uniform standards for disseminating and use of health care information.[1546]

In 2000, rules designed to protect medical information were promulgated by the Clinton administration. However, these rules were amended in 2002 to permit certain health-related information to be shared without patient consent including their treatment and payment for certain marketing purposes. These new rules include certain privacy protections:

- Patients must be given notice of their rights under HIPPA by hospitals as well as how their medical information will be used.[1547]
- Patients have a right to see, copy, or correct inaccuracies in their medical records.[1548]
- When a covered entity uses or discloses protected health information from another covered entity, a covered entity must "make reasonable efforts to limit protected health information to the minimum necessary to accomplish the intended purpose of the use, disclosure, or request."[1549]
- Health-care providers are prohibited from disclosing an individual's health information to their employers.[1550]
- individuals may choose not to have their names and health information publicly listed in a hospital's directory.[1551]
- Patients may request that their medical records are not shared. However, no consent is required for a patient's medical records to be transferred between doctors' offices for the purpose of medical treatment. A covered entity "is permitted to use or disclose protected health information" for "treatment, payment, or health

---

[1545]   29 U.S.C. § 1181(a)(2) (2000).
[1546]   42 U.S.C. §§ 1320a–7c, 1395ddd, 1395b–5.
[1547]   45 C.F.R. 164.528.
[1548]   45 C.F.R. 164.524(b); 45 C.F.R. 164.526.
[1549]   45 C.F.R. 164.502(b)(1).
[1550]   45 C.F.R. 164.508(a)(1); 45 C.F.R. 164.504(a); 45 C.F.R. 164.504(c)(3).
[1551]   45 C.F.R. 164.510(a).

care operations" without a patient's consent. The use of medical information for certain marketing activities is permitted.[1552]

1.b. Genetic Information Nondiscrimination Act of 2008, Pub. L. No. 110-233, 122 Stat. 881. The Genetic Information Nondiscrimination Act prohibits discrimination on the basis of genetic information with respect to health insurance and employment. The act also prohibits employers from discriminating on the basis of predictive genetic information.[1553] Under the act, employers and insurers are prohibited from requiring applicants to submit to genetic tests, would have to adhere to strict use and disclosure requirements, and are subject to penalties for violating the privacy policy.[1554] The act intends to enable and encourage individuals to undergo genetic screening, counseling, testing, and new therapies to advance genetic research. In terms of privacy, the act also prevents health insurers from denying coverage or adjusting premiums because of an individual's predisposition to a genetic condition.[1555]

The U.S. House of Representatives passed the bill 420 to 3, but the Senate has yet to vote on the bill.[1556]

1.c. Substance Abuse Privacy, 42 U.S.C. § 290dd-2 (2000). Under 42 U.S.C. § 290dd-2, medical records maintained by any federal substance-abuse program that contains certain patient information—identity, diagnosis, treatment, etc.—is required to be maintained as confidential.[1557] The statute allows the use of records by medical personnel, and makes exceptions to the confidentiality requirement in the case of court orders, and patient's consent.[1558] Moreover, there is a further exception to the confidentiality requirement in the case of audits and research but required

---

[1552] 45 C.F.R. 164.502(a)(1)(ii); 45 C.F.R. 164.506(a); 45 C.F.R. 164.501.
[1553] Genetic Information Nondiscrimination Act of 2008, § 202.
[1554] *Id.*
[1555] *Id.* § 2753. *See* Brandon Keim, *Genetic Protections Skimp on Privacy, Says Gene Tester,* WIRED, May 23, 2008, http://blog.wired.com/wiredscience/2008/05/genetic-protect. html (last visited June 23, 2008). This article points out several potential gaps in the act, including lack of protection for life insurance and long term disability applicants. There is a lack of clarity as to whether the act supersedes state laws. Also, if there is a surge in demand for genetic testing, these companies will have more information to distribute to entities, including law enforcement, that are not restricted by the act or other laws.
[1556] S. 358, 110th Cong. (2007).
[1557] 42 U.S.C. § 290dd–2(a).
[1558] 42 U.S.C. § 290dd–2(b)(c).

that the patients identities are not disclosed.[1559] Violators of the statute are subject to a fine.[1560]

1.d. Veterans Health Administration Privacy Policy, 38 U.S.C. § 7332 (West Supp. 2005). Under 38 U.S.C. § 7332 medical records maintained by the Veterans Health Administration containing certain patient information—patient identity, diagnosis, treatment etc.—for certain illnesses including drug and alcohol abuse, Human Immunodeficiency Virus infection, or sickle-cell anemia must remain confidential.[1561] Exceptions of the confidentiality requirement exist in the case of patient consent, emergency treatment, management and financial audits, as well as court orders.[1562]

2. Financial, Credit, and Consumer Records

2.a. Bank Secrecy Act, 31 U.S.C. §§ 5311–5330 (2000). This act reduces citizens' right to privacy concerning banking information. Financial institutions are required by the federal government to monitor customers, maintain records, and report personal financial transactions that "have a high degree of usefulness in criminal, tax and regulatory investigations and proceedings."[1563] "Suspicious activity reports" must be filed with the Treasury Department's Financial Crimes Enforcement Network ("FinCEN").[1564] Financial-institution reporting is secret, done without the knowledge or consent of an institution's customers. Reports of suspicious activity are available electronically to every U.S. attorney's office and to fifty-nine law-enforcement agencies, including the FBI, the Secret Service, and the Customs Service. Law-enforcement agencies need not suspect an actual crime before accessing a report. Additionally, no court order, warrant, subpoena, or even written request is needed to view these reports.[1565]

[1559] 42 U.S.C. § 290dd–2(b)(2)(B).
[1560] 42 U.S.C. § 290dd–2(f).
[1561] 38 U.S.C. § 7332(a)(1).
[1562] 38 U.S.C. § 7332(b).
[1563] 12 U.S.C. § 1951.
[1564] 31 U.S.C. § 5318(g)(1). *See also* Annunzio-Wylie Anti-Money Laundering Act, 102 Pub. L. No. 550, 106 Stat. 4044 (1992) (codified in various sections of 12, 18, 31 and 42 U.S.C.).
[1565] *See* sources cited *supra* note 790.

2.b. Fair Credit Reporting Act of 1970 ("FCRA"), 15 U.S.C. §§ 1681–1681u (2000). Congress enacted the FCRA to protect consumers from the disclosure of inaccurate and arbitrary personal information held by consumer reporting agencies.[1566] The FCRA regulates the disclosure of personal information, but it does not restrict the amount or type of information that can be collected. Under the FCRA, consumer reporting agencies may disclose personal information to third parties only under specified conditions. Additionally, information may be released to a third party with the written consent of the subject of the report or when the reporting agency has reason to believe that the requesting party intends to use the information:

- for a credit, employment, or insurance evaluation;
- in connection with the grant of a license or other governmental benefit; or
- for another "legitimate business need" involving the consumer.[1567]

2.c. Fair and Accurate Credit Transactions Act of 2003 ("FACTA"), Pub. L. No. 108-159, 117 Stat. 1952 (2003) (amending 15 U.S.C. §§ 1681–1681u). The congressional rationale of augmenting the Fair Credit Reporting Act of (15 U.S.C. § 1681 et seq.) with FACTA was to reduce instances of identity theft. Among FACTA are provisions that are designed to alert consumers and other procedures designed to detect and prevent identity theft.[1568] However, Congress also effectively barred states from adopting stronger laws.[1569]

FACTA prevents medical creditors from "obtain[ing] or us[ing] medical information pertaining to a consumer in connection with any determination of the consumer's eligibility, or continued eligibility, for credit."[1570] But there are exceptions, and federal banking agencies were directed to issue regulations to cover uses of medical information to protect "legitimate operational, transactional, risk, consumer, and other needs."[1571]

2.d. Gramm-Leach-Bliley Act of 1999 ("GLBA"), Pub. L. No. 106-102, 113 Stat. 1338 (1999) (codified at 15 U.S.C. §§ 6801–6809). The GLBA is

---

[1566]   31 U.S.C. § 1681(b).
[1567]   15 U.S.C. § 1681(b)(f).
[1568]   15 U.S.C. §§ 1681c–1, 1681m.
[1569]   15 U.S.C. § 1681t(b).
[1570]   15 U.S.C. § 1681b(g)(2).
[1571]   15 U.S.C. § 1681b(g)(5)(A).

one of the most comprehensive consumer financial-privacy statutes in U.S. history.[1572] It imposes strict obligations and restrictions on financial institutions in disclosing the personal financial information of customers to nonaffiliated third parties.[1573]

The GLBA regulates the privacy of personally identifiable, nonpublic financial information disclosed to nonaffiliated third parties by financial institutions. The act requires written or electronic notice of the categories of personal information collected, the categories of people the information will be disclosed to, the consumer's opt-out rights, and the company's confidentiality policy. The act also requires administrative, technical, and physical safeguards to protect the security and privacy of information.

2.e. Section 7216 of the Internal Revenue Code, 26 U.S.C. § 7216. Section 7216 of the Internal Revenue Code prohibits anyone who is involved in the preparation of tax returns from knowingly or recklessly disclosing or using the tax-related information provided other than in connection with the preparation of such returns. Anyone who violates this provision may be subject to a fine or even imprisonment. The regulations under section 7216 provide an exemption from this law for tax-return preparers who disclose taxpayer information to a third party for the purpose of having that third party process the return. Note that there is no requirement in section 7216 or its regulations that a preparer inform the client that a third-party provider is being used. In addition, section 7525 provides a client with a privilege similar to the attorney-client privilege when the client makes certain tax-related disclosures to, among others, certified public accountants ("CPAs").[1574]

2.f. Right to Financial Privacy Act of 1978, 12 U.S.C. §§ 3401–3422 (2000). The Right to Financial Privacy Act was Congress's response to a U.S. Supreme Court decision finding that bank customers had no legal right to privacy in financial information of theirs held by financial institutions.[1575] The statutes are largely procedural in nature in that they require agencies to provide notice to individual bank customers, as well as an opportunity to object before a bank or other financial institution

---

[1572] WESTBY, *supra* note 376, at 19.
[1573] *Id.*
[1574] 26 U.S.C. § 825(a)(1).
[1575] *See* United States v. Miller, 425 U.S. 435(1976) (holding that there is no Fourth Amendment right of an individual with respect to their bank records that could be vindicated by a challenge to the validity of the subpoenas).

can disclose personal financial information. The Act, however, allows financial information to be revealed by mere written requests.[1576]

The Right to Financial Privacy Act was designed to protect the confidentiality of personal financial records by creating a statutory Fourth Amendment protection for bank records. The relevant section (12 U.S.C. § 3402) states that:

> no Government authority may have access to or obtain copies of, or the information contained in the financial records of any customer from a financial institution unless the financial records are reasonably described

and—

(1) such customer has authorized such disclosure in accordance with section 3404 of this title;
(2) such financial records are disclosed in response to an administrative subpoena or summons which meets the requirements of section 3405 of this title;
(3) such financial records are disclosed in response to a search warrant which meets the requirements of section 3406 of this title;
(4) such financial records are disclosed in response to a judicial subpoena which meets the requirements of section 3407 of this title; or
(5) such financial records are disclosed in response to a formal written request which meets the requirements of section 3408 of this title.[1577]

The statute prevents banks from requiring customers to authorize the release of financial records as a condition of doing business and states that customers have a right to access a record of all disclosures.[1578]

3. Educational Records

3.a. Family Educational Rights and Privacy Act of 1974 ("FERPA"), 20 U.S.C. § 1232g (2000). FERPA was enacted by Congress in 1974 with the intent of providing students or their parents various rights to inspect

---

[1576] 12 U.S.C. § 3408.
[1577] 12 U.S.C. § 3402.
[1578] 12 U.S.C. § 3404.

student records, and to request any corrections they believe to be incorrect or misleading.[1579] Moreover, student records may not be released without permission, except under certain circumstances.[1580] FERPA applies only to educational agencies and institutions that receive funds from the U.S. Department of Education.[1581]

Generally, schools must have written permission from the parent or eligible student in order to release any information from a student's education record. However, FERPA allows schools to disclose those records, without consent, to the following parties:[1582]

- School officials with a legitimate educational interest
- Other schools to which a student is transferring
- Specified officials for audit or evaluation purposes
- Appropriate parties in connection with financial aid to a student
- Organizations conducting certain studies for or on behalf of the school
- Accrediting organizations
- Appropriate officials in cases of health and safety emergencies
- State and local authorities, within a juvenile justice system, pursuant to specific state law

FERPA also allows schools to disclose records without consent to comply with a judicial order or lawfully issued subpoena.[1583]

Schools may disclose, without consent, "directory information" such as a student's name, address, telephone number, etc.[1584] However, schools must tell parents and eligible students about directory information and give parents and eligible students a reasonable amount of time to request that the school not disclose directory information about them.[1585] Schools must notify parents and eligible students annually of their rights under FERPA.[1586] The actual means of notification (special letter, PTA bulletin, student handbook, or newspaper article) is left to the discretion of each school.

[1579]   31 U.S.C § 1232g(2).
[1580]   31 U.S.C § 1232g(5)(b).
[1581]   31 U.S.C § 1232g(a)–(b).
[1582]   34 C.F.R. § 99.31 (2007).
[1583]   31 U.S.C § 1232g(b)(1)(j).
[1584]   31 U.S.C § 1232g(a)(5)(a).
[1585]   31 U.S.C § 1232g(a)(5)(b).
[1586]   34 C.F.R. 99.7.

Colleges and universities comply with these regulations by dealing exclusively with the student. Bills for tuition are an exception. Since student bills are financial records, involving yet another set of regulations, institutions are allowed to communicate with parents about financial records if the student authorizes the school to do so. Such authorization, however, applies only to financial records and may never include academic or other student records.[1587]

4. Personal Identity Information and Personally Sensitive Information

4.a. Brady Handgun Violence Prevention Act ("Brady Law"), (Pub. L. 103-159, 107 Stat. 1536, enacted 1993-11-30) codified at 18 U.S.C. § 921–922. The Brady Handgun Violence Prevention Act requires gun dealers to submit information about prospective buyers to a federal computer system to prevent sales to convicted felons, fugitives, and other disqualified persons from purchasing firearms. The information includes the potential purchaser's name, sex, race, date of birth, and state of residence. One provision mandates that law enforcement agencies "shall not disclose any such form or the contents thereof to any person or entity, and shall destroy each such form and any record of the contents thereof no more than 20 days from the date such form is received."[1588]

4.b. Cable Communications Policy Act of 1984 ("Cable Act"), Pub. L. 98-549, 98 Stat. 2780 (codified at 47 U.S.C. §§ 521–59 (2000)). The Cable Act places restrictions the collection, maintenance, and dissemination of subscriber data by cable systems operators.[1589] It specifically prohibits operators from collecting subscriber information without prior consent, unless it is needed to render service, detect unauthorized reception, is disclosed pursuant to a court order, or is made for other "legitimate business activitie[s]."[1590] The Cable Act requires operators to notify subscribers of what personal information is collected, how it is used, the length of time it is retained by the operator, how and to whom it is disclosed.[1591]

[1587]   31 U.S.C § 1232g(a)(1)(C)(i).
[1588]   18 U.S.C. § 923(g)(3)(B).
[1589]   47 U.S.C. § 551(a).
[1590]   47 U.S.C. § 551(c).
[1591]   47 U.S.C. § 551(a).

And cable operators must destroy any personal data collected when it is longer needed for the purpose for which it was collected.[1592]

4.c. Census Confidentiality, 13 U.S.C. § 9 (2000). Under 13 U.S.C. § 9, information provided for the census may only be used for its initial statistical purpose, and may not be published in a way that would allow an individual to be identified.

4.d. Children's Online Privacy Protection Act of 1998 ("COPPA"), Pub.L. 105-277, 112 Stat. 2581–728 (codified at 15 U.S.C. §§ 6501–6506 (2000)). COPPA regulates the collection of personal information on the Internet from children. It protects the privacy of children under the age of thirteen by requesting parental consent for the collection or use of any personal information of the users.[1593]

Some of the key requirements of the act that Web site operators must follow include:

- acquiring "verifiable parental consent" before collecting personal information from a child under the age of thirteen;[1594]
- disclosing to parents any information collected about their children by the Web site;[1595]
- providing a right to revoke consent and have information deleted;[1596]
- limiting the collection of personal information when a child participates in online games and contests;[1597] and
- protecting the confidentiality, security, and integrity of any personal information that is collected online from children.[1598]

4.e. Driver's Privacy Protection Act of 1994, 18 U.S.C. §§ 2721–2725 (2000). This act prohibits states from disclosing personal information, such as an individual's photograph, Social Security number, driver's license identification number, name, address, telephone number, or medical or disability information, with certain exceptions.

4.f. Employee Polygraph Protection Act of 1988, Pub. L. 100-347, 102 Stat. 646 (codified at 29 U.S.C. §§ 2001–2009 (2000)). This act prohibits most private employers from using lie-detector tests either for preemployment

---

[1592]   47 U.S.C. § 551(e).
[1593]   15 U.S.C. § 6502(b)(1).
[1594]   15 U.S.C. § 6502(b)(1)(A)(ii).
[1595]   15 U.S.C. § 6502(b)(1)(A)(i).
[1596]   15 U.S.C. § 6502(b)(1)(B)(ii).
[1597]   15 U.S.C. § 6502(b)(1)(C).
[1598]   15 U.S.C. § 6502(b)(1)(D).

screening or during the course of employment.[1599] Exceptions, however, are made for private security-service firms and pharmaceutical manufacturers, and FBI contractors.[1600] The law does not apply to federal, state, or local governments. In the cases where polygraph testing is permitted, the testers are subject to strict standards regarding the length and conduct of the test.[1601]

4.g. Fair Credit Reporting Act of 1970 (see 2.b).

4.h. Fair and Accurate Credit Transactions Act of 2003 (see 2.c).

4.i. False Identification Crime Control Act of 1982 ("FICCA"), Pub. L. No. 97-398, 96 Stat. 2009 (codified at 18 U.S.C. §§ 1028, 1738 (2000)). FICCA was the product of a ten-year legislative process that prohibits the production, transfer, or possession of any document-making instrument used to produce false identification.[1602] FICCA also provides penalties for (1) knowingly and unlawfully producing or transferring an identification document or false identification document; (2) possessing five or more false identification documents; (3) possessing false identification documents with the intent to defraud the United States; or (4) possessing an identification document that appears to be a U.S. document with knowledge that it is stolen or produced without authority.[1603]

4.j. Genetic Information Nondiscrimination Act of 2007 (see 1.b).

4.k. Identity Theft and Assumption Deterrence Act of 1998, Pub. L. No. 105-318, 112 Stat. 3007 (codified at 18 U.S.C. § 1028 (2000)). This act amends FICCA to encompass computer-aided false-identity crimes. It expands the scope of the fraudulent-identification-document crime to include document transfers by electronic means.[1604]

4.l. Substance Abuse Privacy (see 1.c).

4.m. Video Privacy Protection Act of 1998 ("VPPA"), Pub. L. No. 100-618, 102 Stat. 3195 (codified at 18 U.S.C. § 2710 (2000)). The VPPA prohibits videotape service providers from knowingly disclosing personal information, such as titles of rented videocassettes, without the individual's written authorization.[1605] Congress passed the VPPA following the controversy that arose when Judge Robert Bork's video-rental records were

---

[1599] 29 U.S.C. § 2002.
[1600] 29 U.S.C. § 2006.
[1601] 29 U.S.C. § 2007(b).
[1602] 18 U.S.C. § 1028(a).
[1603] *Id.*
[1604] 18 U.S.C. § 1028(c)(3).
[1605] 18 U.S.C. § 2710(b)(1).

released during his Supreme Court nomination hearings. Although a private individual would likely be able to bring suit for a common-law invasion of privacy, a public figure like Judge Bork would probably not prevail, because the First Amendment would probably protect the information contained in his rental record.

4.n. Identity Theft Penalty Enhancement Act of 2003, Pub. L. No. 108-275, 118 Stat. 831 (codified at 47 U.S.C. § 1028A (West. Supp. 2006). The act adds the substantive offense of "aggravated identity theft," caring a minimum sentence of two years.[1606] Aggravated identity theft occurs when a person uses the identification of another person in the course of an enumerated felony.[1607] Such enumerated felonies include, *inter alia*: theft of public money; false statements while acquiring a firearm; mail fraud; immigration, nationality, passport, and citizenship violations; and false social security statements.[1608]

4.o. Internet False Identification Act of 2000, Pub. L. No. 106-578, 114 Stat. 3075 (codified at 18 U.S.C. § 1028). The IFIA further amended the FICCA to include computer-aided false identification including computer templates in the prosecution of identity theft.[1609]

4.p. Telephone Consumer Protection Act of 1991 ("TCPA") Pub. L. No. 102-243, 105 Stat. 2394 (codified principally at 47 U.S.C. § 227 (2000)). The TCPA is the principal law governing the conduct of telephone solicitations. Among its provisions are restrictions on the use of automatic telephone dialing systems. Specifically, they may not be used to dial the number of any emergency "medical physician or service office, health care facility, poison control center, or fire protection or law enforcement agency;" any patient rooms at hospitals or old-age homes; or any number assigned to a service for which the customer is charged.[1610] The act creates a private cause of action for its enforcement.[1611] Moreover, the TCPA does not preempt state law or regulations covering telemarketing.[1612] Both the Ninth and Fourth Circuit Courts of Appeal upheld the constitutionality of the TCPA's restrictions.[1613]

[1606] 18 U.S.C. § 1028A(a)(1).
[1607] *Id.*
[1608] 18 U.S.C. § 1028A(c).
[1609] 18 U.S.C. § 1028(d)(1)–(2).
[1610] 47 U.S.C. § 227(b)(1)(A)(i)–(iii).
[1611] 47 U.S.C. § 227(b)(3).
[1612] 47 U.S.C. § 227(e).
[1613] *See* Moser v. FCC, 46 F.3d 970 (9th Cir. 1995) *cert. denied*, 515 U.S. 1161 (1995); Destination Ventures Ltd. v. FCC, 46 F.3d 54 (9th Cir. 1995).

5. Personal Communications

5.a. Cable Communications Policy Act of 1984 (see 4.b).

5.b. Controlling the Assault of Non-Solicited Pornography and Marketing Act of 2003 ("CAN-SPAM Act"), Pub L, No. 08-187, 117 Stat. 2699 (2003) (codified at 15 U.S.C. §§ 7701-7713 and 18 U.S.C. § 1037 (West Supp. 2006)). Aside from requiring unsolicited e-mails to include opt-out instructions and to include the sender's physical address, the statute authorizes the FTC to establish a "do-not-e-mail" registry.[1614]

5.c. Communications Decency Act of 1996 ("CDA") Pub. L. No. 104-104, 110 Stat. 56, 133–43 (codified in scattered sections of 47 U.S.C. and 18 U.S.C.). The pertinent section reads:

(1) Treatment of publisher or speaker.—No provider or user of an interactive computer service shall be treated as the publisher or speaker of any information provided by another information content provider.[1615]

The provisions of the CDA that dealt with restrictions on obscene speech were declared unconstitutional in *Reno v. ACLU*.[1616] The provision dealing with immunity for Internet service providers, however, has survived.

In the case of *Zeran v. America Online*,[1617] the Fourth Circuit found that a service provider was not liable for failing to remove defamatory material from the Web, even after notice. A series of cases interpreting the CDA have immunized Internet sites that do not provide actual content.

5.d. Communications Assistance for Law Enforcement Act of 1994 ("CALEA"), Pub. L. No. 103-414, 108 Stat. 4279 (codified at 47 U.S.C. §§ 1001–10 (2000)). CALEA was enacted with the intent of protecting public safety and national security by ensuring that law enforcement agencies have the ability to conduct electronic surveillance. This is done by requiring that telecommunications operators modify and design their equipment and services so that they have surveillance capabilities. "Telecommunications carriers" for purposes of the statute include common carriers, facilities-based broadband Internet access providers, and providers of interconnected

---

[1614]   15 U.S.C. § 7708.
[1615]   47 U.S.C. § 230(c)(1).
[1616]   521 U.S. 844 (1996).
[1617]   129 F.3d 327 (4th Cir. 1997).

Voice over Internet Protocol (VoIP) service.[1618] When CALEA was passed in 1994, it was the first time that private telecommunications companies were required to modify their equipment and services to facilitate government surveillance.

5.e. Electronic Communications Privacy Act of 1986 ("ECPA"), Pub. L. No. 99-508, Oct. 21, 1986, 100 Stat. 1848 (codified at 18 U.S.C. §§ 2510, 2521, 2701, 2710, 3117 3121, 3126)). The ECPA was an amendment to Title III of the Omnibus Crime Control and Safe Streets Act of 1968. It is aimed at preventing invasions into individuals' privacy by the government. However, the ECPA law also forbids private electronic communications operators from divulging their contents. The ECPA generally prohibits the use of pen registers and trap-and-trace without a court order with the exceptions of system testing and to record fraud.[1619]

5.f. Communications Act of 1934, 47 U.S.C. §§ 151–713 (2000). The Communications Act of 1934 and amendments to that act cover a broad range of issues relating to privacy, including protection of telecommunications, cable, and cell phone information.[1620]

5.g. Section 222 of the Telecommunications Act of 1996, Pub. L. No. 104-104, 110 Stat. 56 (codified at 47 U.S.C. § 222 (2000)). Section 222, entitled "Privacy of Customer Information," states generally that "[e]very telecommunications carrier has a duty to protect the confidentiality of proprietary information of, and relating to . . . customers." Section 222 places restrictions on the use of, disclosure of, and access to certain customer information.

In 1998, the FCC issued an opt-in regulation requiring customers to opt-in prior to companies using their customer data. The Tenth Circuit Court of Appeals, however, ruled the opt-in regulation unconstitutional in violation of the First Amendment.[1621]

5.h. Telephone Consumer Protection Act of 1991 (see 4.p).

5.i. Wireless Communications and Public Safety Act of 1999 ("911 Act").[1622] The 911 Act amended privacy provisions in the Telecommunications Act of 1996 to allow location information to be used for emergency-services purposes.

[1618]   47 U.S.C. § 1001(8).

[1619]   18 U.S.C. § 3121(a)–(b).

[1620]   Amendments relating to privacy include Privacy of Customer Information, 47 U.S.C. § 222 (2006) and Protections of Subscriber Privacy, 47 U.S.C. § 551(2006).

[1621]   U.S. West, Inc. v. FCC, 182 F.3d 1224 (10th Cir. 1999), *cert. denied*, 530 U.S. 1213 (2000) (vacating the Commission's implementation of opt-in).

[1622]   47 U.S.C. § 615a (2000).

Enhanced 911, or E911, is an FCC program that requires mobile phone services to be able to track and communicate the locations of users. GPS tracking is used in E911 service. Although E911 allows emergency-service providers to locate callers, E911 also allows third parties to track phones using the GPS signal. For example, parents can track their child's location.[1623]

6. Computer Use or Computer-Generated Information

6.a. Computer Fraud and Abuse Act of 1984, L. 98-473, 98 Stat. 2190 (codified at 18 U.S.C. § 1030 (Supp. 2001)). The Computer Fraud and Abuse Act makes certain activities designed to access a "federal interest computer" illegal.

> Whoever . . . knowingly causes the transmission of a program, information, code or command, and as a result of such conduct, intentionally causes damage without authorization, to a protected computer . . . [or] knowingly and with intent to defraud traffics . . . in any password or similar information through which a computer may be accessed without authorization . . . shall be punished as provided in subsection (c) of this section.[1624]

The Patriot Act amended the Computer Fraud and Abuse Act with both procedural and substantive changes that may influence future prosecutions. Some changes will make it easier for law enforcement to investigate computer crimes, fight terrorism, and fight cyberterrorism. The title and purpose of the Patriot Act are the only apparent limits to these modifications.[1625]

6.b. Computer Matching and Privacy Protection Act of 1988 ("CMPPA"), Pub. L. No. 100-503, 102 Stat. 2507 (codified at 5 U.S.C. § 552a(o) (2000)). The CMPPA amended the Privacy Act of 1974 by prohibiting disclosures of personal information contained in databases to any government or private agency for "use in a computer matching

---

[1623] Amy Harmon, *Cellphones That Track Kids Click with Parents*, SEATTLE TIMES, Dec. 21, 2003, *available at* http://seattletimes.nwsource.com/html/nationworld/2001820367_track21.html.

[1624] 18 U.S.C. § 1030(a).

[1625] Ellen S. Podgor, *Computer Crimes and the USA PATRIOT Act*, CRIM. JUST., Summer 2002, at 60, *available at* http://www.abanet.org/crimjust/cjmag/17-2/crimes.html (last visited May 9, 2008).

program."[1626] As amended by the CMPPA, the Privacy Act now requires agencies involved in computer matching programs to, *inter alia*:

- state "the purpose and legal authority" of the program;[1627]
- state "the justification for the program and [its] anticipated results;"[1628]
- describe the information and records used in the matching program;[1629]
- state the starting and completion dates of the project;[1630]
- provide notice procedures for individualized notice;[1631]
- provide procedures for the retention and destruction of records, and their security.[1632]

6.c. E-Government Act of 2002, Pub. L. No. 107-347, 116 Stat. 2899 (codified at 44 U.S.C. §§ 3501–3521 (West Supp. 2005). The E-Government Act establishes many requirements for computer and Internet use within the federal government. With respect to privacy, the key requirement is that agencies must conduct privacy impact assessments.[1633] Agencies must assess the reasons for holding an individual's information, with whom the information will be shared, the duration it is to be retained, and its intended use.[1634] Unlike the Privacy Act of 1974, whose applicability is limited to U.S. citizens and legal residents, the E-Government Act of 2002 applies more broadly to "individuals."[1635]

The Office of Management and Budget issued guidelines for what should be addressed in a privacy impact assessment: the specific information collected, the purpose for collection, the intended use of the information, a list of the parties with which the information may be shared, notice regarding the collection of information, security provisions, and whether a system of records notice has been created pursuant to the Privacy Act.[1636]

[1626] 5 U.S.C. § 552a(o)(1).
[1627] 5 U.S.C. § 552a(o)(1)(A).
[1628] 5 U.S.C. § 552a(o)(1)(B).
[1629] 5 U.S.C. § 552a(o)(1)(C).
[1630] *Id.*
[1631] 5 U.S.C. § 552a(o)(1)(D).
[1632] 5 U.S.C. § 552a(o)(1)(D)–(E).
[1633] E-Government Act of 2002 § 208(b)(1).
[1634] Mortensen & Kelly, *supra* note 752.
[1635] *Id.* § 12:4.1.
[1636] *Id.* § 12:4.2.

Additional privacy protections in the act include prohibitions on the disclosure of information obtained for statistical purposes and the requirement that federal agencies post machine-readable privacy policies on their Web sites.[1637]

6.d. Freedom of Information Act ("FOIA") (see 8.e).

6.e. Privacy Act of 1974, Pub. L. No. 93-579, 88 Stat. 1896 (codified at 5 U.S.C. 552a).[1638] The Privacy Act applies only to federal governmental agencies[1639] that maintain information that can be used to identify an individual.[1640] The act restricts the disclosure of personal information, provides individuals with the right to access the contents of their files, and provides the right to seek amendment or correction of inaccurate information.[1641]

The Department of Justice notes that "the Act's imprecise language, limited legislative history, and somewhat outdated regulatory guidelines have rendered it a difficult statute to decipher and apply."[1642]

7. Business Information

7.a. Economic Espionage Act of 1996 ("EEA"), Pub. L. No. 104-294, 110 Stat. 3488 (codified at 18 U.S.C. 1831–39). Congress enacted the EEA to prosecute individuals who steal trade secrets. The EEA broadly defines "trade secrets" as:

> all forms and types of financial, business, scientific, technical, eco-nomic, or engineering information, including patterns, plans, com-pilations, program devices, formulas, designs, prototypes, methods, techniques, processes, procedures, programs, and codes, whether tangible or intangible, and whether stored, compiled, or memorial-ized physically, electronically, graphically, photographically, or in writ-ing, if—(A) the owner has taken reasonable measures to keep such information secret, and (B) the information derives independent

---

[1637] E-Government Act of 2002 §§ 208(c)(2), 212(e)(4).

[1638] 5 U.S.C. § 552a (2000).

[1639] The definition of "agency" does not encompass the offices included within the Executive Office of the President, whose sole function is to advise and assist the president. Dale v. Executive Office of President, 164 F. Supp. 2d 22, 25 (D.D.C. 2001).

[1640] *See* Mortensen & Kelly, *supra* note 752.

[1641] Westby, *supra* note 376, at 15.

[1642] Privacy Act Overview, May 2004 Edition, http://www.usdoj.gov/oip/04_7_1.html (last visited May 9, 2008).

economic value, actual or potential, from not being generally known to, and not being readily ascertainable through proper means by, the public.[1643]

The EEA makes it a crime when an individual knowingly "steals, or without authorization appropriates, takes, carries away, or conceals, or by fraud, artifice, or deception obtains a trade secret."[1644] The EEA also contains provisions to protect the trade secrets in court proceedings. Violators must forfeit proceeds stemming from the crime, and a court may order the forfeiture of any property used to commit or to facilitate the commission of the crime.[1645] For more serious violations of the EEA, a defendant can be imprisoned for up to fifteen years or fined up to $500,000 or both.[1646]

7.b. Employee Polygraph Protection Act (see 4.f).

7.c. Freedom of Information Act ("FOIA") (see 8.e).

8. Exemptions from Public Records and Protection Against Public Intrusions

8.a. Census Confidentiality (see 4.c).

8.b. Computer Matching and Privacy Protection Act (see 6.b).

8.c. Computer Security Act of 1987, Pub. L. No. 100-235, 101 Stat. 1724 (codified at 15 U.S.C. 271–278h) (1988)). The act defines "sensitive information" as "information, the loss, misuse, or unauthorized access to or modification of which could adversely affect the national interest or the conduct of Federal programs, or the privacy to which individuals are entitled under [the Privacy Act] . . ."[1647] The act also requires that minimum standards be established for federal information systems.[1648]

8.d. E-Government Act of 2002 (see 6.c).

8.e. Freedom of Information Act of 1966 ("FOIA") Pub. L. No. 89-554, 80 Stat. 383 (codified at 5 U.S.C. 552). The FOIA requires federal agencies to make information publically available. There are, however, exceptions to FOIA that protect privacy interests from disclosure. A federal agency may withhold information about individuals in personnel and medical

---

[1643] 18 U.S.C. § 1839(3)(A)–(B).
[1644] 18 U.S.C. § 1831(a)(1).
[1645] 18 U.S.C. § 1834.
[1646] 18 U.S.C. § 1831(a).
[1647] 18 U.S.C. § 278g–3.
[1648] 18 U.S.C. § 278g–3.(a).

files and similar files the disclosure of which would constitute a clearly unwarranted invasion of personal privacy".[1649] Another exemption allows agencies to withhold records compiled for law-enforcement purposes.[1650]

8.f. Paperwork Reduction Act of 1995, Pub. L. No. 104-13, 109 Stat. 163 (codified at 44 U.S.C. 3501–20). The PRA established Office of Information and Regulatory Affairs within the Office of Management and Budget.[1651] The OIRA is required to promulgate guidance for and oversight of federal agencies' information-management activities.[1652]

The act also requires federal agencies to ensure compliance with the Privacy Act and to coordinate management of the requirements of FOIA, the Privacy Act, the Computer Security Act, and related management laws.

8.g. Privacy Act of 1974 (see 6.e).

8.h. Privacy Protection Act of 1980, Pub. L. No. 96-440, 94 Stat. 1879 (codified at 42 U.S.C. 2000aa et seq.). The Privacy Protection Act mainly deals with protecting First Amendment freedom-of-the-press values. The act prohibits "a government officer or employee, in connection with the investigation or prosecution of a criminal offense, to search for or seize any work product materials possessed by a person reasonably believed to have a purpose to disseminate to the public a newspaper, book, broadcast, or other similar form of public communication, in or affecting interstate or foreign commerce."[1653] There, however, is an exception to the prohibition if there is probable cause that the possessor of the materials is involved in a criminal offense.[1654]

8.i. Section 1983 of the Civil Rights Act of 1871 (codified at 42 U.S.C. § 1983). Section 1983 of the Civil Rights Act provides:

> Every person who under color of any statute, ordinance, regulation, custom, or usage, of any State or Territory or the District of Columbia, subjects, or causes to be subjected, any citizen of the United States or other person within the jurisdiction thereof to the deprivation of any rights, privileges, or immunities secured by the Constitution and laws, shall be liable to the party injured in an action at law, suit in equity, or other proper proceeding for redress, except that in any

---

[1649] 5 U.S.C. § 552(b)(6).
[1650] 5 U.S.C. § 552(b)(7).
[1651] 44 U.S.C. § 3503.
[1652] 44 U.S.C. § 3504.
[1653] 42 U.S.C. § 2000aa(a).
[1654] 42 U.S.C. § 2000aa(a)(1).

action brought against a judicial officer for an act or omission taken in such officer's judicial capacity, injunctive relief shall not be granted unless a declaratory decree was violated or declaratory relief was unavailable."[1655]

Section 1983 jurisprudence is extremely complicated, but has been expanded to apply to causes of action relating to privacy rights and surveillance.[1656]

8.j. Social Security Number Confidentiality Act of 2000, Pub. L. No. 106-433, 114 Stat. 1910 (codified at 31 U.S.C. § 3327 (2000)). This act prohibits Social Security numbers from being visible on or through unopened mailings or other checks or drafts issued by the Treasury Department.

9. Private Intrusions

9.a. Controlling the Assault of Non-Solicited Pornography and Marketing Act of 2003 ("CAN-SPAM") (see 5.b).

9.b. False Identification Crime Control Act of 1982 (see 4.i).

9.c. Identity Theft and Assumption Deterrence Act of 1998 (see 4.k).

9.d. Identity Theft Penalty Enhancement Act (see 4.n).

9.e. Section 7216 of the Internal Revenue Code (see 2.e.).

9.f. Internet False Identification Act of 2000 (see 4.o).

9.g. Paperwork Reduction Act of 1995 (see 8.f).

9.h. Privacy Act of 1974 (see 6.e).

9.i. Privacy Protection Act of 1980 (see 8.h).

9.j. Social Security Number Confidentiality Act of 2000 (see 8.j).

9.k. Video Voyeurism Prevention Act of 2004.[1657]

The VVPA makes it a crime "to capture an image of a private area of an individual without their consent . . . under circumstances in which the individual has a reasonable expectation of privacy . . . ."[1658] "Private area" includes the "naked or undergarment clad genitals, pubic area, buttocks, or female breast."[1659] Moreover, under the act, a reasonable expectation of privacy includes both a public and private dimension. The VVPA defines reasonable expectation of privacy as "circumstances in which a reasonable

---

[1655]   42 U.S.C. § 1983.
[1656]   See supra notes 779–81 and accompanying text.
[1657]   18 U.S.C. § 1801 (Supp. 2004).
[1658]   18 U.S.C. § 1801(a).
[1659]   18 U.S.C. § 1801(b)(3).

person would believe that a private area of the individual would not be visible to the public, regardless of whether that person is in a public or private place.[1660] Cedric Laurant, formerly of the Electronic Privacy Information Center, commented on the law: "Previous state laws did not prohibit activities like taking a picture up a woman's skirt, when the woman was in a public place. . . . This [law] will specifically target that kind of activity, which should mean people will have more privacy."[1661]

10. Statutes Authorizing Governmental Intrusions

10.a. Bank Secrecy Act (see 2.a).

    10.b. Communications Assistance for Law Enforcement Act of 1994 ("CALEA") (see 5.d).

    10.c. Computer Fraud and Abuse Act of 1994 (see 6.a).

    10.d. Electronic Communications Privacy Act of 1986 (see 5.e).

    10.e. Foreign Intelligence Surveillance Act of 1978 ("FISA") Pub. L. No. 95-511, 92 Stat. 1783 (codified at 50 U.S.C. §§ 1801–1811). Intercepting private communications during the course of an ordinary criminal investigation has traditionally been viewed as a violation of privacy. In *United States v. U.S. District Court*,[1662] the Supreme Court stated:

> Given those potential distinctions between Title III criminal surveillances and those involving the domestic security, Congress may wish to consider protective standards for the latter which differ from those already prescribed for specified crimes in Title III. Different standards may be compatible with the Fourth Amendment if they are reasonable both in relation to the legitimate need of Government for intelligence information and the protected rights of our citizens.[1663]

In 1978, Congress passed the FISA, the statutory framework governing the procedures by which electronic surveillance and physical searches are conducted for foreign intelligence investigations.

[1660] 18 U.S.C. § 1801(b)(5)(B).

[1661] Mark S. Sullivan, *Law May Curb Cell Phone Camera Use*, PCWORLD, July 23, 2004, *available at* http://www.pcworld.com/article/id,117035-page,1/article.html (last visited May 9, 2008).

[1662] States v. United States District Court ("*Keith*"), 407 U.S. 297 (1972).

[1663] *Id.* at 322–23.

Traditionally, under the Fourth Amendment, a search warrant must be based on a probable cause belief that an individual is engaged in criminal activity. FISA, however, only requires that belief that "the acquisition of the contents of communications transmitted by means of communications used exclusively between or among foreign powers.[1664] However, if the target of an investigation is a "U.S. person," there still must be probable cause to believe that their activities involve espionage. Furthermore, a U.S. citizen may not be determined to be an agent of a foreign power "solely upon the basis of activities protected by the First Amendment to the Constitution of the United States."[1665]

FISA also has a minimization requirement. Prior to the enactment of the Patriot Act, FISA-obtained information could be used in criminal proceedings so long that the "primary purpose" of the investigation was to collect foreign intelligence.[1666] In a number of instances, however, there have overlaps between foreign intelligence gathering and criminal investigations. A common minimization procedure is known as an "information-screening wall." These "walls" require a disinterested to review the information gathered by FISA surveillance, to screen it, and only pass on information that might be relevant evidence.[1667]

The Foreign Intelligence Surveillance Court ("FISC") is a special court composed of seven federal district court judges and exercises jurisdiction over "applications for and grant orders approving electronic surveillance anywhere within the United States."[1668] Under the FISA, the Department of Justice reviews applications for warrants made by agencies prior to submitting them to the FISC. The attorney general also must approve all FISA applications.[1669] The application must contain, *inter alia*,

- the identity of the target of the surveillance, and the nature of the information sought;[1670]

[1664]   50 U.S.C. § 1802(a)(1)(A)(i).

[1665]   50 U.S.C. § 1861(a).

[1666]   Foreign Intelligence Surveillance Act of 1978 §§ 1801(h), 1804(a)(5), 1804(a)(7)(B), 1805(a)(4). *See also* United States v. Truong Dinh Hung, 629 F.2d 908, 912–13, 916 (4th Cir. 1980) (holding that evidence obtained pursuant to FISA where the primary purpose is a criminal investigation is inadmissible in court).

[1667]   STEPHEN J. SCHULHOFER, RETHINKING THE PATRIOT ACT: KEEPING AMERICAN SAFE AND FREE 37–38 (2005).

[1668]   50 U.S.C. § 1803. *See also* 50 U.S.C. § 1822(c) (granting FISC jurisdiction over physical searches conducted pursuant to FISA).

[1669]   50 U.S.C. §§ 1804(a)(2), (e).

[1670]   50 U.S.C. § 1804(a)(3), (6).

- a "statement of the facts and circumstances relied upon by the applicant to justify his belief that—(A) the target of the electronic surveillance is a foreign power or an agent of a foreign power; and (B) each of the facilities or places at which the electronic surveillance is directed is being used, or is about to be used, by a foreign power or an agent of a foreign power;"[1671]
- the proposed minimization procedures.[1672]

The case records are sealed and may not be revealed. There is no requirement that executed warrants be returned. Nor is there any certification requirement that surveillance was conducted pursuant to the warrant and its proposed "minimization" protocol. The FISA makes provision for review of FISC decisions by the Foreign Intelligence Surveillance Court of Review (FISCR).

10.f. Omnibus Crime Control and Safe Streets Act of 1968, Pub. L. No. 90-351, 82 Stat. 197 (codified at 18 U.S.C. § 2510 et seq.). The act makes it a crime for one who "intentionally intercepts, endeavors to intercept, or procures any other person to intercept or endeavor to intercept, any wire, oral, or electronic communication."[1673] However, the act also grants the Attorney General the right to apply for electronic surveillance in the course of investigating certain enumerated criminal offenses.[1674]

10.g. USA PATRIOT Act, Pub. L. No. 107-56, 115 Stat. 272 (codified in various sections of 18, 31, and 42 U.S.C.). The Patriot Act is a sweeping piece of legislation which amends several enactments protecting personal privacy. One key provision is the lowering of the FISA standard relating to intelligence investigations. Patriot Act section 218 lowers the preexisting FISA standard that "*the purpose*" of surveillance is to gather foreign intelligence to the lower threshold of requiring that foreign intelligence gathering be "a *significant* purpose" of surveillance.[1675] The constitutionality of the "significant purpose standard" was considered by the Foreign Intelligence Surveillance Court (FISC).

[1671] 50 U.S.C. § 1804(a)(4)(A)–(B).
[1672] 50 U.S.C. § 1804(a)(5).
[1673] 18 U.S.C. § 2511(1)(a).
[1674] 18 U.S.C. § 2516.
[1675] 50 U.S.C. § 1804(a)(7)(B). *See generally* William C. Banks, *And the Wall Came Tumbling Down: Secret Surveillance After the Terror*, 57 U. Miami L. Rev. 1147, 1174–81 (2003) (discussing the erosion of the foreign intelligence and criminal investigation dichotomy).

Title II of the Patriot Act amends the Omnibus Crime Control and Safe Streets Act to allow "roving wiretap, allowing the intercept of communications made by the target of an investigation without having to specify the particular telephone line or computer being monitored."[1676] The Patriot Act moreover liberalizes the use of pen registers and trap-and-trace devices. The FISA requirement that the surveillance be pursuant to "any investigation to gather foreign intelligence information or information concerning international terrorism" was replaced with the requirement that "any investigation to obtain foreign intelligence information not concerning a United States person or to protect against international terrorism or clandestine intelligence activities, provided that such investigation of a United States person is not conducted solely upon the basis of activities protected by the first amendment to the Constitution."[1677]

The scope of the Patriot Act is extremely broad and it affects numerous pieces of preexisting laws protecting privacy including:

- the Electronic Communications Privacy Act of 1986;
- the Computer Fraud and Abuse Act of 1984;
- the Foreign Intelligence Surveillance Act of 1978;
- the Family Educational Rights and Privacy Act of 1974;
- the Money Laundering Control Act of 1986;
- the Immigration and Nationality Act of 1952;
- the Money Laundering Control Act of 1986;
- the Bank Secrecy Act of 1970;
- the Right to Financial Privacy Act of 1978;
- the Fair Credit Reporting Act of 1970.

[1676] 18 U.S.C. § 2518(11).
[1677] 50 U.S.C. § 1842(a).

APPENDIX II

Privacy Protections in State Constitutions[1678]

Congress and the states have enacted laws to protect individuals' privacy in various specific areas, such as medical and financial records, and courts have determined a right to privacy in certain areas. State constitutions provide another source of protection. Constitutions in ten states—Alaska, Arizona, California, Florida, Hawaii, Illinois, Louisiana, Montana, South Carolina, and Washington—*expressly* recognize a right to privacy. In other states, court decisions have established constitutional rights of privacy.

Alaska	art. I, § 22	"The right of the people to privacy is recognized and shall not be infringed. The legislature shall implement this section."
Arizona	art. II, § 8	"No person shall be disturbed in his private affairs, or his home invaded, without authority of law."
California	art. I, § 1	"All people are by nature free and independent and have inalienable rights. Among these are enjoying and defending life and liberty, acquiring, possessing, and protecting property, and pursuing and obtaining safety, happiness, and privacy."

[1678] From the Web site of the National Conference of State Legislatures, http://www.ncsl.org/programs/lis/privacy/stateconstpriv03.htm (last visited May 9, 2008). Provisions dealing only with search and seizure have been deleted.

Florida	art. I, § 23	"Every natural person has the right to be let alone and free from governmental intrusion into the person's private life except as otherwise provided herein. This section shall not be construed to limit the public's right of access to public records and meetings as provided by law."
Hawaii	art. I, § 6	"The right of the people to privacy is recognized and shall not be infringed without the showing of a compelling state interest. The legislature shall take affirmative steps to implement this right."
Illinois	art. I, § 12	"Every person shall find a certain remedy in the laws for all injuries and wrongs which he receives to his person, privacy, property or reputation. He shall obtain justice by law, freely, completely, and promptly."
Louisiana	art. I, § 5	"Every person shall be secure in his person, property, communications, houses, papers, and effects against unreasonable searches, seizures, or invasions of privacy. No warrant shall issue without probable cause supported by oath or affirmation, and particularly describing the place to be searched, the persons or things to be seized, and the lawful purpose or reason for the search. Any person adversely affected by a search or seizure conducted in violation of this Section shall have standing to raise its illegality in the appropriate court."
Montana	art. II, § 10	"The right of individual privacy is essential to the well-being of a free society and shall not be infringed without the showing of a compelling state interest."

South Carolina	art. I, § 10	"The right of the people to be secure in their persons, houses, papers, and effects against unreasonable searches and seizures and unreasonable invasions of privacy shall not be violated, and no warrants shall issue but upon probable cause, supported by oath or affirmation, and particularly describing the place to be searched, the person or thing to be seized, and the information to be obtained."
Washington	art. I, § 7	"No person shall be disturbed in his private affairs, or his home invaded, without authority of law."

APPENDIX III

Examples of Consumer Privacy Policies

Macy's Privacy Statement

This policy was last updated on June 4, 2006.

What Information Do We Collect?

We collect various types of information depending upon how you use our site.

- When you order from us, we collect your name, billing address, shipping address, email address, phone number, and credit card number (with expiration date) or gift card number. We also gather information on the person who will receive any gift you send (e.g., that person's name and address) and we will retain a record of your purchases. In addition, if you are a registered user and have signed in when you enter this information, it will automatically be saved in your Wallet and/or Address Book for ease of reference.
- When you become a macys.com registered user, we collect your name, mailing address, email address, birth date and password. This information is gathered to make your shopping experience as a registered user as quick and easy as possible.

- When you enter a sweepstakes or contest online, we usually collect your name, address, email address, and phone number. We also may ask you for additional information, such as your age, interests, product preferences, or zip code.
- When you submit a question to customer service, we need your email address to respond, and you also may provide us with various additional information to help us answer your question.
- We also may receive some information about you from other sources and may add it to your account information. For example, we might get your updated address from a shipper or information on your preferences from another Web site conducting a promotion or event with us.
- When you apply for a Macy's credit card, you will be asked to provide your name, address, email address, phone number, and other information needed to assess your creditworthiness and verify your identity, such as social security number and employer. This information is required to process your application. The personal information you provide is transmitted through a secure server using SSL encryption. To apply for a Macy's credit card and review the separate privacy policy that applies to your Macy's credit card account, click here.
- We may acquire customer lists from other parties so that we may invite new people to visit macys.com. Our policy is to acquire only lists of people who have indicated that they are willing to receive email offers. Also, each time we send an email offer, we provide people with the opportunity to opt out of receiving future email offers.
- We have carefully selected a company, Coremetrics, to assist us in better understanding how people use our site. macys. com will place cookies on your computer to collect information. The information that is collected through these cookies tells us things like which search engine referred you, how you navigated around our site, what you browsed and purchased and what traffic is driven by banner ads and emails.
- Coremetrics analyzes the information it collects from macys. com and returns it to us through a secure web connection. We use the information to help us understand your interests in our

web site and how to better serve you. It also helps us provide you with more personalized product offerings. macys.com does not allow Coremetrics to collect credit card, username or password information.

- Coremetrics may only use your personal information to perform services for us. It may not share your personal information with anyone else, or use it for any other purpose, except on an aggregate, non-personal basis (in other words, the information will not be identified with you). Coremetrics is required to maintain all of the information it collects and analyzes securely and in confidence.
- As a visitor to macys.com, you may choose to opt-out of Coremetrics' analysis of your browsing and purchasing behavior on our site. You may also choose to continue to benefit from the improved shopping experience that the Coremetrics analysis allows us to provide, but maintain your anonymity. To learn more about the various levels of privacy and confidentiality you can select with respect to Coremetrics on this site and to exercise your opt-out choices, click here.
- Please note that Coremetrics collects data on our site using first-party data collection. As a result, blocking cookies served from third-party domains will **not** block these first-party macys.com cookies. You need to follow the opt-out process specified (see paragraph above) in order to opt-out of Coremetrics data collection.
- What Are Cookies and Do We Use Them? A cookie is a small piece of information sent by a Web site that is saved on your hard disk by your computer's browser. It holds information a site may need to interact with you and personalize your experience. At macys.com, we use two kinds of cookies: session cookies and persistent cookies.
- Session cookies exist only for as long as your browser remains open. Once you exit your browser, they go away. We use session cookies to maintain information we need to have in order for you to shop at macys.com. For example, the Session ID cookie that we ask your browser to hold retains the ID for your shopping bag. Without the Session ID cookie, you can't add merchandise to your bag and carry it to Checkout.

- Persistent cookies, in contrast, last from visit to visit; they do not go away when you exit your browser. At macys.com, we use persistent cookies to give you a more personalized shopping experience and to help you navigate our store more efficiently. We will use your information to enhance your site experience. However, you can use our site without accepting a persistent cookie. To do so, you should set your browser options to reject persistent cookies. Alternatively, you can set your browser to notify you when you receive a cookie, which gives you the opportunity to decide whether you want to accept it or not. In many instances, the Help button on your browser toolbar will tell you how you can take these steps.
- Cookies can be used by a Web site to recognize you. But that does not necessarily mean any personal information is stored in the cookies. At macys.com, we store no personal information about you in the cookies. Anything you choose to tell us about yourself (such as your address and email address) is stored safely and separately on our secured servers, and you need to provide a password to access it.
- We also use cookies to look at how groups, rather than individuals, use our Web site. In our physical stores, we can observe which aisles and departments are most heavily trafficked and determine what displays or sales are the most successful. Then, we can identify ways to improve the customer experience. On the Web, cookies help us develop a similar understanding so that we can continue to improve the arrangement, product offerings, and merchandise placement you see at macys.com.

How Do We Use Your Information?

We may use your information in a number of ways, including the following:

- In order to serve you better, we may combine the information you provide us online, in our stores and through our catalogs. We use that information to improve your overall shopping experience.

- To improve the content on our Web site. For example, we may use cookies to find out which parts of our site or our products are visited most often.
- To enhance your online shopping experience. For example, we may use it to recognize you and welcome you to the site.
- For marketing and promotional purposes. For example, we send out email and direct mail to our online and store customers about products or events that we think may be of interest to them. We also may send you offers for discounts or free services (e.g., free gift wrap or shipping) on our site or in our stores.

Do We Share Your Information?

The information gathered may be shared with the Macy's, Inc. family of companies, which include Macy's and Bloomingdale's. We also share the information with third parties, including responsible companies with which we have a relationship. For example:

- When you make a purchase, we may share information about you and your transaction with other companies for the purpose of processing your transaction, including fraud prevention, vendor direct shipping and credit card authorization.
- WeddingChannel (www.weddingchannel.com) operates the website where you can access the Macy's bridal registry (the "Macy's Wedding & Gift Registry") or register for your own wedding. When you use that Web site, Macy's Wedding & Gift Registry, macys.com and WeddingChannel receive your information. Please note that WeddingChannel is a separate company; it is not part of the Macy's, Inc. family.
- Some of our vendors may work closely with us to create a vendor shop within the macys.com site or to ship your order directly to you. In certain instances, we may share certain information about you with that vendor (e.g., if you decide to buy their products).
- You also may make a purchase from macys.com through a link from another Web site or search engine and may use their express checkout tool to do so. When you do, please be

aware that both macys.com and that Web site or search engine will receive your information.

- In some cases, macys.com may enter into a co-branding relationship with another Web site that offers you products or services that supplement macys.com's assortment (e.g., flowers). In those cases, you may link from macys.com to another site to purchase the item. In that case, both macys.com and the other Web site may receive your information.
- macys.com may team with another Web site to conduct a sweepstakes or other event (e.g., a live Web chat). In those cases, each of the participating Web sites may collect or receive personal information from you.
- For some of our products, macys.com may provide you with a link to the supplier of that product so that you may get further information. If you link to the supplier's site, the supplier may collect or receive information about you.
- Like other companies, macys.com may use third party advertising companies to serve ads (e.g., banners or links) on its behalf. These companies may employ cookies and action tags (also known as single pixel gifs or web beacons) to measure advertising effectiveness. Any information that these third parties collect via cookies and action tags is anonymous. If you would like more information about this practice and your choices, click here.

In most of the above situations, these third parties will receive your information because you will be visiting their Web sites or using their links and, in doing so, you may provide information directly to them. You therefore should refer to their privacy policies to understand how they handle your information and what kinds of choices you have.

Macys.com also may share your personal information with outside companies that perform services for macys.com. For example, we may retain an outside company to manage a database containing certain customer information or to create and distribute an email offering. In those situations, the outside party is performing work for macys.com, and macys.com takes appropriate steps designed to ensure your information is used only to provide the services requested by macys.com, and not for other purposes.

Additionally, macys.com may share account or other information when we believe it is necessary to comply with law or to protect our interests or property. This may include sharing information with other companies, lawyers, credit bureaus, agents or government agencies in connection with issues related to fraud, credit, or debt collection.

And in the event that some or all of the business assets of macys. com are sold or transferred, we generally would transfer the corresponding information about our customers.

Finally, macys.com may share your personal information with unrelated outside companies so that they can directly market their products or services to you if we feel that a company offers products or services that we believe may be of interest. We also may provide you with the opportunity to sign up on our Web site to receive such email offers.

What Choices Do You Have Regarding the Use of Your Information?

We provide you with a number of choices regarding our handling of your personal information.

If you do not want to receive email from macys.com and/or do not want us to share your information with unrelated third parties for marketing purposes, please submit a request electronically by doing the following:

Please click here to change your privacy options via email.

- "Please do not send me email" or
- "Keep my email address private" or

Or, to opt-out of email, you can click on the unsubscribe link and hit send at the bottom of any macys.com email communication.

Note: Once you have submitted your request you should assume that it has been successfully received and your request is being processed. Please allow us 10 business days from when the request was received to complete the removal, as some of our promotions may already have been in process before you submitted your request.

If you shop at our Macy's stores and wish to be removed from the list of customers that receive direct mail or telemarketing calls, please either:

- write to FACS Customer Service, P.O. Box 8215, Mason, OH 45040, or
- call Customer Service toll-free at 1-888-529-2254.

If you choose to write to us, please include your name, address and credit card account number (if you have one), and state one of the following:

- "NO MAIL OFFERS" (if you don't want to receive offers by mail);
- "NO PHONE OFFERS" (if you don't want to receive offers by phone); or
- "NO PHONE OR MAIL OFFERS" (if you don't want to receive either)

Because customer lists often are prepared well in advance of an offering (sometimes 3–4 months before the offer is made), you may continue to receive some offers after you send us a request not to use your information for specified marketing purposes. We appreciate your patience and understanding in giving us time to carry out your request.

You also may use the address and phone number above to request that we not disclose your personal information to unrelated third parties for marketing purposes. If you choose to write to us, please include your name, address and credit card account number (if you have one) and state "NO THIRD PARTY SHARING" in your request.

Is My Information Secure?

Macys.com is committed to doing its best to maintain the security of information collected on our site. To try to prevent unauthorized access, maintain data accuracy, and ensure the correct use of information, we have put in place the appropriate physical, electronic, and managerial procedures to safeguard and secure the information we collect online.

Private account and customer information is located on a secured server behind a firewall; it is not directly connected to the Internet.

Encryption is a process by which a message or information is scrambled while it is in transit to macys.com. It is based on a key that has two different parts, public and private. The public part of the key is distributed to those with whom you want to communicate.

The private part is for the recipient's use only. So long as you use a browser that allows for encryption, when you send personal information to us, you use a public key to encrypt your personal information. If your information is intercepted during the transmission, it is scrambled and very difficult to decrypt. Once we receive your encrypted personal information, we use the private part of our key to decode it.

Bank of America Privacy Statement for 2008

1. Making the security of information a priority

Keeping financial information secure is one of our most important responsibilities. We maintain physical, electronic and procedural safeguards to protect Customer Information. Appropriate employees are authorized to access Customer Information for business purposes only. Our employees are bound by a code of ethics that requires confidential treatment of Customer Information and are subject to disciplinary action if they fail to follow this code.

2. Collecting your information

We collect and use various types of information about you and your accounts to service your accounts, save you time and money, better respond to your needs, and manage our business and risks.

   Customer Information is categorized in the following six ways:

A. Identification Information—information that identifies you such as name, address, telephone number and Social Security number.

B. Application Information—information you provide to us on applications and through other means that will help us determine if you are eligible for products you request Examples include assets, income and debt.

C. Transaction and Experience Information—information about transactions and account experience, as well as information about our communications with you. Examples include account balances, payment history, account usage and your inquiries and our responses.

D. Consumer Report Information—information from a consumer report. Examples include credit score and credit history.

E. Information from Outside Sources—information from outside sources regarding employment, credit and other relationships that will help us determine if you are eligible for products you request. Examples include employment history, loan balances, credit card balances, property insurance coverage and other verifications.

F. Other General Information—information from outside sources, such as data from public records, that is not assembled or used for the purpose of determining eligibility for a product or service.

As required by the USA PATRIOT Act, we also collect information and take actions necessary to verify your identification.

3. Managing information about you

Managing information within Bank of America

Bank of America is made up of a number of companies, including financial service providers such as our brokerage company and credit card company, and nonfinancial companies such as our operations and servicing subsidiaries.

Bank of America may share any of the categories of Customer Information among our companies. For example, sharing information allows us to use information about your ATM, credit card and check card transactions to identify any unusual activity and then contact you to determine if your card has been lost or stolen.

We occasionally receive medical or health information from a customer if, for example, a customer applies for insurance from us. We also may obtain information from insurance support organizations not affiliated with Bank of America that prepare and provide reports to others as well as to us. We do not share medical or health information among our companies, except to maintain or collect on accounts, process transactions, service customer requests or perform insurance functions, to the extent permitted by law.

Managing information with companies that work for us

We may share any of the categories of Customer Information with companies that work for us, including companies located outside the United States. All nonaffiliated companies that act on our behalf and receive Customer Information from us are contractually obligated to keep the information we provide to them confidential, and to use the Customer Information we share only to provide the services we ask them to perform. These companies may include financial service providers such as payment processing companies, and nonfinancial companies such as check printing and data processing companies.

In addition, we may share any of the categories of Customer Information with companies that work for us in order to provide marketing support and other services, such as a service provider that distributes marketing materials. These companies may help us to market our own products and services or other products and services that we believe may be of interest to you. Please note that some of our own companies may provide marketing support and other services for us as well.

Sharing information with third parties (for customers with credit cards and Sponsored Accounts)

We may share Identification Information, Transaction and Experience Information, as well as Other General Information we collect about each of your (1) Bank of America credit card account(s) and (2) Sponsored Accounts at Bank of America, with selected third parties.

(1) Credit card account information, whether co-branded or not, may be shared with third parties.
(2) Sponsored Account information may be shared with third parties. Sponsored Accounts are non-credit card accounts or services provided by Bank of America that are also endorsed, co-branded or sponsored by other organizations.

Examples of these organizations include colleges, sporting teams, retailers and other affinity organizations, such as charities. Sponsored Accounts may include deposit accounts or other banking services provided by Bank of America, such as a savings account co-branded with an automobile club. You will know whether an account is a Sponsored Account by the appearance of the name or logo of the sponsoring organization on account materials, such as statements and marketing materials.

We may share information about credit cards and Sponsored Accounts with selected third parties including:

- Financial services companies (such as insurance agencies or companies and mortgage brokers, and organizations with whom we have agreements to jointly market financial products);

- Nonfinancial companies (such as retailers, travel companies and membership organizations); and
- Other companies (such as nonprofit organizations).

The sharing of information, as described in this section, is limited to credit card and Sponsored Account information. Please see Section 4, *Honoring Your Preferences* to learn how you may choose to opt out of this sharing.

Disclosing information in other situations

We also may disclose any of the categories of Customer Information to credit bureaus and similar organizations and when required or permitted by law. For example, Customer Information may be disclosed in connection with fraud prevention or investigation, risk management and security, and recording mortgages in public records.

4. Honoring your preferences
You have choices when it comes to how Bank of America shares and uses information.

Sharing information with third parties (for customers with credit cards and Sponsored Accounts)

If you have a Bank of America credit card or Sponsored Account, you may request that we not share information about these accounts with third parties. If you request that we not share information with third parties, we may still share information:

- Where permitted or required by law as discussed in Section 3 under *Disclosing information in other situations;*
- With our service providers as discussed in Section 3 under *Managing information with companies that work for us;* and
- With other financial companies with whom we have joint marketing agreements.

Sharing among the Bank of America family of companies

You may request that Application Information, Consumer Report Information and Information from Outside Sources not be shared among Bank of America companies.

For sharing among Bank of America companies, each customer may tell us his or her preferences individually, or you may tell us the preferences for any other customers who are joint account owners with you.

Direct Marketing

You may choose not to receive direct marketing offers—sent by postal mail, telephone and/or e-mail—from Bank of America. These preferences apply to all marketing offers from us and from companies working for us. To minimize the amount of telephone solicitation our customers receive, Bank of America does not offer nonfinancial products and services through telephone solicitations. Direct marketing offers from us may include information about products and services we believe may be of interest to you.

If you elect not to receive direct marketing offers by postal mail, telephone and/or e-mail, please note that we may continue to contact you as necessary to service your account and for other nonmarketing purposes. You may also be contacted from your client relationship manager or assigned account representative, if applicable. Bank of America may also continue to provide marketing information in your regular account mailings and statements, including online and ATM communications.

Each customer may opt out of each direct marketing option individually. Since marketing programs may already be in progress, it may take up to 12 weeks for your opt out to be fully effective. When you opt out of direct marketing by postal mail or telephone, your opt out will last for five (5) years. After that, you may choose to renew your opt out for another five-year period.

APPENDIX IV

"There Should Be a Law!": Questions and Answers from Real Life

Is it legal for a supermarket to disclose that the wife of a political candidate shops at the store?

No federal law explicitly prohibits the disclosure of this information, and it is unlikely that state law would particularly address this information. A disclosure of this information may be contrary to the supermarket's privacy policy, however. The FTC considers a merchant's acting contrary to its privacy policy to be an unfair trade practice and has enforced similar matters, albeit when violations affect more consumers.[1679] An isolated disclosure, however, probably would not lead the FTC to act.

May a merchant create an individualized consumer profile of items purchased and sell this information?

For those who shop online, it is not news that merchants create consumer profiles based on one's purchases. Some online merchants will use the information to provide new purchase recommendations to the consumer, which can be quite useful.

[1679] *See* Benita A. Kahn & Heather J. Enlow, *The Federal Trade Commission's Expansion of the Safeguards Rule*, 54 FED. LAW., Sept. 2007, at 39 (discussing the FTC's enforcement of unfair trade practices regarding the protection of personal information).

However, what may be news is that merchants may sell information about your purchases if they don't promise not to. This is more troubling in the case of online purchases, as opposed to in-store purchases. Online, a merchant may collect information that cannot be gleaned from a credit-card swipe, such as a customer's shipping address, home phone number, and e-mail address.

In the case of in-store purchases, typically the only information a merchant has access to is the information contained on the face of a credit card. The information contained on the magnetic strip of a credit card contains no more personally identifiable information than appears on the face of the card.[1680] The utility of associating just a name with purchases is questionable (e.g., did John Smith #1 purchase these items, or was it John Smith #2?).

Merchants may associate a customer's personal information with purchase information for chargeback purposes. No federal law seems to prevent a merchant from using this information for other purposes.

State law governs whether the merchant may request or require additional information to process the credit card. In California, for example, the merchant may not request any additional information from the card-holder for a standard point-of-sale purchase.[1681]

Is it legal for a public utility company to disclose a customer's Social Security number?

Federal law prohibits federal and state employees from disclosing a person's Social Security number.[1682] The statute, however, does not appear to prevent municipal employees from disclosing such information. State law may also prohibit the disclosure of Social Security numbers.

At least one state court has recognized a Social Security number as "private and confidential information" protected under that state's

---

[1680] The ISO 7813 standard, which defines the data fields for credit cards, states that the magnetic information contains the account number, the name of the account holder, and the expiration date, among other nonidentifiable information. Wikipedia, ISO 7813, http://en.wikipedia.org/wiki/ISO_7813 (last visited May 20, 2008).

[1681] CAL. CIV. CODE § 1747.08(a) (Deering 2007). Exceptions to this statute include transactions in which a credit card is used to make a deposit to secure future payment, to make a cash advance, and to make a purchase that requires shipping, delivery, or installation of the purchased goods. Id. § 1747.08(c).

[1682] 42 U.S.C. § 405(c)(2)(c)(viii)(I), (III) (2007).

consumer-protection law, holding that a tenant is not required to provide a landlord this information to renew a lease.[1683] If other courts followed the reasoning of this holding, a Social Security number could be more widely viewed as private information protected from disclosure.

Can a retail store sell a consumer's purchase record to a data broker?

Yes; however, the FTC may view this as an unfair trade practice if the practice violates the store's privacy policy.[1684] There is no law that prevents the store from sharing statistical data after identifying information has been removed. However it is often possible to identify a person even after information has been removed.[1685]

May law enforcement use information obtained from a data broker?

Yes, and they do.[1686] By using data brokers, the government is easily able to collect and use information for which it might need a search warrant to collect itself. Data collected and maintained by data brokers, however, may be inaccurate and difficult to amend.[1687]

May the federal government monitor the content of a citizen's e-mail?

Yes, but the monitoring procedure varies. If the messages the government seeks are downloaded from the mail server and stored on a user's computer,

---

[1683] Meyerson v. Prime Realty Servs., LLC, 796 N.Y.S.2d 848 (Sup. Ct. 2005).
[1684] See Albrecht, supra note 674 (discussing supermarkets' use of consumer information obtained through store loyalty cards).
[1685] Id. at 536–37 (discussing the possibility of "data reidentification").
[1686] See, e.g., Security Focus, U.S. Police Using Data Brokers, http://www.securityfocus.com/brief/233 (last visited May 9, 2008).
[1687] See, e.g., Dennis v. BEH-1, LLC, 504 F.3d 892 (9th Cir. 2007) (discussing the plaintiff's difficulty in having inaccurate information in his credit report corrected after a state court misreported a judgment against the plaintiff in public records); see also CHRIS JAY HOOFNAGLE, PRIVACY SELF REGULATION: A DECADE OF DISAPPOINTMENT (2005), available at http://epic.org/reports/decadedisappoint.pdf (including a letter from a data broker to a data subject brazenly stating that the subject has no rights). Data aggregators rely on the accuracy of data from underlying sources.

the government must obtain a search warrant to access the user's computer. However, upon request, the government can require an Internet service provider to preserve evidence and maintain a copy of downloaded messages.[1688] If messages are stored on a remote server, for example, through the use of Web mail or a Microsoft Exchange account, law enforcement may access the content of messages stored for over 180 days by using a search warrant, administrative subpoena, or court order. For messages stored for fewer than 180 days, a warrant is necessary. Although notice to the user is required when using an administrative subpoena or court order,[1689] a district court may grant a delay of up to 90 days before the user is notified of the order.[1690]

In 2008, the Ninth Circuit ruled that a user has no reasonable expectation of privacy in the to and from addresses of e-mails or in the IP addresses of Web sites visited.[1691] The Court reasoned that this information is analogous to phone numbers dialed, in which a person cannot maintain a reasonable expectation of privacy.[1692] The Court asserted:

> [E]-mail and Internet users have no expectation of privacy in the to/from addresses of their messages or the IP addresses of the Web sites they visit because they should know that this information is provided to and used by Internet service providers for the specific purpose of directing the routing of information.[1693]

The court analogized to earlier cases to suggest that a person does have a reasonable expectation of privacy in the contents of e-mails and in the URLs of Web sites visited.[1694] If other courts follow the Ninth Circuit's reasoning, which is likely given that the opinion relies on settled Supreme

---

[1688] 18 U.S.C. § 2703(f) (2007).

[1689] *Id.* § 2703(b)(1)(B).

[1690] *Id.* § 2705. Further extensions of the delay of notification may be granted by the court. *Id.* § 2705(a)(4).

[1691] United States v. Forrester, 512 F.3d 500, 510–11 (9th Cir. 2008). The Court explained IP addresses: "Every computer or server connected to the Internet has a unique IP address. A website typically has only one IP address even though it may contain hundreds or thousands of pages." *Id.* at 510 n.5.

[1692] *Id.* at 510. In *Smith v. Maryland,* 442 U.S. 735, 745–46 (1979), the Supreme Court stated that the use of a pen register, which records the numbers dialed from a phone, does not constitute a search for Fourth Amendment purposes. The Court asserted that "[a]ll telephone users realize that they must 'convey' phone numbers to the telephone company, since it is through telephone company switching equipment that their calls are completed." *Id.* at 742.

[1693] *Forrester,* 512 F.3d at 510.

[1694] *Id.* at 511, n.6.

Court precedent, a person will not have a reasonable expectation of privacy in e-mail to and from addresses or IP addresses.

May a pharmacy sell information about a customer's nonprescription purchases to a data broker?

Yes. Although HIPAA prohibits the wrongful disclosure of individually identifiable health information,[1695] nonprescription purchase information probably does not qualify as protected information under the statute.[1696] Therefore, information about the purchase of condoms, yeast-infection cream, or enema bags probably would not be protected.

Can a data broker or credit-reporting agency sell information to a landlord or prospective employer?

In enacting the Fair Credit Reporting Act, Congress made the finding that "[t]here is a need to insure that consumer reporting agencies exercise their grave responsibilities with fairness, impartiality, and a respect for the consumer's right to privacy."[1697] However, there are many exceptions. The credit-reporting agency can sell information to any party if the subject of the credit report authorizes the release of the information in writing.[1698] But in order for a prospective employer to use the information, the employer must provide additional disclosures.[1699] Most concerning, however, is that a credit-reporting agency may provide a report to any business that has a "legitimate business need for the information" either in connection with

---

[1695] 42 U.S.C. § 1320d-6 (2000).
[1696] 42 U.S.C. § 1320d(6) states:
   The term "individually identifiable health information" means any information, including demographic information collected from an individual, that: (a) is created or received by a health care provider, health plan, employer, or health care clearinghouse; and(b) relates to the past, present, or future physical or mental health or condition of an individual, the provision of health care to an individual, or the past, present, or future payment for the provision of health care to an individual, and:
   (i) identifies the individual; or
   (ii) with respect to which there is a reasonable basis to believe that the information can be used to identify the individual.
[1697] 15 U.S.C. § 1681(a)(4) (2000).
[1698] *Id.* § 1681b(a)(2).
[1699] *Id.* § 1681b(b).

a transaction initiated by the consumer or for account-review purposes.[1700] Thus, according to FTC commentary, "a consumer report may be obtained on a consumer who applies to rent an apartment, offers to pay for goods with a check, applies for a checking account or similar service, seeks to be included in a computer dating service, or who has sought and received over-payments of government benefits that he has refused to return."[1701]

[1700] *Id.* § 1681b(a)(3)(F).
[1701] 16 C.F.R. § 600 app. (2007).

INDEX

Marion Brechner Citizen Access Project, 242 n.1304
Nice Parking, Dude, 74–75 n.354
PeopleFind, 32 n.129
PlateWire, 74–75 n.354
PollingReport.com, 50 n.216
Privacilla.org, 150 n.749; 155 n. 790; 311
Privacy International scoring of Web sites, 299
Privacy Rights Clearinghouse, 244 n.1312
ReverseAuction, 158
RudePeople, 74–75 n.354
Spokeo.com, 53 n.239
Toysmart.com, 199 n.1074
USA People Search, 28 n.103
Whosarat.com, 75–76 n.359; 276 n.1431; 278
Wikipedia, 75
wink.com, 53 n.239
Zabasearch.com, 53
Zillow.com, 53 n.237
Webster v. Reproductive Health Servs., 270 n.1402
Weinberger, Ellis, 23 ns.75–78
Weinberger, Goldman v., 15 n.41
Westby, Jody R., 79 ns.376, 377; 80 n.380; 301 ns.1535, 1536; 302 ns.1537,1538; 320 n.1572; 331 n.1641
Westinghouse Electric Corp., United States v., 126
West v. Media Gen. Convergence, Inc., 182 n.964
Whalen v. Roe, 17 n.51; 125; 127
Whaley v. County of Tuscola, 207 n.1121; 208 n.1122; 209
White, White v., 149 n.738
White v. Samsung Elec. Am., Inc., 164 n.843; 175 n.917
White v. White, 149 n.738
Whitman, James Q., 80 ns.383, 384; 273; 274; 275 ns.1426–1429
Whitney v. California, 112
Whosarat.com, 75–76 n.359; 276 n.1431; 278
Wigginton, Doe v., 127
Wikipedia, 75
Williams, Glen, 252–253
Williams, State v., 23 n.83

Williams v. City of Minneola, 188; 195 n.1044; 202; 252–253; 296 n.1516
Wilson, Joseph Burstyn, Inc. v., 239
Windsor v. Fed. Executive Agency, 52 n.228
Winfield v. Div. of Pari-Mutual Wagering, 67 n.324; 294 n. 1508
Wink.com, 53 n.239
Wireless Communications and Public Safety Act of 1999 (911 Act), 148 ns.722, 726; 313; 328–329
Wiretap, information obtained with, 58 n.270
Wiretap Act, 31; 117; 289 n. 1486
Wisconsin, 163–164 n.836; 165 n.845; 224
Witherspoon, Reese, 196–197
Woflson v. Lewis, 286 n.1472
Wooley v. Maynard, 115 n.558
Worldwide libel, 81
World Wide Web. *See* Internet; Web sites
World Wide Web Consortium (W3C), 78–79 n.370
Worley, Kelley v., 179 n.948
Wright, Danaya C., 240 n.1295
Wrongful genetic testing, 44
Wu, Tim, 99 n.484; 299 n.1529
Wugmeister, Miriam, 95 n.467; 96 n.477

Y

Yinsi, 95 n.461
Youens, Liam, 254–255

Z

Zabasearch.com, 53
Zacchini, Hugo, 230
Zacchini v. Scripps-Howard Broadcasting, 230 n.1225–1228
Zarsky, Tal Z., 2 n.8
Zeller, Tom Jr., 29 n.109
Zeran v. America Online, Inc., 35 ns. 145, 146; 276 n.1431
Zetter, Kim, 2 n.5
Zhu, Guobin, 95 n.460
Zillow.com, 53 n.237
Zimberlin, Winona, 68 ns.326, 328; 69 n.332
Zimmerman, Diane L., 7 n.35; 182 n.962; 187 n.995; 237
Zoeller, Fuzzy, 75 n.356
Zoning laws, 19 n.59
Zuckman, Jill, 270 n. 1403